Jennifer
JENNIFER LEVINE R.N., B.A.
1521 Wood Moor Drive, Fort Wayne, Ind. 46804

D1301814

THE PROCESS OF CHILD DEVELOPMENT

COMMENTARY

How much of childhood development is dependent on external stimuli and how much comes from natural internal growth? What are the normal stages of development, and how can they be differentiated from the abnormal? What are the dynamics of parent-child relationships during the first year of infancy? Are differences in male and female development biologically or culturally determined? How do children internalize moral codes?

These are but a few of the questions explored in *The Process of Child Development*. This volume includes the most stimulating work in the field—the celebrated general developmental principles of Anna Freud, Jean Piaget's influential theories of of intellectual growth, Margaret Mahler's seminal work on the separation-individuation process, and Charlotte Buhler's classic model of human development, as well as several studies on individual infant behavior and articles on sexual differences in development and the problem of adolescence.

Bringing together the work of seventeen renowned authorities, this work provides a timely overview of one of the most rapidly expanding frontiers of human knowledge.

THE PROCESS OF CHILD DEVELOPMENT

Edited by

Peter B. Neubauer, M.D.

New York • Jason Aronson • London

Acknowledgments and Copyright Notices

Alissi, A. S. "Concepts of Adolescence," *Adolescence*, 7:28 (1972), 490-510.
Bayley, Nancy. "On the Growth of Intelligence," *American Psychologist*, 1955, *10*: 805-818. Copyright © 1955 by the American Psychological Association. Reprinted by permission.
Bühler, C. "The Course of Human Life as a Psychological Problem," *Human Development 11*: 184-200 (Karger, Basel, 1968).
Freud, Anna. "The Concept of Developmental Lines," from *The Writings of Anna Freud*, Vol. 6; Copyright © 1965 by International Universities Press. Reprinted by permission of the publisher.
Hutt, C. "Sex Differences in Human Development," *Human Development 15*: 153-170 (Karger, Basel 1972).
Kohlberg, L. "The Development of Children's Orientations Toward a Moral Order," *Vita humana 6*: 11-33 (Karger, Basel, 1963).
Mahler, M. S. "Rapprochement Subphase of the Separation-Individuation Process," *The Psychoanalytic Quarterly*, Vol. XLI, No. 4:487-506 (1972).
Murphy, Gardner. "Kurt Lewin and Field Theory." Reprint with permission from the *Bulletin of the Menninger Clinic*, Vol. 30, No. 6, pp. 358-367. Copyright © 1966 by the Menninger Foundation.
Piaget, Jean. "Piaget's Theory," in *Carmichael's Manual of Child Psychology*, Vol. 1, P. H. Mussen, ed. New York: Wiley, Copyright © 1970. Reprinted by permission of John Wiley & Sons, Inc. (A shorter version of this chapter was originally published in the *International Journal of Psychology*. Reprinted by permission of the International Union of Psychological Science and Dunod Editeur, Paris.)
Sander, L. W., G, Stechler, H. Julia, and P. Burns. "Primary Prevention and Some Aspects of Temporal Organization in Early Infant-Caretaker Interaction," in *Infant Psychiatry: A New Synthesis*, E. N. Rexford, L. W. Sander, and T. Shapiro, eds., in press, Yale University Press, New Haven.
Thomas, Alexander and Stella Chess. "Development in Middle Childhood," *Seminars in Psychiatry*, 4:4 (November) 1972, pp. 331-341. Reprinted by permission of Grune & Stratton, Inc. and the authors.
Thornburg, Hershel. "Adolescence: A Re-interpretation," *Adolescence*, 5:20 (1970) 463-484.
Watson, J. B. "Experimental Studies on the Growth of the Emotions," *Pedagogical Seminary*, 1925, *32*: 328-348.
Weil, Annemarie, "The First Year; Metapsychological Inferences of Infant Observation," Copyright © 1976 by Annemarie Weil.
Werner, Heinz. "The Concept of Development from a Comparative and Organismic Point of View," D. B. Harris, ed., *The Concept of Development*. Minneapolis: University of Minnesota Press. Copyright © 1957 by the University of Minnesota.
Wolff, P. H. "The Role of Biological Rhythms in Early Psychological Development." Reprint with permission from the *Bulletin of the Menninger Clinic*, Vol. 31, No. 4, pp. 197-218, Copyright © 1967 by the Menninger Foundation.
Zender, M. A., and B. F. Zender, "Vygotsgy's View About the Age Periodization of Child Development," *Human Development 17*:24-40 (Karger, Basel, 1974).

Originally published as a quality paperback by New American Library, Inc.

New Printing 1983

ISBN: 0-87668-674-9

Library of Congress Catalog Number: 84-45122

Manufactured in the United States of America.

Contents

Introduction

Any ''Reader'' not only expresses the formulations in the field that are considered to be representative of present-day thinking and that highlight the new findings, but is also an expression of the editor's interests, his own point of view, resulting in special selections and preferences. Therefore, it is important that the editor explain the rationale behind his choices.

The term ''human development'' is very often used quite loosely in referring to any statement of psychic function or to any process of interaction that may occur at any time in the life of a human being. Thus any personality change or adjustment is very often represented as reflecting the development of a human being. For instance, if a person shows an adjustment to his marriage, some may refer to his ''development'' in marriage. The editor of this reader has used the term ''human development'' in a much narrower sense to mean those processes of change which are part of the blueprint of developmental sequences and organizations reflecting the growth, maturation and development of a human being. It is assumed that each species has its own built-in developmental program from infancy through adult life. In this sense development is characterized by three dimensions: (1) The beginning, or that state of early organization out of which further change occurs. This can be referred to as the genetic dimension, that is to say, the dimension concerned with exploring the beginning conditions from which the developmental processes take place and which influence further mental and psychic evolvement. It does not refer to genes or constitution. (2) The end product of development. In what direction does the developmental process move in order to achieve maturity in adult life? This implies an *aim* in development and an importance in understanding this aim in order to be able to differentiate normality from abnormality in the developmental process. (3) The process of change. What are the laws that govern the human developmental sequences? Very often the most central facets of the theory of development involve this third dimension.

There are general notions that have been accepted as characterizing the changes that occur under the auspices of development. There are those changes which proceed from the earliest undifferentiated organization to the most highly differentiated. We see the infant's responses to be more global in nature and as development proceeds to become more specific. Differentiation proceeds in the direction of specificity of response. Moreover, we assume that the developmental process does not occur in a linear form, but rather reveals stages of organization or phases. Thus a certain discontinuity is built in. This process assumes that earlier organizations are given up and replaced later by more complex organizations, that a new hierarchy of significance is achieved which leaves behind the less differentiated and the less specific functions and responses. While there is also some continuity of function in certain areas, we can also see discontinuity. When a child, for instance, changes from crawling to the upright position, one can assume that a qualitative change has occurred which affects his relationship to himself and the outside world and that this new condition is sufficiently different so that one can infer a new stage in the child's maturation and development. While the child is still able only to crawl, his whole developmental force pulls him toward the exercising and the maintenance of the upright modality. What is true for motor skills is also true for many psychic and mental functions.

This book does not attempt to present a comprehensive, inclusive picture of those who have made contributions to empirical findings about development or of those who have contributed to the theory of development. It does not try to represent all schools of development, nor all those scientists who have made outstanding individual contributions. Rather, we selected authors who have had a significant influence on present theory of development and those who at present are making new contributions which may influence future thinking in the field. There are very few who attempt to create new schools at the present time. The effort seems to be rather in the direction of accumulating new data, particularly in the area of infant research. This may bring about a better understanding of the predispositions of the child and of the factors that will transform predispositions into dispositions and patterns of functioning which become part of stable mental and psychic organizations. We do not need to point out that often enough theories of development consider only childhood and neglect the investigation of developmental changes that occur during adult life. From infancy through death, there is a built-in timetable of changes. If we view development in these terms, we must explore changes that occur in early and middle adult life and certainly those that govern old age.

When we use the term "maturation" we refer to all those changes which are relatively connected with biological conditions, the maturation of the central nervous system, tooth development, and so forth. When we refer to development in terms of processes that are in close relationship with environmental interactions, maturation and development together are considered as expressions of the growth of an individual. Any outline of the developmental process must therefore take into account the environmental conditions that have direct relevance to the developmental process. One would need a systematic outline of the environment, the cultural values and the family organization within which a child's development takes place. We have mentioned the assumption that development occurs through a built-in timetable and blueprint that is species-specific and that therefore has physiologically determined characteristics. It is clear that the content of the human experience, the conflicts of the developmental conditions and the processes of regulation that determine phase organization are co-determined by the environment within which the developmental process takes place.

It would therefore be of interest to present aspects of development that can be observed in various societies and cultures and that therefore express the relatively stable and unchangeable internal conditions. Similarly, one could present those variations in the environment which have proven to have a direct effect on the developmental process, the timing of the emergence of phases, the appropriate content of the phase versus the specific conflicts and the mode of resolution of these conflicts.

In the papers included we have emphasized authors who attempt to outline general conditions of development over those who attempt to describe the environmental variations that contribute to developmental change. Furthermore, we have selected contributions that address themselves to normal development rather than those that investigate deviant and pathological development.

We have organized the papers into sections. The section headings, "Developmental Concepts," "Cognitive Development," "Clinical Issues" and "Special Issues," are not an attempt at a systematic presentation of schools or of one special area, but rather groupings of selections from the works of various authors that will contribute to an understanding of the wide scope which opens up as one explores human development.

We thought that a short introduction to each of these sections might assist the reader's thinking. We hope that the References at the end of each paper will also assist in the examination of additional contributions that will round out the presentations included here. Some of the papers present advanced findings from the authors' research, and the bibliographies will suggest readings about the studies that are the background for the material presented. We consider it important to set before the reader presentations which reflect various levels of theoretical formulation, and therefore some papers will be easier to read than others. We have included some papers which were written quite some time ago, either because of their historical significance or because they highlight changes which have occurred in the newer formulation of developmental issues or theories in development.

I wish to thank Inge King, who so conscientiously and intelligently contributed as my assistant to the preparation of this collection.

I. DEVELOPMENTAL CONCEPTS

This section addresses itself specifically to developmental theories. For this section I have included papers that will permit a historical view of concepts of development, and furthermore I have selected authors who base their findings on psychological research or on clinical investigations and exploration through therapeutic intervention. It is of interest to note the differences in the concepts based on this source of data gathering. There are researchers that limit themselves to the study of processes of development, and there are those who formulate developmental concepts as a ''by-product'' of pathological disorder, or of deviant development.

Some of the papers in this section are closer to observable data, and others present concepts on a more abstract level of theory—formation. My intention is to show these variations of positions and the resulting divergent views.

I have chosen as the first paper A. S. Alissi's ''Concepts of Adolescence,'' because it gives an almost editorial overview of the concepts of this developmental stage. In addition, the author links the adolescence processes with cultural and social factors and therefore demonstrates that development does not proceed by itself, but can be understood only in the context of the environment. The formulations presented are on a descriptive level; they reflect a desire to synthesize concepts and to bridge the difference between the schools, and to do it in a way that allows realistic implementations.

The second paper, by Anna Freud, is a chapter from her book *Normality and Pathology in Childhood: Assessments of Development*. For many decades Anna Freud has been interested in expanding the psychoanalytic theory of development. Her notion that development is a primary task of childhood has provided new criteria to assess normality and pathology and led her to new theoretical and clinical formulations.

Through the analysis of adults, Sigmund Freud was able to propose distinct stages of libidinal development by reconstructing the early childhood of his patients. Anna Freud, as a child analyst (engaged in many services for children) and from direct observation of children in many circumstances, has enlarged the body of information about the development of children.

Psychoanalytic theory proposes a number of "points of view" which permit the systematic organization of data. There is the dynamic point of view, which deals with the interaction of psychic forces and with the motivational component of psychic functions; the economic point of view, which deals with the emergence of stable psychic organizations, the id, ego and superego and their relationships, with one another and with the outside world; and then there is the genetic point of view, which deals with the emergence of health and pathology in the light of conditions which favor one or the other. This last metapsychological consideration includes the developmental consideration that has come more and more into the foreground of theoretical and clinical interest.

In the chapter chosen, Anna Freud proposes "lines of development" as a way of understanding developmental processes. These "lines" are not isolated areas of psychic functioning, but a result of many related factors. They were selected by Anna Freud because each relates to a major function that undergoes continuous change during the course of development. The lines, too, are interrelated, and the specific ways in which they interact permit a clearer differentiation of normal from abnormal development.

Erik Erikson, who is not represented in this section because his work is so widely quoted, proposes an epigenetic developmental principle, thus broadening developmental theory by viewing the individual in the context of the family and of society.

"Kurt Lewin and Field Theory" is a review paper by Gardner Murphy. Since he writes about the significant contribution of Kurt Lewin, I will summarize Gardner Murphy's own position. He is a researcher of wide interests in many areas of psychology and development, this supported by his intent to formulate a theory that brings together all the relevant factors from various theories and to integrate them in order to study man in his complex behavior. He outlines three stages in development: the undifferentiated wholeness, the stage of differentiated function and finally the stage of integration. He sees the need of man to become more and more specific over time and refers to the concept of canalization, which permits the interplay between need and environment. Thus he investigates the "life space" within the individual. He assumes that the structure of the environment is built within the person. Murphy has also made substantial contributions to the theoretical and experimental aspects of parapsychology.

Since Murphy has explored the individual in his environmental context, it is particularly suitable that he discuss Kurt Lewin, who has addressed himself to building a field theory in which the person and environment are part of the same psychological field.

Kurt Lewin was closely connected with those who founded the Gestalt psychology. He applied the field concepts from physics to psychology and at the same time explored the dynamics of group functioning, and he combined both into one theoretical frame of reference. He defines the concept of field as "the totality of coexisting facts which are conceived of as mutually interdependent." The life space for him is seen as encompassing both the individual and the environment as separate units. Lewin was guided by his conviction that social events are as real as physical facts and as such can be studied realistically. The term "group dynamics" was introduced by Kurt Lewin.

Heinz Werner's paper, "The Concept of Development from a Comparative and Organismic Point of View," is a continuation of an approach represented by Kurt Lewin and others of the "organic" school. The Gestalt psychology explored the structural aspects—that is, the relationship of parts or details to the whole. This approach was different from a "mechanistic" view, which studied items and variables. Heinz Werner's organic view insisted that "the study of mental patterns should take precedence over the study of elements." This proposition has a significant influence on the theory and research of development. He also advocated the comparative method—the uncovering of the similarities between earlier cultures, children and modern man.

Gardner Murphy, Kurt Lewin and Heinz Werner therefore follow a similar path and share many propositions.

John B. Watson's paper, "Experimental Studies on the Growth of the Emotions," was written by a man who has extraordinary historical significance. This paper, based on a lecture, was written in 1925. The reason for including it is that it gives us a view of early observations of behavior and Watson's propositions to explain these observations. His behavioristic approach was an attempt at objectivity. He looked at behavior "as it is" and tried to delineate certain correlations in the relationship between environmental conditions and the responses of the individual. Read today, this paper profiles more clearly the limitations of such an approach—the absence of motivational forces, the complexity of interactional systems, and so forth.

Since this section begins with a paper on adolescence, I thought a paper that returns to this concern might facilitate a comparison of the various concepts proposed in the other presentations in this section.

Hershel Thornburg, in "Adolescence: A Re-interpretation," reviews many ideas and quotes Havighurst's "Ten Accomplishments Necessary to Move into Adult Life." Some will be reminded of Anna Freud's "lines of development." These lists of accomplishments, from dependence to independence, from play to work, from self-centeredness to social responsibility, are the same. The difference is that Havighurst describes them as aims of development in order to reach maturity, whereas Anna Freud's lines of development serve as a yardstick to study the processes of change and the interlocking of these lines with each other. Thornburg's paper also documents the observation that studies of adolescence seem to focus on the environment as it influences adolescent conflicts and the search for a new identity in this stage of development.

In this section one can therefore find concepts based on different views of "life" and its reference to development. These are examples of different approaches to the study of developmental processes; the "how one looks at it" determines the "how one studies it." These papers should interest the reader not only for their developmental concepts but also for their research methods.

1. Concepts of Adolescence*

A. S. Alissi, DSW
DIRECTOR OF RESEARCH
C. F. MENNINGER MEMORIAL HOSPITAL, TOPEKA

Not long ago, a newspaper article carried the caption "Astrologer Charts Teen Scene: New Key to Generation Gap?" The article gave an account of a Los Angeles astrologer who used the changing planetary relationships in the cosmos to explain the generation gap, dropout scene, hippie movement, and rebellion on the campuses. The planet Venus, which is a sign of love and a strong force in this era, was used to explain the flower children's search for love and the existence of a love generation.

The theory is indeed inviting, but perhaps falsely assures us that whatever our quandary may be, it is not of our own making. It is also discouraging to think that man will never be able to affect such phenomena until he has the wherewithal to manipulate the planets—which is, to use an apt phrase, an Herculean task. Although there are people who take this view seriously, the unique appeal of such simple, self-contained theories becomes more obvious as we engage in our own struggle in this paper to review some of the modern-day prevailing concepts of adolescence.

Our brief overview will highlight some of the more plausible concepts and theories which may be applied to the full range of adolescent experiences. Although these may appear to be refined, and "established," we can be misled if we fail to take into account certain built-in problems in conceptualizing. Actually, the development of effective conceptual tools has been a slow and tedious process in the behavioral sciences. Simply we have been unable to invent adequate means to portray social reality in its totality.

This should not surprise us, however, for it is true that we never see things in their total concreteness. We see only certain aspects—those that we have been taught to abstract using the currency of our own cultural symbols. As Walter Lippman expressed in his famous aphorism "First we

*Presented at Sixth Annual Conference of American Association for Child Care in Hospitals in New York City, May, 1971.

look, then we name, and only then do we see." A group of young people standing arm in arm cluttering entrances to buildings and singing songs in unison brings certain reactions after they are defined as "demonstrators"! The responses would indeed be different were they defined as strolling carolers, bearing messages of good cheer.

This is another way of saying that we do not respond to stimuli but rather to our definitions of the stimuli.

What passes for knowledge and understanding then must center on how we arrive at these definitions. In exploring the sociology of knowledge, Manheim introduced the notion of *relationism,* which stated that truth is not necessarily a fixed commodity but is predicated on the historical and situational context in which it is found. As cross-cultural studies have repeatedly demonstrated, our own involvement and narrowed cultural frame of reference in a sense institutionalizes our own distortions of the truth. As Hall puts it, "Culture hides much more than it reveals, and strangely enough what it hides, it hides most effectively from its own participants" (20, p. 39). And so it is with the helping professions, where even the most careful descriptions of adolescence are not automatically objective—for all behavioral definitions have pre-established connotations. The mere fact of describing a particular adolescent behavior as "ambivalent" reveals a psychoanalytic conceptual bias. We must, therefore, be sensitive to our own frame of reference, which is, as is true of all social inventions, subject to time and place distortions.

In short, what we see or ignore depends on the concepts available to us. We have a ready-made "package deal" set of concepts when it comes to American teenagers. We thus have an image of the teenager which serves as a prophecy we are altogether too eager to fulfill as selected aspects are highlighted and others blotted out that are not conveniently covered by the label. The prefabricated conceptual molds and packages come in all sizes and shapes. One set forces us to recognize anti-establishmentism, the generation gap, and contradicting subcultural values. A second set calls attention to dependency, ambivalence, psychosexual conflicts, resurging oedipal conflicts. And still another sets us searching for anomie in the social system, status deprivations, and role confusions.

It would be more realistic to develop a "do-it-yourself concept kit" which would seek to see all that is possible by applying a blend of concepts selected not because they are pre-established in our minds but because they are tailored to account for the particular behavior in question and are therefore closer to the truth of the matter.

This is, in my estimation, the hallmark of the professional—an ability to find and apply the most workable combination of concepts tailor-made to fit the problem at hand. It follows then that this capacity will vary depending on the range and depth of his repertoire. No matter how creative he may feel, a mechanic cannot do much with only a Phillips screwdriver and pair of pliers. Similarly, those with a limited inventory of narrowly focused concepts and theories will be handicapped in that they lack the range necessary to apply to real life problems. The richer the repertoire of conceptual tools the practitioner has at his disposal, the more likely he will be able to discover the combination that will be successful for understanding and dealing with practical problems.

Scientific Concepts

The behavioral sciences have for some time now been searching for concepts, hypotheses, and theories which will effectively integrate both psychological and sociological explanations of behavior. While human behavior involves both aspects, the distinctive ways in which the sciences have grown have consistently favored separate approaches. The study of adolescence has similarly been influenced by these developments and for this reason is perhaps better understood when examined in terms of these traditional fields of study.

Adolescence as a Stage in Individual Development

The earliest efforts to establish a separate psychology of adolescence can be traced to G. Stanley Hall (19). Extending Darwin's evolutionary doctrine, Hall's theory of recapitulation held that each individual grows through stages of development which reenact or recapitulate the history of mankind. Where infancy reenacts the prehistoric stage, and childhood the cave-dwelling stage, adolescence reenacts the transitional stage, which is characterized by rebellion, storm and stress. Hall was optimistic about adolescence, for he held that if any higher stage of development of the race were to occur, it would not come out of adult life but would come through increased development of the adolescent stage, which was in his words "the bud and promise for the race" (21, p. 50).

Biological determinism is also evidenced in the work of Arnold Gesell

(17), whose descriptions of age trends have been widely accepted as norms in the United States. In his view, the basic direction of growth is fashioned by maturational forces and developmental changes which oscillate along a spiral course through progression and partial regression. Fairly detailed descriptions of adolescent physical and mental development from year to year are spelled out which are characterized by alternating stages of calmness and storm. Wilfred Zeller (3) introduced the idea of a *body gestalt* to signify the changes in the total complex of body functions which accounted for corresponding psychological changes. Secondary sex characteristics at puberty, for example, involve more comprehensive body changes leading to disharmony of body gestalt resulting in increased impulsivity, nervousness and overcritical attitudes. To the followers of Ernst Kretschmer (3), on the other hand, predispositions to major psychological tendencies corresponded to body types, and hence the degree of turbulence found in adolescence was sufficiently explained by the existence of differing body types.

The more psychologically oriented approaches tend to highlight specific kinds of experiences relating to personality development, cognition, values, perceptions and attitudes. Oswald Kroh (3), for example, was impressed with psychological aspects of consciousness at different stages of development and advanced the concept of *phase structure* to emphasize the totality of personality throughout the process. In his view, the adolescent personality develops a theoretical view of the world and deeper understanding of life. On the other hand, Edward Spranger (3) saw adolescence as a period of transition in which a hierarchy of values is established. Three kinds of changes are inwardly experienced. There are radical and dramatic changes in self-perception, a gradual adoption of cultural values, and finally, an achievement of self-disciplined and actively sought-after goals.

A most comprehensive examination of the deveopment of cognition stems from Jean Piaget and his colleague Barbel Inhelder (23, 29). Systems of thought are, in their view, evolved from a gradual internalization of action. Whereas the child reasons on the basis of objects called *concrete operations,* the adolescent is able to reason on the basis of symbols or verbal propositions called *formal thought* or *propositional operations*. The stage of cognitive development the adolescent achieves involves the ability to deal with propositional logic, to grasp metaphors, and to reason about thought itself. From the developmental point of view, limitations and capabilities of adolescent cognition are intimately involved in all adolescent experience. For example, his ability to distinguish between what is and what could be permeates his social view, whereas his newly found introspective powers may lead to heightened self-consciousness in his private view (11).

Herbert Cross (7), among others, maintains that a person's concepts can be ordered according to certain patterns of organization into what might be called conceptual systems. Developmental progression is seen to move through degrees of abstractness from the concrete, inflexible, rigid to the abstract, flexible, and creative. Assessing an adolescent's conceptual level of development and the context of his training environment are both acknowledged as crucial variables in the adolescent experience.

Without a doubt, though, the psychoanalytic theories continue to provide the richest source of concepts for understanding adolescence. The classical psychoanalytic view of adolescence holds that the biological changes during puberty upset a balance which has existed between the ego and id during latency. Adolescence is a time in which the increased impulses confront a relatively weak ego. Most evident during adolescence is the resurgence of the oedipal complex which brings with it derivatives of pregenital drives, oral, anal impulses and aggressive drives. Related to the oedipal situation is the adolescent's task of freeing himself from the dependency of parents. Detachment from the incestuous objects is marked by rejection, resentment, and hostility towards parents and other authorities.

The meaning of eruption and turmoil during adolescence is important. Upset behavior is seen to be an external indication of internal adjustments taking place, and these are taken to be signs of *normal* growth. Hence, the very nature of adolescence interrupts peaceful growth and it is therefore normal for the adolescent to be inconsistent, unpredictable, and to fluctuate between opposites. Conversely, when there is a steady equilibrium during adolescence, there is abnormality (16).

In general, adolescence seems to offer a second chance where new forces are released and restructuralization takes place. The orthodox psychoanalytic position has, of course, been modifed by Erikson, Fromm, Horney, Sullivan, and others who emphasized the role of social factors in the developmental processes.

Erikson's (12) concept of ego identity in particular has stimulated much current interest. It has been said that the problem of identity is for our times what the problem of sex seemed to be for Freud's. As used by Erikson, the concept referred to the relationship between what a person appears to be in the eyes of others with what he feels he is. It represents the search for an inner continuity and sameness which matches the outer social circumstances.

The term "identity crisis" was first used to describe a type of breakdown of inner controls found among a group of psychiatric patients. The same kinds of central disturbances were noted in conflicted young people who were experiencing a sense of confusion in themselves. Thus, the term "identity crisis" has taken on a normative meaning when applied to adolescence. The word "crisis" does not connote impending catastrophe but rather a necessary turning point at a "crucial moment" where development must move one way or another "managing resources of growth, recovery, and further differentiation" (13).

In the main, the identity concept concentrates on the fusion of a variety of elements such as identification, capacities, opportunities, and ideals into a viable self-definition. Adolescents vary in the tempo in which an identity is found. Some may crystallize identity too early or too narrowly to avoid diffusion. Others do not seem to find themselves and try out various identities existing in a kind of psychosocial moratorium.

In their clinical work, behavioral therapists have challenged this unconscious determinism of the psychoanalytic variety and argue that the symptoms or undesirable behavior patterns are learned in the same way as other habits. These can be unlearned by applying the same principles. As Albert Mehrabian puts it, "It is easier to act yourself into a new way of thinking than to think yourself into a new way of acting" (27, p. 143). Whereas the various stage theories discussed assume that behavior can be categorized into relatively fixed discrete sequences related to maturational processes and socialization forces, the social learning theorists stress individual differences. Moreover, intra-individual continuities are noted in early development, inasmuch as marked changes in behavior are seen to occur only as a result of abrupt alternations in social training and are rarely found in most individuals during the pre-adult years (2, p. 25).

Social Perspective on Adolescence

In contrast to the focus on the individual adolescent, the sociological approach focuses on the social and cultural determinants which in a sense create the adolescent condition. According to this view, social structure and culture in American society conjoin to induce adolescence, which essentially is an experience of passing through an unstructured and ill-defined phase that lies between childhood and adulthood. This void or gap in the social structure stems largely from two factors: a finely established division of labor with its complex technical status structure; and the failure of the cultural system to provide a meaningful ideology which would result in a strong identity and feeling of purpose. The emotional instability and general turbulence associated with adolescence arises, then, out of the indeterminate status of the adolescent in the social structure rather than from innate constitutional causes (31).

Certain sociological approaches do, however, share an interest in the developmental aspects of adolescence along with the stage theories previously discussed. According to John Barron Mays (25), the developmental tasks to be achieved by the adolescent within society's unstructured framework include efforts to somehow come to terms with society by getting an education, job, and starting a family; to come to terms with oneself in developing an identity, and individual talents; and to come to terms with life as a whole by acquiring a moral code and general religious beliefs. Robert Havighurst's (22) well-known list of essential developmental tasks more specifically points up skills, knowledge, and attitudes which must be mastered by the growing adolescent to avoid maladjustment and social disapproval in future years. To Kingsley Davis (9), adolescence represents a phase of development where physical maturity moves far ahead of social maturity. As society becomes more complex, the gap becomes greater, and adult status is delayed as adolescence is prolonged despite physical and mental preparedness for adulthood.

Allison Davis (8) employed socialization as a key concept to refer to a continuous process of social reinforcement and punishment affecting growth and development. Fears of punishment resulted in what he termed *socialized anxiety,* which serves to help individuals adapt to the demands of society. Socialized anxiety increases during adolescence as the adolescent faces new responsibilities while at the same time he is expected to delay normal gratifications. In the process, adolescents develop a new awareness of societal values. According to Davis, socialized anxiety, however, varied with social class, which accounts for behavioral differences in the stratification system.

Victor Gioscia (18) used the concept of *achrony* to depict a general state of frustration where there is a gap between role of behavior and role of fulfillment of expectations in a social structure which simultaneously demands and prevents the adoption of adult status. He arrived at the concept in his study of adolescent drug addiction, where it was seen that drug use produced an illusion of timelessness representing a kind of flight away from culturally accepted definitions of the normal flow of time.

Adolescents in our culture, who have not adopted a set of norms which can be synchronized with the pace of modern urban culture, will be subjected to achrony.

Unless the social and cultural systems are altered, adolescence will continue to represent a period of instability which is more or less a normal state. Stable attitudes are difficult to achieve largely because societies only intermittently and in special cases give recognition to youth. The Komsomols of Soviet Russia, the Israeli Kibbutz, and the Nazi youth organizations serve as examples of how adolescence experiences can be structured politically and ideologically. While the exporting of American "teenageism" is recognized, adolescence is symptomatic of any well-developed and affluent society. England has its teddy boys, Rockers, and Mods; Russia its *stilyagi;* Japan its thunder boys; France and Germany their Americanized "teenagers"; and so on. In this view, underdeveloped societies in the process of industrialization can expect to create their share of the adolescent phenomena in the future (32).

There is an aphorism that an adolescent is one who, if not treated as an adult, acts like an infant. If role expectations are poorly defined, the resulting confusions may induce the teenager to seek clear roles. If the adult status is not available, childhood behavior may be the only alternative.

A somewhat different view is presented by Edgar Friedenberg (15), who sees society as manipulating the adolescent into patterns of mass conformity. Society "dampens out" questioning, conflict, rebellion and all that is stressful during adolescence. Not having experienced the stress and strain, the adolescent is deprived of the opportunity to establish his real identity. Adolescence as a developmental phenomenon is minimized and is, in his view, *vanishing*. Current youth protestors with deep commitments may be positive reminders that idealism is not dead but is "entrusted afresh to each new generation" (25, p. 118). On the other hand, the "new alienation" has been interpreted by Kenneth Keniston as a "form of rebellion without a cause, of rejection without a program, or of refusal of what is without a vision of what should be" (24, p. 6).

The role of the youth culture or peer group in helping its members achieve full adult status is, of course, an important consideration. According to Eisenstadt (10), training in the family is insufficient for moving in the wider society insofar as it no longer is the basic unit in the division of labor, nor does it perform political, economic, or religious functions. Hence, family training in itself is not adequate for developing full identity and social maturity. Age-homogeneous youth groups serve in this sense to help in the transition from what is described as the "particularism" of the family to the "universalism" of the larger society.

The adolescent subculture then serves as a link between childhood and adulthood, and according to James Coleman (5) is fast becoming a distinctive life style with a language and value system of its own. Society is now not confronted with a set of individuals to be socialized into adulthood but instead is faced with an adolescent social system which offers a united front in resisting adult intervention.

Finally, there is the phenomenon of the youthful *counter-culture* as advanced by Theodore Roszak (31). The concept refers to an amorphous generation unit of dissenting young people who deplore the dehumanizing forces of a technological society with its accompanying credo "never let happen naturally and enjoyably what can be counterfeited by the technician." The counter-culture represents a "healthy instinct" refusing to participate personally and politically in practices which violate human sensibilities. In Roszak's words,

> Most of what is presently happening that is new, provocative and engaging in politics, education, the arts, social relations (love, courtship, family, and community) is the creation either of youth who are profoundly, even fanatically, alienated from the parental generation, or of those who address themselves primarily to the young. (31, p. 1)

Doubtless, this brief overview of psychological and sociological perspectives does not represent a thorough review of the literature. By necessity it tends to highlight only certain features of the concepts considered, and therefore may be biased to favor our overall argument that we lack integrated comprehensive models for dealing with the real world. It might help for us to more broadly examine what appears to be currently happening to us to see what clues this might give us for moving toward more integrated approaches. The dialogue surrounding the generation gap might prove insightful in this regard.

The Generation Gap and the Current Dialogue

Many talk about the change in status from childhood to adulthood as though it were a discrete step forward resembling the pubescent rites of passage described in anthropology textbooks. This of course is not true, for our society has a system which is haphazard and ambiguous at best. Upon reaching the age of twelve, children gain the dubious status of paying adult fares on trains and airlines and adult rates at movies and theaters. At sixteen, he is largely freed from the protection of child labor laws and is able to secure a driver's license but is seldom legally responsible as an adult. At eighteen, he can go to war, and indeed he may very well be forced to enjoy this privilege and yet he cannot enter a bar to drink, and in many states cannot marry without parental consent. On reaching twenty-one, he achieves the legal status of adulthood. But interestingly enough, a number of youth beyond this age are still financially dependent as they are forced to prolong their education and training in schools of higher education (6).

Much of our effort to deal constructively with adolescence in modern society is based on the assumption that most of the problems associated with this stage of life will somehow disappear if we could only "bridge the generation gap" (1). This implies that the ideal relationship between the older and younger generations should be one of consensus and harmony. Further, it is assumed that the major responsibility for creating such consensus and harmony depends largely on the purposeful actions of the members of the older generation. Presumably, the gap to be bridged is one in which the older generation maintains a key role in the socialization process to insure that cherished values, knowledge and skills are available to the younger generation. Success then implies the maintenance of a smooth functioning social system which is relatively free from disruption. This is sought in spite of how outmoded the social structure itself may have become. As one author put it, "More hung up on youth than any nation on earth, we are also more determined that youth is not to enter into history without paying the price of that adulteration we call adulthood" (30, p. 188).

But in many ways, today's adolescents prefer to be nonparticipants of the past and have indeed become "dropouts from history." In spite of pamperings, briberies, put-downs, tongue-lashings, and promises of a bright and shiny future, youths are refusing to reenact the past and may not even desire to keep the system intact. They are what Leslie Fiedler refers to as "the new mutants" who face life with a new logic of its own.

> Not only do they reject the Socratic adage that the unexamined life is not worth living, since for them precisely the unexamined life is the only one worth enduring at all. But they also abjure the Freudian one: "Where id was, ego shall be," since for them the true rallying cry is, "Let id prevail over ego, impulse over order," or—in negative terms—"Freud is a Fink!" (14, p. 207)

In contrast to his earlier counterpart, today's adolescent often feels no need to hide or disguise his rebellious deeds out of deference to god and motherhood. He announces his activities matter-of-factly with the subtlety of a sledge hammer. And his escapades contribute directly to the growing inferiority complex and amateur status of his parents.

And as the saying goes, the only premarital experiences current adolescents deny themselves is the experience of learning how to cook.

Others have suggested that perhaps society gets the kind of children it deserves or even secretly wants. Erikson, for example, stated, "If our children disappoint us, it is because the world we have created for them—which influences their values and perceptions—disappoints us even more" (28, p. 1). There are clear signs that youth has reached a level of disgust at having been made "scapegoats for adult apathy, indifference," and lack of honesty and courage in dealing with life's problems.

But perhaps our postindustrial society has signaled the beginning of a still more profound revelation which in Margaret Mead's (26) view represents an entirely new cultural stage in our history. Beginning with a postfigurative culture where children learned primarily from their forebears, and moving to a cofigurative culture in which both children and adults learned from their peers, we are now entering a prefigurative culture in which adults learn also from their children. No matter how remote or simple the society, nowhere in the world are there elders who know what the youth know. Whereas in the past, the older generation could lend experience to guide youth through life, today's elders cannot provide this help because there simply are no guides. Youth, therefore, takes on a new authority in dealing with what is a mutually experienced unknown future.

The impact of this insight for adults is highlighted in an observation by June Bingham:

> Those now over 40 were often burdened by their late-Victorian and pre-Freudian parents with a harsh conscience, a tendency to overblame themselves. They are sandwiched between a generation that questioned too little and a generation that questions too much. They themselves never had the white meat of the turkey. When they were children, the best parts were saved, as a matter of course, for the adults; by the time they grew up, the best parts were being saved, as a matter of course, for the children. Having been children in an adult-centered world, they are now adults in a child-centered world." (4, p. 427)

Our society is structured in accordance with our outmoded ways of thinking about one another. And our incapacity to learn to think differently leads to the suppression of some of our most vital elements. The rebellion of youth is mostly seen as a threat to an established order essential to the well-being of adults. However, it is through the process of rebelling that the adolescent asserts his own self-identity and adds meaning to his life. In short, any upheaval is viewed negatively by the adult while at the same time it may be "functional" and beneficial for the adolescent.

One does not bridge the generation gap by merely eliminating tensions. The older generation has to make room economically, politically, and emotionally if the adolescent is ever to realize his own potential. But, this does not call for the full-blown free expression of adolescent rebellion and all that implies. Instead, one must create conditions whereby the social structure is supported or modified so that *both* the older and the younger generation can work through *their* conflicts within a relatively stable climate.

Doubtless, this will not occur easily. The conflicts between generations exist because we are consistent in the way we feel about one another. Changes will not occur until we are able to invent new ways of seeing, imagining and describing ourselves relative to one another.

Synthesizing Concepts

It is not possible here to fully explore how to bring together the diverging concepts into more meaningful forms in practice. We may illustrate only a few areas where a conscious effort to integrate concepts in practice could lead to changing perspectives. Most essential in the process is the need to become aware of the basic assumptions underlying our services. This is important because unrecognized assumptions have a habit of blocking from our view new and unique potentials. They act as cultural blinders which are most costly in terms of what is systematically overlooked rather than what is specifically stated. We have become accustomed to think that orthodox Freudians set about to resolve oedipal conflicts, Adlerians seek to alter compensatory strivings, Rankians try to resolve separation anxieties, Rogerians seek to bridge the gaps between the real and ideal self, while the Existentialists continue to reach for self-awareness.

The ways agencies organize around conceptual frameworks, and institutionalize procedures to perpetuate them, reinforce conceptual bias and hamper efforts to integrate approaches. Thus, in spite of efforts to refer and coordinate services at all levels of practice, the fact remains that knowledge and skills developed in one approach are not available in usable form to those practicing in the other. The outcome is that the client remains fragmented in spite of even the most sophisticated efforts to develop services which intervene simultaneously at different target points.

The bridging of the generation gap, we have asserted, calls for the creation of stable conditions which will permit both adults and youths to work out tensions and provide youths with the opportunity to experience new statuses and roles. A step toward synthesizing our concepts would be achieved if we could organize our thinking around certain core themes. For example, if the focus is on providing opportunities for newly created places in society for youths, then one could select across the traditional boundaries of behavioral sciences to incorporate what is known about the identity crisis with our knowledge of how the social structure is unfortunately patterned so as to prevent the emergence of meaningful statuses and roles. Instead of treating individual pathology or manipulating social systems, the aim would be on using knowledge of the social structure to come down to cases in directly helping the adolescent. The focus then will be on finding ways to help him search out his individual potential, not however as a passive participant in the social setting. Indeed, it is vital that he be encouraged to become actively engaged with other adolescents and with adults, changing expectations and creating new and meaningful transitional places for youth in the society.

One cannot overemphasize the need to view adolescents and adults as an interacting unit, for to separate them in our thinking distorts their true nature. Insofar as the interaction of the two becomes the basic unit of concern, new guides for development will become apparent. For example, this might move us away from the trend towards specializing services aimed at particular age groups. Those who typically work with adolescents may become less identified with them as it becomes apparent that success would depend more on developing skills in influencing the nature of *interaction* which exists between the younger and older generations.

Activities would be redirected at those points in everyday life where youths and adults come together. Most educational programs, youth-service agencies, and neighborhood and community centers will have to drastically revise their programs. This is a far cry from the traditional involvement of youth in such activities as youth councils, which are so often characterized by adult manipulation, paternalism, and authoritative control. On the contrary, adolescents along with adults will have to share responsibility in the schools, agency centers, and in economic and political activity as well. The important point is that the adolescent become a contributing part of his environment with structured positions and well-defined expectations. This would suggest new positions in decision-making or policy-making groups, carrying responsibility for service projects and economic enterprises, lobbying for changing legislation—in short, a greatly expanded involvement in *things that matter*.

Part of the focus would be on changing the adult's traditional expectations to encourage the acceptance of adolescent upheavals as a natural state of affairs in social relations. This may call for educational programs aimed at reevaluating negative reactions which arise among adults and which tend to strain relations and cloud the real issues. It would suggest institutionalizing conflicts through new opportunities for community debate, and shared problem-solving activities in significant arenas where community standards influence the behavior of youths. In the search for individual solutions to the identity problem the adolescent would be encouraged to invent significant roles for himself in dealing with issues of concern.

It is admittedly difficult to project in any clear way how services might look if they were reorganized around different sets of concepts. Interestingly enough this in itself tells us something. We become so accustomed to the familiar programs and the traditional ways of thinking about them that even as they become outmoded or ineffective they continue to influence our judgment, blocking easy access to new insights and fresh approaches.

Conclusion

We have stressed the need to create new social conditions to help both older and younger generations work out intergenerational tensions. The new conditions should also provide for the assumption of new statuses by the younger generation within a climate of stability. The means for achieving this vary according to the particular concepts and theories which are used. None tells the complete story nor does any correspond completely with the real world. It is, therefore, vital that the assumptions underlying them be fully explored, for in the final analysis they provide the distinctive flavor which characterizes practice methods and techniques. The great task is modifying, combining, and integrating newer concepts into more inclusive frameworks which more realistically reflect life experiences.

REFERENCES

1. Alissi, Albert S. "Bridging the Concept Gap in Work with Youth," *Children*, 1971, Vol. 18, No. 1, pp. 13-18.
2. Bandua, Albert, and Richard H. Walters. *Social Learning and Personality Development*. New York: Holt, Rinehart & Winston, 1963, 329 pp.
3. Beller, E. Kuno. "Theories of Adolescent Development," in James F. Adams, ed., *Understanding Adolescence*. Boston: Allyn and Bacon, 1968, pp. 70-100.
4. Bingham, June. "The Intelligent Square's Guide to Hippieland," in Simon Dinitz, Russell R. Dynes, and Alfred C. Clarke, eds., *Deviance*. New York: Oxford University Press, 1969, pp. 418-427.
5. Coleman, James. *The Adolescent Society*. New York: The Free Press of Glencoe, 1961, 368 pp.
6. Committee on Adolescence, Group for the Advancement of Psychiatry, *Normal Adolescence*. New York: Charles Scribner's Sons, 1968, 127 pp.
7. Cross, Herbert. "Conceptual Systems Theory Application to Some Problems of Adolescents," *Adolescence*, 1967, Vol. II, No. 6, pp. 153-165.
8. Davis, Allison. "Socialization and Adolescent Personality," in *Adolescence: Yearbook of the National Society for the Study of Education*, 1944.
9. Davis, Kingsley. "Adolescence and the Social Structure," in Jerome M. Seidman, ed., *The Adolescent*. New York: Holt, Rinehart & Winston, 1960, 870 pp.
10. Eisenstadt, S. N. *From Generation to Generation*. Glencoe, Illinois: The Free Press, 1956, 357 pp.
11. Elkind, David. "Cognitive Development in Adolescence," in James F. Adams, ed., *Understanding Adolescence*. Boston: Allyn and Bacon, 1968, pp. 128-158.
12. Erikson, Erik H. *Children and Society*. New York: W. W. Norton & Co., Second Edition, 1963, 445 pp.
13. Erikson, Erik H. *Identity: Youth and Crisis*. New York: W. W. Norton & Co., 1968, 336 pp.
14. Fiedler, Leslie A. "The New Mutants," in Alex Klein, ed., *Natural Enemies?* Philadelphia: J. B. Lippincott Co., 1969, pp. 206-217.
15. Friedenberg, Edgar Z. *The Vanishing Adolescent*. Boston, Mass.: Beacon Hill, 1959, 144 pp.
16. Freud, Anna. "Adolescence," *The Psychoanalytic Study of the Child*. Vol. 13, New York: International University Press, 1958, pp. 255-278.
17. Gesell, Arnold, Frances L. Ilg., and Louise B. Ames. *Youth: The Years from Ten to Sixteen*. New York: Harper, 1956.
18. Gioscia, Victor J. "Adolescence, Addiction, and Achrony," in Robert Endleman, ed., *Personality and Social Life*. New York: Random House, 1967, pp. 330-345.
19. Grinder, Robert E., and Charles E. Strickland. "G. Stanley Hall and the Social Significance of Adolescence," in Robert E. Grinder, ed., *Studies in Adolescence*. New York: Macmillan Co., 1963, pp. 3-16.
20. Hall, Edward T. *The Silent Language*. New York: Fawcett World Library, 1959, 192 pp.
21. Hall, Granville Stanley. *Adolescence*. Vol. II, New York: Appleton & Co., 1904.
22. Havighurst, Robert J. *Developmental Tasks and Education*. New York: Longmans, Green, 1951.
23. Inhelder, Barbel, and Jean Piaget. *The Growth of Logical Thinking from Childhood Through Adolescence*. New York: Basic Books, 1958.
24. Keniston, Kenneth. *The Uncommitted: Alienated Youth in American Society*. New York: Harcourt, Brace & World, 1960.
25. Mays, John Barron, *The Young Pretenders*. New York: Schocken Books, 1965, 206 pp.
26. Mead, Margaret. *Culture and Commitment: A Study of the Generation Gap*. New York: Doubleday & Co., 1970, 91 pp.

27. Mehrabian, Albert. *Tactics of Social Influence*. Englewood Cliffs, New Jersey: Prentice-Hall, 1970, 152 pp.
28. Schickil, Richard: "Why Youth Seeks New Values," in Alexander Klein, ed., *Natural Enemies?*, Philadelphia: J. B. Lippincott Co., 1969, pp. 1-10.
29. Muuss, Rolf E. "Jean Piaget's Cognitive Theory of Adolescent Development," *Adolescence*, 1967, Vol. II, No. 7, pp. 285-310.
30. Poirier, Richard. "The War Against the Young," in Alexander Klein, ed., *Natural Enemies?*, Philadelphia: J. B. Lippincott Co., 1969, pp. 172-189.
31. Roszak, Theodore. *The Making of a Counter Culture*. Garden City, New York: Doubleday & Co., 1968, 303 pp.
32. Sebald, Hans. *Adolescence: A Sociological Analysis*. New York: Appleton-Century-Crofts, 1968, 537 pp.

2. The Concept of Developmental Lines

Anna Freud
DIRECTOR
HAMPSTEAD CHILD THERAPY CLINIC

For useful answers to the parents' questions concerning developmental issues, the external decisions under consideration need thus to be translated into their internal implications. This cannot be done if drive and ego development are viewed in isolation from each other, necessary as this is for purposes of clinical analysis and theoretical dissection.

So far, in our psychoanalytic theory, the developmental sequences are laid down only with regard to particular, circumscribed parts of the child's personality. Concerning the development of the sexual drive, for example, we possess the sequence of libidinal phases (oral, anal, phallic, latency period, preadolescence, adolescent genitality) which, in spite of considerable overlapping, correspond roughly with specific ages. With regard to the aggressive drive we are already less precise and are usually content to correlate specific aggressive expressions with specific libidinal phases (such as biting, spitting, devouring with orality; sadistic torturing, hitting, kicking, destroying with anality; overbearing, domineering, forceful behavior with the phallic phase; inconsiderateness, mental cruelty, dissocial outbursts with adolescence, etc.). On the side of the ego, the analytically known stages and levels of the sense of reality, in the chronology of defense activity and in the growth of a moral sense, lay down a norm. The intellectual functions themselves are measured and graded by the psychologist by means of the age-related scales of the various intelligence tests.

Without doubt we need more for our assessments than these selected developmental scales which are valid for isolated parts of the child's personality only, not for its totality. What we are looking for are the basic interactions between id and ego and their various developmental levels, and also age-related sequences of them which, in importance, frequency, and regularity, are comparable to the maturational sequence of libidinal stages or the gradual unfolding of the ego functions. Naturally, such sequences of interaction between the two sides of the personality can be best established where both are well studied, as they are, for example, with regard to the libidinal phases and aggressive expressions on the id side and the corresponding object-related attitudes on the ego side. Here we can trace the combinations which lead from the infant's complete emotional dependence to the adult's comparative self-reliance and mature sex and object relationships, a gradated developmental line which provides the indispensable basis for any assessment of emotional maturity or immaturity, normality or abnormality.

Even if perhaps less easily established, there are similar lines of development which can be shown to be valid for almost every other area of the individual's personality. In every instance they trace the child's gradual outgrowing of dependent, irrational, id- and object-determined attitudes to an increasing ego mastery of his internal and external world. Such lines—always contributed to from the side of both id and ego development—lead, for example, from the infant's suckling and weaning experiences to the adult's rational rather than emotional attitude to food intake; from cleanliness training enforced on the child by environmental pressure to the adult's more or less ingrained and unshakable bladder and bowel control; from the child's sharing possession of his body with his mother to the adolescent's claim for independence and self-determination in body management; from the young child's egocentric view of the world and his fellow beings to empathy, mutuality, and companionship with his contemporaries; from the first erotic play on his own and his mother's body by way of the transitional objects (Winnicott, 1953) to the toys, games, hobbies, and finally to work, etc.

Whatever level has been reached by any given child in any of these respects represents the results of interaction between drive and ego-superego development and their reaction to environmental influences, i.e., between maturation, adaptation, and structuralization. Far from being theoretical abstractions, developmental lines, in the sense here used, are historical realities which, when assembled, convey a convincing picture of an individual child's personal achievements or, on the other hand, of his failures in personality development.

Prototype of a Developmental Line: From Dependency to Emotional Self-Reliance and Adult Object Relationships

To serve as the prototype for all others, there is one basic developmental line which has received attention from analysts from the beginning.

This is the sequence which leads from the newborn's utter dependence on maternal care to the young adult's emotional and material self-reliance—a sequence for which the successive stages of libido development (oral, anal, phallic) merely form the inborn, maturational base. The steps on this way are well documented from the analyses of adults and children, as well as from direct analytic infant observations. They can be listed, roughly, as follows:

1. The biological unity between the mother-infant couple, with the mother's narcissism extending to the child, and the child including the mother in his internal "narcissistic milieu" (Hoffer, 1952), the whole period being further subdivided (according to Margaret Mahler, 1952) into the autistic, symbiotic, and separation-individuation phases with significant danger points for developmental disturbances lodged in each individual phase;
2. the part object (Melanie Klein), or need-fulfilling, anaclitic relationship, which is based on the urgency of the child's body needs and drive derivatives and is intermittent and fluctuating, since object cathexis is sent out under the impact of imperative desires, and withdrawn again when satisfaction has been reached;
3. the stage of object constancy, which enables a positive inner image of the object to be maintained, irrespective of either satisfactions or dissatisfactions;
4. the ambivalent relationship of the preoedipal, anal-sadistic stage, characterized by the ego attitudes of clinging, torturing, dominating, and controlling the love objects;
5. the completely object-centered phallic-oedipal phase, characterized by possessiveness of the parent of the opposite sex (or vice versa), jealousy of and rivalry with the parent of the same sex, protectiveness, curiosity, bids for admiration, and exhibitionistic attitudes; in girls a phallic-oedipal (masculine) relationship to the mother preceding the oedipal relationship to the father;
6. the latency period, i.e., the postoedipal lessening of drive urgency and the transfer of libido from the parental figures to contemporaries, community groups, teachers, leaders, impersonal ideals, and aim-inhibited, sublimated interests, with fantasy manifestations giving evidence of disillusionment with and denigration of the parents ("family romance," twin fantasies, etc.);
7. the preadolescent prelude to the "adolescent revolt," i.e., a return to early attitudes and behavior, especially of the part-object, need-fulfilling, and ambivalent type;

8. the adolescent struggle around denying, reversing, loosening, and shedding the tie to the infantile objects, defending against pregenitality, and finally establishing genital supremacy with libidinal cathexis transferred to objects of the opposite sex, outside the family.

While the details of these positions have long been common knowledge in analytic circles, their relevance for practical problems is being explored increasingly in recent years. As regards, for example, the much-discussed consequences of a child's separation from the mother, the parents or the home, a mere glance at the unfolding of the developmental line will be sufficient to show convincingly why the common reactions to, respectively, the pathological consequences of such happenings are as varied as they are, following the varying psychic reality of the child on the different levels. Infringements of the biological mother-infant tie (phase 1), for whatever reason they are undertaken, will thus give rise to separation anxiety (Bowlby, 1960) proper; failure of the mother to play her part as a reliable need-fulfilling and comfort-giving agency (phase 2) will cause breakdowns in individuation (Mahler, 1952) or anaclitic depression (Spitz, 1946), or other manifestations of deprivation (Alpert, 1959), or precocious ego development (James, 1960), or what has been called a "false self" (Winnicott, 1955). Unsatisfactory libidinal relations to unstable or otherwise unsuitable love objects during anal sadism (phase 4) will disturb the balanced fusion between libido and aggression and give rise to uncontrollable aggressivity, destructiveness, etc. (A. Freud, 1949). It is only after object constancy (phase 3) has been reached that the external absence of the object is substituted for, at least in part, by the presence of an internal image which remains stable; on the strength of this achievement temporary separations can be lengthened, commensurate with the advances in object constancy. Thus, even if it remains impossible to name the chronological age when separations can be tolerated, according to the developmental line it can be stated when they become phase-adequate and nontraumatic, a point of practical importance for the purposes of holidays for the parents, hospitalization of the child, convalescence, entry into nursery school, etc.[1]

There are other practical lessons which have been learned from the same developmental sequence, such as the following:

[1] If, by "mourning" we understand not the various manifestations of anxiety, distress, and malfunction which accompany object loss in the earliest phases but the painful, gradual process of detaching libido from an internal image, this, of course, cannot be expected to occur before object constancy (phase 3) has been established.

that the clinging attitudes of the toddler stage (phase 4) are the result of preoedipal ambivalence, not of maternal spoiling;

that it is unrealistic on the part of parents to expect of the preoedipal period (up to the end of phase 4) the mutuality in object relations which belongs to the next level (phase 5) only;

that no child can be fully integrated in group life before libido has been transferred from the parents to the community (phase 6). Where the passing of the oedipus complex is delayed and phase 5 is protracted as the result of an infantile neurosis, disturbances in adaptation to the group, lack of interest, school phobias (in day school), extreme homesickness (in boarding school) will be the order of the day;

that reactions to adoption are most severe in the later part of the latency period (phase 6) when, according to the normal disillusionment with the parents, all children feel as if adopted and the feelings about the reality of adoption merge with the occurrence of the "family romance";

that sublimations, foreshadowed on the oedipal level (phase 5) and developed during latency (phase 6), may be lost during preadolescence (phase 7), not through any developmental or educational failure, but owing to the phase-adequate regression to early levels (phases 2, 3, and 4);

that it is as unrealistic on the part of the parents to oppose the loosening of the tie to the family or the young person's battle against pregenital impulses in adolescence (phase 8) as it is to break the biological tie in phase 1, or oppose pregenital autoerotism in the phases 1, 2, 3, 4, and 7.

Some Developmental Lines Toward Body Independence

That the ego of an individual begins first and foremost as a body ego does not imply that bodily independence of the parents is reached earlier than emotional or moral self-reliance. On the contrary: the mother's narcissistic possessiveness of her infant's body is matched from the child's side by his archaic wishes to merge with the mother and by the confusion concerning body limits which arises from the fact that in early life the distinctions between the internal and external world are based not on objective reality but on the subjective experiences of pleasure and unpleasure. Thus, while the mother's breast, or face, hands, or hair, may be treated (or maltreated) by the infant as parts of his own organization, his hunger, his tiredness, his discomforts are her concern as much as they are his own. Although for the whole of early childhood the child's life will be dominated by body needs, body impulses, and their derivatives, the quantities and qualities of satisfactions and dissatisfactions are determined not by himself but by environmental influence. The only exceptions to this rule are the autoerotic gratifications which from the beginning are under the child's own management and, therefore, provide for him a certain circumscribed measure of independence of the object world. In contrast to these, as will be shown below, the processes of feeding, sleeping, evacuation, body hygiene, and prevention of injury and illness have to undergo complex and lengthy developments before they become the growing individual's own concern.

From Suckling to Rational Eating

A long line has to be passed through before a child arrives at the point where, for example, he can regulate his own food intake actively and rationally, quantitatively and qualitatively, on the basis of his own needs and appetites and irrespective of his relations to the provider of food, and of conscious and unconscious fantasies. The steps on the way are approximately as follows:

1. Being nursed at the breast or bottle, by the clock or on demand, with the common difficulties about intake caused partly by the infant's normal fluctuations of appetite and intestinal upsets, partly by the mother's attitudes and anxieties regarding feeding; interference with need satisfaction caused by hunger periods, undue waiting for meals, rationing or forced feeding set up the first—and often lasting—disturbances in the positive relationship to food. Pleasure sucking appears as a forerunner, by-product of, substitute for, or interference with feeding;
2. weaning from breast or bottle, initiated either by the infant himself or according to the mother's wishes. In the latter instance, and especially if carried out abruptly, the infant's protest against oral deprivation has adverse results for the normal pleasure in food. Difficulties may occur over the introduction of solids, new tastes and consistencies being either welcomed or rejected;
3. the transition from being fed to self-feeding with or without implements, "food" and "mother" still being identified with each other;
4. self-feeding with the use of spoon, fork, etc., the disagreements with the mother about the quantity of intake being shifted often to

the form of intake, i.e., table manners; meals as a general battleground on which the difficulties of the mother-child relationship can be fought out; craving for sweets as a phase-adequate substitute for oral sucking pleasures; food fads as a result of anal training, i.e., of the newly acquired reaction formation of disgust;

5. gradual fading out of the equation food-mother in the oedipal period. Irrational attitudes toward eating are now determined by infantile sexual theories, i.e., fantasies of impregnation through the mouth (fear of poison), pregnancy (fear of getting fat), anal birth (fear of intake and output), as well as by reaction formations against cannibalism and sadism;
6. gradual fading out of the sexualization of eating in the latency period, with pleasure in eating retained or even increased. Increase in the rational attitudes to food and self-determination in eating, the earlier experiences on this line being decisive in shaping the individual's food habits in adult life, his tastes, preferences, as well as eventual addictions or aversions with regard to food and drink.

The infant's reactions to the changes in phase 2 (i.e., to weaning and to the introduction of new tastes and consistencies) reflect for the first time his leaning toward either progression and adventurousness (when new experiences are welcomed) or a tenacious clinging to existing pleasures (when every change is experienced as threat and deprivation). It is to be expected that whichever attitude dominates the feeding process will also become important in other developmental areas.

The equation food-mother, which persists through phases 1-4, provides the rational background for the mother's subjective conviction that every food refusal of the child is aimed at her personally, i.e., expresses the child's rejection of her maternal care and attention, a conviction which causes much oversensitiveness in handling the feeding process and underlies the battle about food on the mother's side. It explains also why in these phases food refusal and extreme food fads can be circumvented by temporarily substituting a stranger, i.e., a noncathected or differently cathected person, for the maternal figure in the feeding situation. Children will then eat, in hospital, in nursery school, or as visitors, but this will not cure their eating difficulties at home, in the presence of the mother. It explains also why traumatic separations from the mother are often followed by refusal of food (rejection of the mother substitute), or by greed and overeating (treating food as a substitute for mother love).

The eating disturbances of phase 5, which are not related to an external object but are caused by internal, structural conflicts, are not affected by either the material presence or the material absence of the mother, a fact which can be utilized for differential diagnosis.

After phase 6, when the arrangements for food intake have become the mature individual's personal concern, the former food battle with the mother may be replaced by internal disagreements between the manifest wish to eat and an unconsciously determined inability to tolerate certain foods, i.e., the various neurotic food fads and digestive upsets.

From Wetting and Soiling to Bladder and Bowel Control

Since the desired aim on this line is not the comparatively intact survival of drive derivatives but the control, modification, and transformation of the urethral and anal trends, the conflicts between id, ego, superego, and environmental forces become particularly obvious.

1. The duration of the first phase, during which the infant has complete freedom to wet and soil, is determined not maturationally but environmentally, i.e., by the mother's timing of her interference, in which she in her turn is under the influence of personal needs, familial, social, or medical conventions. Under present conditions this phase may last from a few days (training from birth based on reflex action) to two or three years (training based on object relatedness and ego control).

2. In contrast to phase 1, the second phase is initiated by a step in maturation. The dominant role in drive activity passes from the oral to the anal zone, and due to this transition the child stiffens his opposition to any interference with concerns which have become emotion 'ly vital to him. Since in this phase the body products are highly cathected with libido, they are precious to the child and are treated as "gifts" which are surrendered to the mother as a sign of love; since they are cathected also with aggression, they are weapons by means of which rage, anger, disappointment can be discharged within the object relationship. In correspondence to this double cathexis of the body products, the toddler's entire attitude toward the object world is dominated by ambivalence, i.e., by violent swings between love and hate (libido and aggression not fused with each other). This again is matched on the ego side by curiosity directed toward the inside of the body, pleasure in messing, molding, play with retaining, emptying, hoarding, as well as dominating, possessing, destroying, etc. While the trends shown by the children in this phase are fairly uniform, the actual events vary with the differences in the mother's attitude. If she succeeds in remaining sensitive

to the child's needs and as identified with them as she is usually with regard to feeding, she will mediate sympathetically between the environmental demand for cleanliness and the child's opposite anal and urethral tendencies; in that case toilet training will proceed gradually, uneventfully, and without upheavals. On the other hand, such empathy with the child in the anal stage may be impossible for the mother due to her own training, her own reaction formations of disgust, orderliness, and punctiliousness, or other obsessional elements in her personality. If she is dominated by these, she will represent the demand for urethral and anal control in a harsh and uncompromising manner and a major battle will ensue, with the child as intent to defend his right over unrestricted evacuation as the mother is on achieving cleanliness and regularity and with them the rudiments and *sine qua non* of socialization.

3. In a third phase the child accepts and takes over the mother's and the environment's attitudes to cleanliness and, through identification, makes them an integral part of his ego and superego demands; from then onward, the striving for cleanliness is an internal, not an external, precept, and inner barriers against urethral and anal wishes are set up through the defense activity of the ego, in the well-known form of repression and reaction formation. Disgust, orderliness, tidiness, dislike of dirty hands guard against the return of the repressed; punctuality, conscientiousness, and reliability appear as by-products of anal regularity; inclinations to save, to collect, give evidence of high anal evaluation displaced to other matters. In short, what takes place in this period is the far-reaching modification and transformation of the pregenital anal drive derivatives which—if kept within normal limits—supply the individual personality with a backbone of highly valuable qualities.

It is important to remember in respect to these achievements that they are based on identifications and internalizations and, as such, are not fully secure before the passing of the oedipus complex. Preoedipal anal control remains vulnerable and, especially in the beginning of the third phase, remains dependent on the objects and the stability of positive relations to them. For example, a child who is trained to use the chamberpot or toilet in his home does not exchange them automatically for unfamiliar ones, away from the mother. A child who is severely disappointed in his mother, or separated from her, or suffering from object loss in any form, may not only lose the internalized urge to be clean but also reactivate the aggressive use of elimination. Both together will result in incidents of wetting and soiling which appear as "accidents."

4. It is only in a fourth phase that bladder and bowel control become

wholly secure. This is brought about when the concern for cleanliness is disconnected from object ties and attains the status of a fully neutralized, autonomous ego and superego concern.[2]

From Irresponsibility to Responsibility in Body Management

That the satisfaction of such essential physical needs as feeding and evacuation[3] remains for years under external control and emerges from it in such slow steps corresponds well with the equally slow and gradual manner in which children assume responsibility for the care of their own body and its protection against harm. As described at length elsewhere (A. Freud, 1952), the well-mothered child leaves these concerns largely to the mother, while he allows himself attitudes of indifference and unconcern, or, as a weapon in a battle with her, downright recklessness. It is only the badly mothered or the motherless who adopt the mother's role in health matters and play "mother and child" with their own bodies as the hypochondriacs do.

On the positive progressive line, here too, there are several consecutive phases to be distinguished from each other, though our present knowledge of them is more sketchy than in other areas.

1. What comes first, as a maturational step in the first few months of life, is an alteration in the direction of aggression from being lived out on the body to being turned toward the external world. This vital step sets limits to self-injury from biting, scratching, etc., although indications of such tendencies can also be seen in many children as genuine remnants at later ages.[4] The normal forward move happens partly due to the setting up of the pain barrier, partly due to the child's answering to the mother's libidinal cathexis of his body with a narcissistic cathexis of his own (according to Hoffer, 1950).

2. What makes itself felt next are the advances in ego functioning such as orientation in the external world, understanding of cause and effect, control of dangerous wishes in the service of the reality principle. Together with the pain barrier and the narcissistic cathexis of the body, these newly acquired functions protect the child against such external dangers as water, fire, heights, etc. But there are many instances of

[2]See H. Hartmann (1950b) on "secondary autonomy of the ego."

[3]Also sleep.

[4]Such remnants should not be confused with the later "turning of aggression against the self," which is not a defect in maturation but a defense mechanism used by the ego under the impact of conflict.

children where—owing to a deficiency in any one of these ego functions—this advance is retarded so that they remain unusually vulnerable and exposed if not protected by the adult world.

3. What comes last normally is the child's voluntary endorsement of the rules of hygiene and of medical necessities. So far as the avoidance of unwholesome food, overeating, and keeping the body clean are concerned, this is inconclusive here since the relevant attitudes belong to the vicissitudes of the oral and anal component instinct rather than to the present line. It is different with the avoidance of ill-health or the compliance with doctor's orders concerning the intake of medicines, and motor or dietary restrictions. Fear, guilt, castration anxiety, of course, may motivate any child to be careful (i.e., fearful) for the safety of his body. But when not under the influence of these, normal children will be remarkably uncompromising and obstructive in health matters. According to their mothers' frequent complaints, they behave as if they claimed it as their right to endanger their health while they left it to their mothers to protect and restore it, an attitude which lasts often until the end of adolescence and may represent the last residue of the original symbiosis between child and mother.

Further Examples of Developmental Lines

There are many other examples of developmental lines, such as the two given below, where every step is known to the analyst, and which can be traced without difficulty, either through working backward by reconstruction from the adult picture, or through working forward by means of longitudinal analytic exploration and observation of the child.

From Egocentricity to Companionship

When describing a child's growth in this particular respect, a sequence can be traced which runs as follows:

1. a selfish, narcissistically oriented outlook on the object world, in which other children either do not figure at all or are perceived only in their role as disturbers of the mother-child relationship and rivals for the parents' love;
2. other children related to as lifeless objects, i.e., toys which can be handled, pushed around, sought out, and discarded as the mood

demands, with no positive or negative response expected from them;

3. other children related to as helpmates in carrying out a desired task such as playing, building, destroying, causing mischief of some kind, etc., the duration of the partnership being determined by the task, and secondary to it;
4. other children as partners and objects in their own right, whom the child can admire, fear, or compete with, whom he loves or hates, with whose feelings he identifies, whose wishes he acknowledges and often respects, and with whom he can share possessions on a basis of equality.

In the first two phases, even if cherished and tolerated as the baby by older siblings, the toddler is by necessity asocial, whatever efforts to the contrary the mother may make; community life at this stage may be endured but will not be profitable. The third stage represents the minimum requirement for socialization in the form of acceptance into a home community of older siblings or entry into a nursery group of contemporaries. But it is only the fourth stage which equips the child for companionship, enmities and friendships of any type and duration.

From the Body to the Toy and from Play to Work

1. Play begins with the infant as an activity yielding erotic pleasure, involving the mouth, the fingers, vision, the whole surface of the skin. It is carried out on the child's own body (autoerotic play) or on the mother's body (usually in connection with feeding) with no clear distinction between the two, and with no obvious order or precedence in this respect.

2. The properties of the mother's and the child's body are transferred to some soft substance, such as a nappy, a pillow, a rug, a teddy, which serves as the infant's first plaything, the transitional object (according to Winnicott, 1953) which is cathected both with narcissistic and with object libido.

3. Clinging to one specific transitional object develops further into a more indiscriminate liking for soft toys of various kinds which, as symbolic objects, are cuddled and maltreated alternately (cathected with libido and aggression). That they are inanimate objects, and therefore do not retaliate, enables the toddler to express the full range of his ambivalence toward them.

4. Cuddly toys fade out gradually, except at bedtime, when—in their capacity as transitional objects—they continue to facilitate the child's passing from active participation in the external world to the narcissistic withdrawal necessary for sleep.

In daytime their place is taken increasingly by play material which does not itself possess object status but which serves ego activities and the fantasies underlying them. Such activities either directly gratify a component instinct or are invested with displaced and sublimated drive energies, their chronological sequence being approximately the following:

a. toys offering opportunities for ego activities such as filling-emptying, opening-shutting, fitting in, messing, etc., interest in them being displaced from the body openings and their functions;
b. movable toys providing pleasure in motility;
c. building material offering equal opportunities for construction and destruction (in correspondence with the ambivalent trends of the anal-sadistic phase);
d. toys serving the expression of masculine and feminine trends and attitudes, to be used
    i. in solitary role play,
    ii. for display to the oedipal object (serving phallic exhibitionism),
    iii. for staging the various situations of the oedipus complex in group play (provided that stage 3 on the developmental line toward companionship has been reached).

Expression of masculinity can be taken over also by the ego activities of gymnastics and acrobatics, in which the child's entire body and its skillful manipulation represent, display, and provide symbolic enjoyment from phallic activities and phallic mastery.

5. Direct or displaced satisfaction from the play activity itself gives way increasingly to the pleasure in the finished product of the activity, a pleasure which has been described in academic psychology as pleasure in task completion, in problem solving, etc. By some authors it is taken as the indispensable prerequisite for the child's successful performance in school (Bühler, 1935).

The exact manner in which this pleasure in achievement is linked with the child's instinctual life is still an open question in our theoretical thinking, although various operative factors seem unmistakable such as imitation and identification in the early mother-child relationship, the influence of the ego ideal, the turning of passive into active as a mechanism of defense and adaptation, and the inner urge toward maturation, i.e., toward progressive development.

That pleasure in achievement, linked only secondarily with object relations, is present in very young children as a latent capacity is demonstrated in a practical manner by the successes of the Montessori method. In this nursery school method the play material is selected so as to afford the child the maximum increase in self-esteem and gratification by means of task completion and independent problem solving, and children can be observed to respond positively to such opportunities almost from the toddler stage onward.

Where this source of gratification is not tapped to the same degree with the help of external arrangements, the pleasure derived from achievement in play remains more directly connected with praise and approval given by the object world, and satisfaction from the finished product takes first place at a later date only, probably as the result of internalization of external sources of self-esteem.

6. Ability to play changes into ability to *work*[5] when a number of additional faculties are acquired, such as the following:

a. to control, inhibit, or modify the impulses to use given materials aggressively and destructively (not to throw, to take apart, to mess, to hoard), and to use them positively and constructively instead (to build, to plan, to learn, and—in communal life—to share);

b. to carry out preconceived plans with a minimum regard for the lack of immediate pleasure yield, intervening frustrations, etc., and the maximum regard for the pleasure in the ultimate outcome;

c. to achieve thereby not only the transition from primitive instinctual to sublimated pleasure, together with a high grade of neutralization of the energy employed, but equally the transition from the pleasure principle to the reality principle, a development which is essential for success in work during latency, adolescence, and in maturity.

Derived from the line from the body to the toy and from play to work and based predominantly on its later stages are a number of allied activities which are significant for personality development such as daydreaming, games, and hobbies.

[5]What is attempted here is not a definition of work with all its social as well as psychological implications, but merely a description of the advances in ego development and drive control which seem to be the necessary forerunners of any individual's acquisition of the capacity to work.

Daydreaming: When toys and the activities connected with them fade into the background, the wishes formerly put into action with the help of material objects, i.e., fulfilled in play, can be spun out imaginatively in the form of conscious daydreams, a fantasy activity which may persist until adolescence, and far beyond it.

Games: Games derive their origin from the imaginative group activities of the oedipal period (see stage 4, d, iii) from which they develop into the symbolic and highly formalized expression of trends toward aggressive attack, defense, competition, etc. Since they are governed by inflexible rules to which the individual participant has to submit, they cannot be entered successfully by any child before some adaptation to reality and some frustration tolerance have been acquired and, naturally, not before stage 3 on the developmental line toward companionship has been reached.

Games may require equipment (as distinct from toys). Since this is in many instances of symbolic phallic, i.e., masculine-aggressive, significance, it is highly valued by the child.

In many competitive games the child's own body and the body skills themselves play the role of indispensable tools.

Proficiency and pleasure in games are, thus, a complex achievement, dependent on contributions from many areas of the child's personality such as the endowment and intactness of the motor apparatus; a positive cathexis of the body and its skills; acceptance of companionship and group life; positive employment of controlled aggression in the service of ambition, etc. Correspondingly, functioning in this area is open to an equally large number of disturbances which may result from developmental difficulties and inadequacies in any of these areas, as well as from the phase-determined inhibitions of anal aggression and phallic-oedipal masculinity.

Hobbies: Halfway between play and work is the place of the hobbies, which have certain aspects in common with both activities. With play they share a number of characteristics:

a. of being undertaken for purposes of pleasure with comparative disregard for external pressures and necessities;

b. of pursuing displaced, i.e., sublimated, aims, but aims which are not too far removed from the gratification of either erotic or aggressive drives;

c. of pursuing these aims with a combination of unmodified drive energies plus energies in various states and degrees of neutralization.

With working attitudes as described above, the hobbies share the important feature of a preconceived plan being undertaken in a reality-adapted way and carried on over a considerable period of time, if necessary in the face of external difficulties and frustrations.

Hobbies appear for the first time at the beginning of the latency period (collecting, spotting, specializing of interests), undergo any number of changes of content, but may persist as this specific form of activity throughout life.

Correspondence Between Developmental Lines

If we examine our notions of average normality in detail, we find that we expect a fairly close correspondence between growth on the individual developmental lines. In clinical terms this means that, to be a harmonious personality, a child who has reached a specific stage in the sequence toward emotional maturity (for example, object constancy), should have attained also corresponding levels in his growth toward bodily independence (such as bladder and bowel control, loosening of the tie between food and mother), in the lines toward companionship, constructive play, etc. We maintain this expectation of a norm even though reality presents us with many examples to the contrary. There are numerous children, undoubtedly, who show a very irregular pattern in their growth. They may stand high on some levels (such as maturity of emotional relations, bodily independence, etc.) while lagging behind in others (such as play where they continue to cling to transitional objects, cuddly toys, or development of companionship where they persist in treating contemporaries as disturbances or inanimate objects). Some children are well developed toward secondary thought, speech, play, work, community life while remaining in a state of dependency with regard to the management of their own bodily processes, etc.

Such imbalance between developmental lines causes sufficient friction in childhood to justify a closer inquiry into the circumstances which give rise to it, especially into the question how far it is determined by innate and how far by environmental reasons.

As in all similar instances, our task is not to isolate the two factors and to ascribe to each a separate field of influence but to trace their interactions, which may be described as follows:

We assume that with all normally endowed, organically undamaged children the lines of development indicated above are included in their constitution as inherent possibilities. What endowment lays down for them on the side of the id are, obviously, the maturational sequences in the development of libido and aggression; on the side of the ego, less obviously and less well studied, certain innate tendencies toward organization, defense, and structuralization; perhaps also, though we know less still about this, some given quantitative differences of emphasis on progress in one direction or another. For the rest, that is, for what singles out individual lines for special promotion in development, we have to look to accidental environmental influences. In the analysis of older children and the reconstructions from adult analysis we have found these forces embodied in the parents' personalities, their actions and ideals, the family atmosphere, the impact of the cultural setting as a whole. In the analytic observation of young infants it has been demonstrated that it is the individual mother's interest and predilection which act as stimulants. In the beginning of life, at least, the infant seems to concentrate on the development along those lines which call forth most ostensibly the mother's love and approval, i.e., her spontaneous pleasure in the child's achievement and, in comparison, to neglect others where such approval is not given. This implies that activities which are acclaimed by the mother are repeated more frequently, become libidinized, and thereby stimulated into further growth.

For example, it seems to make a difference to the timing of speech development and the quality of early verbalization if a mother, for reasons of her own personality structure, makes contact with her infant not through bodily channels but through talking. Some mothers find no pleasure in the growing infant's adventurousness and bodily unruliness and have their happiest and most intimate moments when the infant smiles. We have seen at least one such mother whose infant made constant and inordinate use of smiling in his approaches to the whole environment. It is not unknown that early contact with the mother through her singing has consequences for the later attitudes to music and may promote special musical aptitudes. On the other hand, marked disinterest of the mother in the infant's body and his developing motility may result in clumsiness, lack of grace in movement, etc.

It was known in psychoanalysis long before such infant observations that depressive moods of the mother during the first two years after birth create in the child a tendency to depression (although this may not manifest itself until many years later). What happens is that such infants achieve their sense of unity and harmony with the depressed mother not by means of their developmental achievements but by producing the mother's mood in themselves.

All this means no more than that tendencies, inclinations, predilections (including the tendency to depression, to masochistic attitudes, etc.) which are present in all human beings can be eroticized and stimulated toward growth through forming emotional links between the child and his first object.

The disequilibrium between developmental lines which is created in this manner is not pathological as such. Moderate disharmony does no more than prepare the ground for the innumerable differences as they exist among individuals from an early date, i.e., it produces the many *variations of normality* with which we have to count.

Applications: Entry into Nursery School as an Illustration

To return to the problems and queries raised by parents which are mentioned above:

With the foregoing points in mind, the child analyst can cease to answer them on the basis of the child's chronological age, a factor which is inconclusive psychologically; or on the basis of the child's intellectual grasp of the situation, which is a one-sided view diagnostically. Instead, he can think in terms of basic psychological differences between the mature and immature, and in terms of lines of development. The child's readiness to meet events such as the birth of a sibling, hospitalization, school entry, etc., is seen then as the direct outcome of his developmental progress on all the lines which have a bearing on this specific experience. If the appropriate stations have been reached, the happening will be constructive and beneficial to the child; if this is not the case, either on all or on some of the lines concerned, the child will feel bewildered and overtaxed and no effort on the part of the parents, teachers, nurses will prevent his distress, unhappiness, and sense of failure which often assume traumatic proportions.

Such a "diagnosis of the normal child" can be illustrated by a practical example, taking—as one for many—the question under which developmental circumstances a child is ready to leave his home surroundings temporarily for the first time, to give up his close proximity to the mother and enter group life in a nursery school without undue distress and with benefit to himself.

Required Status on the Line "from Dependency to Emotional Self-Reliance"

In the not-too-distant past it was assumed that a child who had reached the age of three years six months should be able to separate from his mother on the first day of entry at the outer door of the nursery school building and should adapt to the new physical surroundings, the new teacher, and the new playmates all in one morning. A blind eye was turned toward the distress of the new entrants; their crying for their mothers, their initial lack of participation and cooperation were considered of little significance. What happened under those conditions was that most children went through an initial stage of extreme unhappiness, after which they settled down to nursery school routine. Some others reversed this sequence of events. They began with a period of acquiescence and apparent enjoyment which then, to the surprise of parents and teacher, was followed a week later by intense unhappiness and a breakdown in participation. In their case, the delayed reaction was due to a slower intellectual grasp of the external circumstances. What seems important with regard to both types of reaction is the fact that formerly no thought was given to the way the individual children were affected internally by their respective periods of distress and desolation, and—more important still—that the latter were accepted as inevitable.

As seen from our present point of view, they are inevitable only if developmental considerations are neglected. If, at nursery school entry, a child of whatever chronological age still finds himself at stage 1 or 2 of this developmental line, separation from home and mother, even for short periods, is not age adequate and offends against his most vital need; protest and suffering under these conditions are legitimate. If he has reached *object constancy* at least (stage 3), separation from the mother is less upsetting, he is ready to reach out to new people and to accept new ventures and adventures. Even then, the change has to be introduced gradually, in small doses, the periods of independence must not be too long, and, in the beginning, return to the mother should be open to his choice.

Required Status on the Line Toward Bodily Independence

Some children are extremely uncomfortable in nursery school because they find themselves unable to enjoy any food or drink which they are given, or to use the lavatory for urination or defecation. This does not depend on the type of food offered or on the lavatory arrangements themselves, although the child himself usually uses their strangeness as a rationalization. The real difference between the child's function or disfunction in these respects is the developmental one. On the eating line at least stage 4 of self-feeding should have been reached; on the line to bowel and bladder control, the attitude toward cleanliness belonging to stage 3.

Required Status on the Line Toward Companionship

Any child will be a disturbing element in the nursery school group, and unhappy in himself, before he has attained the stage where other children can be related to at least as helpmates in play (stage 3). He will be a constructive, leading member in the group as soon as he learns to accept other children as partners in their own right, a step which enables him also to form real friendships (stage 4). In fact, if development in this respect is at a lower level, he either should not be accepted in nursery school or, if he has entered, he should be permitted to interrupt attendance.

Required Status on the Line from Play to Work

The child usually enters nursery school at the beginning of the stage when "play material serves ego activities and the fantasies underlying them" (stage 4), and he climbs up the ladder of development gradually through the sequence of toys and materials until at the end of nursery school life he reaches the beginning of "work," which is a necessary prerequisite for entry into elementary school. In this respect it is the task of the teacher throughout to match the child's needs for occupation and expression with the material offered and not to create a sense either of boredom or of failure by lagging too far behind or by anticipating needs before they arise.

So far as the child's ability to *behave* adequately in nursery school is concerned, this depends not on any of the developmental lines described, but in general on the interrelations between his id and ego.

Somewhere in her mind, even the most tolerant nursery school teacher carries the image of the "ideal" nursery child who exhibits no outward signs of impatience or restlessness; who asks for what he wants instead of grabbing it; who can wait for his turn; who is satisfied with his fair share; who does not throw temper tantrums but can stand disappointments. Even if no single child will ever display all these forms of behavior, they will be found in the group, in one or the other pupil, with regard to one or the other aspect of daily life. In analytic terms this means that, at this period, the children are on the point of learning how to master their affects and impulses instead of being at the mercy of them. The developmental tools at their disposal in this respect belong above all to ego growth: advance from primary process to secondary process functioning, i.e., to be able to interpolate thought, reasoning, and anticipation of the future between wish and action directed toward fulfillment (Hartmann, 1947); advance from the pleasure principle to the reality principle. What comes to the help of the child from the side of the id is the age-adequate—probably organically determined—lessening in the urgency of the drives.

3. Kurt Lewin and Field Theory*

Gardner Murphy, Ph.D.
Professor of Psychology
George Washington University

Kurt Lewin is one of the great figures in modern systematic psychology. He delighted in order and system; he thought like a mathematician; he stood for rigor and precision. On the other hand, he was a man of great warmth, charm, devotion, a father or big brother to a rising generation of creative young psychologists first in Germany, then in the United States.

A place was ready in twentieth-century psychology for a man of this stature and of this personal quality. Experimental psychology in the German universities was producing new ideas by the dozens during the first decade of this century. There was the "personalistic psychology" of William Stern, striving to find the uniquely individualistic or personalistic in each quality of an organism's response; there was the experimental psychology of the thought processes, with systematic implications for what Freud called "preconscious" activities, as represented by Külpe at Würzburg; there was the experimental development of projective tests, such as the use of handwriting by Klages; and there was the vivid and challenging new Gestalt psychology of Max Wertheimer.

All these movements, however, represented a common theme, a basic preoccupation with *structure*. Everywhere the older psychologists were accused of piecemeal attention to details, or "atomism"; or, as Dilthey had said, a tendency to rend, anatomize, or dissect *(zergliedern)*. The strain was developing in the direction of a radical new formulation in terms of pattern, order, form, or perhaps most comprehensively, *structure*. Wertheimer's Gestalt psychology began with Wertheimer's interpretation of his experimental studies of the perception of motion: With a stroboscope he showed that when one visual impression is replaced a fraction of a second later by a second one, the *motion* experienced cannot possibly be the sum of the first static impression plus the second, but is a higher-order integration suggesting the presence of true higher-level "cross processes"

*Presented to the Topeka Institute of Psychoanalysis, March 2, 1966.

in the brain. Wertheimer's two brilliant pupils, Wolfgang Köhler and Kurt Koffka, went on to show the broad implications of a form or Gestalt principle for the processes of perceiving, thinking, and indeed growing and learning. Gestalt psychology was a new movement, hardly to be heard during the course of the four years of the First World War, but rapidly making its way thereafter.

Fresh from military service, Kurt Lewin appeared at the University of Berlin as an honors student in mathematics and physics. Here he soon had an opportunity to associate himself with the three great leaders already named, for by an extraordinary coincidence at the University of Berlin all four men—Wertheimer, Koffka, Köhler, and Lewin—did pioneer experiments in the formulation of their ideas in the twenties. Lewin was not quite an orthodox Gestalt psychologist, but he was heart and soul with the new movement, and a contributor to the new development by developing his own special quality of mathematical thinking.

In particular, Lewin had been impressed with the concept of "field" as used in physics and now coming into biology. He was impressed especially with topology, one development in modern mathematics which deals with certain problems of space. We may, for example, draw an irregular curving line that sweeps about and then joins itself, and we may define the properties of the space within and the space without this line without even asking ourselves how big the area is, or whether the contour line is a circle, ellipse, or whatnot. This "Jordan curve" has certain properties, for example, relating to the impossibility of getting from one space to the other without crossing the line; and we may proceed to set up within this space a series of sub-spaces, each of which is bounded and permits communication from one to another *only* if there are open passages, in other words, if the surface is "porous." It occurred to Lewin that many of the phenomena of psychology are based upon areas included and areas excluded, and upon firm or porous barriers from one to the other.

Indeed he proceeded to conceptualize through *topology* the concept of the "life space," the psychological space in which each of us lives. Putting aside for the moment the experience of the passage of time, certainly a very large part, perhaps all of our experience, is organized in some sort of spatial form. This is not simple Euclidean space. We would not apply Euclid's methods of demonstration to its study. It is, however, a kind of space and it can be studied in topological terms.

Let us suppose, for example, that a child very intensely desires to go to the movies after supper. The parents say "no." We may define the life space of the child in terms of the enclosed surface shown below in which the movies represent the goal object on the right, and the arrow represents the child's tension or vector directed towards this fascinating goal. A firm black line, however, represents the parents' veto.

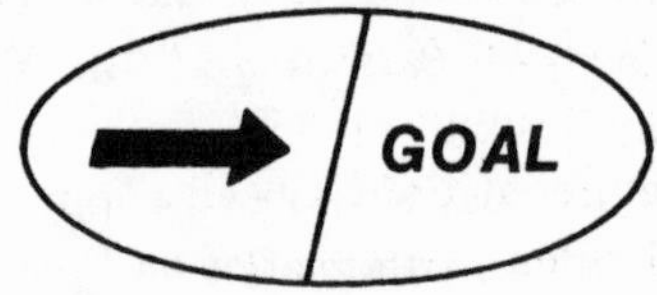

There is no way to get through. We can, however, bring in the further resources of a basically geometrical way of thinking. The child may dream, and lift the whole process to a higher level. Here again in the figure below we have the child with his wishes, and at the higher level we note that the barrier has become porous; the veto of the parents is not absolute in the fantasy world of the dream. The child gets through somehow to the desired goal.

We have already passed beyond the sheer analysis of the formal attributes of psychological space and their representation through a

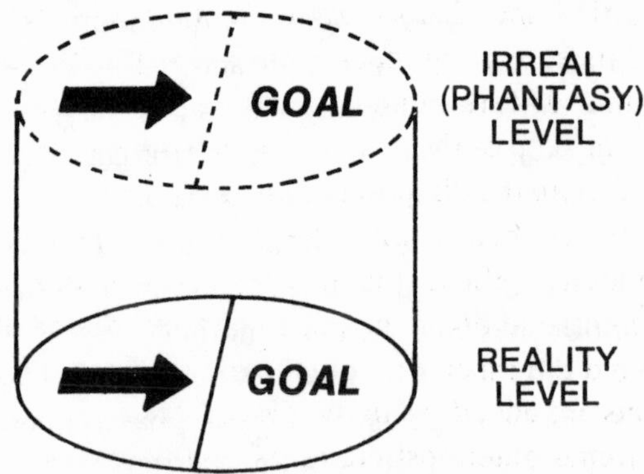

topological scheme; for we have introduced the concept of *goal,* and the associated *vector* which turns any neutral object into a goal. We find ourselves close indeed to the Freudian concept of investment or cathexis. There may, in any representation, be many vectors, many goals, many directed activities. We may consequently proceed to set up a chart to represent now the life space of any one of us at a given time. Suppose, for example, that I wish to get into a society or hobby group, and the question of my really sharing the interests of the other members, the question of my adequacy as a potential member, comes up for consideration. I may be admitted to some, and excluded from others. Our life space is honeycombed likewise with areas into which we cannot move because of age, sex, race, economic circumstances, or dozens of other matters. Each of us lives in a rather tortured and tortuous system of open and semi-open spaces in which we may visualize the vector arrows darting hither and yon, sometimes finding a way through a porous barrier, and sometimes not.

Sometimes the nature of the individual may determine, whether by biological or by social rules, the sub-spaces into which he can move. A mental defective, for example, appears in some of Lewin's studies to be capable of handling certain types of simple repetitive tasks in an easy and disciplined way, but to undergo emotional difficulties as the task changes. Modes of functioning which are "open to" other children are "closed to" the defective child.

We may symbolize the growth process as one of differentiation or progressive subdivision of the whole life space into more and more parts. It may or may not be true that the mind of the newborn, as William James said, is a "blooming, buzzing confusion," but it is certainly a less differentiated world in which impressions from sight, from sound, from the skin, etc., and the upwelling tensions from the vital organs and muscles are less easily identified and sharply named and articulated than in the older child. The child must learn to identify the parts of the body; he must learn to recognize and differentiate sensory and emotional experiences. Ultimately with the help of those around him he gives things names and can control more and more the direction of his learning.

The first figure below indicates the way in which the separate components—motor, reflex, instinctive, etc., whatever we may call them—are differentiated off in the opening weeks of life, as in a system of "scallops" around the inner wall of the Jordan curve. Later on, however, more components are added, as in the second chart below; that is, there are not only the extreme outermost elements, but elements somewhat within, and we go on building in an inner-directed direction until there is only a little of the undifferentiated inner world that has not been marked out, differentiated, recognized, and accepted as part of our most intimate personal experience: the inner world of the person.

Incidentally this conception of *degrees of differentiation,* person by person, is one which has been fruitfully developed recently by Witkin, who has shown that the "field independence" which appears in experimental studies of the process of perceiving—the capacity for sharp separation of each component of a given experience from each other component so that things do not get mixed up—can be traced to a very broad differentiation

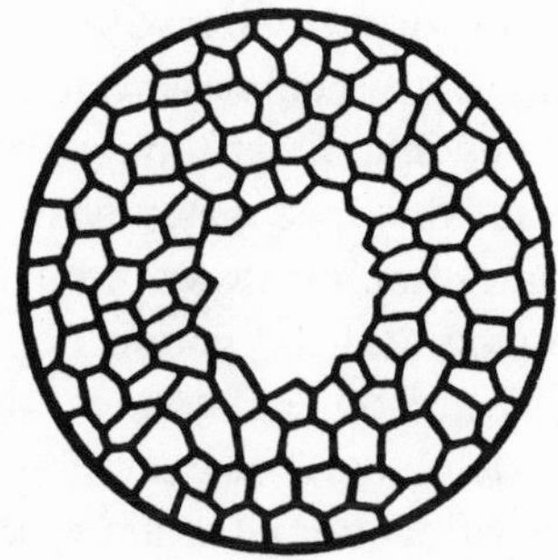

capacity of the person as a whole, a capacity differing notably from one person to another.

But clearly in a quasi-mathematical form of thinking like this, we need to pay more attention to the identification and measurement of the system of tensions. Outstandingly brilliant and influential along these lines is the work of Zeigarnik, done under Lewin's direction at Berlin. She gave her subjects a series of tasks to be carried out in the laboratory, allowing the subjects to complete some of these tasks and in other instances interrupting them before the work was done. Later, after other activities had been carried out, she asked her subjects to recall all the tasks which she had assigned them. She noted a very marked difference between the ability to recall tasks which had been completed and the ability to recall those which had been interrupted. In fact, there were nearly twice as many interrupted tasks recalled as completed tasks. This very strongly suggested that she was right in thinking of each task as involving a tension which had been worked up to a certain level, and which had been discharged when each task had been finished. On the other hand, an undischarged state remained in the case of the interrupted tasks, which revealed their own dynamic when the cue to recall was presented. It is the high level of tension which keeps material ready for reappearance in action or in consciousness.

The Zeigarnik ratio of two to one for interrupted versus uninterrupted tasks has been studied by a long series of later investigators. Some of them indeed showed that the form of the responses and the Zeigarnik ratios will vary with the kind of tension system involved. If, for example, the subject believes that the interruption of the task means he is not doing at all well, this has an utterly different meaning from what would appear when the subject believes he is interrupted because he has already done enough. Similar variations in the tension qualities result naturally in different types of tension patterns.

Another series of studies which won prompt renown were those by Hoppe, who was interested in tension as related to the individual's standard or goal of achievement which he had set for himself, his "aspiration level." A conveyor belt on which there were hooks moved rapidly by and the subject was required to put rings on the hooks. The task could be made easier or harder. As soon as he had completed a task, and had made a certain score, let us say sixty percent of successful placement of the rings on the hooks, he was asked: "How well will you do next time?" The resulting difference score was based upon the average discrepancy between what he had actually done and what he had predicted he would do. It turned out that some people characteristically maintained high difference scores; they would set their own aspiration level far too high to be in accord with reality. On the other hand some individuals set the aspiration level so low that they easily won and there was no real effort towards mastery.

A further illustration of the conception of tension within a walled-in system which, as it mounts, will inevitably produce increased stress somewhere is the study of a group of prisoners who, during long terms, had won considerable credit through good behavior, but who, a few days before their scheduled release, became violent—the very opposite of what a calculated pleasure-pain philosophy would expect. This, of course, is analogous to the psychoanalytic conception of a tendency of high mounting energy to find expression through one or another symptom, often involving the substitution of one immediate object of aggression for another. The appropriate comparisons with the psychoanalytic system are abundant.

I have been describing Lewin's work in Germany up to 1932. In 1932 it was my privilege to meet him at the Columbia University Faculty Club in New York on his way west. The situation in Germany was difficult, but it was not at all certain what was going to happen. When I talked to him he was eager to talk about child psychology, eager to talk of tension and vector psychology as regards mother-child relationships. At the time he had an invitation to Stanford which he accepted, and from which he went on to appointments at the State University of Iowa, at Cornell, and later at the Massachusetts Institute of Technology at Cambridge. From the Stanford appointment onwards, he went on to an unbroken and highly productive period of directing advanced studies, particularly doctoral dissertations at American universities, employing basic field theory concepts.

I will illustrate the trend of his thinking by summarizing several of the best-known experimental studies:

First, the study by Barker, Dembo and Lewin on an attempt to translate psychoanalytic concepts into field theory concepts, and to put them into demonstrable experimental form. Suppose, in the light of our conception of differentiation of the life space, we can conceive of the little child as relatively undifferentiated, with scallops around the edge, so to speak, and the inner region relatively undifferentiated. We may say that a six-year-old boy is a good deal more differentiated than a two-year-old. If now we should wish to test the hypothesis that frustration can lead to regression—that is, a backward movement developmentally to an earlier more primitive, less differentiated form—we may say for the purposes of the test, "Regression is *de*-differentiation," and since we can measure the process of differentiation, or its reverse—*de*-differentiation—we can experimentally frustrate the child and measure the regressive behavior.

Thirty children of nursery school age were rated on "constructiveness." If a toy telephone were used simply as a rattle, this would have low value, but if it were used to carry on an imaginary conversation the score would be high. Scribbling with a crayon would count low, and pretending to write a letter would count high. Children who had been observed and rated in a variety of these situations were then led towards another part of the play area, and shown some fascinating *new* toys such as a "duck pond." But they were only allowed a few moments of play, and were then led away, and confronted again with the old toys on which their play had been rated. In response to this "frustration," they did show an astonishing "regression" in the following terms: The average regression on the constructiveness scale was seventeen months of mental age from an average fifty-five-month level at the beginning. Children had become more "babyish." The method was sufficient then to show that de-differentiation could be expressed in terms of an experimental procedure. It is true that the nine out of the thirty children who did not show this tendency were not easy to interpret in the schema; and that the ideal of "exceptionless validity" towards which these experiments aimed was very difficult to achieve with human material; but perhaps this is comparable to the early abstractions and later qualifications and modifications which are characteristic of all psychology.

Such studies are conceived in "individualistic" terms, the individual child being the subject of observation. There is room, however, in Lewin's field theory for a study of interpersonal responses, and the experimental constitution of groups for experimental purposes. In fact, "group dynamics," a pattern of studying interpersonal relations in work and play situations, was already coming into vogue in the period between the two world wars, and was greatly stimulated by Kurt Lewin.

An outstanding group study carried out during his Iowa period was done in collaboration with Ralph White and Ronald Lippitt. Boys in small groups were preparing masks for a theatrical performance. The leader created, in each group, a special atmosphere which he had thought through and worked out; he set the pace of the group either in terms of *authoritarianism,* or of *laissez faire,* or of *democracy*. The same leaders were trained to play, at different times, these different roles. Each group of boys was observed sometimes under *authoritarian,* sometimes under *laissez faire*, sometimes under *democratic* arrangements. It was possible to show the emergence of social attitudes, varieties of goals, vectors, modes of responding to barriers, etc. Thus, for example, more material was damaged or destroyed under thc pressure of the authoritarian atmosphere. Boys who had had experience in an authoritarian situation, and had then been transferred to a *laissez faire* situation, were inclined to show interpersonal aggression. They actually showed a tendency to beat each other up; and some boys, frightened or disturbed, actually withdrew from the play situation. By charting the course of the behavior from moment to moment, and from session to session, it was possible to show the relation of group atmospheres to individual tension levels and to interactions within the group.

Also during the Iowa period, but a bit later, during World War II, group dynamics were similarly studied in a war-derived pressure situation: Women were currently being asked to buy and prepare the less favored cuts of meat so that the more favored cuts could go to the Armed Forces. Lectures explained how these meats were to be prepared. In a "public opinion" study, the women generally declared themselves convinced. A quiet follow-up a fortnight later showed, however, that they had not changed their buying habits. But another method was available: No lectures were given to the women, but they were simply asked to talk it over and reach their own decision. The interpersonal exchanges and the *group decision* made a real difference; the check-up a fortnight later showed that this group-determined decision *was* being followed out. Group decisions were also successfully studied among women operatives making cloth for uniforms. Despite the fact that these women were all at their supposed "physiological limit" of productivity, a half-hour of discussion among them set a new level or standard towards which they rapidly moved, and which they maintained during the whole course of the later study. It begins to appear clear why it makes sense to speak of "group *dynamics*."

One may easily discern in this brief biographical sketch a movement from sharply defined physical and mathematical issues to very broadly defined issues in social behavior. Lewin's trajectory from the physical to the social was even more dramatic than these words indicate. He had been intensely preoccupied even as a young man with issues of family psychology and of education, and they led him through the Iowa period and the period at the Massachusetts Institute of Technology in the direction of an ever-increasing concern with larger human groups. His studies on group decision were entering wedges into a broad consideration of the psychology of the democratic process. In a manner reminiscent of Heinrich Heine's forecast as to the huge clash which was bound to occur in Germany decades later between democratic and authoritarian forces, he wrote notable papers on "national character," comparing the Germany that he knew with the United States that he knew.

As a Jew he was acutely aware of the danger that anti-Semitism might pass from sheer meanness into mass genocide, and he saw with exceptional clarity the direction in which the group hostilities within a democracy like our own may need intensive scientific analysis if catastrophes are to be prevented. In collaboration, for example, with Ronald Lippitt and Charles Hendry, he set up centers for "action research" in which research on group hostilities was so conceived as to reduce the hostilities in the very process of such investigation. For example, through the Committee on Community Interrelations, later sponsored by the authorities of the city of New York, he studied the prejudice of white against Negro in reference to eating accommodations, and he did one of the first notable studies of the actual effect of the newer integrative legislation upon changing social relationships. In the lucid and charming book of Alfred Marrow entitled *Living Without Hate* can be found a series of these action research studies; studies in which there is not just research and then action, or first action and then research, but an integrated planful study of the situation which both gives knowledge about it and alters it.

If one asks, regarding this or any other study of Lewin's, whether someone else might not have done it, or whether some other theory than field theory might not have sponsored it, the answer is, of course, always "yes." But the fundamental reply is that it was because he was thinking in dynamic field terms, that he was more prone to see large personal and large interpersonal issues in terms of a comprehensive dynamic in which life space, field forces, and the amenability of the situation to experimental control all come to light. I cannot here do justice to the massive impact Kurt Lewin had upon social thinking, but I can at least record the judgment that it was because he was both an incisive thinker and a lover of his fellowmen that he inevitably developed a field theory of social, indeed of international, significance.

4. Experimental Studies on the Growth of the Emotions*

John B. Watson
Director, Psychology Laboratory
Johns Hopkins University (1908-1920)

In my last lecture I told you that the current psychological view of instincts is not in harmony with the experimental findings of the behaviorist. Can the case for the present conception of emotions be made out any better? Probably no subject, unless it be that of instinct, has been more written about than emotions. Indeed the awe-inspiring number of volumes and papers and journals produced by Freudians and post-Freudians in the last twenty years would fill a good-sized room. And yet the behaviorist, as he reads through this great mass of literature, cannot but feel in it a lack of any central scientific viewpoint. Not until his own genetic studies, started less than ten years ago, began to bear fruit, did it become apparent to the behaviorist that he could simplify the problems of emotion and apply objective experimental methods to their solution.

The Behaviorist's Approach to the Problems of Emotion

During the past ten years the behaviorist has approached the problem of emotions from a new angle. In accordance with his usual procedure, he decided, before beginning work himself, to consign to the waste basket the work of his predecessors and to start the problem over again. His observation of adults told him rapidly that mature individuals, both men and women, display a wide group of reactions which go under the general name of emotional. The Negro down South whines and trembles at the darkness which comes with a total eclipse of the sun, often falling on his knees and crying out, begging the Deity to forgive him for his sins. These same Negroes show fear in passing through graveyards at night. They

*Powell Lecture in Psychological Theory at Clark University, January 17, 1925.

show "awe" and "reverence" for charms and relics. They will not burn wood which has been struck by lightning. In rural communities adults and children collect around the home as soon as dusk begins to fall. They often rationalize it by saying that they will get the "misery" from the night air. Situations of the most ordinary kinds judged from our more sophisticated standpoint arouse the strongest kinds of emotional reactions in them.

But let us be even more specific and bring the matter closer home. Here is the list of things a three-year-old youngster in New York fears: darkness, all rabbits, rats, dogs, fish, frogs, insects, mechanical animal toys. This infant may be playing excitedly with blocks. When a rabbit or other animal is introduced, all constructive activity ceases. He crowds towards one corner of his pen and begins to cry out "take it away," "take it away." Another child examined the same day shows a different set. Another may show no fear reactions.

The more the behaviorist goes about examining the sets of reactions of adults, *the more he finds that the world of objects and situations surrounding people brings out more complex reactions than the efficient use or manipulation of the object or situation would call for*. In other words, the object seems to be "charged," seems to bring out thousands of accessory bodily reactions which the laws of efficient habit do not call for. I can illustrate this by the Negro's rabbit foot. For us the rabbit foot is something to be cut off from the carcass of the animal and thrown away. One might toss it to one's dog as a part of his food. But to many of the Negroes the rabbit foot is not an object to be reacted to in this simple way. It is dried, polished, put into the pocket, cared for and guarded jealously. He examines it now and then; when in trouble he calls upon it for guidance and aid, and in general reacts to it not as to a rabbit's foot but in the same way as a religious man reacts to a Deity.

Civilization to some extent has stripped from man these superfluous reactions to subjects and situations, but many still persist, especially in the realm of religion. Bread is something to be eaten when hungry. Wine is something to be drunk with meals or on festive occasions. But these simple objects when fed to the individual at church under the guise of communion, call out kneeling, prayer, bowing of the head, closing of the eyes, and a whole mass of other verbal and bodily responses. The bones and relics of the saints may call out in devout religious individuals a different but entirely homologous (from the standpoint of religion) set of reactions to those the rabbit foot calls out in the Negro. The behaviorist even goes further and investigates his colleague's everyday behavior. He finds that a noise in the basement at night may reduce his next-door neighbors to reactions quite infantile; that many of them are shocked when the Lord's name is "taken in vain," giving as a rationalization that it is irreverent, that punishment will be visited upon the individual so misbehaving. He finds many of them walking away from dogs and horses, even though they have to turn back or cross the street to avoid coming near them. He finds men and women picking out impossible mates without being able to rationalize the act at all in any way. In other words, if we were to take all of life's objects and situations into the laboratory and were to work out a physiologically sound and scientific way of reacting to them (experimental ethics may approach this some day) and call these forms the norm or standard, and were then to examine the man's everyday behavior in the light of such norms, we would find divergence from them the rule. Divergence takes the form of accessory reactions, slowed reactions, nonreactions (paralysis), blocked reactions, negative reactions, reactions not sanctioned by society (stealing, murder, etc.), reactions belonging to other stimuli (substitute).[1] It seems fair to call all of this group *emotional* without further defining the word at the present time.

Now as you know, we haven't physiologically standardized norms of reactions as yet. There is some approach to it. Progress in physical sciences has done much towards standardizing our way of reacting to day and night, the seasons, the weather. We no longer react to a tree struck by lightning as accursed. We no longer think that we have any advantage over our enemy when we come in possession of his nail parings, hair and excrement. We no longer react to the blue of the heavens above as a kingdom in which supermundane beings dwell (at least some of us hardy souls do not!). We no longer react to distant and almost invisible mountains as being the homes of gnomes and fairies. Science, geography and travel have standardized our responses. Our reactions to foods are becoming

[1]Examples:

Of accessory reactions: The subject does the task quickly and correctly but he becomes pale, he may even cry, urinate or defecate, his mouth glands may become inactive. He reacts steadily and correctly in spite of his emotional state. Other examples of accessory reaction are whistling, talking, singing while at work.

Of negative reactions: He may show fear at food—push it away, he may fumble and drop his work, or react with too much or too little energy. Response to questions comes slowly or very rapidly.

Of negative reactions: He may show fear at food—push it away or run away from it himself. Instead of the ordinary reactions to dog or horse, the subject may walk away from them. Phobias belong in this group.

Of reaction not sanctioned by society: The subject may in "heat of anger," for example, commit murder, injure property. I have in mind here all acts which the law punishes but where it tempers justice with mercy because of emotional factors.

Of reactions belonging to other stimuli: All homosexual reactions; all sex attacks by sons upon their mothers; all sex reactions to fetishes, etc. Emotional responses of parents to children masquerading under the guise of natural affection.

There are of course, legions of responses we call "emotional," that cannot be listed under any one of these headings.

standardized through the work of the food chemist. We no longer think of any particular form of food as being "clean" or "unclean." We think of it now as fulfilling or not fulfilling definite bodily requirements.

Our social reactions, however, remain unstandardized. There is even no historical guide. Professor Sumner, of Yale, has well pointed this out. According to him, every conceivable kind of social reaction has at one time or another been considered the "normal" and unemotional way of acting. One woman could have many husbands; one man many wives; the offspring could be killed in times of famine; human flesh could be eaten; sacrifice of offspring could be made to appease Deities; you could lend your wife to your neighbor or guest; the wife was acting properly when she burned herself on the pyre that consumed her husband's body.

Our social reactions are not standardized any better today. Think of our 1925 accessory responses when we are in the presence of our parents, in front of our social leaders. Think of our hero worship, our veneration of the intellectual giant, the author, the artist, the church! Think of the way we behave in crowds, at masked parties (Ku Klux as well as social)—at football and baseball games, at elections, in religious revivals (conversions, antics of the holy rollers, etc.), in grief at the loss of loved objects and people. We have a host of words to cover these accessory reactions—reverence, love of family, of God, of church, of country; respect, adulation, awe, enthusiasm. When in the presence of many of these emotional stimuli we act like infants.

How the Behaviorist Works: The complicated nature of all these adult responses makes it hopeless for the behaviorist to begin his study of emotion upon adults. He has to study emotional behavior genetically.

Suppose we start with three-year-olds—we will go out into the highways and byways and collect them and then let us go to the mansions of the rich. We bring them into our laboratory. We put them face to face with certain situations. Suppose we first let a boy go alone into a well-lighted playroom and begin to play with his toys. Suddenly we release a boa constrictor or some other animal. Next we may take him to a dark room and suddenly start a miniature bonfire with newspapers. I cannot take time to tell you all of the stage settings used by the behaviorist in experiments of this type. As you can see we can set the stage so that we can duplicate almost any kind of life situation.

But after testing him alone in all these situations we must test him again when an adult, possibly father or mother, is with him—when another child of his own age and sex is nearby, when another child of the opposite sex accompanies him, when groups of children are present.

In order to get a picture of his emotional behavior, we have to test separation from mother. We have to test him with different and uncustomary foods, with strange people to feed him, with strange nurses to bathe him, clothe him and put him to bed. We must rob him of his toys, of things he is playing with. We must let a bigger boy or girl bully him, we must put him in high places, on ledges (making injury impossible however), on the backs of ponies or dogs.

I am giving you a picture of how we work just to convince you of its simplicity, naturalness and accuracy—that there is a wide field for objective experimentation.

Brief Summary of Results of Such Tests

One of the sad things we find by such tests is that even at three years of age many (but not all) of the children are shot through with all kinds of useless and actually harmful reactions which go under the general name *emotional*.

They are afraid in many situations.[2] They are shy in dozens of others. They go into tantrums at being bathed or dressed. They go into tantrums when given certain foods—or when a new nurse feeds them. They go into crying fits when the mother leaves them. They hide behind their mother's dress. They become shy and silent when visitors come. A characteristic picture is to have one hand in the mouth and the other grasping the mother's dress. One fights every child that comes near. He is called a bully, a ruffian, sadistic. Another cries and runs away if a child half his size threatens him. His parents call him a coward and his playmates make him the scapegoat.

Whence Arise These Varied Forms of Emotional Response?

A child three years of age is very young. Must we conclude that emotional reactions are hereditary? Is there an hereditary pattern of love, of fear, rage, shame, shyness, humor, anger, jealousy, timidity, awe,

[2]Mrs. Mary Cover Jones reports that in the work with the older children at the Heckscher Foundation, the frog, especially when it suddenly jumps, is the most potent stimulus of all in bringing out fear reactions. The most pronounced reactions were called out from the children by an animal when it was come upon suddenly. For this reason the smaller animals were often left around the room concealed in boxes. General manipulation of objects in the room lead the child sooner or later to the sudden uncovering of the animal.

reverence, admiration, cruelty? Or are these just *words* to describe general types of behavior without implying anything as to their origin? Historically they have been considered hereditary in origin. To answer the question scientifically, we need new methods of experimentation.

Experiments upon the Origin and Growth of Emotional Reactions

In our experimental work we early reached the conclusion that young children taken at random from homes both of the poor and of the well-to-do do not make good subjects for the study of the origin of emotions. Their emotional behavior is too complex. Fortunately we have been able to study a number of strong healthy children belonging to wet nurses in hospitals, and other children brought up in the home under the eye of the experimenters. Several of these children were observed from approximately birth through the first year, others through the second year and two or three children through the third year. I wish to give you an account of these studies.

In putting these hospital-reared children through emotional situations we usually had the older ones sit in a small infant's chair. If the infant was very small—too young to sit up—we allowed it to sit in the lap of the mother or that of an attendant.

Reactions to Animals (a) in the Laboratory: We first took the children to the laboratory and put them through the routine of tests with various animals. We had the laboratory so arranged that they could be tested in the open room, alone; with an attendant; with the mother. They were tested in the dark room, the walls of which were painted black. This room was bare of furniture. It offered an unusual situation in itself. In the dark room we had conditions so arranged that we could turn on a light behind the infant's head or illuminate the room with the light in front of and above the infant. The infants were always tested one at a time. The following group of situations was usually presented:

First, a lively black cat, invariably affectionately aggressive, was shown. The cat never ceased its purring. It climbed over and walked around the infant many times during the course of each test, rubbing its body against the infant in the usual feline way. So many false notions have grown up around the response of infants to furry animals that we were surprised ourselves to see these youngsters *positive always* in their behavior to this proverbial "black cat." Reaching out to touch the cat's fur, eyes and nose was the invariable response.

A rabbit was always presented. This, likewise, in every case called out manipulatory responses and nothing else. Catching the ears of the animal in one hand and attempting to put them in its mouth was one of the favorite responses.

Another furry animal invariably used was the white rat. This, possibly on account of its size and whiteness, rarely called out continued fixation of the eyes of the infant. When, however, the animal was fixated, reaching occurred.

Airedale dogs, large and small, were also presented. The dogs were also very friendly. The dogs rarely called out the amount of manipulatory response that an animal the size of the cat and rabbit called out. Not even when the children were tested with these animals in the dark room, either in full illumination or with a dim light behind their heads, was any fear response evoked.

These tests on children not emotionally conditioned proved to us conclusively that the classical illustrations of hereditary responses to furry objects and animals are just old wives' tales.

Next a feathery animal was used, usually a pigeon. The pigeon was presented first in a paper bag. This was a rather unusual situation even for an adult. The bird struggled and in struggling would move the bag around the couch. Oftentimes it would coo. While the pigeon was rattling and moving the paper bag about, the child rarely reached for the bag. The moment, however, the pigeon was taken into the experimenter's hands, the usual manipulatory responses were called forth. We have even had the pigeon moving and flapping its wings near the baby's face. This can be done easily by holding the pigeon by its feet, head down. Under these conditions even an adult will sometimes dodge and flinch a bit. When the wings fanned the infant's eyes, blinking was usually called out. Hesitation in response and failure to reach occurred. When the bird quieted down, reaching began.

Another form of test which we have often made under these same conditions was the lighting of a small newspaper bonfire both out in the open room and in the dark room. In several cases when the paper first caught fire, the infant reached eagerly toward the flame and had to be restrained. As soon, however, as the flame became hot, reaching and manipulatory responses died down. At such times the infant may sit with hands partly up in a position that looks almost like the start of the shading reaction that the adult uses when coming too close to a fire. There isn't much question that this type of habit would have developed if the experiment had been repeated often. It probably is entirely similar to the reaction animals and humans make to the sun. When the sun gets too hot and they are not active they move into whatever shade is available.

(b) To Animals in Zoological Parks: On several occasions hospital-reared children, and home-reared children whose emotional history was known, have been taken to zoological parks—always as a first experience. The children under observation were not pronounced in any of their reactions in the zoological park. Every effort was made to give them a good presentation of those animals which apparently have played considerable part in the biological history of the human. For example, a great deal of time was spent in the primates' house. Considerable time was spent also in the rooms where reptiles, frogs, turtles and snakes were kept. In such tests I have never got the slightest negative reaction to frogs and snakes, although the jumping frog, where children have been conditioned, is an extremely strong stimulus in bringing out fear responses, as will be shown in the next chapter.

In the summer of 1924, I took my own two children to the Bronx Zoological Park. The older child, B, was a boy two and a half years of age. The younger child, J, was a boy seven months of age. The younger child was without conditioned emotional fear responses. The older child had been conditioned but in a known way. For example, the first time he was taken into water up over his neck, he showed fear (I am sure that the so-called fear of the water is the same type of response that we get from loss of support). Before his trip to the park he had seen horses, dogs, cats, pigeons, English sparrows, sea gulls, toads, worms, caterpillars and butterflies. He had developed no negative responses to any of these animals except the dog. Once a dog had attacked him and thereafter he was partly conditioned to dogs, but this fear had not transferred to other animals or to woolly toys or mechanical animals. In everyday life he began immediately to play with every animal (other than the dog) as soon as it came within his ken. Much to the distress of his mother, he would often bring to her worms and caterpillars of every description. Even to the hoptoad he showed not the slightest negative response.

In going to the Bronx Zoological Park, we had to take a ferry, and this was his first experience on a large boat. Before this trip he had been in a canoe with me several times. The first time I took him out in the canoe, it was a little rough and the canoe was a tippy one. I got him out about 300 yards. A small wave struck us and he stiffened up a bit and said, "Daddy, too much water." I then took him closer in and paddled around the shore line for a while. All fear responses to the canoe disappeared, although even now he sits pretty close and pretty tight when out in it. Shortly after his first trip in the canoe, he took the trip in question to the zoological park. On the ferry almost the same type of behavior developed. We got about halfway over. He was leaning down and looking at the passage of the water. Suddenly he looked up and said, "Mamma, too much water; Billy not afraid." But his general behavior belied his words somewhat.

In the zoological park he showed a tremendous eagerness to go after every animal he saw and we took him religiously to every cage, pen and yard. The animals that brought out his greatest reluctance to leave were a pair of chimpanzees. They were having a gorgeous time. They were carrying armfuls of hay up the chains of the swing. After getting to the seat they tried to slip the hay underneath them. Then suddenly they would swing down and catch each other's hands, drop and hit the floor with a bang.

The animals calling out the most excited verbal response were the elephants; and next came the gaudily colored tropical birds. Every reaction to every animal was positive.

The behavior of the seven-month-old baby was that of resigned boredom throughout the whole afternoon. Not once was any response shown, either positive or negative. Now and then the set fixation of the eyes was noticed. The birds seemed to bring out the most prolonged fixation.

We think that we have carried these experiments far enough on infants, the genesis of whose emotional behavior we know, to uphold our main contention that when fear responses occur in the presence of all objects and situations such as we have described they are always conditioned.

Are we to conclude from this work that in infants there are no *unlearned* reactions of a kind that might give us a starting point for building up emotional behavior?

Evidence for Three Types of Unlearned Beginnings of Emotional Reactions

I feel reasonably sure that there are three different forms of response that can be called out at birth by three sets of stimuli. Don't misunderstand me if I call these responses "fear," "rage" and "love." Let me hasten to assure you that while I use the words fear, rage and love, I want you to strip them of all their old connotations. Please look upon the reactions we designate by them just as you look upon breathing, heart beat, grasping and other unlearned responses studied in the last chapter.

The facts follow.

FEAR

Our work upon infants, especially those without cerebral hemispheres, where the reaction is more pronounced, early taught us that loud sounds almost invariably produced a marked reaction in infants from the very moment of birth. For example, the striking of a steel bar with a hammer will call out a jump, a start, a respiratory pause, followed by more rapid breathing with marked vasomotor changes, sudden closure of the eye, clutching of hands, puckering of lips. Then occur, depending upon the age of the infant, crying, falling down, crawling, walking or running away. I have never made a very systematic study of the range of sound stimuli that will call out fear responses. Not every type of sound will do it. Some extremely low-pitched, rumbling noises will not call them out, nor will the very high tones of the Galton whistle. In the half-sleeping infant of two or three days of age I have called them out repeatedly by suddenly crinkling a half of a newspaper near its ear, and by making a loud, shrill, hissing sound with the lips. Pure tones, such as those obtained from the tuning fork at any rate, are not very effective in calling them out. Considerably more work must be done upon the nature of the auditory stimulus as well as upon the separate part reactions in the response before the whole stimulus-response picture is complete.[3]

The other stimulus calling out this same fear reaction is loss of support—*especially when the body is not set to compensate for it*. It can best be observed in newborns just when they are falling asleep. If dropped then, or if the blanket upon which they lie is suddenly jerked, pulling the infant along with it, the response invariably occurs.

In infants only a few hours old this fear reaction is quickly "fatigued." In other words, if the same sound or the same kind of loss-of-support stimulus is frequently applied, you can often call out the reaction only once. After a few moments' rest those same stimuli are again effective.

[3]I have found only one child out of many hundreds worked with in whom a fear response cannot be called out by loud sounds. She is well developed, well nourished, and normal in every way. There were no fear reactions to any other stimuli. The nearest approach to fear I saw was at the sight and sound of an opening and closing umbrella. I have no explanation to offer for this exception.

Even in the case of the adult human and higher mammals, loss of support when the individual is not set for it calls out a strong fear reaction. If we have to walk across a slender plank, naturally as we approach it the muscles of the body are all set for it, but if we cross a bridge which remains perfectly steady until the middle has been reached and then suddenly begins to give way, our response is very marked. When this happens in the case of a horse, one can with difficulty get him to cross bridges again. There are many horses in the country bridge-shy. I am sure the same principle is operative when a child is rapidly let out into deep water for the first time. The buoyancy of the water actually throws him off his balance. Even when the water is warm there is a catching of the breath, clutching with the hands and crying.

RAGE

Have you ever had the never to be forgotten experience when proudly walking across a crowded street holding your two-year-old daughter's hand of having her suddenly pull you in some other direction? And when you quickly and sharply jerked her back and exerted steady pressure on her arm to keep her straight did she then suddenly stiffen, begin to scream at the top of her voice, and lie down stiff as a ramrod in the middle of the street, yelling with wide open mouth until she became blue in the face, and continuing to yell until she could make no further sound? If you have not, any picture of rage behavior must appear lifeless to you.

Possibly you have seen the large village bully take some child, down him and hold his arms and legs so closely to his body that the child could not even struggle. Have you watched the youngster stiffen and yell until he became blue in the face?

Did you ever notice the sudden changes that come into the faces of men when they are jostled and suddenly and unduly crowded in the street cars and railway trains? *Hampering of bodily movement* brings out the series of responses we call rage. This can be observed from the moment of birth but more easily in infants ten to fifteen days of age. When the head is held lightly between the hands; when the arms are pressed to the sides; and when the legs are held tightly together, rage behavior begins. The unlearned behavior elements in rage behavior have never been completely catalogued. Some of the elements, however, are easily observed, such as the stiffening of the whole body, the free slashing movements of hands, arms and legs, and the holding of the breath. There is no crying at first, then the mouth is opened to the fullest extent and the breath is held until the face appears blue. These states can be brought on without the pressure in any case being severe enough to produce the slightest injury to the child. The experiments are discontinued the moment the slightest blueness appears in the skin. All children can be thrown into such a state and the reactions will continue until the irritating situation is relieved, and sometimes for a considerable period thereafter. We have had this state brought out when the arms are held upward by a cord to which is attached a lead ball not exceeding an ounce in weight. The constant hampering of the arms produced by even this slight weight is sufficient to bring out the response. When the child is lying on its back it can occasionally be brought out by pressing on each side of the head with cotton wool. In many cases this state can be observed quite easily when the mother or nurse has to dress the child somewhat roughly or hurriedly.

Love

The study of this emotion in the infant is beset with a great many difficulties on the conventional side. Our observations consequently have been incidental rather than directly experimental. The stimulus to *love responses* apparently is stroking of the skin, tickling, gentle rocking, patting. The responses are especially easy to bring out by the stimulation of what, for lack of a better term, we may call the erogenous zones, such as the nipples, the lips and the sex organs. The response in an infant depends upon its state; when crying the crying will cease and a smile begin. Gurgling and cooing appear. Violent movements of arms and trunk with pronounced laughter occur in even six-to-eight-month-old infants when tickled. It is thus seen that we use the term "love" in a much broader sense than it is popularly used. The responses we intend to mark off here are those popularly called "affectionate," "good-natured," "kindly," etc. The term "love" embraces all of these as well as the responses we see in adults between the sexes. They all have a common origin.

Are There Other Unlearned Responses of These Three General Types?

Whether these three types of response are all that have an hereditary background we are not sure. Whether or not there are other stimuli which will call out these responses we must also leave in doubt.[4] If our observations are in any way complete, it would seem that emotional reactions are quite simple in the infant and the stimuli which call them out quite few in number.

These reactions which we have agreed, then, to call fear, rage and love, are at first quite indefinite. Much work remains to be done to see what the various part reactions are in each and how much they differ. They are certainly not the complicated kinds of emotional reaction we see later on in life, but at least I believe *they form the nucleus out of which all future emotional reactions arise*. So quickly do they become conditioned, as we shall show later, that it gives a wrong impression to call them hereditary modes of response. It is probably better to just keep to the actual facts of observation thus;

(Ordinarily called Fear:)

(U)S	(U)R
Loss of support Loud sounds	Checking of breathing, "jump" or start of whole body, crying, often defecation and urination (and many others not worked out experimentally. Probably the largest group of part reactions are visceral).

(Ordinarily called Rage:)

(U)S	(U)R
Restraint of bodily movement	Stiffening of whole body, screaming, temporary cessation of breathing, reddening of face changing to blueness of face, etc. It is obvious that while there are general overresponses, the greatest concentration of movement is in the visceral field. Blood tests of infants so manhandled show that there is an increase in blood sugar. This means probably an increase in the secretion of the adrenal glands —release of increased output of adrenalin.

[4]For example, I am uncertain what the relationship is between the fear reactions we have been describing and the reactions called out by very hot objects, ice cold water, and other noxious stimuli.

(Ordinarily called Love:)

(U)S	(U)R
Stroking skin and sex organs, rocking, riding on foot, etc.	Cessation of crying; gurgling, cooing and many others not determined. That visceral factors predominate is shown by changes in circulation and respiration, erection of penis, etc.

If we think of these *unlearned* (so-called emotional) responses in the terms of these simple formulae, we cannot go very far wrong.

How Our Emotional Life Becomes Complicated

How can we square these observations with those which show the enormous complexity in the emotional life of the adult? We know that hundreds of children are afraid of the dark, we know that many women are afraid of snakes, mice and insects, and that emotions are attached to many ordinary objects of almost daily use. Fears become attached to persons and to places and to general situations, such as the woods, the water, etc. In the same way the number of objects and situations which can call out rage and love become enormously increased. Rage and love at first are not produced by the mere sight of an object. We know that later on in life the mere sight of persons may call out both of these primitive emotions. How do such "attachments" grow up? How can objects which at first do not call out emotions come later to call them out and thus greatly increase the richness as well as the dangers of our emotional life?

Since 1918 we have been at work upon this problem. We were rather loath at first to conduct such experiments, but the need of this kind of study was so great that we finally decided to experiment upon the possibility of building up fears in the infant and then later to study practical methods for removing them. We chose as our first subject Albert B, an infant weighing twenty-one pounds, at eleven months of age. Albert was the son of one of the wet nurses in the Harriet Lane Hospital. He had lived his whole life in the hospital. He was a wonderfully "good" baby. In all the months we worked with him we never saw him cry until after our experiments were made!

Before turning to the experiments by means of which we built up emotional responses in the laboratory, it is necessary for you to recall all that I tried to tell you on the conditioning of reflexes. I am going to assume that you know that when you establish a conditioned reaction, you must have a fundamental stimulus to start with which will call out the response in question. Your next step is to get some other stimulus to call it out. For example, if your purpose is to make the arm and hand jerk away every time a buzzer sounds, you must use the electric shock or other noxious stimulus each time the electric buzzer is sounded. Shortly, as you know, the arm will begin to jump away when the buzzer is sounded just as it jumps away when the electric shock is given. We already know now that there is an unconditioned or fundamental stimulus which will call out the fear reaction quickly and easily. It is a loud sound. We determined to use this just as we use the electric shock in experiments on the conditioned motor and glandular reflexes.

Our first experiment with Albert had for its object the conditioning of a fear response to a white rat. We first showed by repeated tests that nothing but loud sounds and removal of support would bring out fear response in this child. Everything coming within twelve inches of him was reached for and manipulated. His reaction, however, to a loud sound was characteristic of what occurs with most children. A steel bar, about one inch in diameter and three feet long, when struck with a carpenter's hammer produced the most marked kind of reaction.

Our laboratory notes[5] showing the progress in establishing a conditioned emotional response are given here in full:

> Eleven months, three days old. (1) White rat which he played with for weeks was suddenly taken from the basket (the usual routine) and presented to Albert. He began to reach for rat with left hand. Just as his hand touched the animal the bar was struck immediately behind his head. The infant jumped violently and fell forward, burying his face in the mattress. He did not cry, however.
>
> (2) Just as his right hand touched the rat the bar was again struck. Again the infant jumped violently, fell forward and began to whimper.

On account of his disturbed condition no further tests were made for one week.

> Eleven months, ten days old. (1) Rat presented suddenly without sound. There was steady fixation but no tendency at first to reach for it. The rat was then placed nearer, whereupon tentative reaching movements began with the

[5]See the original paper by Rosalie Rayner and John B. Watson, *Scientific Monthly*, 1921, p. 493.

right hand. When the rat nosed the infant's left hand the hand was immediately withdrawn. He started to reach for the head of the animal with the forefinger of his left hand but withdrew it suddenly before contact. It is thus seen that the two joint stimulations given last week were not without effect. He was tested with his blocks immediately afterwards to see if they shared in the process of conditioning. He began immediately to pick them up, dropping them and pounding them, etc. In the remainder of the tests the blocks were given frequently to quiet him and to test his general emotional state. They were always removed from sight when the process of conditioning was under way.

(2) Combined stimulation with rat and sound. Started, then fell over immediately to right side. No crying.

(3) Combined stimulation. Fell to right side and rested on hands with head turned from rat. No crying.

(4) Combined stimulation. Same reaction.

(5) Rat suddenly presented alone. Puckered face, whimpered and withdrew body sharply to left.

(6) Combined stimulation. Fell over immediately to right side and began to whimper.

(7) Combined stimulation. Started violently and cried, but did not fall over.

(8) Rat alone. The instant the rat was shown the baby began to cry. Almost instantly he turned sharply to the left, fell over, raised himself on all fours and began to crawl away so rapidly that he was caught with difficulty before he reached the edge of the mattress.

Surely this proof of the conditioned origin of a fear response puts us on a natural science grounds in our study of emotional behavior. It is a far more prolific goose for laying golden eggs than is James' barren verbal formulation. It yields an explanatory principle that will account for the enormous complexity in the emotional behavior of adults. We no longer in accounting for such behavior have to fall back upon heredity.

The Spread or Transfer of Conditioned Responses

Before the above experiment on the rat was made, Albert had been playing for weeks with rabbits, pigeons, fur muffs, the hair of the attendants and false faces. What effect will conditioning him upon the rat have upon his response to these animals and other objects when next he sees them? To test this we made no further experiments upon him for five days. That is, during this five-day period he was not allowed to see any of the above objects. At the end of the sixth day we again tested him first with the rat to see if the conditioned fear response to it had carried over. Our notes are as follows:

> Eleven months, fifteen days old.
>
> (1) Tested first with blocks. He reached readily for them, playing with them as usual. This shows that there has been no general transfer to the room, table, blocks, etc.
>
> (2) Rat alone. Whimpered immediately, withdrew right hand and turned head and trunk away.
>
> (3) Blocks again offered. Played readily with them, smiling and gurgling.
>
> (4) Rat alone. Leaned over to the left side as far away from the rat as possible, then fell over, getting up on all fours and scurrying away as rapidly as possible.
>
> (5) Blocks again offered. Reached immediately for them, smiling and laughing as before.

This shows that the conditioned response was carried over the five-day period. Next we presented in order a rabbit, a dog, a sealskin coat, cotton wool, human hair and a false face:

> (6) Rabbit alone. A rabbit was suddenly placed on the mattress in front of him. The reaction was pronounced. Negative responses began at once. He leaned as far away from the animal as possible, whimpered, then burst into tears. When the rabbit was placed in contact with him he buried his face in the mattress, then got up on all fours and crawled away, crying as he went. This was a most convincing test.
>
> (7) The blocks were next given to him, after an interval. He played with them as before. It was observed by four people that he played far more energetically with them than ever before. The blocks were raised high over his head and slammed down with a great deal of force.
>
> (8) Dog alone. The dog did not produce as violent a reaction as the rabbit. The moment fixation of the eyes occurred the child shrank back and as the animal came nearer he attempted to get on all fours but did not cry at first. As soon as the dog passed out of his range of vision he became quiet. The dog was then made to approach the infant's head (he was lying down at the moment). Albert straightened up immediately, fell over to the opposite side and turned his head away. He then began to cry.
>
> (9) Blocks were again presented. He began immediately to play with them.
>
> (10) Fur coat (seal). Withdrew immediately to the left side and began

to fret. Coat put close to him on the left side, he turned immediately, began to cry and tried to crawl away on all fours.

(11) Cotton wool. The wool was presented in a paper package. At the ends the cotton was not covered by the paper. It was placed first on his feet. He kicked it away but did not touch it with his hands. When his hand was laid on the wool he immediately withdrew it but did not show the shock that the animals or fur coat produced in him. He then began to play with the paper, avoiding contact with the wool itself. Before the hour was up, however, he lost some of his negativism to the wool.

(12) Just in play W., who had made the experiments, put his head down to see if Albert would play with his hair. Albert was completely negative. The other two observers did the same thing. He began immediately to play with their hair. A Santa Claus mask was then brought and presented to Albert. He was again pronouncedly negative, although on all previous occasions he had played with it.

Our notes thus give a convincing proof of spread or transfer.

We have here further proof in these transfers that conditioned emotional responses are exactly like other conditioned responses. If we condition a man or lower animal by regular conditioned reflex methods, say, to a tone A of a given pitch, almost any other tone will at first call out the response. By continuing the experiment—say by always feeding when tone A is sounded but never when any other tone is sounded—you soon get the animal to the point where it will respond only to A. This would be a differential conditioned response.

I am sure that in these cases of transfer or spread of conditioned emotional responses the same factors are at work.

I believe, although I have never tried the experiments, that we could set up just as sharp a differential reaction in the emotional field as we can in any other. I mean by this merely that if the experiment was long continued we could bring the fear reaction out sharply whenever the rat was shown but never when any other furry object was shown. If this were the case, we should have a differential conditioned emotional response. This seems to be what happens in real life. Most of us in infancy and in early youth are in the undifferentiated emotional state. Many adults, especially women, remain in it. All primitive peoples remain in it (superstitions, etc.). But educated adults by the long training they get in manipulating objects, handling animals, working with electricity, etc., reach the second or differentiated stage of the conditioned emotional reaction.

There is thus, if my reasoning is correct, a thoroughly sound way of accounting for transferred emotional responses—and for the Freudians' so-called "free-floating affects." When conditioned emotional responses are first set up, a wide range of stimuli (in this case all hairy objects) physically similar will at first call out the response and so far as we know will continue to call it out unless experimental steps (or a very fortunate series of environmental settings) are taken to bring the undifferentiated conditioned response up to the differentiated stage. *In the differentiated stage only the object or situation you were conditioned upon originally will call out the response.*

Summary

We must see that there is just as little evidence for a wholesale inheritance of these complicated patterns of response commonly called *emotional* as there is for the inheritance of those called *instinctive*.

Possibly a better way to describe our findings is to say that in working over the whole field of the human infant's reaction to stimuli, we find that certain types of stimuli—loud sounds and removal of support—produce a certain general type of response, namely, momentary checking of breath, a start of the whole body, crying, marked visceral responses, etc.; that another type of stimulus, holding or restraint, produces crying with wide-open mouth, prolonged holding of breath, marked changes in circulation and other visceral changes; that a third stimulus, stroking the skin, especially in the sex areas, produces smiling, changes in respiration, cessation of crying, cooing, gurgling, erection and other visceral changes. Attention is called to the fact that responses to these stimuli are not mutually exclusive—many of the part reactions are the same.

These unconditioned stimuli with their relatively simple unconditioned responses are our starting points in building up those complicated conditioned habit patterns we later call our emotions. In other words, emotional reactions are built in and order like most of our other reaction patterns. Not only do we get an increase in the number of stimuli calling out the response (substitution) through direct conditioning and through transfers (thus enormously widening the stimulus range), but also we get marked additions to and modifications of the responses themselves.

Another set of factors increasing the complexity of our emotional life must be taken into account. The same object (for example a person) can become a substitute stimulus for a fear response in one situation and a little later a substitute stimulus for a love response in another, or even for a rage response. The increasing complexity brought about by these factors soon gives us an emotional organization sufficiently complicated to satisfy even the novelist and the poet.

I am loath to close until I have introduced, parenthetically at least, one additional thought. The thought is that notwithstanding the fact that in all emotional responses there are overt factors such as the movement of the eyes and the arms and the legs and the trunk, *visceral and glandular factors predominate*. The "cold sweat" of fear, the "bursting heart," "the bowed head" in apathy and grief, the "exuberance of youth," the "palpitating heart" of the swain or maiden, are more than mere literary expressions, they are bits of genuine observations.

I want to develop the thesis sometime that society has never been able to get hold of these implicit concealed visceral and glandular reactions of ours, or else it would have schooled them in us, for, as you know, society has a great propensity for regulating all of our reactions. Hence most of our adult overt reactions—our speech, the movements of our arms, legs and trunk—are schooled and habitized. Owing to their concealed nature, however, society cannot get hold of visceral behavior to lay down rules and regulations for its integration. It follows as a corollary from this that we have no names, no words with which to describe these reactions. They remain unverbalized. One can describe in well-chosen words every act of two boxers, two fencers, and can criticize each individual detail of their responses, because there are verbal manuals of procedure and practice in the performance of these skillful acts. But what Hoyle has laid down the rules by which the separate movements of our viscera and glands must take place when in the presence of our lady love?

Because, then, of the fact that we have never verbalized these responses, a good many things happen to us *that we cannot talk about. We have never learned how to talk about them. There are no words for them.* The theory of the unverbalized in human behavior gives us a natural-science way of explaining many things the Freudians now call "unconscious complexes," "suppressed wishes" and the like. In other words, we can now come back to natural science in our study of emotional behavior. Our emotional life grows and develops like our other *sets of habits*. But do our emotional habits once implanted suffer from disuse? Can they be put away and outgrown like our manual and verbal habits? Until very recently we had no facts to guide us in answering these questions.

5. The Concept of Development from a Comparative and Organismic Point of View*

Heinz Werner

G. Stanley Hall Professor of Genetic Psychology

Clark University

The field of developmental psychology, as it is conceived here, transcends the boundaries within which the concept of development is frequently applied: development is here apprehended as a concept not merely applicable to delimited areas such as child growth or comparative behavior of animals, but as a concept that proposes a certain manner of viewing behavior in its manifold manifestations. Such a developmental approach to behavior rests on one basic assumption, namely, that wherever there is life there is growth and development, that is, formation in terms of systematic, orderly sequence. This basic assumption, then, entails the view that developmental conceptualization is applicable to the various areas of life science, and is potentially useful in interrelating the many fields of psychology.

The developmental approach has, of course, been clearly of tremendous heuristic value in systematizing certain aspects of biological phenomena in various fields of life science such as comparative anatomy, neurophysiology, and embryology. Analogously, developmental psychology aims at viewing the behavior of all organisms in terms of similar genetic principles. However, this aim of developmental psychology is perhaps even farther-reaching than that of developmental biology. Developmental psychology does not restrict itself either to ontogenesis or phylogenesis, but seeks to coordinate within a single framework forms of behavior observed in comparative animal psychology, in child psychology, in psychopathology, in ethnopsychology, and in the general and differential psychology of man in our own culture. Eventually, in linking

*From: D. B. Harris, ed., *The Concept of Development* (Minneapolis: Univ. of Minnesota Press, 1957), pp. 125-48.

these variegated observations, it attempts to formulate and systematically examine experimentally testable hypotheses.

In order to clarify and evolve its conceptual framework, developmental psychology has to search for characteristics common to any kind of mental activity in the process of progression or regression. In this comparative venture one has to be wary of the error made by early evolutionists such as Haeckel and G. Stanley Hall, who sought to treat as materially identical various developmental sequences when the data warranted only the assertion of similarity or parallelism. The statement, for instance, that the individual recapitulates in his development the genesis of the species, and the attempt to identify childlike and abnormal forms of behavior, have, in their extreme formulation, aroused just criticism, but criticism which has spread more and more toward undermining comparative developmental psychology as a discipline.

Between the extremes, on the one hand, of viewing as identical various developmental sequences, and on the other, of denying completely any comparability among them, some beginnings toward a theory of development have been made. These beginnings take into account the formal similarities in these various developmental sequences as well as material and formal differences distinguishing each developmental sequence from another.

The Orthogenetic Principle of Development

Developmental psychology postulates one regulative principle of development; it is an orthogenetic principle which states that wherever development occurs it proceeds from a state of relative globality and lack of differentiation to a state of increasing differentiation, articulation, and hierarchic integration.[1] This principle has the status of an heuristic definition. Though itself not subject to empirical test, it is valuable to developmental psychologists in leading to a determination of the actual range of applicability of developmental concepts to the behavior of organisms.[2]

We may offer several illustrations of how this orthogenetic principle is applied in the interpretation and ordering of psychological phenomena.

[1]This, of course, implies "directiveness." It seems to us, therefore, that one must on logical grounds agree with E. S. Russell (33) that organic development cannot be defined without the construct of "directiveness."

[2]In regard to the following discussion, see item 47 in the References.

According to this principle, a state involving a relative lack of differentiation between subject and object is developmentally prior to one in which there is a polarity of subject and object. Thus the young child's acceptance of dreams as external to himself, the lack of differentiation between what one dreams and what one sees, as is found in psychosis, or in some nonliterate societies, the breakdown of boundaries of the self in mescaline intoxication and in states of depersonalization—all of these betoken a relative condition of genetic primordiality compared to the polarity between subject and object found in reflective thinking. This increasing subject-object differentiation involves the corollary that the organism becomes increasingly less dominated by the immediate concrete situation; the person is less stimulus-bound and less impelled by his own affective states. A consequence of this freedom is the clearer understanding of goals, the possibility of employing substitutive means and alternative ends. There is hence a greater capacity for delay and planned action. The person is better able to exercise choice and willfully rearrange a situation. In short, he can manipulate the environment rather than passively respond to the environment. This freedom from the domination of the immediate situation also permits a more accurate assessment of others. The adult is more able than the child to distinguish between the motivational dynamics and the overt behavior of personalities. At developmentally higher levels, therefore, there is less of a tendency for the world to be interpreted solely in terms of one's own needs and an increasing appreciation of the needs of others and of group goals.

Turning to another illustration, one pertaining to concept formation, we find that modes of classification that involve a relative lack of differentiation between concept and perceptual context are genetically prior to modes of classification of properties relatively independent of specific objects. Thus, a color classification that employs color terms such as "gall-like" for a combination of green and blue, or "young leaves" for a combination of yellow and green, is genetically prior to a conceptual color system independent of objects such as gall or young leaves.

It may be opportune to use this last example as an illustration of the comparative character of the developmental approach. That the color classification attached to specific objects involves a mode of cognition genetically prior to a classification independent of specific objects is, of course, consistent with the main theoretical principle of development. In regard to the comparative character of our discipline, however, it does not suffice for us merely to find this type of classification more typical of the man of lower civilization than of the man of higher. The anthropological data point up the necessity of determining whether there is a greater prevalence of such primitive color conceptualization in areas where cognition can be readily observed in terms of lower developmental levels, e.g., in the early phases of ontogenesis. Experimental studies on young children have demonstrated the greater prevalence of concrete (context-bound) conceptualization with regard not only to color but to many other phenomena as well. Again, to take organic neuropathology as an example, in brain-injured persons we find, as Goldstein, Head, and others have stressed, a concretization of color conceptualization symptomatic of their psychopathology; similar observations have been made on schizophrenics.

At this point we should like to state that a comprehensive comparative psychology of development cannot be achieved without the aid of a general experimental psychology broadened through the inclusion of developmental methodology and developmental constructs. There have appeared on the scene of general psychology beginnings of an extremely significant trend toward the studying of perception, learning, and thinking, not as final products but as developing processes, as temporal events divisible into successive stages. Such ''event psychology,'' as one may call it, introduces the dimension of time as an intrinsic property into all experimental data. It stands thus in contrast to approaches, like that of classical psychophysics, in which the treating of successive trials as repetitive responses eliminates as far as possible sequential effects. European psychologists, particularly in Germany and Austria, have turned to the direct study of emergent and developing mental phenomena (34, 42, 46). For instance, using a tachistoscope, we may study the developmental changes in perception which occur when the time of exposure is increased from trial to trial. In studies of this sort, such developmental changes, or ''microgenesis,'' of percepts are predictable from a developmental theory of the ontogenesis of perception. Some of the ensuing parallels between microgenesis and ontogenesis might be summarized as follows (5): In both microgenesis and ontogenesis the formation of percepts seems, in general, to go through an orderly sequence of stages. Perception is first global; whole-qualities are dominant. The next stage might be called analytic; perception is selectively directed toward parts. The final stage might be called synthetic; parts become integrated with respect to the whole. Initially perception is predominantly ''physiognomic.''[3] The physiognomic quality of an object is experienced prior to any details. At this

[3]In regard to this term, see item 44 (p. 69) and item 45 (p. 11) of the References.

level, feeling and perceiving are little differentiated. Again, in the early stages of development imaging and perceiving are not definitely separated.

There is another important technique of studying the emergence and formation of perception. This method was originally utilized in Stratton's well-known experiments in which a person wearing lenses had to adjust to a world visually perceived as upside down. More recently, Ivo Kohler of the Innsbruck Laboratory has utilized this method in extremely significant long-range experiments. He studies stages of perceptual adaptation to a world visually distorted in various ways by prisms or lenses (16, 17, 49). Again, these perceptual formation stages are found to conform to ontogenetic patterns. Ontogenetic studies have made it reasonably certain that the experience of space and spatial objects grows through stages which can be grossly defined. There appears to be an early sensorimotor stage of spatial orientation, succeeded by one in which objects emerge in terms of "things-of-action" (44), where perceptual qualities of things are determined by the specific way these things are handled. For instance, a chair is that object which has a "sitting tone" (Uexküll). A later stage is that of highly objectified or visualized space where the spatial phenomena are perceived in their rather "pure" visual form and form relations.

Keeping these ontogenetic states in mind, it is most enlightening to follow the reports of the subjects used in the Innsbruck Laboratory as they move from level to level in developmental order, adjusting themselves to a disarrayed world. First, they learn to master space on a sensorimotor level; that is, they are able to move about without error. But, though they may be able to ride a bicycle quite skillfully, the visual world as such may, at this stage, still be extremely confused, upside down, or crooked. The further development toward visual adaption shows some remarkable features: the objects seem to fall into two classes, things-of-action and purely visual things. The observer conquers first the things-of-action and only later purely visual things. For instance, observers wearing prisms which invert left and right can see an object already in correct position if it is part of their own actions, but incorrectly—that is, reversed—when purely visually grasped. In a fencing situation, a subject sees his own sword correctly pointing toward the opponent, but at a moment of rest it becomes visually inverted, pointing toward himself. By the same token, a little later in development any object-of-action, such as a chair or a screwdriver, whether it is actually handled or not, is correctly transformed, whereas purely visual objects, such as pictures or printed words, remain reversed. Only at a last stage the differences disappear, and complete transformation of the visual world is achieved.

Another area of general psychology where genetic methodology has been fruitfully applied is that of problem-solving behavior. Whereas Wertheimer's contribution to productive thinking, outstanding as it was, remains essentially agenetic, the signal importance of Duncker's work (7) lies in its genetic methodology. Duncker studied the problem-solving process in terms of genetic stages which follow each other according to developmental laws well established for ontogenesis.[4]

Uniformity Versus Multiformity of Development

The orthogenetic law, being a formal regulative principle, is not designed to predict developmental courses in their specificity. To illustrate, it cannot decide the well-known controversy between Coghill's and Windle's conceptions (6, 50) concerning ontogenesis of motor behavior. According to Coghill, who studied the larval salamander, behavior develops through the progressive expansion of a perfectly integrated total pattern, and the individuation within of partial patterns that acquire varying degrees of discreteness. Windle's conception, derived from the study of placental mammals, is that the first responses of the embryo are circumscribed, stereotyped reflexes subsequently combined into complex patterns. It may be possible to reconcile, under the general developmental law, both viewpoints as follows: The development of motor behavior may, depending on the species or on the type of activity, involve either the differentiation of partial patterns from a global whole and their integration within a developing locomotor activity (Coghill) or the integration of originally juxtaposed, relatively isolated global units which now become differentiated parts of a newly formed locomotor pattern (Windle). In both cases there are differentiation and hierarchic integration, although the specific manifestations differ.[5]

Now, it is precisely this polarity between the uniformity of a general regulative principle and the multiformity of specific developmental changes that makes the study of development necessarily a comparative discipline. If we were merely to seek the ordering of changes of behavior in terms of a universal developmental principle, developmental theory might

[4]Duncker has also clearly seen one aspect of creative thought processes, hitherto little recognized, namely, the fact that successful problem-solving depends not only on the ability to progress along new ways, but also on the ability to regress back to a point from which new development can take place. In other words, he has observed a most important genetic principle, that of oscillatory activity in terms of progression and regression. (See the last section of this paper.)

[5]Cf. the excellent discussion by Barron, presented at the Chicago Conference on Genetic Neurology (2).

still be of interest to the philosophy of science and theoretical psychology, but it would be of far lesser value to empirical psychology.

In order to get a clearer picture of what is involved here, it might be advantageous to refer to one of our studies, namely, that of the development of the acquisition of meaning, by the use of a word-context test (48).

In this experiment eight- to thirteen-year-old children had the task of finding the meaning of an artificial word which was embedded successively in six verbal contexts. For instance, one such artificial word was "corplum." After each of these six sentences the child was interrogated concerning the meaning of the artificial word.

The six sentences in which "corplum" (correct translation: "stick" or "piece of wood") appears, are as follows: (1) A corplum may be used for support. (2) Corplums may be used to close off an open place. (3) A corplum may be long or short, thick or thin, strong or weak. (4) A wet corplum does not burn. (5) You can make a corplum smooth with sandpaper. (6) The painter used a corplum to mix his paints.

Now, the task confronting the subjects in the word-context test is essentially the synthesis of the cues from a set of six contexts for the purpose of forming a general meaning of the word, that is, a meaning applicable to all six sentences. The success of such an operation is reflected in two kinds of results. The first shows a steady and continuous increase in the achievement of a correct solution with increasing age. The second reflects changes in the underlying patterns of operation. As to the first point, there is a developmental increase in achievement which signifies the increasing capacity for hierarchization, that is, for integrating the various cues within a common name. However, the finding concerning a steady rise in achievement of correctness was, for us, not the most important result. Our main aim was to study the processes underlying such achievement. We were far more concerned with detecting the fact that conceptual synthesis is not achieved by a unitary pattern of operations, but that there are various sorts of processes of synthesis which differ from each other developmentally. The lower forms were found to emerge, to increase, and then to decrease during intellectual growth, yielding finally to more advanced forms of generalization (48, p. 97).

Studies of this sort inform us that the workings of the orthogenetic law as a uniform, regulative principle have to be specified through the ordering and interpretation of the multiform operations. Such a view implies the rejection of a tacit assumption made by many child psychologists that the measured achievement always reflects unequivocally the underlying operations, or that overt achievement is necessarily a true gauge of the developmental stage. This assumption is untenable; the same achievement may be reached by operations genetically quite different (41). An analysis of types of operations rather than measurement merely in terms of accuracy of performance often reveals the truer developmental picture.[6] In fact, a greater accuracy in certain circumstances may even signify a lower developmental level, as in the case of a decorticate frog who shows greater accuracy in catching flies than the normal frog. Gottschaldt (10) presented normal and mentally deficient eight-year-old children with the task of constructing squares or rectangles from the irregular pieces into which these figures had been cut. The normal children had difficulties with the test because they tried to relate the figuratively unrelated pieces to the end form. Operating on a purely mechanical level, the mentally deficient children matched the edges of the same length and thus performed quicker and with fewer errors. Again, a thinker oriented toward and capable of highly abstract thought may be at a disadvantage in certain concrete tasks of concept formation, compared with a concretely thinking person.

Continuity Versus Discontinuity of Development

The orthogenetic principle of increase in differentiation and hierarchic integration is not meant to imply continuous progress as the exclusive characteristic of developmental change. A good deal of the controversy centering in the continuity-discontinuity problem appears to be due to a lack in clarification of these terms. In particular, there has been considerable confusion about two different aspects of change. One is the quantitative aspect of change. Here the problem of continuity versus discontinuity is related to the measurement—in terms of gradual or abrupt increase with time—of magnitude, of efficiency, of frequency of

[6]It is not accidental that out of the immense field of potentially great significance for developmental psychology, the two main areas emphasized by psychologists in this country were the area of intelligence and the area of learning. They were chosen because they were clearly amenable to rigid quantification on a continuum in terms of more or less. The success of workers in these fields obtained by statistical treatment of overt behavior and the successes in practical application have reinforced the conviction that outside the rather trivial notion of continuous increase in achievement with increase in age, developmental theory is not needed. In regard to intelligence testing the evaluation of G. Stanley Hall, the father of comparative genetic psychology, still seems to hold: Intelligence tests and measurements, he stated, have done a great work in applying psychology to life and industry but have added scarcely a scintilla to our knowledge of human development (11, p. 450). As to the situation in the area of learning, it seems significant that a man as deeply informed as Hilgard, in a well-balanced evaluation of this field of research, comes to the conclusion that undue stress on quantification may lead to a collapse when underlying processes are not understood (13, p. 328).

occurrence of a newly acquired operation in an individual or in a group. The other aspect concerns the qualitative nature of changes. Here the problem of continuity versus discontinuity centers in the question of the reducibility of later to earlier forms—emergence—and the transition between later and earlier forms—intermediacy.

It seems that discontinuity in terms of qualitative changes can be best defined by two characteristics: "emergence," i.e., the irreducibility of a later stage to an earlier; and "gappiness," i.e., the lack of intermediate stages between earlier and later forms. Quantitative discontinuity,[7] on the other hand, appears to be sufficiently defined by the second characteristic.

Now it seems that in many discussions, particularly among psychologists, the quantitative and qualitative forms of continuity and discontinuity have not been clearly kept apart. Thus, a change may be discontinuous in terms of quality but may become distinguishable (e.g., measurable) only gradually; i.e., there may be a continuous quantitative increase, such as in frequency of occurrence or in magnitude. For instance, the attempt of the young child to walk on two legs is discontinuous with four-limb locomotion, though the successive actual attempts may show gradual progress toward precision and success.[8] In accordance with our definition given above, two-legged locomotion cannot be reduced to four-limbed locomotion, and, furthermore, there is limitation in regard to intermediate steps.

Another related mistake is that of accepting smallness of change, whether qualitative or quantitative, as an indicator of continuity. For instance, the genetic changes termed "mutation" may be very slight, but there has to be "discontinuity inasmuch as there are no intermediate forms between the unchanged and the changed.[9] This significant fact in mutation, namely, discontinuity, says Schroedinger, "reminds a physicist of

[7]To facilitate distinction and alleviate confusion, I would suggest substituting "abruptness" for quantitative discontinuity, reserving the term "discontinuity" only for the qualitative aspect of change. It also appears feasible to distinguish between two types of emergence: (a) emergence of a single operation, e.g., abstract function, (b) emergence of a novel pattern of operation. A novel pattern may emerge as a consequence of new operations that enter the pattern, or it may also emerge through a reorganization of the existing characters within a certain pattern, through a changing dominance between these existing characters, etc. One may note here some analogies between psychological emergence and biogenetic emergence coming about (a) through mutant genes, and (b) through changes in local constellations of genes.

[8]Such paradoxical coexistence of qualitative discontinuity and gradualness of appearance (progression) seems to pertain to developmental changes of various kinds. For instance, regenerative development of transplanted tissue is either determined according to the domicile within which the transplant is embedded (place-wise) or according to the original extraction of the transplant (origin-wise). This determination is an all-or-none phenomenon; however, visible differentiation is not instantaneously evident but progressive (26, pp. 70f).

[9]Schroedinger, p. 34 (37). Schroedinger points out that Darwin was mistaken in regarding the small, continuous chance variations within a species as the basis of evolution by natural selection. These variations (e.g., length of awn in a pure-bred crop) cannot be formants of a new species because they are not inheritable.

quantum theory: no intermediate energies occurring between two neighboring energy levels. He would be inclined to call de Vries's mutation theory . . . the quantum theory of biology." Because of the smallness of change, in developmental psychology as well as in developmental biology, one often will find it possible to argue for discontinuity only on the basis of extensive data accumulated in extensive temporal sequences; discontinuity in change may then be concluded after a trait has become sufficiently distinct in terms of frequency, permanency, and magnitude.

Other factors that are often not clearly recognized for their importance in determining sequences as either continuous or discontinuous are (a) the handling of the data and (b) the nature of the universe of discourse.

Concerning the first factor, it should be realized that discontinuous process changes typical in individual development may be obscured by averaging developmental achievement scores of individuals to secure a composite curve for a group which then suggests continuous growth.[10]

Another fallacy in deriving continuity of behavioral development from group scores has been most recently discussed by Lashley (21) in regard to a particular feature of the usual mental tests, namely, the heterogeneity (discontinuity) of the items which the test patterns comprise. Lashley's criticism implies that discontinuity of processes may be obscured by interpreting developmental data on the assumption that variations in achievement can be based only on variations in a single underlying process. As noted before, the achievement of correctness on our word-context test shows a steady increase with age, whereas underlying processes give a picture of the rise and decline of more or less primitive operations and the abrupt rise of an adult type of generalization around ten or eleven years of age. Reference should be made here to the important study by Nancy Bayley (3) concerning mental development during the first three years. She could show that in terms of accumulated scores there was a steady increase with age; however, a further analysis of the test items in terms of underlying operations revealed a shift from one type of function ("sensorimotor") to a qualitatively different type ("adaptive") occurring at approximately nine months of age.

Secondly, it should be recognized that it is the universe of discourse, the interpretational frame within which the material is grasped, that often determines the ordering in terms of continuity or discontinuity. To illustrate by an analogy, one may represent the relation between color hues in physical terms, i.e, wavelength, that change continuously within the

[10]Lecomte DuNoüy (8) in his remarkable book, *Biological Time*, takes the extreme view that continuity always is "manufactured" by our treatment of the data: "one of the roles of consciousness is to manufacture continuity from discontinuity."

range of visibility. Within the psychological frame of reference, however, there is discontinuity. The gradual variation from blue to green is discontinuous with the gradual variation from green to yellow, which, in turn, is discontinuous with the gradual variation from yellow to red.

There is no logical necessity for a concordance in terms of continuity between the quantitative and qualitative aspects of any developmental series. A discontinuous (epigenetic) qualitative change may become distinct gradually; that is, it does not need to be "saltatory" in a quantitative sense, if by that word is meant that a new form or function becomes suddenly overt. Nor does unevenness—spurt versus depression—of any growth curve necessarily point to novel process formation. However, though we have to beware of confusing quantitative discontinuity-continuity with qualitative discontinuity-continuity, quantitative unevenness may, possibly more often than not, point to qualitative discontinuity or emergent evolution. We may illustrate this from Paul Weiss's discussion (40) on embryonic growth: "An obstacle to simple mathematical treatment of growth is its lack of continuity; for embryonic growth advances unevenly, in spurts and jumps, with intermittent depressions. These depressions correspond to phases of intensive histological differentiation" (p. 44). Furthermore, if embryonic growth curves in terms of weight are compared with progress in terms of differentiation and morphogenesis, one finds that both kinds of progressions advance unevenly, but, that "maxima of differentiation coincide with minima of growth." From this, Weiss concludes that "acceleration of differentiating activity is attended by retardation of growth activity, or in other words, that there is some antagonism between differentiation and growth" (p. 134).[11]

Weiss's observations point to an important instance where the saltations and depressions of "accumulating" activity (growth in terms of quantitative discontinuity) appear to be vicariously related to morphogenetic processes directed toward the production of "discrete discontinuous . . . cell types which are not connected by intergradation"—development in terms of qualitative discontinuity (p. 98).

Quite possibly there are analogies to this vicarious correspondence between quantitative growth and qualitative development on the level of psychological behavior. To illustrate, one such analogy might be found in a frequent observation concerning certain phases of speech development.

[11]One may note the possibility of discriminating between "growth" as a process of accumulation versus "development" defined by differentiation.

There appears to occur between the stage of babbling and that of naming, a period during which vocalizing is depressed (22, p. 82). It seems plausible to interpret this period as one during which the awareness of sound patterns as verbal symbols emerges. Once this novel operation has emerged, the child bursts forth with naming, increasing its vocabulary at a swiftly accelerating rate.

In conclusion, it seems to me that development cannot be comprehended without the polar conceptualization of continuity and discontinuity. Within the ''universe of discourse'' in which the orthogenetic law is conceived, development, insofar as it is defined as increase in differentiation and hierarchization is, ideally, continuous. Underlying the increase in differentiation and integration are the forms and processes which undergo two main kinds of changes: (a) quantitative changes which are either gradual or abrupt, and (b) qualitative changes which, by their very nature, are discontinuous.[12]

Unilinearity Versus Multilinearity of Development

The orthogenetic law, by its very nature, is an expression of unilinearity of development. But, as is true of the other polarities discussed here, the ideal unilinear sequence signified by the universal developmental law does not conflict with the multiplicity of actual developmental forms. As implied in the conclusion of the preceding section, coexistence of unilinearity and multiplicity of individual developments must be recognized for psychological just as it is for biological evolution. In regard to human behavior in particular, this polarity opens the way for a developmental study of behavior not only in terms of universal sequence, but also in terms of individual variations, that is, in terms of growth viewed as a branching-out process of specialization or aberration.

To illustrate, ''physiognomic'' perception appears to be a developmentally early form of viewing the world, based on the relative lack of distinction between properties of persons and properties of inanimate things (44, pp. 67f). But the fact that in our culture physiognomic perception, developmentally, is superseded by logical, realistic, and technical conceptualization, poses some paradoxical

[12]For further discussion of the continuity-discontinuity problem, see Bertalanffy, ch. 12 (4); DuNoüy (8); Huxley, ch. 5 (14); Lillie (23); Novikoff (27); Simpson, ch. 14 (39); Schneirla (35, 36).

problems, such as, What genetic standing has adult aesthetic experience? Is it to be considered a "primitive" experience left behind in a continuous process of advancing logification, and allowed to emerge only in sporadic hours of regressive relaxation? Such an inference seems unsound; it probably errs in conceiving human growth in terms of a simple developmental series rather than as a diversity of individual formations, all conforming to the abstract and general developmental conceptualization. Though physiognomic experience is a primordial manner of perceiving, it grows, in certain individuals such as artists, to a level not below but on a par with that of "geometric-technical" perception and logical discourse.

Fixity Versus Mobility of Developmental Level of Operation

The assumption that all organisms normally operate upon a relatively fixed and rather sharply circumscribed developmental level appears to be tacitly accepted by many psychologists. A contrary view is that all higher organisms manifest a certain range of genetically different operations. This means, for instance, that a child of a certain age or an adult, depending on the task or on inner circumstances, may, qua normal, perform at genetically different levels. Furthermore, there is, so to speak, not only "horizontal" differentiation but also "vertical" differentiation; that is, the more mature compared with the less mature individual has at his disposal a greater number of developmentally different operations.

It should be recognized that these views are not necessarily antagonistic; i.e., fixity as well as mobility of levels of operation coexist as polar principles of development. The principle of fixity is implied in, or can be inferred from, the intrinsic trend of any evolution toward an end stage of maximum stability. Such maximum stability, as the end stage of a developmental sequence, implies the ceasing of growth; that is, implies the permanency, for instance, of specialized reaction patterns, or automatization of response. But the principle of fixity would finally lead to rigidity of behavior if not counterbalanced by the polar principle of mobility. As most generally conceived, mobility implies "becoming" in contrast to "being"; it implies that an organism, having attained highly stabilized structures and operations may or may not progress further, but if it does, this will be accomplished through partial return to a genetically earlier, less stable level. One has to regress in order to progress. The intimate relation of regression to progression appears succinctly expressed in the statement of one of the early evolutionists, Richard Owen (32). On interpreting the resemblance of the embryo to the phylogenetic ancestry, Owen said: "We perceive a return to the archetype in the early embryological phases of development of the highest existing species, or ought rather to say that development starts from the old point" (p. 108).

An impressive illustration of the relation between renewed development and regression on the biological level can be found in the process of regeneration. Such regeneration, as extensively studied at the amphibian level, consists of two phases, regressive as well as progressive. The progressive phase—analogous to normal embryonic development—starts with the formation of the "blastema" or regenerative bud. But prior to progression there is regression. The regressive phase involves de-differentiation of already specialized cells (26, p. 3). Another probable source for blastema formation is reserve cells, that is, cells that have remained at a low state of differentiation (40, p. 466). It is noteworthy that power of regeneration, being associated with capacity to de-differentiate, is, in general, inversely correlated with the organism's ontogenetic or phylogenetic status of differentiatedness (26, p. 62).

In speculating by analogy from biological events of this sort to human behavior one might argue that in creative reorganization, psychological regression involves two kinds of operations: one is the de-differentiation (dissolution) of existing, schematized or automatized behavior patterns; the other consists in the activation of primitive levels of behavior from which undifferentiated (little-formulated) phenomena emerge.

The polar conceptualization of normal levels of operation in terms of fixity-mobility appears thus closely linked to another polar-distinction, namely, that involved in the relation between lower and higher levels of operation. In regard to this relation, one particular problem among many has aroused considerable interest. It concerns the degree of fixity or mobility of an operation emerging at a certain level, in relation to developmentally later forms of operation.

As mentioned before, development, whether it concerns single function, complex performances, or the totality of personality, tends toward stabilization. Once a certain stable level of integration is reached, the possibility of further development must depend on whether or not the behavioral patterns have become so automatized that they cannot take part in reorganization. We may refer here to Rapaport's concept of "apparatus" (31, p. 76) or to Piaget's concept of "schema" (30). The individual, for instance, builds up sensorimotor schemata, such as grasping, opening a box, and linguistic patterns; these are the goal of early learning at first, but later on become instruments or apparatuses for handling the environment. Since no two situations in which an organism finds itself are alike, the usefulness of these schemata in adaptive behavior will depend on their stability as well as on their pliability (a paradoxical "stable flexibility").

Furthermore, if one assumes that the emergence of higher levels of operations involves hierarchic integration, it follows that lower-level operations will have to be reorganized in terms of their functional nature so that they become subservient to higher functioning. A clear example of this is the change of the functional nature of imagery from a stage where images serve only memory, fantasy, and concrete conceptualization, to a stage where images have been transformed to schematic symbols of abstract concepts and thought.

Differential Versus General Developmental Psychology: Individuality as a Problem of Developmental Psychology

At Clark University we are becoming increasingly impressed with the fruitfulness of the developmental frame of reference for the study of group and individual differences. We may illustrate this approach to the many problems which are in need of investigation by referring to a few studies on cognitive organization.

One problem concerns the over-all maturity status of the individual, that is, his cognitive level of operation under optimal conditions, and the stability of this level under varying internal and external conditions. Friedman, Phillips, and their co-workers at Worcester State Hospital and at Clark University have constructed a genetic scoring system of the Rorschach test founded on developmental theory, and standardized through an ontogenetic study of children. The scoring system is based essentially on the occurrence and frequency of "genetically low" and "genetically high" scores. Restricting ourselves here mainly to the various whole and detail responses, genetically low responses are those which indicate amorphous, diffuse, or confabulatory percepts where little attention is given to part relations and to perception of contours. The genetically high percepts are reflected in the responses whereby the percept is that of a precisely formed unit with integrated parts, where the whole is composed of relatively independent sub-wholes brought together in an integrated fashion. Applying this developmental scoring analysis to the responses of 160 children of from three to eleven years of age, Hemmendinger found the basic principle of development confirmed. That is, with age there is a decrease of the undifferentiated diffuse whole and detail responses along with an increase of the highly articulated, well-integrated whole and detail responses. There is further an interesting shift from the early whole responses toward small detail responses between the ages of about six and eight; later on there is a decline in favor of the integrated whole responses (12).

This genetic scoring method has been utilized for the gauging of developmental levels of cognitive organization in normal and deviant persons in studies carried out at Worcester State Hospital, Clark University, and Boston University.[13] According to the theory, the most severely impaired groups should here show the genetically lowest responses, and there should be a decrease of these responses and an increase in the genetically high responses with less impaired or unimpaired groups. The evidence is in good agreement with this expectation (see Figures 1 to 4). It was found that the genetic scores of the hebephrenic-catatonic schizophrenics resembled those of children three to five years of age. The paranoids were similar to children six to ten years of age; the psychoneurotics were intermediate between the ten-year-olds and normal adults (9, 28, 38).

We may add at this point that for the study of individual differences in their developmental aspects, experimental methods other than those based on ontogenesis have become available. Among these, probably the most

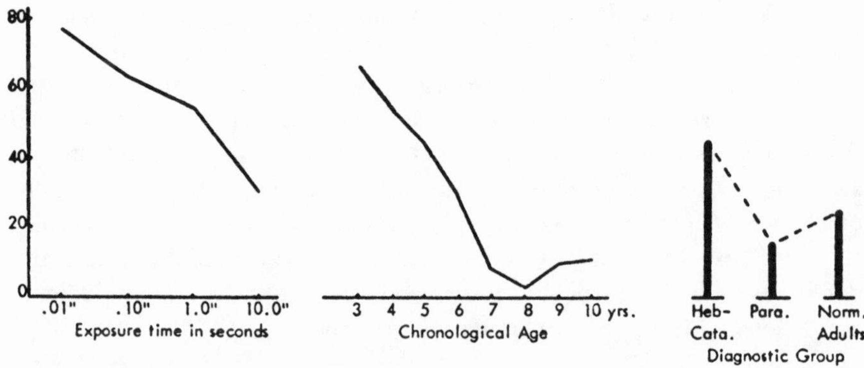

Figure 1. Median percentage of whole responses in normal adults at tachistoscopic exposures, and in children and diagnostic groups at full exposure, of the Rorschach.

[13]The illustrations given here refer to perceptual organization. For some of our pertinent studies on language behavior, see items 1, 9, 15, 24, 45, and 47 of the References.

promising method is that of "microgenesis." This method, already mentioned above, is based on the assumption that activity patterns, percepts, thoughts, are not merely products but processes that, whether they take seconds, or hours, or days, unfold in terms of developmental sequence.

To study microgenesis of perception, Framo presented the Rorschach cards to 80 normals. Twenty subjects in each of four groups viewed the

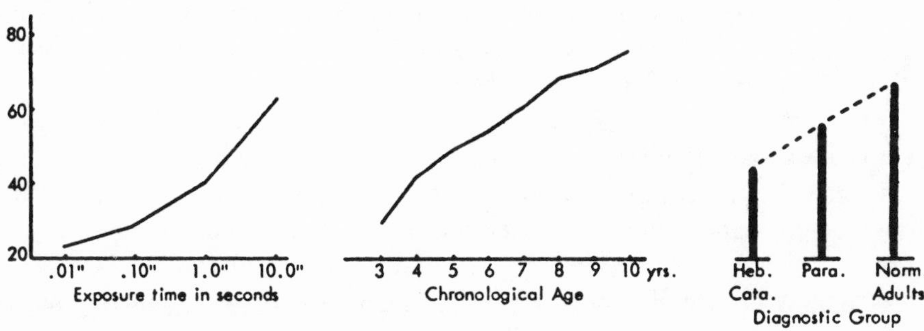

Figure 2. Median percentage of usual detail responses in normal adults at tachistoscopic exposures, and in children and diagnostic groups at full exposure, of the Rorschach.

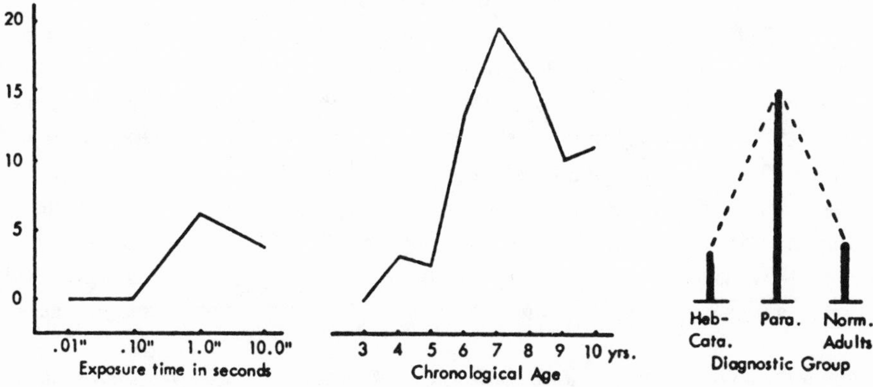

Figure 3. Median percentage of rare detail responses in normal adults at tachistoscopic exposures, and in children and diagnostic groups at full exposure, of the Rorschach.

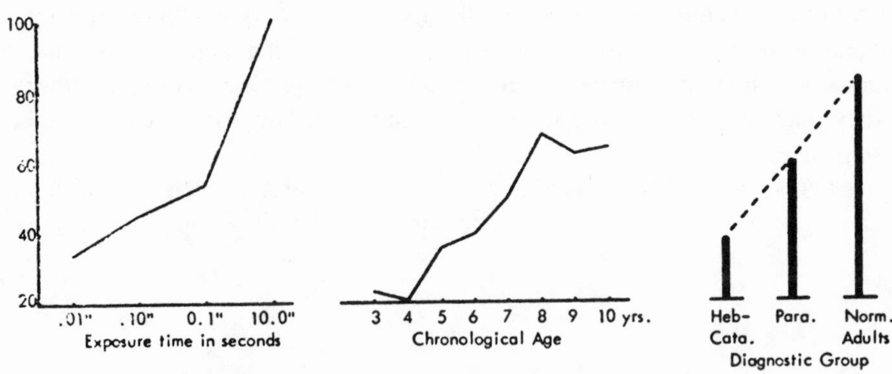

Figure 4. Percentage of developmentally mature whole responses of all whole responses in normal adults at tachistoscopic exposures, and in children and diagnostic groups at full exposure, of the Rorschach.

cards at exposures of 0.01 second, 0.1 second, 1 second, and 10 seconds, respectively. A comparison of the responses in this study with the ontogenetic data obtained by Hemmendinger show striking agreements (29).[14]

The overall conclusion is that the responses of the clinical groups represent various, more or less immature levels of perceptual development as compared to those of normals.

This evidence is supplemented by a study which E. Freed carried out under the direction of Leslie Phillips (29). Freed hypothesized that hebephrenic and catatonic schizophrenics would fail to show increased differentiation with time. Using the same design as Framo, he exposed the Rorschach to a group of 60 hebephrenic-catatonic schizophrenics, 15 at each of four exposure times. At the shortest exposure time their performance was not grossly different from that of the normal adults, but as exposure time was increased these schizophrenics increasingly lagged behind in the development toward perceptually mature responses (see Figure 5). It can be concluded, therefore, that unlike the normal subjects, these schizophrenic groups did not utilize the increases in exposure time to improve their perceptual adequacy and integration.[15]

If we combine the notions and the evidence in terms of ontogenesis, microgenesis, and regression, we may conclude that perceptual processes

[14]Figures 1 to 4 show the W. D. and Dd responses and the genetically high responses (Mature W%, Mature D%) for (a) microgenetic changes and (b) ontogenetic changes, and (c) the responses of hebephrenic-catatonic schizophrenics, paranoids, and normals under the usual Rorschach Test conditions.

[15]Another area of abnormal behavior to which the microgenetic methodology has been applied is that of speech pathology. Experiments on apprehension of tachistoscopically presented words by normal subjects suggest that paraphrasic naming is related to microgenetically early stages of name formation (46).

develop and come to a halt at different levels. At what level the processes stop depends on such conditions as age, experience, and complexity of stimuli, and on the normal or pathologic maturity status of a person. Thus, it might be said that by evaluating the Rorschach responses of a person through genetic scores, one tests the level of perceptual formation to which such a person under optimal time conditions progresses.

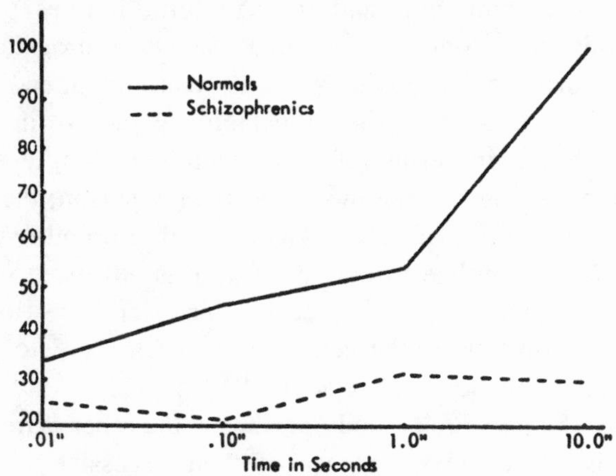

Figure 5. Median percentage of developmentally mature whole responses for normals and schizophrenics at four exposure times.

Not only has degree of psychiatric intactness been found to correspond to levels of development, but preliminary work at Worcester suggests that forms of symptom expression can also be ordered to the developmental sequence, as indicated by the genetic Rorschach scores. Thus, a number of studies have shown that persons whose symptoms are characterized by immediacy of overt reaction function at developmentally lower levels than those whose symptomatology represents displacement to more mediated forms of behavior. This has been shown by Misch, who found that a directly assaultive group is developmentally lower than a group of individuals who only threaten to assault (25). Similar findings have been obtained by Kruger (19) for subjects who demonstrate overt sexual perversion in contrast to those who only fear that they may act in a sexually perverse fashion. In addition, Kruger found that those patients who made a serious suicidal attempt were developmentally lower than those who only threatened to commit suicide.

Another developmental aspect of individuality that is in need of experimental and clinical study concerns what one might call the genetic stratification or the developmental heterogeneity of a person. Developmental stratification means that a person is structured into spheres of operations which differ in regard to developmental level. Still another aspect concerns the flexibility of a person to operate at different levels depending on the requirements of a situation.

In a particular way, it seems to us, this aspect of flexibility is connected with a further problem of individuality, namely, that of creativity. Now creativity, in its most general meaning, is an essential feature of emergent evolution, and this, in turn, implies progression through reorganization. Since we assume that such progress through reorganization cannot be achieved without "starting anew," that is, without regression, it follows that a person's capacity for creativity presupposes mobility in terms of regression and progression. The hypothesis would then be that the more creative the person, the wider his range of operations in terms of developmental level, or in other words, the greater his capacity to utilize primitive as well as advanced operations. This hypothesis is currently being tested at Worcester State Hospital and Clark University by means of the genetic Rorschach scores of relatively creative versus relatively noncreative adults.[16]

It might also be possible to study persons at the other extreme end of mobility, that is, those who, because of their excessive yearning for security, are coping with the environment in terms of rigidly formalized behavior. In this regard the work by the Swedish psychologist Ulf Krogh (18) seems very suggestive. He studied the microgenesis of complex pictures with various groups of people. Among other results he found that persons such as the compulsion-neurotics, whose reaction patterns to the environment are inordinately formalized, are lacking in microgenetic mobility, that is, they are lacking the intermediate steps that are normally present during the unfolding of percepts.

We should like, then, to conclude with this observation: The original aim of developmental theory, directed toward the study of universal genetic changes, is still one of its main concerns; but side by side with this concern, the conviction has been growing in recent years that developmental conceptualization, in order to reaffirm its truly organismic character, has to expand its orbit of interest to include as a central problem the study of individuality.

REFERENCES

1. Baker, R. W. "The Acquisition of Verbal Concepts in Schizophrenia: A Developmental Approach to the Study of Disturbed Language Behavior." Unpublished Ph.D. thesis, Clark University, 1953.

[16]The study, well advanced, is being carried out by C. Hersch.

2. Barron, D. H. "Genetic Neurology and the Behavior Problem," in P. Weiss, ed., *Genetic Neurology*, pp. 223-31. Chicago: University of Chicago Press, 1950.
3. Bayley, N. "Mental Growth during the First Three Years," *Genet. Psychol. Monogr.*, Vol. 14 (1933), No. 1, p. 92.
4. Bertalanffy, L. *Modern Theories of Development*. London: Oxford University Press, 1933.
5. Bruell, J. "Experimental Studies of Temporally Extended Perceptual Processes and the Concept of 'Aktualgenese,' " in a symposium on *The Developmental Viewpoint in Perception*, A. P. A. Meetings, Washington, D. C., 1952. Mimeogr. copy, Clark University.
6. Coghill, G. E. *Anatomy and the Problem of Behavior*. New York: Macmillan, 1929.
7. Duncker, K. "On Problem-solving," *Psychol. Monogr.*, Vol. 58 (1945), No. 5, pp. ix + 113.
8. DuNoüy, P. Lecomte, *Biological Time*. New York: Macmillan, 1937.
9. Friedman, H. "Perceptual Regression in Schizophrenia: An Hypothesis Suggested by the Use of the Rorschach Test." *J. Genet. Psychol.*, Vol. 81 (1952), pp. 63-98.
10. Gottschaldt, K. "Aufbau des Kindlichen Handelns," *Schrift. Entwickl. Psychol.*, Vol. 1 (1954), p. 220. Leipzig: Barth.
11. Hall, G. S. *Life and Confessions of a Psychologist*. New York: Appleton, 1923.
12. Hemmendinger, L. "A Genetic Study of Structural Aspects of Perception as Reflected in Rorschach Responses." Unpublished Ph.D. thesis, Clark University, 1951.
13. Hilgard, E. R. *Theories of Learning*, New York: Appleton, 1948.
14. Huxley, J. *Evolution*. London: Allen & Unwin, 1944.
15. Kaplan, B. "A Comparative Study of Acquisition of Meanings in Low-Educated and High-Educated Adults." Unpublished M.A. thesis, Clark University, 1950.
16. Kohler, I. *Über Aufbau and Wandlungen der Wahrnehmungswelt*. Wien: Rudolph M. Rohrer, 1951.
17. ———. "Umgewöhnung im Wahrnehmungsbereich," *Die Pyramide*, Vol 5 (1953), pp. 92-95, Vol. 6 (1953), pp. 109-13.
18. Krogh, U. "The Actual-Genetic Model of Perception-Personality," *Stud. Psychol. Paedag.*, Series altera, Vol. 7 (1955), p. 394. Lund: Gleerup.
19. Kruger, A. "Direct and Substitute Modes of Tension-Reduction in Terms of Developmental Level: An Experimental Analysis by Means of the Rorschach Test." Unpublished Ph.D. thesis, Clark University, 1955.
20. Lane, J. E. "Social Effectiveness and Developmental Level," *J. Personal.*, Vol. 23 (1955), pp. 274-84.
21. Lashley, K. S. "Persistent Problems in the Evolution of Mind," *Quart. Rev. Biol.*, Vol. 24 (1949), pp. 28-42.
22. Lewis, M. M. *Infant Speech*. New York: Harcourt, 1936.
23. Lillie, R. S. "Biology and Unitary Principle," *Philos. Sci.*, Vol. 18 (1951), pp. 193-207.
24. Mirin, B. "A Study of the Formal Aspects of Schizophrenic Verbal Communication," *Genet. Psychol. Monogr.*, Vol. 52 (1955), No. 2. pp. 149-90.
25. Misch, R. "The Relationship of Motoric Inhibition to Developmental Level and Ideational Functioning: An Analysis by Means of the Rorschach Test." Unpublished Ph.D. thesis, Clark University, 1953.
26. Needham, A. E. *Regeneration and Wound Healing*. New York: Wiley, 1952.
27. Novikoff, A. B. "The Concept of Integrative Levels and Biology," *Science*, Vol. 101 (1945), pp. 209-15.
28. Peña, C. "A Genetic Evaluation of Perceptual Structurization in Cerebral Pathology," *J. Proj. Tech.*, Vol 17 (1953), pp. 186-99.
29. Phillips, L., and J. Framo. "Developmental Theory Applied to Normal and Psychopathological Perception," *J. Personal.*, Vol. 22 (1954), pp. 464-74.
30. Piaget, J. *Play, Dreams, and Imitation in Childhood*. New York: Norton, 1951.

31. Rapaport, D. "The Conceptual Model of Psychoanalysis," *J. Personal.*, Vol. 20 (1951), pp. 56-81.
32. Russell, E. S. *Form and Function*. London: Murray, 1916.
33. ———. *The Directiveness of Organic Activities*. Cambridge: Cambridge University Press, 1945.
34. Sander, F. "Experimentelle Ergebenisse der Gestalt Psychologie," *Bar. ü.d. Kongr. f. Exper. Psychol.*, Vol. 10 (1928), 23-87.
35. Schneirla, T. C. "A Consideration of Some Conceptual Trends in Comparative Psychology." *Psychol. Bull.*, Vol. 6 (1952), pp. 559-97.
36. ———. "Problems in the Biopsychology of Social Organization," *J. Abn. and Soc. Psychol.*, Vol. 41 (1946), pp. 385-402.
37. Schroedinger, E. *What is Life?* Cambridge: Cambridge University Press, 1951.
38. Siegel, E. L. "Genetic Parallels of Perceptual Structurization in Paranoid Schizophrenia." Unpublished Ph.D. thesis, Clark University, 1950.
39. Simpson. G. G. *The Meaning of Evolution*. New Haven: Yale University Press, 1950.
40. Weiss, P. *Principles of Development*. New York: Holt, 1939.
41. Werner, H. "Process and Achievement," *Harvard Educ. Rev.*, Vol. 7 (1937), pp. 353-68.
42. ———. "Musical Microscales and Micromelodies," *J. Psychol.*, Vol. 10 (1940), pp. 149-56.
43. ———. "Experimental Genetic Psychology," in P. Harriman, ed., *Encyclopedia of Psychology*, pp. 219-35. New York: Philosophical Library, 1944.
44. ———. *Comparative Psychology of Mental Development*, rev. ed. Chicago: Follet, 1948.
45. ———, ed., *On Expressive Language*. Worcester: Clark University Press, 1955.
46. ———. "Microgenesis in Aphasia," *J. Abn. and Soc. Psychol.*, Vol. 52 (1956), pp. 347-53.
47. ———, and B. Kaplan. "The Developmental Approach to Cognition: Its Relevance to the Psychological Interpretation of Anthropological and Ethnolinguistic Data." Mimeogr. paper, Clark University, 1955.
48. ———. "The Acquisition of Word Meanings: A Developmental Study," *Monogr. Soc. Res. Child Developm.*, Vol. 15 (1952), No. 1, p. 120.
49. ———, and S. Wapner, "The Innsbruck Studies on Distorted Visual Fields in Relation to an Organismic Theory of Perception," *Psychol. Rev.*, Vol. 62 (1955), pp. 130-38.
50. Windle, W. F., and J. E. Fitzgerald. "Development of the Spinal Reflex Mechanism in Human Embryos," *J. Comp. Neurol.*, Vol. 67 (1937), pp. 493-509.

6. Adolescence: A Re-interpretation

Hershel Thornburg
PROFESSOR OF SOCIOLOGY
UNIVERSITY OF ILLINOIS AT CHICAGO CIRCLE

Adolescence has been traditionally thought of as the period of transition from childhood to adulthood, from the onset of puberty to voting age, from dependency to self-direction. Friedenberg describes adolescence as follows:

> Adolescence is the period during which a young person learns who he is, and what he really feels. It is a time in which he differentiates himself from the culture; though on the culture's terms. It is the age at which, by becoming a person in his own right, he becomes capable of deeply felt relationships to other individuals, perceived clearly as such. (1959, p. 9)

Jersild has defined adolescence as:

> A period during which the growing person makes the transition from childhood to adulthood. While it is not linked to any precise span of years, adolescence may be viewed as beginning roughly when young people begin showing signs of puberty and continuing until most of them are sexually mature, have reached their maximum growth in height, and have approximately reached their full mental growth as measured by intelligence tests. The period . . . includes the years from about the age of twelve to the early twenties. (1963, p. 5)

While such definitions give a general description of the stage of adolescent development, factors within today's society cause us to look for a more relevant definition of the adolescent period of life. The best definitions most likely will come from adolescents themselves. Philosophical and theoretical definitions of the adolescent age may give a behavioral-expectancy framework, but most likely its adequacy will depend on our ability to assess youth's ideas about today's problems.

Many of our problems today are a result of the very progress we have made. The adolescents who make our youth culture are the post-World War II babies who have constantly been bombarded with industrialization, technology, automation, television, a shift from rural to urban life, increasing affluence, advanced scientific discoveries, the space age, the atomic age, an impending leisure-time-for-work-time age, greater communication and mobility, sexual liberalization, and increasing prerequisites for educational and occupational realizations.

The impact of social advancement may be analyzed by looking at the biological, psychological, and cultural bases which may contribute to changing adolescent behavior. If, indeed, a new basis in any of these three areas now exists, then it seems only fair to evaluate youth in terms of contemporary advancements rather than previous ages. While many psychologists have observed different developmental behaviors of the adolescent, the most thorough and systematic categorization of adolescent developmental tasks was advanced in Robert Havighurst's *Developmental Tasks and Education* (1952) in which he describes a series of tasks which should be accomplished during the adolescent period of life.

Developmental Tasks in Adolescence

Developmental tasks may be defined as skills, knowledge, functions or attitudes which an individual should acquire within a specific period of his life. Havighurst sees these as being acquired through (1) physical maturation, (2) cultural expectations, and (3) personal aspirations. These forces "set for the individual a series of developmental tasks which must be mastered if he is to be a successful human being" (1952, p. 4). Therefore, in specific reference to the adolescent, the following developmental tasks are advanced by Havighurst (1952, pp. 33-71) as necessary accomplishments in order to move successfully into early adulthood.

1. Achieving new and more mature relations with age-mates of both sexes.
2. Achieving a masculine or feminine social role.
3. Accepting emotional independence of parents and other adults.
4. Achieving assurance of economic independence.
5. Accepting one's physique and using the body effectively.

6. Selecting and preparing for an occupation.
7. Preparing for marriage and family life.
8. Developing intellectual skills and concepts necessary for civic competence.
9. Desiring and achieving socially responsible behavior.
10. Acquiring a set of values and an ethical system as a guide to behavior.

Havighurst describes some tasks as arising primarily from physical maturation. Tasks 1 and 2, which accompany the onset of puberty, have a strong biological base. Other competencies, such as emotional maturity (Task 3), occupational selection (Task 6), and developing intellectual skills (Task 8), are also strongly influenced by physical maturation. Some tasks are resolved by the adolescent in view of personal and cultural expectations. Such tasks as striving for economic independence (Task 4), marriage (Task 7), gaining social responsibility (Task 9), and acquiring values (Task 10) are characteristic of identity striving.

Most tasks, including those with a strong biological basis, are affected by social approvals and disapprovals. Furthermore, society has appropriate times for certain developmental tasks to be worked out by the adolescent. Inability to accomplish a task within the allotted time interval compounds the learning of such a task, sometimes to the point of nonresolution within the individual himself. Therefore, in light of (1) society's attempt to help the individual learn tasks, (2) the rapid social and technological changes that have been made since World War II, and (3) the continuing change within our contemporary society, it seems necessary to reevaluate adolescent developmental tasks in respect to our existing society.

Task One: Learning Appropriate Relationships with Peers[1]

Goal: To learn effective relationships among members of the same sex and opposite sex. To build within capabilities of understanding the adult sex role.

Biological Basis: Male and female sexual development during early adolescence builds the base for late adolescent sexual maturity.

[1]The author acknowledges that the task definition format originated with Dr. Havighurst, and is used here because of its adequacy in describing the tasks.

Psychological Basis: The process of heterosexual involvements is instrumental in learning proper sex roles, many of which are effective during childhood. Group social activities develop around ages 11-12. Couple dating and double dating is an increasingly important activity among the 13-14 age group. Intimacy and often sexual involvement peaks in many youths by age 16.

Our culture sets a pattern for expected adolescent social behaviors. As groups of adolescents move into their own subcultures these patterns may vary from that designated by the larger society. It has always been thought that by high school, boys and girls should be socializing with the opposite sex, an idea that is not out of line with the accomplishment of Task 1.

Havighurst (1952) suggests that from the age of 13 or 14 most boys and girls are preoccupied with social activities and experimentation. He suggests that from their own sex they learn to behave as adults among adults and with the opposite sex they learn adult social skills. Around 14-16, Havighurst sees the more intimate type of companionship developing.

Yet, there are increasing evidences that heterosexual social roles are beginning at an earlier age. Martinson's (1968) research indicates that children are feeling pressures from their parents to date and attend many heterosexual functions by the sixth grade. A more popular account is that of *Esquire*'s "Micro-boppers" (Braun, 1968) which is a descriptive but somewhat overexaggerated article about adultlike behaviors (business investments, computer playtime, television commercial-making, martinis, and sexual candidness) of the 9-13 age group. Yet, it gives you a glimpse of what merchandisers are capitalizing on, without much thought of the psychosexual conflicts into which youths are thrown.

Physically, the average girl has her adolescent growth spurt shortly after age 10, with the peak being reached around age 12. During this time two significant things occur: (1) around 10.5 years breast enlargement begins, with full development usually occurring within three years. (2) Approximately 80% of the girls reach menarche between ages 11.5 and 14.5 (Meredith, 1967). These increased body changes, combined with industry's appeals to 10-11-year-old femininity, have thrown many girls into a social-sexual role earlier than in previous generations.

One additional factor contributes to an earlier adolescent socialization: the new public school organizational "middle-school" movement, a reorganization of school districts to include a school for grades 5-8 or 6-8. A 1967-68 survey revealed that in the past decade more than 1,100 school districts have adopted this organizational plan (Alexander, 1968).

While it is not yet certain, it is highly probable that the social impact of having 10-13-year-old students in one school will greatly increase the earlier socialization of youths.

Task Two: Learning the Appropriate Masculine and Feminine Social Role

Goal: To be aware of appropriate adult sex roles, acceptable by one's self and society.

Biological Basis: At pubescence the growth patterns of male and female become distinctively clear as each develops characteristics necessary to the sex role he or she must fulfill in life.

Psychological Basis: The alternative roles within our society today do not stress the male-masculine/female-feminine roles as they once did. Boys still find it easy to fit into a role society has designated for them, only now it is a competitve role as females are placing less stress on the wife-mother role and greater emphasis on acceptable alternative role behaviors.

Havighurst sees the necessity of a boy accepting the idea of becoming a man and a girl accepting the idea of becoming a woman. The traditional roles suggested in his book (1952) are work roles for men and wife-mother roles for women, with dependence on a man for support. However, social changes have given today's woman more freedom than was permitted in earlier generations. The result has been less pressure on the adolescent girl to accept the traditional feminine role.

Two factors contribute to a shift from clearly distinct to less definitive sex roles. They are: (1) movement of the female from the home to many roles outside the home, and (2) dress modes that are considered asexual rather than either masculine or feminine.

The growth of industrial centers, with accompanying concentration of population in urban areas, and the shift from extended or rurally located families to nuclear (urban) families, has resulted in an increasing individualism and less definite masculine and feminine roles within and external to the home. In 1890, 4.5% of the married women in America worked. By 1940, just prior to World War II, this figure had risen to 16.7%. In 1961, 34% of the married women were working (Coleman, 1965). A 1962 government report stated that the number of women 14 years and over who were gainfully employed had risen steadily from 25%

in 1949 to 35% in 1960 (Summary Report, 1962). These statistics reveal a lessening emphasis on the female accepting the traditional wife-mother role. Therefore, quite clearly, education and occupational opportunity have provided the female with alternate role possibilities.

Changing dress modes have probably had a more significant effect on men than on women. Our society has become more tolerant of the in-between types of appearance. Winick (1969) refers to this as sexual crisscrossing. He points out that since World War II clothing and appearance have become increasingly unisexual. Regarding men, Winick states:

> Men are wearing colorful and rakishly epauleted sports jackets, iridescent fabrics, dickies, and bibbed and pleated shirts of fabrics like batiste and voile.
>
> Men's trousers are slimmer and in many instances are worn over girdles of rubber and nylon. Ties are slender and often feminine. The old reliable grey fedora has given way to softer shapes and shades, sometimes topped by gay feathers. Sweaters are less likely to have the traditional V-neck than the boat neck adopted from women's fashions. Padded shoulders on a suit are as out-of-date as wide lapels and a tucked-in waist. The new look is the soft, slender, straight-line silhouette that also characterizes the shift, which has been the major woman's dress style of the 1960's. (1969, p. 20)

It is difficult to say what effect this may have on man's masculinity, but it certainly does not make masculinity as obvious with some as it once did. Several studies recently conducted regarding parent-youth interaction that boys' long hair and dress are a major source of conflict (Phi Delta Kappan, 1969; Generations Apart, 1969) which might cause one to at least hypothesize that observable male-masculinity and female-femininity is still desired by many.

Task Three: Learning Acceptance and Use of One's Own Body

Goal: To become aware of one's body so it may be viewed with pride and satisfaction; to regard one's body well enough that appropriate social use is extended.

Biological Basis: Termination of childhood is marked by endocrine changes, which results in an increase in growth rates for breasts, ovaries, and uterus in girls and size of testes, scrotum, and penis in boys. Additional pubertal changes include menstruation by girls, voice change by boys, and pigmented and axillary hair by both around 12 years of age.

Psychological Basis: A major problem which one encounters during this period is the beginning of learning how to channel sexual energy and drive into socially acceptable behaviors. It is often compounded by (1) physical attractiveness, (2) accelerated physical growth, and (3) parental protectiveness, that leaves dubious reactions to early adolescent acceptance of one's body.

If adolescents are to accept themselves and learn how to use their bodies socially, two questions must be resolved. First, "How can I handle the biological changes and newly acquired sexual capabilities within myself?" Second, "What are the acceptable ways to use my body within my social environment?"

An awareness of what changes will take place is most beneficial to the adolescent. Adolescent girls experience the beginnings of breast development about 10.5 years, pigmented hair development in the pubic area about 11, and menarche about 12. Boys initially experience growth in testes and penis around 12 and pigmented pubic hair around 13, which are part of their growth spurt which begins about 12.5 years and peaks around 14 (Meredith, 1967). Winter (1969) has listed changes during adolescence by sex, which are in Table 1.

Table 1

Changes During Adolescence by Sex[2]

Girls	*Boys*
Growth in pubic hair	Growth in pubic hair
Growth of hair under arms	Growth of hair under arms
Light growth of hair on face	Heavy growth of hair on face
Light growth of hair on body	Heavy growth of hair on body
Slight growth of larnyx	Considerable growth of larnyx
Moderate lowering of voice	Considerable lowering of voice
Eruption of second molars	Eruption of second molars
Slight thickening of muscles	Considerable thickening of muscles
Widening of hips	Widening of shoulders
Increase in perspiration	Increase in perspiration
Development of breasts	Slight temporary development of breasts around nipples
No change in hairline	Receding hairline at temples
Menstrual cycle	Involuntary ejaculations
No change in neck size	Enlargement of neck
Growth of ovaries and uterus	Growth of penis and testicles

[2]Reprinted by permission of the publisher.

Many adolescent attitudes toward the body come from comparison with other adolescents. Differences typically cause anxiety. Research has shown they are particularly concerned with height, weight, fatness, thinness, facial blemishes, largeness or smallness of hips and breasts in girls, and smallness or largeness of the genitals in boys (Angelino and Mech, 1955). Our society emphasizes physical appearance and maturation. The closer a person's body fits the "normal," the greater the social reinforcement. For those youths whose bodies do not fit the norm, anxiety may occur, often resulting in negative self-feelings. As Havighurst expressed it, it makes the adolescent question "Am I normal?" (1952, p. 40).

Society prefers its girls to look feminine and be attractive to boys. It also wants its boys to be masculine, to gain recognition among other boys, and to be popular with girls. Adolescent anxiety toward personal appearance can be reduced if youths can learn to accept themselves. To be proud and satisfied with one's self is an important developmental task.

Task Four: Behavioral and Emotional Independence of Parents and Other Adults

Goal: To break infantile ties and develop more independent adolescent relationships with parents. To develop behavioral autonomy as a basis for an emerging values system.

Biological Basis: As an adolescent becomes older, interests broaden and activities outside the home increase. The primary biological basis is chronological age, although an increasing sexual maturation may enhance broadened interests.

Psychological Basis: As adolescents develop more peer relationships they begin exercising behavioral independence. In so doing, they often run into conflicts with parents and the adult world. Their physical maturation causes them to want less controls and inhibitions from parents. Social skills learned through peer interaction facilitates an increasing self-responsibility for one's actions and creates a degree of emotional as well as behavioral independence.

The task of becoming independent has always been a difficult one for American adolescents. The ambivalent conflict is affected by the need to relinquish childhood ties on the one hand and to find sufficient independent behaviors that do not overpower the adolescent on the other. The more rapid and drastic the change, the more the adolescent will experience conflict. Therefore, while it is well and good that youths learn to throw off habits of dependency on adults, it should not be without some parental guidance.

Society desires an adequately functioning adult. This begins in childhood as parents allow their children to exercise initiative and responsibility that will later permit them to make their own way with minimal dependence on their parents. This can be enhanced if parents have an awareness of their child's need to become autonomous. Families which do are usually characterized by warmth and concern, and democratic household procedures. With today's changing society and an increasing confrontation with the "generation gap," the problems of behavioral autonomy are emphasized.

Task Five: Striving Toward Economic Independence

Goal: Learning the effective use of limited economic resources in preparation for earning a living, thus achieving economic independence in adulthood.

Biological Basis: None. Full physical strength may facilitate, but is not necessary to, the accomplishment of this task.

Psychological Basis: Today's youths find a delay in the fulfillment of this task. The lessening number of manual jobs and the increasing educational requirements for many jobs have forced postponement of gaining economic independence for many youths. With the perpetuation of the middle class value of doing a full day's work combined with a dissatisfied delay of entering the occupational field, the assurance of knowing that you are capable of earning your own way is delayed, often resulting in anxiety or self-doubts.

During adolescence, making some preparation for economic independence becomes a tremendously important but difficult task. Our highly technological and industrialized society, which features computers and automation, makes it increasingly difficult for our adolescents to get work experience while they are growing up. If it were possible for adolescents to have direct and successful work experiences it could lend much to the accomplishment of this task.

Achieving assurance of economic independence is obviously related to occupational opportunity. Automation has reduced the number of unskilled jobs to 5% of all available jobs (Wolfbein, 1964) to say nothing of the number of semiskilled and skilled jobs that are now obsolescent.

Then, there are slightly over one million youths 16-21 years old who are out of school and unemployed (Summary Report, 1962). Affluence has told another group of youths that it is not necessary to have a job during adolescence. Therefore, for youths that fall into these areas there is limited, if any, opportunity to gain the assurance of personal capability to be economically independent. For such youths, both economic independence and occupation become either distant or unrealistic goals. In some cases, this task is unresolved until an occupational choice has been determined or a person has completed some type of post-high-school training or education.

Task Six: Vocational Selection and Preparation

Goal: To become aware of the changing occupational world. To prepare for an occupation which is realistic and meaningful.

Biological Basis: None. By the time an adolescent has the opportunity to learn and apply occupational skills, he has an accompanying physical maturation.

Psychological Basis: By the time students reach the twelfth grade they have formulated fairly definite ideas about what they want to do occupationally. With a reduction in skilled jobs, youths are more involved in specific educational programs which will open occupational fields to them.

During adolescence, decisions regarding an occupational choice are tremendously important. It is the time, as Gold and Douvan put it, when the "child presumably becomes critically aware of the work life—of the need to choose a vocation toward which he can gear education, and other instrumental activities, of the variety of work roles, of the relationship that binds adulthood, economic independence, and vocational responsibility into a tight nexus" (1969, p. 255). This task is compounded by our highly industrialized and technological society, which prolongs adolescence. The number of adolescent jobs available is limited, quite often meaningless, and of little practical usefulness.

Job experience during adolescence may have a positive relationship to subsequent occupational choice. In a study done by Slocum and Empey (1959), it was found that meaningful work experience had an effect on occupational choice. Most studies have been done on aspirational levels of students. In general, students tend to aspire to a high goal (Garrison, 1955). In many cases this has been influenced by the underlying cultural pressure that indicates a man's worth is directly related to a man's occupation and his ability to be successful in it.

In other youths, aspirations are affected by their needs. Just as needs may influence choice, needs may change, which in turn realign occupational goals. To discern one's needs and one's goal during adolescence is a difficult task, especially since most youths are exhorted to go to college, or to take training in addition to high school before entering the job market. As a result two conditions exist.

First, due to technological advances many skilled, semi-skilled and unskilled jobs no longer exist. In 1952, Havighurst stated, "Employers want workers who can read and write, and when the labor supply is plentiful, employers like to insist on a high school diploma as a prerequisite. This is a convenient way of selecting people who can learn a new job fairly rapidly" (pp. 47-48). Today, this is no longer true. Employers are considerably more selective and occupational requirements are more stringent. The result is a prolongation of the adolescent's selecting, preparing, and actually becoming involved in the occupational world.

A second important facet of this development task is that it is becoming increasingly vital for adolescent girls. Many opportunities exist today for women which did not exist prior to the 1960's. Therefore, many jobs once awarded the male are now given to females if they have the necessary job qualifications. The task for females is relatively new but more complex than it is for men, because they (1) must discern occupational choices that are most accessible to them, and (2) many females still regard any occupational choice as a tentative one, depending upon whom they marry and his vocational field.

In analysis, the occupational world is more difficult to enter today than it has been before. Occupational mobility, job obsolescence, and changing job requirements point out the importance of adolescent awareness of the changing occupational world. Indeed, perhaps the most successful career prototype hinges around the adolescent who acquires transferable occupational skills.

Task Seven: Preparing and Accepting the Role of Marriage and Family Life

Goal: To become attached to a member of the opposite sex. To develop an understanding of the varying relationships in marriage and family life.

Biological Basis: Physical and sexual maturation facilitates the attachment of the sexes.

Psychological Basis: Adolescents must experience the naturalness of sexual attractiveness to the opposite sex. As an attachment becomes stronger, attitudes toward sexual involvement, marriage, and rearing a family begin emerging. The more aware one is of the involvement and commitment necessary, the more realistic will be the emerging attitudes.

Marriage is held as the core of social life. Attitudes and values toward marriage vary according to the culture and social class influencing the individual. The varying patterns of marriage and attitudes toward the marital relationship point out an increasing need for family life education.

Learning an appropriate sex role in marriage involves the acceptance and understanding of socially approved adult male and female roles. This problem often focuses around using the sex drive in a socially acceptable manner. Within today's society sexual morality is shifting, and this points out the necessity of youths learning sex and family life information from reliable sources. Otherwise, much confusion in the adult sex role can arise from misinformation and ignorance (Thornburg, 1969b).

Youths see confusion in today's sexual morality. Problems arise in connection with petting and premarital intercourse that sometimes appear insoluble. In our society there is no single sex code that is appropriate. Therefore, it is difficult to know what will emerge when different standards are suggested by one's peers, parents, or church. Through the conflict, youths would profit if they could see marriage in a variety of dimensions other than sex. The more broadly based the marriage, the greater are the chances of putting all dimensions into a wholesome perspective.

Task Eight: Developing a Social and Civic Intelligence

Goal: To have an intelligent awareness of social factors in order to live within one's society. To prepare for and accept the role of a citizen.

Biological Basis: Most adolescents have reached their maximum intellectual potential by age 15, thus adult intelligence can be exercised.

Psychological Basis: Inasmuch as learning social and civic skills usually follows the learning of academic skills, this task is usually not accomplished before late adolescence. Regarding social competencies, it is necessary for the adolescent to relate his well-being to his family and to their social position. Good civic intelligence is learned through understanding what society gives to the adolescent and, in turn, what the adolescent may give to society. Individual mental capabilities vary tremendously, thus what is learned as a social or civic skill by one person might not be learned by another person because of his inability to comprehend.

Certain intellectual strengths other than academic are needed in order to develop a balanced maturity toward social and civic functions. Garrison (1955) cites the lack of opportunity for adolescents to get involved, other than during wartime, as not aiding youth in developing civic attitudes toward freedom, work, politics, government, law, and human relations. Garrison (1966) finds it equally important to understand one's own possibilities and limitations in order to function effectively within the social order.

Today's youths live in a complex society where social order often becomes confused and civic responsibility is lost in the apparent inconsistencies of our political structure. Yet, when man becomes complex, it is often not possible to restore him to a simple being; rather it may become necessary for people to learn new skills to cope with him.

One such skill includes the ability to tolerate ambiguity. Not all things are black and white today. Not every question that is asked can be answered. The indefiniteness of many social and civic matters requires a tolerant citizenship.

Another skill needed in today's youth is the ability to delay gratification (Hollister, 1966). Constantly we hear demands for immediate action, and ultimatums. We get the democratic process confused with the necessity of immediately satisfying our protesting youth. They need to understand that some things take time, whether we like it or not.

A third socially intellectual skill is worthy of mention—the ability to tolerate seemingly insoluble problems within our society. Currently civil rights and the Viet Nam war are examples of this need. When the answers to these social and political problems will come is uncertain. The ability of the individual to cope with them can strengthen a person's personal frame of reference.

It must be remembered that such social and civic intelligence is not as easily learned as are other educational or occupational skills. The very fact that all people do not have the capacity for acquisition of such skills must be honored in our society.

Task Nine: Acquiring Personal Values and Ethics

Goal: To attain a value structure which will serve as a guide to behavior. To acquire an ethical philosophy as a guide for decisions.

Biological Basis: None. This task involves a learning, rather than a maturation basis.

Psychological Basis: An individual's value system starts forming early through the social-psychological processes of the family. During adolescence, one's values are tested through experience outside the home. It is during this time that most adolescents find out how closely their values are to their parents' or how much value autonomy they are experiencing. Associated with values is a person's basic philosophy of life. Through considering one's parents, peers, religion, philosophy, and ideals, a value hierarchy emerges and serves as a reference point for adolescent, and subsequent adult, behavior.

A common problem among youths today is the search for identity. In the process a person typically asks questions regarding the who, what, and where of himself. The goal becomes finding one's role in the total life experience.

Disillusionment with today's social structure has caused youths to examine morality, religion, and other traditional questions. Since the 1940's there has appeared to be a decrease in religious interest, and people have sought out philosophies of life without religion as the focal point. It has been an attempt to develop new ethical codes and practices. Recent research indicates that there is an increasing concern for religion by today's youths (Thornburg, 1969a). As with so many other things, religion is viewed as meaningless, and youths find no help within its framework.

Subsequently, youth involvement in issues today has often stemmed from an inability to sort out the superfluous and the traditional. No longer do many enduring values have much significance. Rather than to experience parental value systems and then modify them as one's needs demand, youths are rejecting such value systems, labeling them as traditional, conservative, stifling, etc. Such descriptions have not aided much in solving their dilemma.

Adolescents need a personal reference point. While they may become disenchanted with that which their parents or society build into them, it is still necessary for them to have a value structure in order to know what changes are necessary for an individual to make. Through this process each person can emerge with a personal value system—one which will allow many indefinite and ambiguous questions to be resolved. It is the process of being one's self—morally, ethically, philosophically.

Since adolescence has important long-term effects, and since adolescence today is an increasingly longer period, it is necessary to reevaluate the adolescent's developmental tasks to facilitate the interpretation and transmission of his culture in a way conducive to the total growth of youth. Regardless of the stressful experiences the adolescent encounters, the nature of such experiences may have crucial long-range effects on his growth. If the adolescent is aware of what is expected of him, he may better focus on his tasks. Interpreting such tasks in light of contemporary society lends significance to the accomplishment of them. Thus, the functioning adolescent evolves into the functioning adult.

REFERENCES

Alexander, W. M. "The Middle-School Movement," *Theory into Practice,* 1968, 7, 114-17.

Angelino, H. and Mech, E. V. " 'Fears and Worries' Concerning Physical Changes: A Preliminary Survey of 32 Females," *Journal of Psychology,* 1955, 39, 195-98.

Braun, S. "Life-styles: The Micro-bopper," *Esquire,* 1968, 69 (3), 103-106; 22-24.

Coleman, J. S. *Adolescents and the Schools.* New York: Basic Books, 1965.

Friedenberg, E. Z. *The Vanishing Adolescent.* New York: Dell Publishing Company, 1959.

Garrison, K. C. "Developmental Tasks and Problems of the Late Adolescent Period," *Education,* 1955, 76, 232-35.

Garrison, K. C. *Psychology of Adolescence.* New York: Prentice-Hall, 1966.

Generations Apart. New York: Columbia Broadcasting System, 1969.

Gold, M., and E. Douvan, eds., *Adolescent Development.* Boston: Allyn & Bacon, 1969.

Havighurst, R. L. *Developmental Tasks and Education.* New York: Longmans, Green and Company, 1952.

Hollister, W. G. "Preparing the Minds of the Future." *National Association of Secondary Principals Bulletin,* 1966, 50, 30-50.

The Impact of Urbanization on Education. Washington, D.C.: Government Printing Office, 1962.

Jersild, A. T. *The Psychology of Adolescence,* 2nd ed. New York: Macmillan, 1963.

Martinson, F. M. "Sexual Knowledge, Values and Behavior Patterns of Adolescents," *Child Welfare,* 1968, 48, 405-410; 426.

Meredith, H. V. "A Synopsis of Pubertal Changes in Youth," *Journal of School Health,* 1967, 37, 171-76.

Phi Delta Kappan, 1967, 48 (7), 354.

Slocum, W. L., and L. T. Empey. *Occupational Planning by Young Women.* Pullman, Wash.: Bulletin 568, Agricultural Experimental Station, State College of Washington, 1959.

Thornburg, H. D. "Student Assessment of Contemporary Issues," *College Student Survey,* 1969a, 3 (1), 1-5; 22.

Thornburg, H. D. *Sex Education in the Public Schools.* Phoenix: Arizona Education Association, 1969b.

Winick, C. "The Beige Epoch: Depolarization of Sex Roles in America," *The Annals of the American Academy of Political and Social Science,* 1969, 376, 18-24.

Winter, G. D. "Physical Changes During Adolescence," in G. D. Winter, and E. M. Nuss, eds., *The Young Adult.* New York: Scott, Foresman, and Company, 1969, 85-89.

Wolfbein, S. L. "Labor Trends, Manpower, and Automation," in H. Borow, ed., *Man in a World at Work.* Boston: Houghton Mifflin, 1964.

II. COGNITIVE DEVELOPMENT

The area of cognition has continued to sustain great interest in developmental psychology. It permits easier empirical exploration than, let's say, affect or unconscious motivation. The method of study is more precise and the findings more measurable. Moreover, Jean Piaget has contributed so much in this area on which further investigations can rest. The examination of this single area of psychic development permits many investigators to discern the laws of developmental changes, although rate or the timing or the structural formation may differ from those of other psychological areas. Today this field of investigation offers much new understanding.

First, there is Nancy Bayley's paper, "On the Growth of Intelligence." This is an excellent review paper which discusses many aspects of cognition, different tests and research investigations. Bayley summarizes the many modes of testing intelligence at various levels of development, and explains problems which emerge as one uses these tests. She discusses the correlation of intelligence in childhood with the intellectual functioning of adults. Bayley reviewed the concept of "the Constant IQ"; if this is accepted one may conclude that the IQ of infants gives a measure of the intelligence of the individual through life. But the finding is that intellectually precocious babies leveled down and the low IQ of some can substantially increase over time; thus new amendment to the original concept had to be made. Therefore, she explores the "Problems in Constructing Curves of Growth in Intelligence"—and the changing intellectual process into adult life.

The next paper is by Lawrence Kohlberg, who has contributed so much to the understanding of developmental processes. His study is "The Development of Children's Orientations Toward a Moral Order: Sequences in the Development of Moral Thought." Kohlberg has chosen here to follow the evolution of one aspect of development, morality. Viewed developmentally, it proceeds through stages and sequences and allows us to see the progression toward more stable internalized concepts. This study, too, combines the direct study of children with the formation of developmental theory. Connections can be seen here between the author's theory and Piaget's, as well as psychoanalytic propositions concerning superego development. Kohlberg bases his work on the concepts of Piaget. He transfers the cognitive stages to the moral thought sequential stages. At the same time new findings made Kohlberg alter some of this earlier proposition. In this paper he compares carefully his steps with those outlined on Piaget. Later he applied this approach to the study of sex identity and differences.

Surely you will expect Piaget's theory to be represented. We chose a selection written by Piaget himself. Here he places his theoretical propositions in the context of developmental processes, and he outlines the basis on which he formulated his original findings. He chose the advantage of studying cognition independently of other psychic functions, such as affect. This delineation was undertaken in order to provide a focus, with the realization that his experiments and the resultant findings, when applied clinically, must be correlated with the larger fabric of development. Piaget's work has influenced a whole generation of investigators, and has led to many applications in the clinical and educational service areas. Many attempts have been made to integrate or at least coordinate his findings with other theories of development. Like Werner, Piaget believed that one can study processes as they follow "logical" organization, and to extend this thought, that the development of logical thinking is an expression of that organization. He too believed in the Gestalt approach, and he studied forms of equilibrium: predominance of parts, which will lead to the disturbance of the whole, the predominance of the whole, with the consequence of deviating the parts, and the appropriate interplay of both whole and parts. Some of his best-known works are on the child's theories about life, on the child's language development and causal reasoning.

His interest in "mental embryology" led to one of his major contributions, namely the problem of a genetic epistemology. These endeavors continue to influence present-day psychological thought in most basic areas. His concepts of intellectual operations in childhood have also opened up new approaches to methods of studies. His stages of cognitive development have great clinical implications, for they permit the assessment of normal versus abnormal development, and a better understanding of "organic" disorders.

7. On the Growth of Intelligence*

Nancy Bayley

Research Psychologist Emeritus
Institute of Human Development
University of California, Berkeley

One of the primary objectives of the Berkeley Growth Study (20) has been to study the processes of the development of intelligence as measured by tests. During the 25 years since the study was started, there has been continual change in psychologists' ideas and theories about intelligence. As a result, some of the changing theories and emphases are reflected in the series of reports that have been made on the growth of intelligence in these children. What is more, by their very nature these longitudinal studies have themselves contributed something to our knowledge of, and theories about, intellectual development and functioning.

I should like here to review the data from the Berkeley Growth Study, together with some related material, as they bear on our knowledge of the growth of intelligence.

The Concept of the Constant IQ

In early studies the intelligence quotient was found to be very practical: it served as an easily understood index of a child's relative ability, an index by which he could be compared with other children the same age or in the same grade at school. It was found that as a rule the IQ changed very little when a child was retested a week or a month or a year or two later. This gave people great confidence in the IQ's "constancy." Furthermore, there are advantages in being able to classify a child and have him remain as classified. But this very stability of scores over certain short periods of the life span led to the assumption that intelligence is a basic entity which changes only by accretions and decrements in quantity with childhood growth, adult stability, and senescent decline. Of course this is

*Presidential address read at the May 1954 meeting of the Western Psychological Association.

an oversimplified extreme position, though it seems to have been (and still often is) held by many people who have used "IQ Tests" in education and in practice. It is not, however, a position held for long by those who have been actively engaged in studying the nature of intelligence and its growth.

Another result of the concept of the constant IQ has been its extrapolation, both forward and backward from the school-age child, to include all ages, from birth to senescence. If the IQ is constant, then we should be able to classify a child in infancy according to his intellectual potential. We can plan his education, we can make better foster home placements, we can put the feeble-minded into custodial care very young, and so on.

The Selection of Infant Tests

Although the Binet-Simon tests and Kuhlman's American revision included items for the first year of life, little had been done on tests of infants before Gesell set up a normative study at Yale in the early 1920's. When the Berkeley Growth Study started in 1928, we searched the literature for descriptions of infant behavior that would be suitable for evaluating intellectual development during the first year. The list tentatively compiled for our mental tests was heavily loaded with items from Gesell's norms, in the first formulations as published in 1925 (15). Many of these items were closely similar to those listed in other sources, but Gesell had assembled an excellent set of materials on which to test these behaviors. He was also one of the few who had actually tested a fair sample of infants, thus furnishing good preliminary norms. We selected from both the test materials and test items as first described by Gesell, adding items from other sources. In many instances we found it necessary to work out our own standard procedures and criteria of success or failure.

These tentative schedules we applied to the 61 babies of the Berkeley Growth Study, each infant being brought in at monthly intervals, starting at approximately one month of age. Ratings and descriptions were made on each child's responses during the testing situation. The items finally included in the California First Year Mental scale were selected after analysis of their adequacy according to the usual criteria. These criteria include: their occurrence in all or most of the infants; the increasing percentage of success on them with increasing age, for appropriate developmental stages; their internal consistency and correlation with the total behavioral criterion; and their apparent relevance as intellectual, or adaptive, functions.

Prediction from Scores in Infancy

At the outset we had accepted the findings based on school-age children, and assumed that IQ's were constant at all ages. Consequently we were amazed at the precocity of some of the babies whose mothers seemed not very bright, and embarrassed at the poor records of other babies who, by the laws of inheritance, should have done better. But we soon found that our embarrassments and amazements were alleviated with time: a slow baby would forge ahead and redeem his inheritance, a precocious infant often seemed to rest on his laurels while the others caught up with him. We were not too surprised, therefore, when the statistical treatment of the test scores revealed that there was no relation between relative performance in the first few months of life and scores earned at the end of the first year.

When the report on the mental scores of the Berkeley Growth Study children during their first three years (7) was published, it was met by many with skepticism. However, in spite of their failure to conform with established theory, these Berkeley children continued to develop in their own individual ways. What is more, we have corroborative evidence from the records of the children in the Guidance Study, as reported by Honzik (18) and more recently by Honzik, Macfarlane, and Allen (19). Furthermore, these irregularities in mental growth were found to occur in other than Berkeley children. Wherever careful statistics have been applied to comparisons of repeated test scores on infants and very young children the correlations between tests separated by a year or two are low. It is now well established that we cannot predict later intelligence from the scores on tests made in infancy (1, 16). Scores may be altered by such conditions as emotional climate, cultural milieu, and environmental deprivation, on the one hand, and by developmental changes in the nature and composition of the behaviors tested, on the other. These latter factors are the primary concern in this paper.

As the Berkeley Growth Study children grew older we continued to record their progress by successive tests at frequent intervals. We have from time to time reported the results of these tests, along with efforts to find relationships between mental growth and other factors (6). When the children were 8 years old a study of the individual growth records showed that only a fifth of the group had maintained any stability in their relative status over the eight-year span (8). Even these few had unstable Standard Scores during the first two years.

This lack of stability in infant test scores has resulted in various efforts to supplement and to correct the infant tests to make them more predictive. It has been suggested that the scales are not composed of the right kind of test items. However, efforts to devise other, more adequate, scales invariably run into the hard fact that infants exhibit a very limited range of behaviors that can be observed and recorded. The various scales of infant intelligence have a remarkable similarity of content. At first there is little to note beyond evidences of sensory functioning in reacting to appropriate stimuli. One can observe that the one-month-old looks momentarily at a dangling ring, or at a rattle or other small object. Or one can vary the source of the sharp sound that will make him start or blink. A little later the responses are evidenced in motor coordinations: the six-month-old may pick up a one-inch cube or a teaspoon placed in easy reach. There are some early evidences of adaptation to the presented stimuli, of memory from a past experience: the seven-month-old, for example, looks ''aware'' that a fallen toy is no longer there, and when a little older he may turn to look for it on the floor. One can note the progression of vocalizations as they become more complex and then as they are used meaningfully. There is a developing ability to discriminate differences, to be aware of new situations, to recognize differences between members of the family and strangers, and so on.

The question is: Which, if any, among these is the forerunner of later intellectual functions? Which, if any, will predict the individual differences found in school-age children?

One method of testing and selecting predictive items has been to use a later (or ''terminal'') measure of intelligence as the criterion. Scores earned by infants or very young children on individual test items have been correlated with their later IQ's. Those items showing the highest *r*'s with the criterion have in some instances been combined into scales. Theoretically, if other items of similar nature are then devised and added, such a scale can be expanded into an adequate predictive test. This method has been tried on infant scales by L. D. Anderson (2) and by Nelson and Richards (25). They compared successes on items under one year with retest criteria at ages 2 to 5 years. Maurer (22) compared scores on items in tests given children at 3 to 5 years with their scores at 15 years as a criterion. More recently Hastings compared preschool test items with 14- to 18-year scores from our studies at the Institute of Child Welfare (17). In all of these studies some items have proved to be better predictors than others. Hastings selected items from the Guidance Study records and validated them on the Berkeley Growth Study (19 boys and 18 girls). His predictive items were good for the boys, but not for the girls in the validating sample. These boys had a wide range of ability, and thus an unusually large *SD* of scores. Their 2-year performance on a scale made up of good predictors correlated .67 with scores at 16-17 years. The same comparisons for the girls gave an *r* of .34. In general the predictions were better at the later preschool ages.

We have tried to find predictive items from the First Year Scale on the Berkeley Growth Study children. Several years ago, using the six children at each extreme of intelligence as measured at the 14 to 16-year tests, we went through the First Year Scale item by item, noting the age at which each of these 12 children first passed each item. We were able to select 31 items in which the six high-scoring teenagers had, as infants, been two months or more advanced over the six low-scorers. These items were an odd assortment, and there was no evident reason for their superiority over other items. Most of the items occur in the second half year, where there is a fair amount of range in scores. In the first few months very few items had a range of more than two months in age at first passing.

Recently we computed scores for the total Berkeley Growth Study sample on this 31-item scale for three ages: months 6, 9, and 12. The *r*'s of these new point scores with the mean of the intelligence sigma scores at ages 16, 17 and 18 years (for 45 cases) are .09 at 6 months, .32 at 9 months, and .30 at 12 months. We were unable to get significant correlations even though our sample was composed in large part of the cases on whom the items were selected, including all of the extreme cases that would determine a relationship.

So far, none of these efforts has been successful in devising an intelligence scale applicable to children under two years that will predict their later performance. The moderate successes of Maurer and of Hastings have been on items at the two-year level of difficulty or older. Even here the *r*'s are not high enough for accurate prediction on individual children. As far as I know, no one has used these items to set up and standardize an expanded scale. There does seem to be some coherence in the types of function tested by the predictive items. It is interesting to note, too, that those items which are good predictors are often not the items that best characterize a child's current stage of development. It has even been suggested that a scale should combine both types of items and then be scored in two ways—one score for evaluating present status and one for predicting future development.

These findings give little hope of ever being able to measure a stable and predictable intellectual factor in the very young. I am inclined to think that the major reason for this failure rests in the nature of intelligence itself. I see no reason why we should continue to think of intelligence as an integrated (or simple) entity or capacity which grows throughout childhood by steady accretions.

The Changing Organization of Intellectual Processes

Intelligence appears to me, rather, to be a dynamic succession of developing functions, with the more advanced and complex functions in the hierarchy depending on the prior maturing of earlier simpler ones (given, of course, normal conditions of care). The neonate who is precocious in the developing of the simpler abilities, such as auditory acuity or pupillary reflexes, has an advantage in the slightly more complex behaviors, such as (say) turning toward a sound, or fixating an object held before his eyes. But these more complex acts also involve other functions, such as neuro-muscular coordinations, in which he may not be precocious. The bright one-month-old may be sufficiently slow in developing these later more complex functions so as to lose some or all of his earlier advantage. This is the kind of thing that does seem to happen. Scores on tests given a month apart are highly correlated, but the longer the time interval between these baby tests the lower the intertest correlation.

If intelligence is a complex of separately timed, developing functions, then to understand its nature we must try to analyze it into its component parts. One approach to this process has been by factor analysis. Of the two main theories resulting from factor analysis, our data would seem to fit better into some variation of a multiple-factor than a two-factor theory. Or perhaps they fit better a theory that is intermediate, somewhere between the two.

The program of the Berkeley Growth Study has not been carried on in such a way as to make factor analysis on this material practicable. For one thing, the number of cases is too small for the usual factorial procedures. Also, for such a purpose one might have chosen a different or a more extensive series of tests. (As it is, the children have tolerated an amazingly large amount of testing and measuring!)

Nevertheless, some of our findings should point the way to new areas where factorial or other kinds of analysis would be fruitful. I should like to know, for example, where to look for *g* in the infant scales. One might expect *g* to be that factor on which prediction could be based. If *g* is not present at first, then when and how does it appear? Or does *g* itself change as it grows more complex? How do factor loadings distribute themselves in infant scales? Does a heavily loaded first factor show a characteristic developmental process of change?

Richards and Nelson (27), using the Gesell items, at 6, 12, and 18 months, obtained two factors which they called "alertness" and "motor ability." They found age changes in communality of the tests that were in part due to restrictions in the type of items included in the scales at the older ages. This very fact reflects the relatively undifferentiated nature of behavior in the very young. It may be a mistake to try to call any infant behavior before 6 months more characteristically "mental" than, for example, motor. In spite of progressive selection of behaviors observed in intelligence tests, the evidence of a motor factor persists in the early ages of the Stanford-Binet, according to McNemar's factor analysis (23). These studies only scratch the surface of what needs to be done to gain real understanding of the nature of early mental processes.

If the word "intelligence" is best used as a broad general term that we apply to a great variety of mental functions, then we will want to investigate the nature of these functions, their interrelationships and the changes that take place in mental organization with growth. We should expect a given "factor" of intelligence to be more important at one stage of development than at another. As Garrett (14) has shown, in a summary of factor analyses, there is evidence of increasing independence of mental factors as children grow older. Does this trend continue indefinitely? Or do some of these factors become functionally reintegrated as they mature? The studies of Thurstone and others can be most valuable in yielding information on this point. Let us hope they will be continued, over the entire life span, with careful attention to the problem of selecting items to test all relevant mental functions at all ages.

The very fact that the scores of mental growth in individual children tend to exhibit gradual shifts in relative status supports the theory that a changing organization of factors is in process. Something akin to *g*, or a high first-factor loading, must appear soon after the second or third year. The correlations of tests at these ages become positive with the later test scores. After 5 or 6 years children can be reliably classified into broad categories of normal, defective, and bright.[1]

Problems Encountered in Constructing Curves of Growth in Intelligence

The use of intelligence quotients, or standard scores, in studying growth changes in children is helpful in showing a child's shifts in status relative to the norms. But a child's progress, in relation to his own past, is better represented if we can use scores that measure increments or *amounts* of intelligence. Here we run into the problem of comparable units. Lacking absolute units for measuring intelligence, we must settle for some measure of greater or lesser difficulty, or degree of complexity of intellectual functioning. The first, and perhaps still most generally used unit of intelligence is mental age. Such a unit tends to force the same value on a mental age increment of (say) a month, whether it occurs at 6 months of age, at 6 years or 16 years. Thurstone (30), Thorndike (28), and others have tried by various devices to set up units that approximate equality of difficulty at all levels of complexity. This is done usually by comparing the overlapping distributions of scores earned by children of successively older ages. Such units would vary with the test and with the normative sample. In any event, they remain only approximations. When we accept and label them as such, however, they become useful in comparing age changes in ability.

Thurstone applied his method to the Berkeley Growth Study scores on the California First Year and Preschool Scales for the first two years (7). We later extended the scaling through five years, and obtained the curve shown in Figure 1. This curve is positively accelerated for a few months,

[1]Since this paper was read, Hofstaetter has made a factor analysis using the 18-year consistency correlations of my data (3). He obtained three distinct factors: the first is predominant for the first two years, the second between 2 and 4 years, and the third accounts for almost the entire variance after 4 years. He names them: I, Sensory Motor Alertness, II, Persistence, and III, Manipulation of Symbols. This latter is most likely the general intellectual factor that most intelligence tests are designed to measure. These are, of course, global, or total-test characterizations, but they illustrate the complete break between the kinds of function measured in infants and in school-age children. P. R. Hoffstaetter, "The Changing composition of 'intelligence': a Study of *t*-Technique," *J. genet. Psychol.*, 1954, 85, 159-164.)

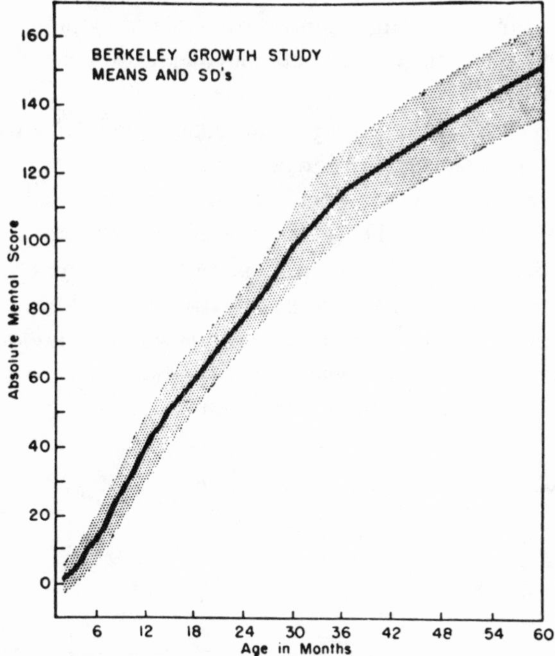

Figure 1. Curve of intelligence, 1 month to 60 months, Berkeley Growth Study, according to Thurstone's method of Absolute Scaling.

then settles into a consistent rapid growth for almost a year, after which there is a gradual slowing down in the rate, though growth continues to be fairly rapid. The curve makes sense in the light of ordinary observations of children's early development. It seems to be a useful approximation, even though one cannot claim absolute equivalence of difficulty of the units at different levels.

Problems of equating different scales. When the children grew older, and an extension of the scale was in order, we ran into another problem. We had to find new tests, adapted to the children's increased mental capacities. At the beginning of the study there had been no well-standardized infant and preschool scales, and we had found it necessary to develop our own. However, good standard tests were available for school-age children. The 1916 revision of the Stanford-Binet was given at 6 years. Since that time we have consistently used standardized tests of intelligence, including the 1916, and both forms of the 1937 Stanford Revision of the Binet, the Terman-McNemar Group test, and the Wechsler-Bellevue Adult Intelligence Scale, Form I. But shifts in scales, with their different norms and units of increment, have complicated the problem of setting up a single continuous scale of mental growth units. This problem has not been solved, but I have approached it tentatively in several ways.

A few years ago, in presenting some data on mental growth for the first 18 years (3), I transposed the early scores into mental age equivalents. These scores, together with the Stanford-Binet mental ages, give us age units from birth to 17 years. The mean mental age curve of the Berkeley Growth Study children is shown in Figure 2. At 17 years, the latest available Stanford-Binet M.A. score for this group, the scores were continuing to increase. However, the rate of growth as expressed in M.A. units has diminished at the later ages. The standard deviations, shown in the lower part of Figure 2, do not increase at a constant rate but are

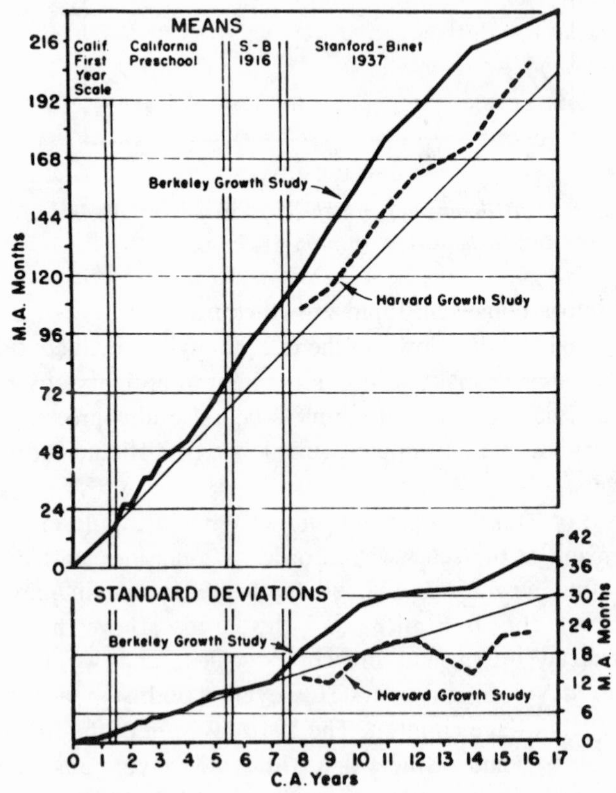

Figure 2. Curves of means and SD's of mental ages, 1 month to 17 years, Berkeley Growth Study. From Bayley (3, p. 169).

relatively large around 10 to 12 years. Similar trends in variability may be found in other samples, and for other tests. This, I have argued (3), reflects a true state of increased variability in intelligence during early adolescence.

The curve of the mean mental ages is in many ways similar, for the same age intervals, to curves constructed by other investigators, using other units of mental growth. The general similarity holds whether the scores are based on longitudinal or cross-sectional samples.

Accordingly, I felt justified in using this longitudinal M.A. curve in conjunction with the Jones and Conrad (21) curve based on cross-sectional data and standard score units, to construct a theoretical curve of the probable course of intelligence from birth to 60 years (5). This curve is shown in Figure 3. It is similar to curves offered by Miles (24), Wechsler (31), and others. However, more recent data on the Berkeley Growth Study, together with data from other studies, raise questions concerning the representativeness of this curve.

The data on the Berkeley Growth Study do not stop at 17 years. The Wechsler-Bellevue Adult intelligence scale was given at 16, 18, and 21 years and we are currently repeating the test at 25 years. A study of the growth of intelligence between 16 and 21 years, as measured by these tests, is now in press (4). The scores were found to increase through 21 years. This was true for each category, at least to 18 years, and for the Efficiency Quotients based on the total test. It was even true of the IQ's. These trends are shown clearly in the curves of the means. The weighted category scores

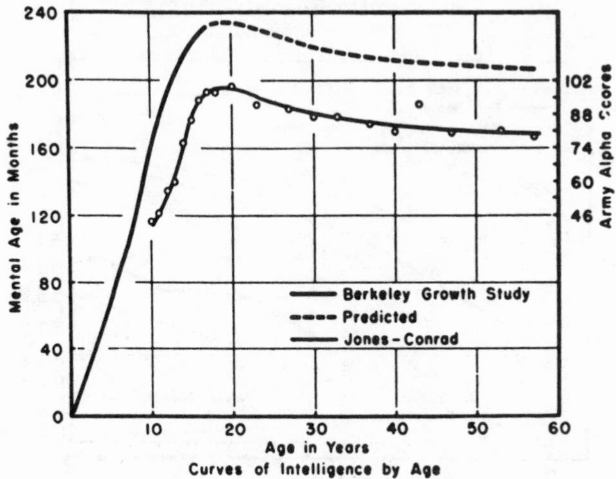

Figure 3. Curves of intellegence by age based on data from the Berkeley Growth Study, and from Jones and Conrad (21). From Ch. 4, p. 170, Theoretical Foundations of Psychology, *H. Helson, ed., D. Van Nostrand, 1951.*

are given in Figure 4; all but one or two are still increasing at 21 years. The total scores in Figure 5 are expressed as quotients: total IQ, and EQ, and

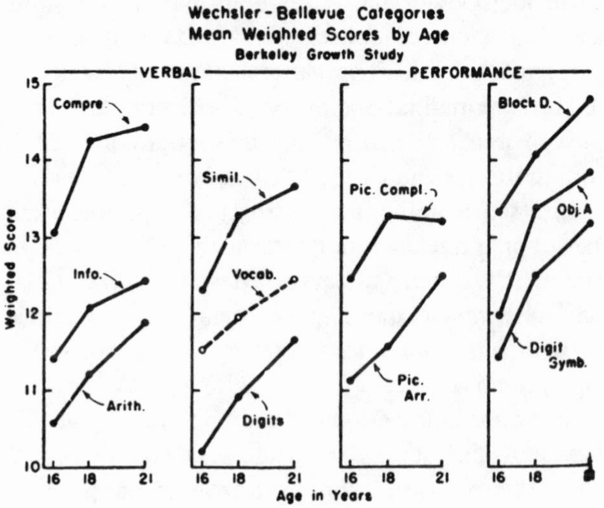

Figure 4. Curves of mean Wechsler-Bellevue category scores, 16, 18, and 21 years, Berkeley Growth Study. From Bayley (4).

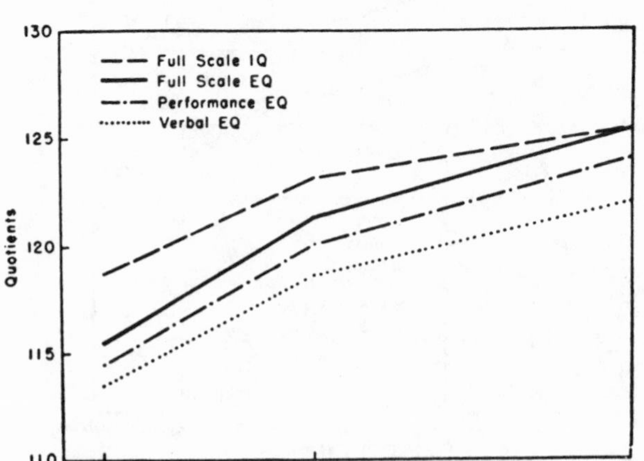

Figure 5. Age curves of Wechsler-Bellevue IQ's and EQ's, Berkeley Growth Study. From Bayley (4).

Verbal and Performance EQ. (The EQ expresses the deviation of the weighted score from the norm for 20-24-year-olds [31].) The gains occurred at all levels of ability within the group. All but one of the 33 subjects made some gain in total weighted score over the five-year period.

These data are in agreement with other investigators' findings on retests of the same individuals. Freeman and Flory (13) and Thorndike (29) have found for different samples, and for different tests, that intelligence scores continue to increase at least to 21 years. Dearborn and Rothney (12) have fitted the Harvard Growth Study data to a curve that, by extrapolation, indicates mental growth would continue to 30 years.

The general appearance of the Wechsler-Bellevue weighted score curve for the Berkeley Growth Study gives the impression that it could very well fit on as a continuation of the 17-year mental age curve. But to put the two curves into a single continuum would require transposing the scores into comparable units. This I have attempted to do, in the hope that it will give at least a rough approximation of the direction of mental growth.

The construction of the 16D Scale. The Berkeley Growth Study tests were scheduled so that alternating forms of the Stanford-Binet were given annually through 12 years and again at 14 and 17 years. The Terman-McNemar Group test was given individually, Form C at 13 years and Form D at 15. The Wechsler-Bellevue was thus dovetailed in, having been given at years 16, 18, and 21. If we assume that the 16-year Wechsler-Bellevue scores earned by these subjects are equivalent in difficulty to a mental age at the 16-year point on their Stanford-Binet mental age curve, we can start at 16 years as a basis for equating the two sets of scores. At the adjacent ages the Stanford-Binet M.A.'s have standard deviations averaging 34 points, while the Wechsler-Bellevue *SD*'s were about 20 and the Terman-McNemar *SD*'s about 19 points.

With these data, starting with the Means and *SD*'s of the 16-year scores, we have constructed a method of transposing the scores from all tests into what may be called 16*D* scores. That is, each child's scores at all ages are expressed in terms of the 16-year standard deviations from the mean score at 16 years.

To do this, a table of equivalents was made by extrapolating the Terman-McNemar scores and interpolating the Stanford-Binet scores, to obtain a 16-year mean, or assumed mean, score for this sample on all three tests. To get comparable standard deviations, for the three tests, the Stanford-Binet M.A. units were reduced by the fraction 20/34, and the Terman-McNemar units were increased by the fraction 20/19. Then, taking an arbitrary score of 140 to represent the 16-year mean, the three scales were related to this new 16*D* scale, point for point so that the 16-year mean would equal 140, while plus and minus one *SD* at 16 years would equal 160 and 120 respectively. This scale can be extended in either direction. All scores for all ages are expressed as deviations from the 16-year level.

The resulting curve, based on the means and *SD*'s of the 16*D* scores, is shown in Figure 6. Whether or not it is a legitimate construct, it looks reasonable, and not too far from the probable trends of growth in intelligence. It would have been better to construct the curve on a more nearly average sample, but at least we may be justified in using the 16*D* scores to apply to the members of the Berkeley Growth Study, as one way of expressing their progress toward, and development beyond, their status at 16 years.

Sixteen years has no particular significance as a point of reference: it was chosen because it was the only age at which the three scales we had used could be approximately equated for this sample. It would have been more satisfying if we could have started at a terminal point, say, conception, or birth, or the age at which scores stop increasing. However, 16 years is one age that has been considered a terminal point, or at least the age beyond which the ratio IQ cannot be used without modification. The score of 140 at 16 years was chosen because, from this figure when the

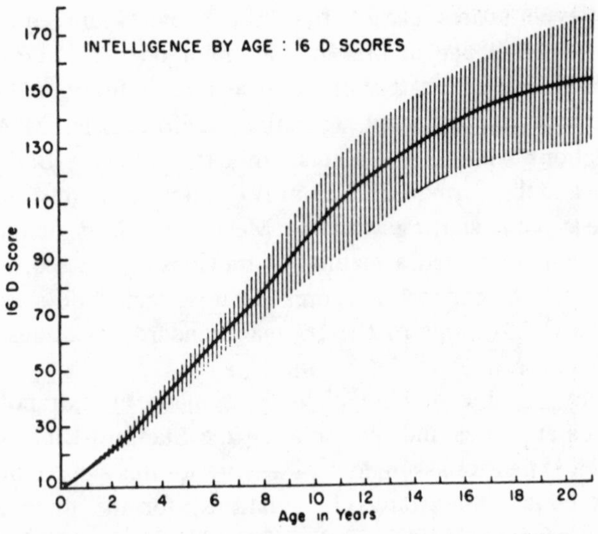

Figure 6. Curves of means and SD's *of Intelligence by 16*D *units, birth to 21 years, Berkeley Growth Study.*

curve is extrapolated downward from the mean score obtained at month one, the curve approximates zero at conception.

The Values and Limitations of Standard Scores and Increment Scores

Standard scores: Individual curves. Let us consider some individual curves of intelligence scores earned by these subjects. In the past we have usually presented individual records in the form of Standard Scores or Sigma Scores for this group. Such scores are very useful for observing a child's changes in performance relative to others his age. We can see his ups and downs, and try to relate them to variable factors, environmental or other, that might have caused the changes. Examples of an individual's relative curves are shown in Figure 7. Here we have presented, for the same child from birth to 18 years, his IQ's and his Standard Scores. We have found that the Standard Scores gave a truer picture of a child's relative status at successive ages, because there were age changes in variability of the IQ's. That is, the variability of the M.A. did not, as had been assumed, increase with age in such a way as to maintain a constant *SD* of 15 or 16 points in the MA/CA ratio. We see in Figure 8 that IQ *SD*'s were greatest at one month and at around 10 to 13 years in this sample; they were least at one year, with a secondary restriction of variability around 6 years. In Figure 9 we have a child who was precocious early, but developed slowly.

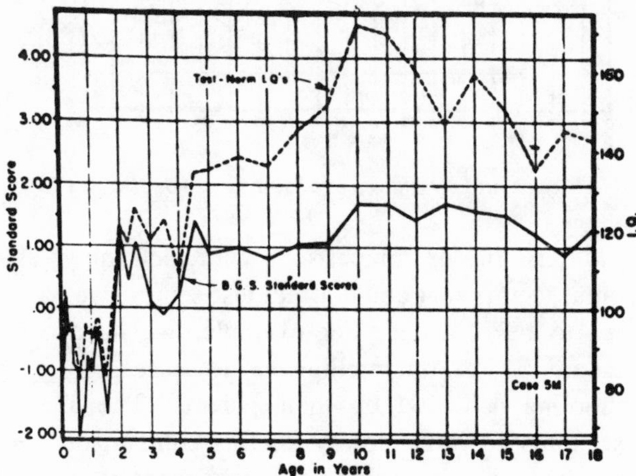

Figure 7. Standard score and IQ curves for case 5M. From Bayley (3, p. 188).

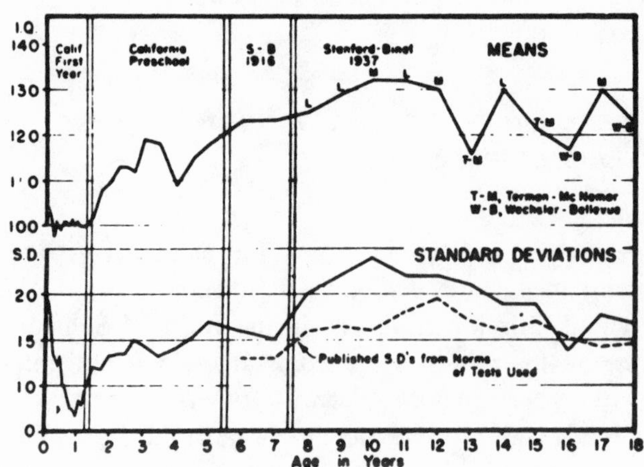

Figure 8. Curves of the means and SD'*s of IQ's, 1 month to 18 years, Berkeley Growth Study. From Bayley (3, p. 171).*

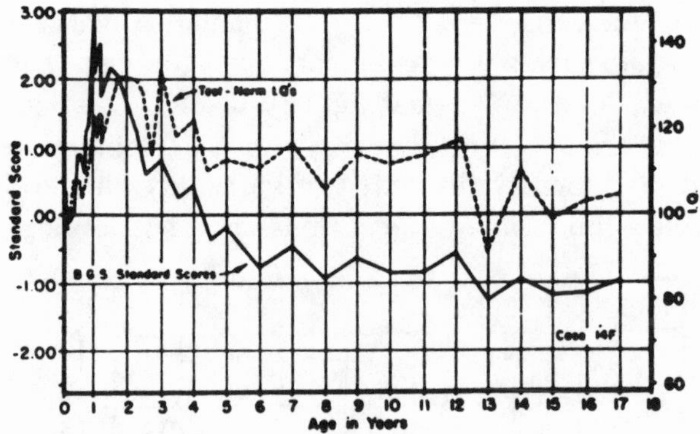

Figure 9. Standard score and IQ curves of case 14F. From Bayley (3, p. 188).

Intercorrelations. In our comparisons with such things as emotional and environmental factors that could affect test scores, we have found the Standard Scores to be of value. For example, we have correlated the children's Standard Scores on intelligence at successive ages with the amount of schooling achieved by their parents. The age changes in correlation (as expressed in Z scores) for this comparison are shown in Figure 10. The infants' scores at first are independent of parental status or negatively correlated, but after 18 months the *r*'s become positive, and by

5 years are about .55. Individual curves in Figure 11 illustrate differences in the ages at which children's scores approach the level of their parents' educational status as expressed in standard scores (9).

Standard scores have been used to correlate mental ability with emotional factors. For example the *r*'s between children's standard scores and the amount of time they spent crying during the period of observation and measurement were at the zero level during the first year. Then, too, the repeated standard scores obtained for one child on intelligence, can be correlated with repeated scores on other variables, using the repeat observations on a single child as a population. For example, I obtained an "Optimal" score for each testing by combining 8 ratings that were indicative of the babies' responsiveness, or attitudes that might affect their performance on the tests (6). The *r*'s between these Optimal scores and intelligence at any one age were close to .30. Twenty of the children had Optimal scores available for from 12 to 15 test ages each, for the age-span between 6 months and 3 years. Using the rank difference method of correlation, rho's were computed for each child between his mental standard scores and his corresponding Optimal scores. These rho's ranged from plus .77 to minus .33. For similarly constructed "Attitude" scores, based on ratings made between 2 and 7 years of age, the individual children's rho's ranged from plus .76 to minus .46.

The wide range of correlations obtained corroborates the impression

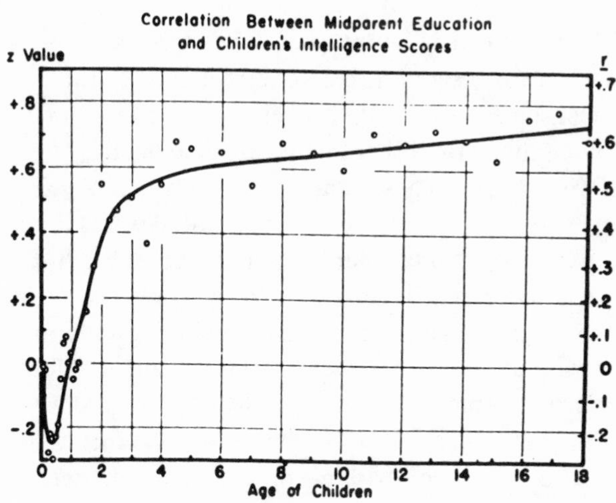

Figure 10. Correlations between children's intelligence scores and parents' education. From Bayley (9, p. 7).

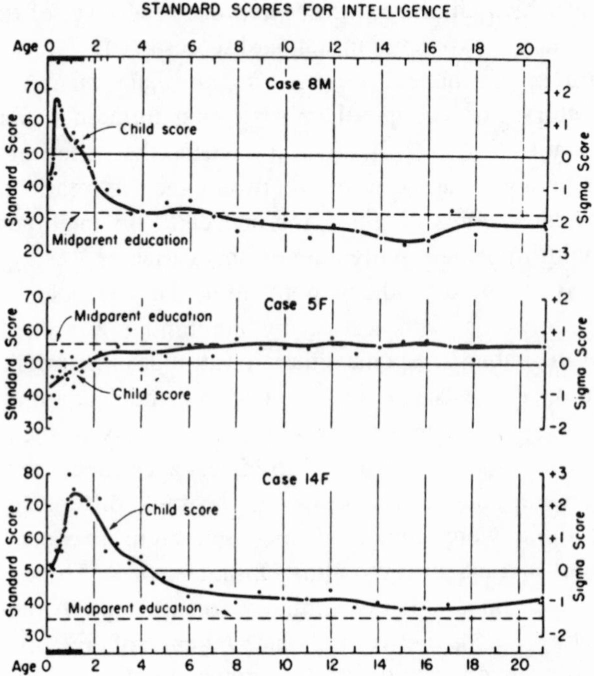

Figure 11. Individual curves of intelligence scores, showing differences in ages at approaching parents' educational level. From Bayley (9, p. 17).

that observable emotional factors and attitudes (seen also in age curves of the different variables), rated at the time of the test, are to some extent related to the test scores, and evidently serve to help or to hinder the child's intellectual functioning. But other factors are also operative in determining a child's shifts in scores. These other factors may, in some cases, be so strong as to override the effects of emotional attitudes, resulting in negative correlations between mental performance and the child's observed responsiveness to the testing situation.

It becomes evident that the intellectual growth of any given child is a resultant of varied and complex factors. These will include his inherent capacities for growth, both in amount and in rate of progress. They will include the emotional climate in which he grows: whether he is encouraged or discouraged, whether his drive (or ego-involvement) is strong in intellectual thought processes, or is directed toward other aspects of his life-field. And they will include the material environment in which he grows: the opportunities for experience and for learning, and the extent to which these opportunities are continuously geared to his capacity to respond and to make use of them. Evidently all of these things are influential, in varying amounts for different individuals and for different stages in their growth. Many of these factors can be studied by observing concomitant variations in Standard Scores.

Individual Differences in Growth Rates

But Standard Scores, and other measures of relative status, have limited usefulness in the study of individual differences in rates of growth. Relative scores tend to make us forget that intellectual growth is a dynamic ongoing process, in which both averages and standard deviations in scores are related to the age of the subjects. It is worthwhile, therefore, to try to present individual curves of growth in units that will emphasize a child's change in relation to himself. Growth curves will enable us to observe a child's periods of fast and slow progress, his spurts and plateaus, and even regressions, in relation to his own past and future.

Such a growth curve has been shown in Figure 11, based on absolute scale units, for the first five years. In Figure 12, I have added two individual curves, superimposed on the curves of the mean and *SD*'s. Both of these boys tend to score above average during their first 18 months. Then case 9M becomes outstandingly superior for a year or two, while 8M suddenly lags behind. Study of the complete sample of individual curves reveals a great variety. There may be plateaus, periods of no growth, and occasionally actual decrements. There may be rapid forging ahead. Each child appears to develop at a rate that is unique for him.

By using the 16*D* scale we are now able to construct individual curves that extend for the entire period of the study. Figure 13 gives 16*D* curves for 5 boys. They cover the age span from one month to twenty-five years. Compared to the later years, the first five years seem very reduced in scope and the curves appear very homogeneous. If they are expanded to the same scale as the Thurstone curves, we find that for any given child both curves show the same periods of acceleration and retardation. The slopes of the Thurstone and the 16*D* curves are somewhat different, but the patterns of accelerations and retardations are generally similar in nature.

Although each child has his own individual pattern of progress, the patterns are not completely random. After the period of infancy there is a strong underlying consistency or constancy. Some children forge ahead and maintain relatively advanced positions after 5 or 6 years of age. Others grow slowly and lag behind. There is some shifting of position, but the changes are gradual over rather long intervals of time. Within such intervals we can expect to obtain fairly constant Standard Scores (IQ's).

It is notable that these five boys have all been tested at 25 years, and all five have continued to improve in their Wechsler-Bellevue scores. The continued growth occurs at all levels of ability. Case 13M, the slowest boy, has had increments in his Wechsler-Bellevue IQ's from 63 at 16 years to 78 at 25 years. This boy spent much of his childhood (ages 10 to 23 years) in an institution for the mentally retarded. When tested at 21 years he had never learned to read more than a few words. Now at 25 he reads, slowly to be sure, but he read aloud without error the Wechsler-Bellevue arithmetic problems.

Similar 16*D* curves are shown in Figure 14 for five girls, four of whom have been tested at 25 years. All but one of the four gained in scores at the 25-year test.

Some of the dips in the individual curves are due to changes in the

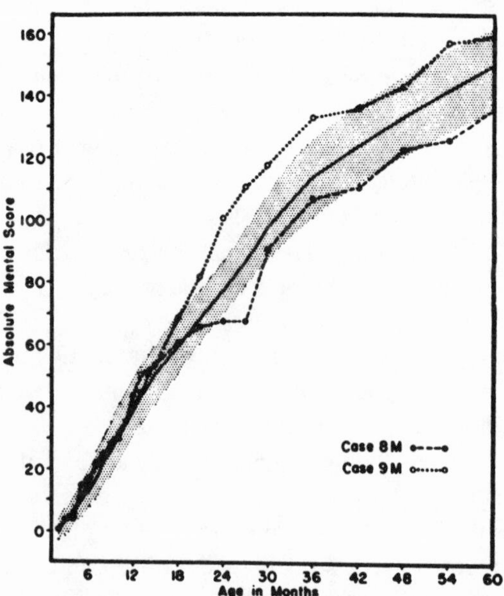

Figure 12. Individual curves of growth in intelligence in absolute scale units, showing contrasting patterns. From Ch. 3, p. 31. H. A. Peterson, S. S. Marzolf, and N. Bayley, Educational Psychology. *New York: Macmillan, 1948.*

tests. For example, those who have trouble in reading make relatively low scores on the Terman-McNemar Group test. But often the irregularities cannot be attributed to changes in the tests used at different ages.

Slight irregularities may reflect temporary conditions of motivation, health, or emotional factors. The more constant shifts require other explanations. Though they may result from prolonged emotional or environmental influences, they may also express inherent tendencies to develop at given rates. I suspect that each child is a law unto himself: in some instances certain factors are more important, while in others different factors play the determining role.

Temporal Changes in Adult Intelligence

The few 25-year scores so far available indicate that the intellectual processes measured by these tests have not yet reached a ceiling. Fourteen out of fifteen subjects tested show continued increments. If these are

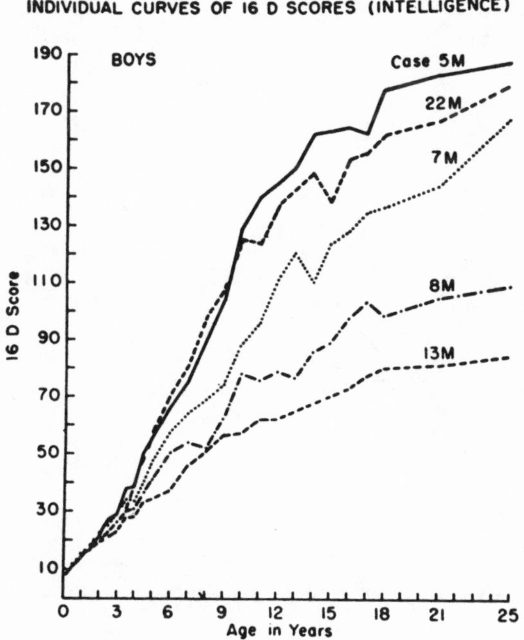

*Figure 13. Individual curves of intelligence (16*D *units) for 5 boys, 1 month to 25 years. Berkeley Growth Study.*

typical cases, what, then, may we venture to predict for the years ahead? The alternative explanation of practice effects from repeating the same test might be offered. But the intervals between repeats on the Wechsler-Bellevue are 2, 3, and 4 years. These are rather long times to remember much about the specific items. Nevertheless, there is probably some residual memory for, or vague familiarity with, the task and the type of solution found at the previous testings. At present we must assume that these factors account for part of the increment.

On the other hand, we have some recent evidence that some intellectual functions do continue to improve with age in adults. When the same individuals are retested after long intervals on the same test or on an alternate form of a test, the scores on the retests are significantly higher. These retests were carried out on superior adults, and their patterns of mental change may be different from those of less able persons.

In a recent study of the adult intelligence of the subjects of the Terman

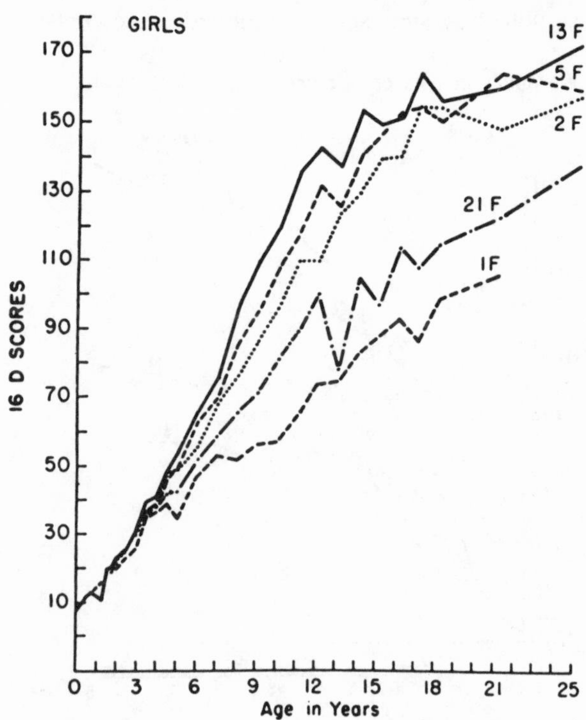

*Figure 14. Individual curves of intelligence (16*D *units) for 5 girls, 1 month to 25 years. Berkeley Growth Study.*

Study of Gifted Children, Bayley and Oden (10) found that scores on the difficult Concept Mastery test increased on a second testing. For a population of over a thousand, composed of Gifted Study subjects and their spouses, comparisons were made between two tests that had been taken about 12 years apart. The increase in scores on the retest averaged about half a standard deviation. The subjects ranged in age from about 20 to about 50 years. When they were grouped into 5-year age intervals, the test-retest scores of all age groups increased, as is shown in Figure 15.

Similar results have been reported by Owens (26) who repeated the Army Alpha test at 50 years on 127 men who had first taken the test as 19-year-old freshmen at Iowa State College. Their scores improved by .55 *SD*'s over the 31-year interval. One can hardly claim practice effects after a lapse of 31 years. Even the 12-year interval of the Terman study is rather long for any such claim: also the Gifted Study subjects were retested on an alternate form, thus ruling out specific memories of items. Furthermore, there were control groups consisting of those who were tested only once, at either the 1940 or the 1951 testing. The differences in mean scores of these groups at the two testings are the same as for the twice-tested groups.

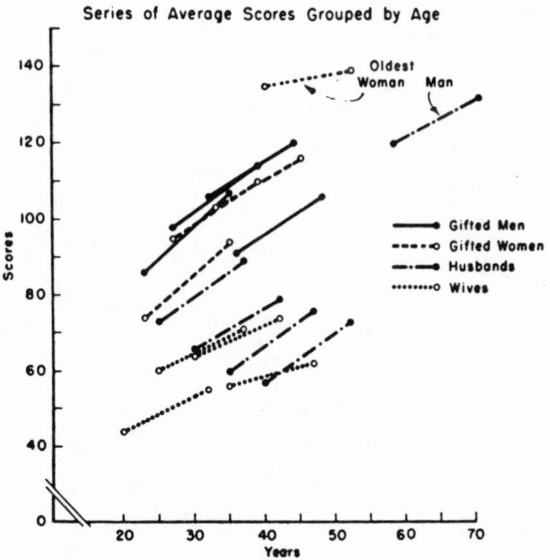

Figure 15. Mean scores on the Concept Mastery test, subjects grouped according to age at first testing of Terman's Gifted Study subjects. First and second tests for each group are connected. From Bayley and Oden (10).

A Suggested Fifty-Year Curve of Intelligence

I have experimented with using the data from these two studies of adults to extend the 16*D* growth curve to 50 years. The subjects of the Berkeley Growth Study are, on the average, a somewhat superior group. Their 16-year Wechsler-Bellevue mean IQ is 117, and their 17-year Stanford-Binet mean IQ is 129. A small group of 25-year-olds who have taken the Concept Mastery earned scores close to the average for the spouses of the Terman subjects at that age. We may assume, then, that this sample is rather similar to the Iowa State freshmen and to the spouses of the Gifted Study subjects, in its general level of test performance. It has, therefore, seemed reasonable to join the data from the Berkeley Growth Study directly to the scores of either of the other studies, in extending the curve, as in Figure 16.

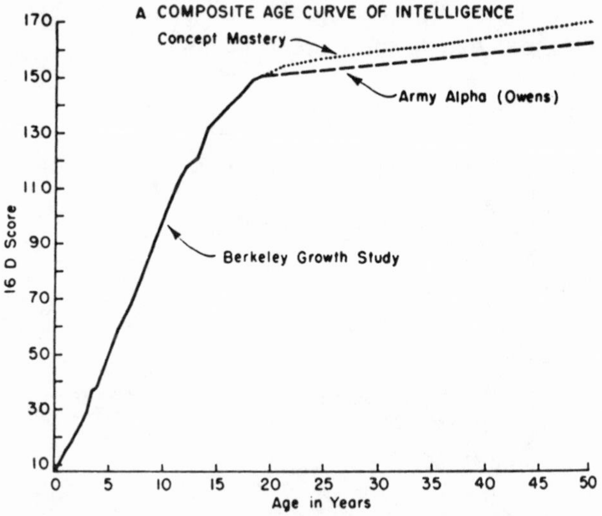

Figure 16. A proposed age curve of intelligence, birth to fifty years. Based on data from the Berkeley Growth Study, the Terman Gifted Study and Owens's Iowa Study.

This joining of the curves has been done for the Iowa study simply by placing the 19-year initial point at 19 years on the 16*D* curve and the 50-year point at the equivalent on the 16*D* scale of an increase of .55 standard deviations.

For the Gifted Study spouses the process was a little more complicated, but it has yielded a series of intermediate points, giving some indication of the probable shape of the curve. To obtain these points, I plotted a series of *SD* increment curves, placing the successively older ages at points on the curves of the younger groups in such a way as to take into account the growth already attained at any new starting age.[2] From these series of overlapping curves, a smoothed curve was drawn, and equivalent 16*D* scores were read off at 5-year intervals.

The resulting two-pronged curve for the 50-year span shows a more modest increment for the Alpha scores of the Iowa men. The Concept Mastery scores of Gifted Study spouses gain a full standard deviation, or about twice as much. Of course, since both of these curves are only approximations, neither may be more correct than the other. The differences are probably due, at least in part, to differences in the testing instrument. The Concept Mastery scale, for one thing, has far more top than the Alpha, and allows for much greater expansion upward.

We have here evidence that tested intelligence, as measured by verbal concepts and abstractions, continues to grow when populations composed primarily of superior adults are retested. Intelligence may also continue to increase in the less bright. Certainly, the less favored members of the Berkeley Growth Study are still improving their scores at 25 years. What is more, in several other studies there is evidence that this phenomenon is not confined to individuals tested at the University of California Institute of Child Welfare. Freeman and Flory (13), for example, divided the children in their study on the basis of scores at 12, 13, and 14, into low and high scorers. At the later ages, 16 and 17 years, the low-scoring group was continuing to improve at a faster rate than the high-scoring group. A recent study by Charles (11) reports retest IQ's for 20 adults who had been diagnosed in childhood as feeble-minded. Their mean childhood Stanford-Binet, 1916, IQ was 58 and their mean adult Wechsler-Bellevue IQ was 81. Charles accounts for this difference in two ways: errors of diagnosis in childhood, and evidence from other studies that people who score low on the Binet test tend to make higher scores on the Wechsler. Similar explanations have been offered for similar findings in other studies. But a mean increase of 23 IQ points amounts to 1.5 *SD*'s of either of the tests used. This is a rather large shift to be attributed to test differences in restriction of scores, to regression phenomena, or to errors in the original test. All 20 individuals improved on the retest. It seems to me quite possible that these people did continue to improve in their mental ability.

[2]That is, the youngest group tested at 20 years and again at 32, with a gain of .4 *SD*. The 25-year initial score of the next older group was then plotted at the 25-year point on the first curve (or at .19 *SD*) and their gain at 37 years was plotted as .33 *SD* above this point (or at .52 *SD*) and so on for successively older groups.

There are many gaps in our knowledge of the nature of intelligence, and many questions remain unanswered concerning age changes in mental organization. In the curve presented in Figure 16, there remains an unanswered discrepancy between the adult portion and data for these ages presented by earlier investigators, who have found decrements in scores with increasing age after about 21 years. In the earlier studies some types of functions held up better than others. Owens found that those abilities that had held up best on the cross-sectional samples were the same ones that increased the most on his retests. The real difference between the conflicting findings seems to lie in the longitudinal as opposed to the cross-sectional method of obtaining scores for successive ages. In the former we have a constant sample whose life experiences, age for age, will have been similar in pervasive environmental conditions, such as wars, technological advances, and methods of education.

If, after taking adequate account of practice effects, the increases still remain, then the next question is to inquire into the nature of the tests, and the extent to which they measure intellectual abilities. Do such tests as the Army Alpha and the Wechsler-Bellevue, for example, measure intelligence in adults? Or do they tend to reflect continued experience in an increasingly enriched environment? Do the younger generations have more opportunity to develop their intellectual capacities than did their parents, or even their older brothers and sisters? Or are we just measuring the effects of increasingly widespread informal education made possible by radio, television, and other modern means of communication?

If, regardless of the cause of the improved scores, they reflect actual degrees of competence outside of the testing situation, then these scores continue to have practical value. Another practical question is: What norms should be used in measuring deterioration resulting from brain injury, or from senescence? Perhaps it will be necessary to compare a present 50-year-old man's score with norms for, say, those who are 50 in 1954, rather than with 50-year norms for other decades.

What normal age changes should we expect in mental organization? The curve presented here is composite. The forms of growth curves vary according to the functions measured. We should expect differences in the steepness of increment and decrement in growth curves of the different functions, and differences in the ages at highest efficiency. These differences have been found consistently in cross-sectional studies. The question raised here is whether more adequate studies, of the same individuals through time, will not show that the age of highest intellectual capacity is later than we thought, and that the decrements in abilities are, correspondingly, deferred.

This curve is offered as an alternative to previously published age-curves of intelligence. I should like to see it tested with further research that would refine, modify, and extend it into a more complete and accurate representation of intellectual changes over the entire life span.

REFERENCES

1. Anderson, J. E. "The Limitations of Infant and Pre-School Tests in the Measurement of Intelligence," *J. Psychol.* 1939, 8, 351-379.
2. Anderson, L. D. "The Predictive Value of Infancy Tests in Relation to Intelligence at Five Years," *Child Develpm.,* 1939, 10, 203-212.
3. Bayley, Nancy. "Consistency and Variability in the Growth of Intelligence from Birth to Eighteen Years," *J. genet. Psychol.,* 1949, 75, 165-196.
4. ———. "Data on the Growth of Intelligence Between 16 and 21 Years as Measured by the Wechsler-Bellevue Scale," *J. genet. Psychol.,* in press.
5. ———. "Development and Maturation," in H. Helson, ed., *Theoretical Foundations of Psychology*. New York: D. Van Nostrand, 1951. Ch. 4, pp. 145-199.
6. ———. "Factors Influencing the Growth of Intelligence in Young Children," *Yearb. nat. Soc. Stud. Educ.,* 1940, 39, 49-79.
7. ———. "Mental Growth During the First Three Years," *Genet. Psychol. Monogr.,* 1933, 14, 92.
8. ———. "Mental Growth in Young Children," *Yearb. nat. Soc. Stud. Educ.,* 1940, 39, 11-47.
9. ———. "Some Increasing Parent-Child Similarities During the Growth of Children," *J. educ. Psychol.,* 1954, 45, 1-21.
10. ———, & Oden, M. H. "The Maintenance of Intellectual Ability in Gifted Adults," *J. Gerontol.,* 1955, 10, 91-107.
11. Charles, D. C. "Ability and Accomplishment of Persons Earlier Judged Mentally Deficient," *Genet. Psychol. Monogr.* 1953, 47, 3-71.
12. Dearborn, W. F., & Rothney, J. W. M. *Predicting the Child's Development*. Cambridge: Sci-Art, 1941.
13. Freeman, F. N., & Flory, C. D. "Growth in Intellectual Ability as Measured by Repeated Tests," *Monogr. Soc. Res. Child Develpm.,* 1937, 2, 116.
14. Garrett, H. E. "A Developmental Theory of Intelligence," *Amer. Psychologist,* 1946, 1, 372-378.
15. Gesell, A. *The Mental Growth of the Pre-School Child*. New York: Macmillan, 1925. Pp. 447.
16. Goodenough, Florence L. *Mental Testing*. New York: Rinehart, 1949. Pp. 609.
17. Hastings, Homer, "The Predictive Value of Individual Items in Preschool Intelligence Tests," unpublished doctor's dissertation, Univ. of California, 1952.
18. Honzik, M. P. "The Constancy of Mental Test Performance During the Preschool Period," *J. genet. Psychol.,* 1938, 52, 285-302.
19. Honzik, M. P., Macfarlane, Jean W., & Allen, L. "The Stability of Mental Test Performance Between Two and Eighteen Years," *J. exper. Educ.,* 1948, 17, 309-324.
20. Jones, H. E., & Bayley, Nancy. "The Berkeley Growth Study," *Child Develpm.,* 1941, 12, 167-173.
21. ———, & Conrad, H. S. "The Growth and Decline of Intelligence: A Study of a Homogeneous Group Between the Ages of Ten and Sixty," *Genet. Psychol. Monogr.,* 1933, 13, 223-294.
22. Maurer, K. M. *Intellectual Status at Maturity as a Criterion for Selecting Items in Preschool Tests*. Minneapolis: Univer. of Minnesota Press, 1946.

23. McNemar, Q. *The Revision of the Stanford-Binet Scale: An Analysis of the Standardization Data*. Boston: Houghton Mifflin, 1942.
24. Miles, R. ''Psychological Aspects of Ageing,'' in E. V. Cowdry, ed., *Problems of Ageing*, 2nd ed. Baltimore: Williams & Wilkins, 1942. Pp. 756-784.
25. Nelson, V. L., & Richards, T. W. ''Fels Mental Age Values for Gesell Schedules,'' *Child Develpm.*, 1940, 11, 153-157.
26. Owens, W. A. ''Age and Mental Abilities: A Longitudinal Study,'' *Genet. Psychol. Monogr.*, 1953, 48, 3-54.
27. Richards, T. W., & Nelson, V. L. ''Abilities of Infants During the First Eighteen Months,'' *J. Genet. Psychol.*, 1939, 55, 299-318.
28. Thorndike, E. L. *The Measurement of Intelligence*. New York: Teachers College, Columbia Univer., 1926.
29. Thorndike, R. L., ''Growth of Intelligence During Adolescence,'' *J. genet. Psychol.*, 1948, 72, 11-15.
30. Thurstone, L. L. ''A Method of Scaling Psychological and Educational Tests,'' *J. educ. Psychol.*, 1925, 16, 433-451.
31. Wechsler, D. *The Measurement of Adult Intelligence*. Baltimore: Williams & Wilkins, 1944.

8. The Development of Children's Orientations Toward a Moral Order: Sequences in the Development of Moral Thought

Lawrence Kohlberg
PROFESSOR OF EDUCATIONAL AND SOCIAL PSYCHOLOGY
HARVARD UNIVERSITY

Since the concept of a moral attitude forms the basic building block of the social psychological theories of Freud (1922), Durkheim (1906), Parsons (1960) and others, there is reason to agree with McDougall (1908) that "the fundamental problem of social psychology is the moralization of the individual by the society."

Following the leads of Freud and Durkheim, most social scientists have viewed moralization as a process of *internalizing* culturally given external rules through rewards, punishments, or identification. Without questioning the view that the end point of the moralization process is one in which conduct is oriented to internal standards, one may well reject the assumption that such internal standards are formed simply through a process of "stamping in" the external prohibitions of the culture upon the child's mind. From the perspective of a developmental psychology such as that of Piaget (1932) or J. M. Baldwin (1906), internal moral standards are rather the outcome of a set of transformations of primitive attitudes and conceptions. These transformations accompany cognitive growth in the child's perceptions and orderings of a social world with which he is continuously interacting.

Directed by this developmental conception of the moralization process, our research has been oriented to the following tasks:

1. The empirical isolation of sequential stages in the development of moral thought.

2. The study of the relation of the development of moral thought to moral conduct and emotion.

3. The application of a stage analysis of moral judgment to subcultural differences as well as pathological deviance in moral orientations.

4. The isolation of the social forces and experiences required for the sequential development of moral orientations.

In the present paper, we shall summarize our findings as they relate to moralization as an age-developmental process, and we shall compare this characterization with that of Piaget.

The Isolation of Six Stages of Development in Moral Thought

Our developmental analysis of moral judgment is based upon data obtained from a core group of 72 boys living in Chicago suburban areas. The boys were of three age groups: 10, 13, and 16. Half of each group was upper-middle class; half, lower to lower-middle class. For reasons to be discussed in the sequel to this paper, half of each group consisted of popular boys (according to classroom sociometric tests), while half consisted of socially isolated boys. All the groups were comparable in IQ.

We have also used our procedures with a group of 24 delinquents aged 16, a group of 24 six-year-olds, and a group of 50 boys and girls aged 13 residing outside of Boston.

The basic data were two-hour tape-recorded interviews focused upon hypothetical moral dilemmas. Both the content and method of the interviews were inspired by the work of Piaget (1932). The ten situations ueed were ones in which acts of obedience to legal-social rules or to the commands of authority conflicted with the human needs or welfare of other individuals. The child was asked to choose whether one should perform the obedience-serving act or the need-serving act and was then asked a series of questions probing the thinking underlying his choice.

Our analysis of results commenced with a consideration of the action alternatives selected by the children. These analyses turned out to shed little light on moral development. Age trends toward choice in favor of human needs, such as might be expected from Piaget's (1932) theory, did not appear. The child's reason for his choice and his way of defining the conflict situations did turn out to be developmentally meaningful, however.

As an example, one choice dilemma was the following:

Joe's father promised he could go to camp if he earned the $50 for it, and then changed his mind and asked Joe to give him the money he had earned. Joe lied and said he had only earned $10 and went to camp using the other $40 he had made. Before he went, he told his younger brother Alex about the money and about lying to their father. Should Alex tell their father?

Danny, a working-class 10-year-old of IQ 98, replied: "In one way it would be right to tell on his brother or his father might get mad at him and spank him. In another way it would be right to keep quiet or his brother might beat him up."

Obviously whether Danny chooses to fulfill his "obligation" to adult authority or to peer loyalty will depend on which action he perceives as leading to the greater punishment. What interests us most, however, is the fact that Danny does not appear to have a conception of moral obligation. His judgments are predictions; they are not expressions of moral praise, indignation, or obligation. From one to the next of the situations presented him, Danny was not consistently "authoritarian" or "humanistic" in his choices, but he was consistent in choosing in terms of the physical consequences involved.

A careful consideration of individual cases eventually led us to define six developmental types of value-orientation. A Weberian ideal-typological procedure was used to achieve a combination of empirical consistency and logical consistency in defining the types. The six developmental types were grouped into three moral levels and labeled as follows:

Level I. Pre-Moral Level

Type 1. Punishment and obedience orientation.
Type 2. Naive instrumental hedonism.

Level II. Morality of Conventional Role-Conformity

Type 3. Good-boy morality of maintaining good relations, approval of others.
Type 4. Authority maintaining morality.

Level III. Morality of Self-Accepted Moral Principles

Type 5. Morality of contract and of democratically accepted law.
Type 6. Morality of individual principles of conscience.

These types will be described in more detail in subsequent sections of this paper. The typology rests upon 30 different general aspects of morality which the children brought into their thinking. One such aspect was the child's use of the concept of rights, another his orientation toward punitive justice, a third his consideration of intentions as opposed to consequences of action, etc. Each aspect was conceived as a dimension defined by a six-level scale, with each level of the scale corresponding to one of the six types of morality just listed.

A "motivational" aspect of morality was defined by the motive mentioned by the subject in justifying moral action. Six levels of motive were isolated, each congruent with one of the developmental types. They were as follows:

1. Punishment by another.
2. Manipulation of goods, rewards by another.
3. Disapproval by others.
4. Censure by legitimate authorities followed by guilt feelings.
5. Community respect and disrespect.
6. Self-condemnation.

These motives fall into three major levels. The first two represent on the verbal level what McDougall (1905) termed "the stage in which the operation of the instinctive impulses is modified by the influence of rewards and punishments." The second two correspond to McDougall's second stage "in which conduct is controlled in the main by anticipation of social praise and blame." The fifth, and especially the sixth, correspond to McDougall's third and "highest stage in which conduct is regulated by an ideal that enables a man to act in the way that seems to him right regardless of the praise or blame of his immediate social environment."

A more cognitive aspect of morality, conceptions of rights, was defined in terms of the following levels:

1. No real conception of a right. "Having a right" to do something equated with "being right," obeying authority.

2. Rights are factual ownership rights. Everyone has a right to do what they want with themselves and their possessions, even though this conflicts with rights of others.

3. Same as the second-level concept but qualified by the belief that one has no right to do evil.

4. Recognition that a right is a claim, a legitimate exception, as to the

actions of others. In general, it is an earned claim, e.g., for payment for work.

5. A conception of unearned, universal individual or human rights in addition to rights linked to a role or status.

6. In addition to level 5 conceptions, a notion of respecting the individual life and personality of the other.

Each of the 50 to 150 moral ideas or statements expressed by a child in the course of an interview could be assigned to one of 180 cells (30 dimensions × 6 levels per dimension) in the classification system. This classification yielded scores for each boy on each of the six types of thought based on the percentage of all his statements which were of the given type. Judges were able to assign responses to the moral levels with an adequate degree of agreement, expressed by product moment correlations between judges ranging from .68 to .84.

In spite of the variety of aspects of morality tapped by the 30 dimensions, there appeared to be considerable individual consistency in level of thought. Thus 15 boys in our original group of 72 were classified (in terms of their modal response) as falling in the first of our six types. On the average, 45% of the thinking of these 15 boys could be characterized as Type 1.

The differences between our age groups offer evidence concerning the developmental nature of the typology. The age trends for usage of the six types of thought are presented in Figure 1.

It is evident that our first two types of thought decrease with age, our next two types increase until age 13 and then stabilize, and our last two types increase until age 16. Analyses of variance of the percentage usage of each type of thought by the 10-, 13-, and 16-year-old groups were carried out.[1] The differences between the three age groups in usage of all types of thought but one (Type 3) were found to be significant beyond the .01 level.

If our stages of moral thinking are to be taken as supporting the developmental view of moralization, evidence not only of age trends, but of sequentiality is required. While the age trends indicate that some modes of thought are generally more difficult or advanced than other modes of thought, they do not demonstrate that attainment of each mode of thought is prerequisite to the attainment of the next higher in a hypothetical sequence.

Because the higher types of moral thought replace, rather than add to,

[1]The means in Figure 1 for age 7 are based on only 12 boys and a limited number of responses per child, compared to the older group.

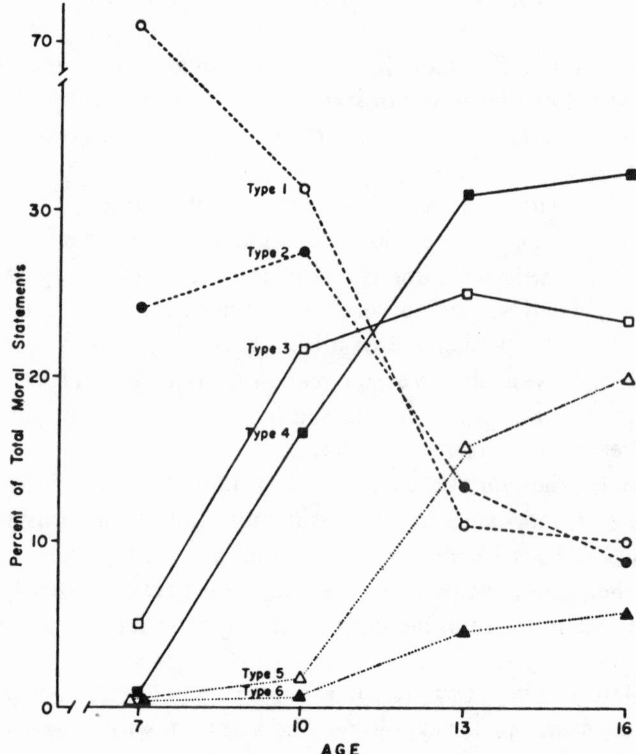

Figure 1. Use of six types of moral judgments at four ages.

the lower modes of thought, the Guttman (1950) scaling technique used by other investigators to establish certain cognitive developmental sequences (Schuessler and Strauss, 1950; Wohlwill, 1960) is not appropriate for our material. A more appropriate statistical model is derived from Guttman's (1954) quasi-simplex correlation matrix. The "simplex" pattern of intercorrelations derives from the expectation that the more two types of thought are separated from one another in a developmental sequence, the lower should be the correlations between them. This expectation can be compared with the actual intercorrelations obtained among the six types of thought.

Each child had a profile showing the percent of his responses that fell within each of the six types of thought. These profiles permitted us to correlate each of the six types of thought with each of the others across the sample of 72 boys, aged 10 to 16. The resulting product-moment correlation matrix is presented in Table I. Each correlation reflects the

TABLE I

Matrix of Intercorrelations Between Six Types of Moral Judgment

Type	1	2	3	4	5	6
1	x					
2	55	x				
3	—41	—19	x			
4	—52	—41	18	x		
5	—52	—58	09	00	x	
6	—37	—43	—29	—07	23	x

extent to which the individuals who use the type of thought identified by the numbers at the left margin of the matrix also use a second type of thought identified by the numbers above the matrix.

The expectation applied to the matrix is that the correlations between two types of thought should decrease as these two types are increasingly separated in the developmental hierarchy. The matrix presented in Table I indicates general agreement with the expectation. The correlations diminish as we move away from the main diagonal entries, whether we go across the columns or down the rows. (The correlations are markedly negative, partially because of the necessity for one percentage score to decrease as another increases.) Furthermore, correlations of types within the three main levels are higher than between levels, supporting our distinction of levels.[2]

The First Two Stages Compared with Piaget's Stages

Our proposed sequence of stages must have logical as well as empirical support. In characterizing our stages, we shall attempt a logical justification of their location in the hierarchy and at the same time, a

[2]These cross-sectional findings need to be supplemented by a longitudinal analysis if we are to accept the stages as a genuine developmental sequence. We are presently engaged in a semilongitudinal analysis, in which we have reinterviewed 54 of our original subjects after a three-year interval. The findings will be reported in a subsequent publication.

comparison of our stages and concepts with Piaget's (1932) theory of developmental stages of moral judgment.[3]

Piaget (1932) starts from a conception of morality as respect for rules, a respect derived from personal respect for the authorities who promulgate and teach the rules. The young child's respect for authority and rules is originally unilateral and absolutistic, but in the 8- to 12-year-olds, this respect becomes mutual, reciprocal and relativistic. Unilateral respect for adults is said to inspire a *heteronomous* attitude toward adult rules as sacred and unchangeable. This attitude is believed to be supported by two cognitive defects in the young child's thought. One defect, egocentrism, the confusion of one's own perspective with that of others, leads to an inability to see moral value as relative to various persons or ends. The other defect, realism, the confusion of subjective phenomena with objective things, leads to a view of moral rules as fixed, eternal entities rather than as psychosocial expectations. The moral ideology resulting from the interaction of heteronomous respect and cognitive realism is described as "moral realism."

Piaget believes that the development of mutual respect toward other individuals in the 8- to 12-year-olds leads to an "autonomous" regard for the rules as products of group agreement and as instruments of cooperative purposes. "Mutual respect" is believed to be associated with the cognitive capacity to differentiate one's own value perspective from that of others (decline of egocentrism) and both of these trends are believed to arise largely through peer-group interaction.

Several of the thirty dimensions characterizing our six types are based on Piaget's conceptions. Our Moral Type 1 shares such characteristics of Piaget's heteronomous as concern for consequences rather than intentions, lack of awareness of relativity of value, definition of right as obedience to authority. These and other Type 1 characteristics are illustrated by an excerpt from an interview with Tommy (age 10, working class, IQ 128). The excerpt also illustrates how the interview method traces back the child's immediate judgments to the unstated but basic assumptions or "principles" behind them.

This portion of the interview is in response to the third of the 10 moral dilemmas:

In Europe, a woman was near death from a special kind of cancer. There was one drug that the doctors thought might save her. It was a form of radium that a druggist in the same town had recently discovered. The

[3]There are a number of other recent typologies of moral judgment relevant to our own, briefly discussed elsewhere (Kohlberg, 1963).

drug was expensive to make, but the druggist was charging ten times what the drug cost him to make. He paid $200 for the radium and charged $2,000 for a small dose of the drug. The sick woman's husband, Heinz, went to everyone he knew to borrow the money, but he could only get together about $1,000, which is half of what it cost. He told the druggist that his wife was dying and asked him to sell it cheaper or let him pay later. But the druggist said: ''No, I discovered the drug and I'm going to make money from it.'' So Heinz got desperate and broke into the man's store to steal the drug for his wife. Should the husband have done that?

The interview proceeded as follows:

''His wife was sick and if she didn't get the drug quickly, she might die. Maybe his wife is an important person and runs a store and the man buys stuff from her and can't get it any other place. The police would probably blame the owner that he didn't save the wife. That would be like killing with a gun or knife.''

(Interviewer: Would it be all right to put the druggist in the electric chair for murder?)

''If she could be cured by the drug and they didn't give it to her, I think so, because she could be an important lady like Betsy Ross, she made the flag. And if it was President Eisenhower, he's important, and they'd probably put the man in the electric chair because that isn't fair.''

(Should the punishment be more if she's an important person?)

''If someone important is in a plane and is allergic to heights and the stewardess won't give him medicine because she's only got enough for one and she's got a sick one, a friend, in back, they'd probably put the stewardess in a lady's jail because she didn't help the important one.''

(Is it better to save the life of one important person or a lot of unimportant people?)

''All the people that aren't important because one man just has one house, maybe a lot of furniture, but a whole bunch of people have an awful lot of furniture and some of these poor people might have a lot of money and it doesn't look it.''

On the one hand we notice Tommy's reasoning ability, his utilitarian calculation of the economics of the greater good. On the other hand we notice that the calculation of value is based on a ''primitive'' assumption as to the basis of moral values. A prosaic and commendable concern about the wife's life is eventually based on the notion that the value of a life is determined by its ''importance'' and that such importance is essentially a function of the amount of furniture owned.

Why are we justified in using the term "primitive" in describing the derivation of the value of life from the value of furniture? Awarding moral value to furniture involves a failure to differentiate the self's point of view from that of others, or to differentiate what the community holds as a shared or moral value (the value of life) and what the individual holds as a private value (the desire for furniture). Such a lack of a sense of subjectivity of value is also suggested by Tommy's definition of culpability in terms of consequences rather than intentions (the wickedness of the druggist depends on his causing the loss of an important life).

It seems warranted then to view our Type 1 responses as reflecting cognitively primitive value assumptions.

Type 1 value assumptions, furthermore, are externalized from the motivational point of view, as indicated by definitions of right and wrong in terms of punishment and conformity to power-figures. As an example, Tommy defines the druggist's wrong in terms of a prediction with regard to punishment, and in terms of conformity to the wishes of important persons.

Such an interpretation of Tommy's responses as involving external motives is open to question, however. Piaget would see these responses as reflecting the young child's deep respect for authority and rules. Piaget sees the young child's morality as externally oriented only in a cognitive sense, not in a motivational sense. According to Piaget, the strong emotional respect the young child feels for authority and rules makes him feel unable to judge for himself, and forces him to rely on external adult sanctions and commands to define what is right and wrong. In the Piaget view, the child is oriented to punishment only because punishment is a cue to what is disapproved by adults or by the "sacred World-Order."

In contrast to Piaget's interpretation, it has seemed to us simpler to start with the assumption that the Type 1 definition of wrong in terms of punishment reflects a realistic-hedonistic desire to avoid punishment, rather than a deep reverence for the adult "World-Order." The children of 10 and older who represent Type 1 morality did not in fact seem to show strong respect for adult authority. A case in point is Danny who, in a situation of conflict between brother and father, defined the right choice in terms of a prediction as to which one would retaliate more heavily. Danny went on to say:

"My brother would say, 'If you tell on me, I'll whip you with my belt real hard.' "

(What would you do then?)

"Well, if I was to tell my Dad if my brother Butchie was still hurting me, my brother Butchie would go find another house to live in."

Danny scores high on various attributes of Piaget's "moral realism," but it is hard to see Danny as expressing what Piaget terms "the sacredness of rules," "unilateral respect for adults," or a "belief in a World-Order."

We have concluded that it is possible to interpret all our observations with regard to "moral realism" without invoking Piaget's notion of the child's sense of the sacredness of authority and rules. This conclusion is consistent with the findings of other studies of Piaget's moral judgment dimensions, as is documented elsewhere (Kohlberg, 1963).

Regardless of the validity of Piaget's interpretation of "moral realism," Piaget's assumption that the young child feels a strong idealized moral respect for adult authority requires direct investigation. Piaget shares this assumption with psychoanalysts, and some form of the assumption seems critical for widely accepted notions as to the early childhood origins of adult neurotic guilt. In collaboration with B. Brener, we attempted a direct study of the validity of the Piaget assumption of "heteronomous respect" to explain the moral judgments of children aged four to eight. Earlier work with children of six and seven indicated that these children defined right and wrong mainly by reference to punishment when faced with simplified versions of our moral dilemmas. Did this indicate a basically "hedonistic" view of right or wrong or did it rather reflect a lack of cognitive resources in answering "why" questions in the context of a concern for conformity to sacred authority (Piaget's view)?

To investigate this issue, 96 children, aged 4, 5, and 7, were confronted with doll-enactments of stories in which disobedience to a rule (or adult) was followed by reward, and other stories in which obedience to a rule was followed by punishment. One such story was of a boy who was ordered to watch a baby on a couch while his mother left the house. The boy in the story proceeded to run out of the house and play outside. The *S* was asked to complete the story. The *S* was told that the mother returned and gave the disobedient boy some candy. *S* was then asked whether the child-doll had done good or bad, and a series of related questions.

In general, the 4-year-olds defined the story act as good or bad according to the reward or punishment rather than according to the rule or adult command. The older children showed considerable conflict, some of the 7-year-olds defining right and wrong in terms of the rule and showing concern about the "injustice" of punishing good and rewarding evil. These older children, however, still explained the rightness and wrongness of the act in relation to sanctions, but took a long-range or probabilistic view of this relation. Disobedience might have been rewarded in that situation, the children said, but in general it would still lead to punishment.

These results, while not consistent with Piaget's assumptions, should not be used to conclude that the moral decisions of 4-5-year-olds are based on crafty hedonism. Only as children reach a level of cognitive development at which the meaning of moral concepts can be differentiated from punishment can they attain either a definite hedonism or a degree of disinterested respect for authority.

The emergence of individualistic hedonism out of such growing cognitive differentiation is suggested by the responses which fall in our Type 2. Just as our first stage of morality coincides descriptively with Piaget's "heteronomous stage" but differs from it in interpretation, so our second stage coincides descriptively with Piaget's autonomous stage but differs from it in interpretation. Like Piaget and others, we found an increase in the use of reciprocity (exchange and retaliation) as a basis for choice and judgment in the years six to ten, though not thereafter. We also found age increases in notions of relativism of value, and in egalitarian denial of the moral superiority of authorities.

These reactions were common enough and well enough associated in our 10-year-olds to help define our Type 2. The tendency to define value relative to private needs is reflected in the response of Jimmy (a 10-year-old working-class boy, IQ 105) to our test situation about mercy-killing. The story continues the plight of the wife dying of cancer as follows:

The doctor finally got some of the radium drug for Heinz's wife. But it didn't work, and there was no other treatment known to medicine which could save her. So the doctor knew that she had only about six months to live. She was in terrible pain, but she was so weak that a good dose of a pain-killer like ether or morphine would make her die sooner. She was delirious and almost crazy with pain, and in her calm periods, she would ask the doctor to give her enough ether to kill her. She said she couldn't stand the pain and she was going to die in a few months anyway.

Should the doctor do what she asks and make her die to put her out of her terrible pain?

Jimmy replied, "It's according to how you look at it. From the doctor's point of view, it could be a murder charge. From her point of view, it isn't paying her to live anymore if she's just going to be in pain."

(How about if there were a law against it?)

"It should be up to her; it's her life. It's the person's life, not the law's life."

In this situation Jimmy defines right action instrumentally, as means to individual values; he defines it relativistically, in relation to the conflicting values of various individuals; and he defines it hedonistically, in terms of "paying" in pleasure and pain. The woman has ownership rights over herself, she is her own property. In more mature types of thought rights are defined relative to duties, the law is seen as defending and defining rights, and the law's respect for the woman's rights represents a respect for her personality and life.

Jimmy also relied heavily on reciprocity in defining role relations as indicated by such remarks as the following:

(Why should someone be a good son?)

"Be good to your father and he'll be good to you."

The advance in cognitive differentiation of this type of response over that of Type 1 seems evident. It seems clear that such definition of value in terms of ego-need and reciprocity of needs is in a sense internal; i.e., it is not simply a reflection of direct teaching by others. It reflects rather Type 2's increasing awareness of its own ego-interests and of the exchange of ego-interests underlying much of social organization.

It also seems evident, however, that the Type 2 modes of thought are far from constituting an adequate or mature basis for morality. We find in a number of our older delinquent boys that further intellectual development seems to carry this Type 2 morality to the cynicism which is its logical end point. For example, John, a bright 17-year-old working-class delinquent (IQ 131), said in response to the story about stealing a drug for one's wife:

"Should the husband steal the drug for his wife? I would eliminate that into whether he wanted to or not. If he wants to marry someone else, someone young and good-looking, he may not want to keep her alive."

John's hedonistic relativism was also associated with a view of rights and law which was the systematic end point of Jimmy's views:

(Should the law make a worse punishment for stealing $500 or for cheating that amount by making a personal loan with no intention to repay it?)

"I don't see that they have a right to decide anything. Who are they? They didn't get robbed and they don't do the stealing. It's vanity, they like the feeling of saying what's right. Laws are made by cowards to protect themselves."

Insofar as John was willing to make judgments not based completely on hedonistic relativism, they involved some notion of equality or reciprocity, e.g.:

"If a buddy of mine loans me something, I'd do anything for him. If he double-crosses me, I'll do anything against him.[4]

From a developmental view, then, the Type 2 morality of need and reciprocity reflects both cognitive advance and a firmer internal basis of judgments than does the Type 1 morality. It does not, however, give rise to any of the characteristics usually attributed to moral judgment, or to a sense of obligation. While possessing the basic attributes stressed by Piaget as characterizing the stage of moral autonomy, this type of thought is not based on mutual (or any other type) moral respect (as Piaget had hypothesized).

The Intermediate Stages of Moral Development

It is clear that Type 1 and Type 2 children do not express attitudes toward "the good" and "the right" like those we take for granted in adults and which we often regard as moral cliches or stereotypes. These stereotypes first appear in our Type 3 and Type 4 preadolescents, whose verbal judgments and decisions are defined in terms of a concept of a morally good person (the implication of labeling Type 3 as a "good boy" morality).

A fairly typical Type 3 "good boy" response to the story about stealing the drug is the following response by Don (age 13, IQ 109, lower-middle class):

"It was really the druggist's fault, he was unfair, trying to overcharge and letting someone die. Heinz loved his wife and wanted to save her. I think anyone would. I don't think they would put him in jail. The judge would look at all sides, and see that the druggist was charging too much."

Don's response defines the issues in terms of attitudes toward the kinds of people involved; "the loving husband," "the unfair druggist," "the understanding judge," "what anyone would do," etc. He assumes that the attitudes he expresses are shared or community attitudes.

Don carries his moral-stereotypical definition of the social world into material not explicitly moral, e.g., into a series of questions we asked concerning the status of various occupational roles. Don tells us:

[4]Such use of reciprocity by delinquents should not be considered evidence of a genuine morality of peer loyality or "mutual respect" however. John says elsewhere, "I'm a natural leader. I understand how kids are made and I just pull the right strings and make monkeys out of them."

"President Eisenhower has done a good job and worked so hard he got a heart attack and put himself in the grave, just about, to help the people."

Don sees expected role-performances as expressions of a virtuous self, and bases respect for authority on a belief in the good intentions and wisdom of the authority figure, rather than in his power. It is also clear that his definition of the good and right has moved from a simple classification of outward acts (Type 1) and their need-related consequences (Type 2) to a definition in terms of "intentions," of inner attitudes of liking and "helping other people" (Type 3), or attitudes of "showing your respect for authority" (Type 4). These concerns imply a definition of good and right which goes beyond mere obedience to rules and authority, and which involves an active concern for the social goals behind the rules.

In terms of motivation, this second level is one in which conduct is controlled in the main by anticipation of praise and blame. Praise and blame are, of course, effective reinforcers even in the child's earliest years. In these early years, however, disapproval is but one of the many unpleasant external consequences of action that are to be avoided. In contrast, our Type 3 and Type 4 pre-adolescents attempt to make decisions and define what is good for themselves by *anticipating* possible disapproval in thought and imagination and by holding up approval as a final internal goal. Furthermore, the pre-adolescent is bothered only by disapproval if the disapproval is expressed by legitimate authorities. This attitude is naively expressed by Andy (age 16, working class, IQ 102) in his reply to the second story about telling one's father about one's brother's lie:

"If my father finds out later, he won't trust me. My brother wouldn't either, but I wouldn't have *a conscience* that he [my brother] didn't."

Andy equates his "conscience" with avoidance of disapproval by authorities, but not by peers. The growth of self-guidance in terms of consciously anticipated moral praise or blame seems to be part of a larger process of development expressed in the active use of moral praise and blame toward others expressed at this stage. There is also a close relationship between approval-sensitivity and what is often termed "identification with authority." This is evident with regard to Andy who tells us:

"I try to do things for my parents, they've always done things for you. I try to do everything my mother says, I try to please her. Like she wants me to be a doctor and I want to, too, and she's helping me to get up there."

Unlike the statements of compliance to the wishes of superiors (as in

Level I), Andy's statements imply an identification of his own goals with his parent's wishes and a desire to anticipate them, somewhat independent of sanctions.

To summarize, we have mentioned the following "cognitive" characteristics of moral definitions at our second level:

a. Moral stereotyping. Definition of the good in terms of kinds of persons and a definition of persons and roles in terms of moral virtues.

b. Intentionalism. Judgments of moral worth based on intentions.

c. Positive, active and empathic moral definition. Duty and moral goodness defined in terms going beyond mere obedience to an actual service to other persons or institutions, or to a concern about the feelings of others.

On the motivational side we have mentioned:

d. Sensitivity to and self-guidance by anticipated approval or disapproval.

e. Identification with authority and its goals.

All of these characteristics imply that moral judgments at this level are based on *role-taking*, on taking the perspective of the other person with legitimate *expectations* in the situation, as these expectations form part of a *moral order*.

For children dominantly Type 3, this order and its associated role-taking is mainly based on "natural" or familistic types of affection and sympathy, as our examples have suggested. For children of Type 4, the moral order is seen as a matter of rules; and role-taking is based on "justice", on regard for the rights and expectations of both rule-enforcers and other rule-obeyers. The distinction between Type 3 and Type 4 styles of role-taking in moral judgment may be illustrated by two explanations as to the wrong of stealing from a store. Carol (13, IQ 108, lower-middle class, Type 3) says:

"The person who owns that store would think you didn't come from a good family, people would think you came from a family that didn't care about what you did."

James (13, IQ 111, lower-middle class, Type 4) says:

"You'd be mad, too, if you worked for something and someone just came along and stole it."

Both Carol and James define the wrong of stealing by putting themselves in the role of the victim. James, however, expresses the "moral indignation" of the victim, his sense that the rights of a community member have been violated, rather than expressing merely the owner's disapproval of the thief as a bad and unloved person. In both, Type 3 and Type 4, regard for rules is based upon regard for an organized social order. For Type 3, this order is defined primarily by the relations of good or "natural" selves; for Type 4 it is rather defined by rights, assigned duties, and rules.

Moral Orientation at the Third Developmental Level

It is often assumed by psychologists that moral conflicts are conflicts between community standards and egoistic impulses. If this were true, it seems likely that the Type 3 and 4 moral orientations would persist throughout life. The story situations we used, however, placed in conflict two standards or values simultaneously accepted by large portions of the community. Many of the children at stages 3 and 4 went to great lengths to redefine our situations in such a way as to deny the existence of such conflicts between accepted norms, no matter how glaringly this conflict was presented. Both types of children took the role of the authority figure in defining right and wrong, tending to insist that the authority figure would adjust the rule in the interests of the various individuals involved.

In contrast, children of Types 5 and 6 accept the possibility of conflict between norms, and they attempt something like a "rational" decision between conflicting norms. This is most clear in our Type 6 children who attempt to choose in terms of moral principles rather than moral rules. Conventional examples of moral principles are the Golden Rule, the utilitarian principle (the greatest good for the greatest number) and Kant's categorical imperative. A moral principle is an obligatory or ideal rule of choice between legitimate alternatives, rather than a concrete prescription of action (Dewey and Tufts, 1936; Kohlberg, 1958). Philosophically such principles are designed to abstract the basic element that exists in various concrete rules, and to form an axiomatic basis for justifying or formulating concrete rules.[5] Moral principles, of course, are not legally or socially prescribed or sanctioned, they are social ideals rather than social realities.

An example of the use of the utilitarian maxim as a moral principle is provided by Tony (age 16, IQ 115, upper-middle class). He is replying to a situation involving a choice of leaving or staying at a civilian air-defense post after a heavy bombing raid may have endangered one's family:

"If he leaves, he is putting the safety of the few over the safety of

[5]It is historically true that all philosophic formulations of moral principles, such as those just mentioned, are variations of a basic prescription to take the role of all others involved in the moral situations.

many. I don't think it matters that it's his loved ones, because people in the burning buildings are someone's loved ones too. Even though maybe he'd be miserable the rest of his life, he shouldn't put the few over the many."

Tony says that leaving the post is wrong, not because of the actual consequences, but because he evaluated the situation wrongly, and "put the few over the many." This is not merely a matter of utilitarian economics but of the requirement of justice that all lives be treated as of equal value.

Moral principles are principles of "conscience," and Type 6 children tend to define moral decisions in these terms. When Type 6 children are asked "What is conscience?" they tend to answer that conscience is a choosing and self-judging function, rather than a feeling of guilt or dread.

A more easily attained "rationality" in moral choice than that of Type 6 is embodied in the Type 5 orientation of social contract legalism. Type 5 defines right and wrong in terms of legal or institutional rules which are seen as having a rational basis, rather than as being morally sacred. Laws are seen as maximizing social utility or welfare, or as being necessary for institutional functioning. It is recognized that laws are in a sense arbitrary, that there are many possible laws and that the laws are sometimes unjust. Nevertheless, the law is in general the criterion of right because of the need for agreement.

While Type 5 relies heavily on the law for definitions of right and wrong, it recognizes the possibility of conflict between what is rationally "right" for the individual actor, and what is legally or rationally right for the society. George (16, upper-middle class, IQ 118) gives a fairly typical response to the questions as to whether the husband was wrong to steal the drug for his dying wife:

"I don't think so, since it says the druggist had a right to set the price since he discovered it. I can't say he'd actually be right; I suppose anyone would do it for his wife though. He'd prefer to go to jail than have his wife die. In my eyes he'd have just cause to do it, but in the law's eyes he'd be wrong. I can't say more than that as to whether it was right or not."

(Should the judge punish the husband if he stole the drug?)

"It's the judge's duty to the law to send him to jail, no matter what the circumstances. The laws are made by the people and the judge is elected on the basis that he's agreed to carry out the law."

George's belief is that the judge must punish even though the judge may not think the act is wrong. This is quite consistent with his belief that the act was individually "just," but legally wrong. It reflects a typical distinction made at this level between individual person and social role, a distinction which contrasts with the earlier fusion of person and role into moral stereotypes. The judge's role is seen as a defined position with a set of agreed-upon rules which the role-occupant contractually accepts on entering office. At the level of definition of role-obligation, then, contract replaces earlier notions of helping the role-partner, just as legality replaces respect for social authority in defining more general norms.

All these aspects of a Type 5 orientation seem to be, in part, reactions to a cognitive advance in social concepts to what Inhelder and Piaget (1958) describe as the level of formal operations. Such a cognitive advance permits a view of normative judgment as deriving from a formal system derived from a set of agreed-upon assumptions. Any given set of norms or roles is then seen as one of many possibilities, so that the major requirement of normative definition becomes that of clarity and consistency.

Implications of the Stages for Conceptions of the Moralization Process

We may now briefly consider some of the implications of our stages for conceptions of the process and direction of moral development. Our age trends indicate that large groups of moral concepts and ways of thought only attain meaning at successively advanced ages and require the extensive background of social experience and cognitive growth represented by the age factor. How is this finding to be interpreted?

From the internalization view of the moralization process, these age changes in modes of moral thought would be interpreted as successive acquisitions or internalizations of cultural moral concepts. Our six types of thought would represent six patterns of verbal morality in the adult culture which are successively absorbed as the child grows more verbally sophisticated.

In contrast, we have advocated the developmental interpretation that these types of thought represent structures emerging from the interaction of the child with his social environment, rather than directly reflecting external structures given by the child's culture. Awareness of the basic prohibitions and commands of the culture, as well as some behavioral "internalization" of them, exists from the first of our stages and does not define their succession. Movement from stage to stage represents rather the way in which these prohibitions, as well as much wider aspects of the social structure, are taken up into the child's organization of a moral order. This order may be based upon power and external compulsion (Type 1), upon a system of exchanges and need satisfactions (Type 2), upon the maintenance of legitimate expectations (Type 3 and 4), or upon ideals or general logical principles of social organization (Types 5 and 6). While these successive bases of a moral order do spring from the child's awareness of the external social world, they also represent active processes of organizing or ordering this world.

We have cited two major results from our quantitative analyses which support this developmental interpretation. The first result was the approximation of the matrix of type intercorrelations to a quasi-simplex form. This suggested that individual development through the types of moral thought proceeded stepwise through an invariant sequence. If our moral types form an invariant sequence, acquisition of a higher type is not likely to be a direct learning of content taught by cultural agents, but is rather a restructuring of preceding types of thought. This interpretation is strengthened by the trend toward negative correlations between the higher and lower types of thought. Such negative relations suggest that higher modes of thought replace or inhibit lower modes of thought rather than being added to them. This in turn suggests that higher types of thought are reorganizations of preceding types of thought.

More strongly than the quantitative data, we believe that the qualitative data and interpretations contained in our stage descriptions makes the notion of developmental transformations in moral thought plausible and meaningful. We have described characteristics of the types which suggest that each type is qualitatively different than previous types. Such qualitative differences would not be expected were development simply a reflection of greater knowledge of, and conformity to, the culture. We have also attempted a logical analysis of the characteristics of the types which allows us to see each type as a conceptual bridge between earlier and later types.

The developmental conception of the moralization process suggested by our analysis of age changes has some definite further implications. Implications as to relations of the development of moral thought to social environmental factors on the one hand, and to the development of moral conduct on the other, will be considered in the sequel to this paper.

Summary

The paper presents an overview of the author's findings with regard to a sequence of moral development. It is based on empirical data obtained mainly from boys aged 10, 13, and 16 in lengthy free interviews around hypothetical moral dilemmas. Ideal-typological procedures led to the construction of six types of moral thought, designed to form a developmental hierarchy. The first two types parallel Piaget's heteronomous and autonomous moral stages, but various findings fail to support Piaget's view that these stages are derived from heteronomous or mutual respect.

More mature modes of thought (Types 4-6) increased from age 10 through 16, less mature modes (Types 1-2) decreased with age. Data were analyzed with regard to the question of sequence, e.g., to the hypothesis that attainment of each type of thought is the prerequisite to attainment of the next higher type. A quasi-simplex pattern of intercorrelations supported this hypothesis.

Such evidence of developmental sequence in moral attitudes and concepts is believed to be of great importance for conceptions of the process of moralization. It indicates the inadequacy of conceptions of moralization as a process of simple internalization of external cultural rules, through verbal teaching, punishment, or identification. In contrast, the evidence suggests the existence of a series of internally patterned or organized transformations of social concepts and attitudes, transformations which constitute a developmental process.

REFERENCES

Baldwin, J. M. *Social and Ethical Interpretations in Mental Development*. New York: Macmillan, 1906.

Dewey, J. and J. Tufts. New York: Holt, 1932.

Durkheim, E. *Sociology and Philosophy*. Glencoe: Free Press, 1953. Originally published 1906.

Freud, S. *Group Psychology and the Analysis of the Ego*. New York: Liveright, 1949. Originally published 1922.

Guttman, L. "The Basis for Scalogram Analysis," in S. A. Stoufer et al., *Measurement and Prediction,* pp. 60-90. Princeton: Princeton University Press, 1950. In P. Lazarsfeld, ed., *Mathematical Thinking in the Social Sciences*. Glencoe: Free Press, 1954.

Inhelder, B. and J. Piaget, *The Growth of Logical Thinking*. New York: Basic Books, 1958.

Kohlberg, L. "The Development of Modes of Moral Thinking and Choice in the Years 10 to 16." Unpublished doctoral dissertation, Chicago, 1958. "Moral Development and Identification," in H. Stevenson, ed., *Child Psychology*. Yearbook of Nat. Soc. for the Study of Education. Chicago: University of Chicago Press, 1963.

McDougall, W. *An Introduction to Social Psychology*. London: Methuen, 1905.

Parsons, T. "The Superego and the Theory of Social Systems," in N. Bell, and E. Vogel, eds., *A Modern Introduction to the Family*. Glencoe: Free Press, 1960.

Piaget, J. *The Moral Judgment of the Child*. Glencoe: Free Press, 1948. Originally published 1932.

Schuessler, K. and A. L. Strauss. "A Study of Concept Learning by Scale Analysis," *Amer. Soc. Rev. 15:* 752-762 (1950).

Wohlwill, J. "A Study of the Development of the Number Concept by Scalogram Analysis," *J. genet. Psychol. 97:* 345-377 (1960).

9. Piaget's Theory*

Jean Piaget†
PROFESSOR OF PSYCHOLOGY
SCHOOL OF PSYCHOLOGY AND EDUCATION
UNIVERSITY OF GENEVA

The following theory of development, which is particularly concerned with the development of cognitive functions, is impossible to understand if one does not begin by analyzing in detail the biological presuppositions from which it stems and the epistemological consequences in which it ends. Indeed, the fundamental postulate that is the basis of the ideas summarized here is that the same problems and the same types of explanations can be found in the three following processes:

a. The adaptation of an organism to its environment during its growth, together with the interactions and autoregulations which characterize the development of the "epigenetic system." (Epigenesis in its embryological sense is always determined both internally and externally.)

b. The adaptation of intelligence in the course of the construction of its own structures, which depends as much on progressive internal coordinations as on information acquired through experience.

c. The establishment of cognitive or, more generally, epistemological relations, which consist neither of a simple copy of external objects nor of a mere unfolding of structures preformed inside the subject, but rather involve a set of structures progressively constructed by continuous interaction between the subject and the external world.

We begin with the last point, on which our theory is furthest removed both

*This chapter was written in French and translated by Dr. Guy Gellerier of the University of Geneva and Professor Jonas Langer of the University of California at Berkeley. We are also grateful to Professors Bärbel Inhelder and Hermione Sinclair for their assistance in the translation.

†The present chapter is, in part, the expansion of an article on my conceptions of development published in *Journal International de Psychologie,* a summary of previous publications, but it also takes into account recent or still unpublished work by the author or his collaborators and colleagues. As a matter of fact, "Piaget's theory" is not completed at this date and the author of these pages has always considered himself one of the chief "revisionists of Piaget." (Author's note)

from the ideas of the majority of psychologists and from "common sense."

I. The Relation Between Subject and Object

1. In the common view, the external world is entirely separate from the subject, although it encloses the subject's own body. Any objective knowledge, then, appears to be simply the result of a set of perceptive recordings, motor associations, verbal descriptions, and the like, which all participate in producing a sort of figurative copy or "functional copy" (in Hull's terminology) of objects and the connections between them. The only function of intelligence is systematically to file, correct, etc., these various sets of information; in this process, the more faithful the critical copies, the more consistent the final system will be. In such an empiricist prospect, the content of intelligence comes from outside, and the coordinations that organize it are only the consequences of language and symbolic instruments.

But this passive interpretation of the act of knowledge is in fact contradicted at all levels of development and, particularly, at the sensorimotor and prelinguistic levels of cognitive adaptation and intelligence. Actually, in order to know objects, the subject must act upon them, and therefore transform them: he must displace, connect, combine, take apart, and reassemble them.

From the most elementary sensorimotor actions (such as pushing and pulling) to the most sophisticated intellectual operations, which are interiorized actions, carried out mentally (e.g., joining together, putting in order, putting into one-to-one correspondence), knowledge is constantly linked with actions or operations, that is, with *transformations*.

Hence the limit between subject and objects is in no way determined beforehand, and, what is more important, it is not stable. Indeed, in every action the subject and the objects are fused. The subject needs objective information to become aware of his own actions, of course, but he also needs many subjective components. Without long practice or the construction of refined instruments of analysis and coordination, it will be impossible for him to know what belongs to the object, what belongs to himself as an active subject, and what belongs to the action itself taken as the transformation of an initial state into a final one. Knowledge, then, at its origin, neither arises from objects nor from the subject, but from interactions—at first inextricable—between the subject and those objects.

Even these primitive interactions are so close-knit and inextricable that, as J. M. Baldwin noted, the mental attitudes of the infant are probably "adualistical." This means they lack any differentiation between an external world, which would be composed of objects independent of the subject, and an internal or subjective world.

Therefore the problem of knowledge, the so-called epistemological problem, cannot be considered separately from the problem of the development of intelligence. It reduces to analyzing how the subject becomes progressively able to know objects adequately, that is, how he becomes capable of objectivity. Indeed, objectivity is in no way an initial property, as the empiricists would have it, and its conquest involves a series of successive constructs which approximate it more and more closely.

2. This leads us to a second idea central to the theory, that of *construction,* which is the natural consequence of the interactions we have just mentioned. Since objective knowledge is not acquired by a mere recording of external information but has its origin in interactions between the subject and objects, it necessarily implies two types of activity—on the one hand, the coordination of actions themselves, and on the other, the introduction of interrelations between the objects. These two activities are interdependent because it is only through action that these relations originate. It follows that objective knowledge is always subordinate to certain structures of action. But those structures are the result of a *construction* and are not given in the objects, since they are dependent on action, nor in the subject, since the subject must learn how to coordinate his actions (which are not generally hereditarily programmed except in the case of reflexes or instincts).

An early example of these constructions (which begin as early as the first year) is the one that enables the 9- to 12-month-old child to discover the permanence of objects, initially relying on their position in his perceptual field, and later independent of any actual perception. During the first months of existence, there are no permanent objects, but only perceptual pictures which appear, dissolve, and sometimes reappear. The "permanence" of an object begins with the action of looking for it when it has disappeared at a certain point *A* of the visual field (for instance, if a part of the object remains visible, or if it makes a bump under a cloth). But, when the object later disappears at *B,* it often happens that the child will look for it again at *A*. This very instructive behavior supplies evidence for the existence of the primitive interactions between the subject and the object which we mentioned (¶1). At this stage, the child still believes that objects depend on this action and that, where an action has succeeded a first time, it must succeed again. One real example is an 11-month-old child who was playing with a ball. He had previously retrieved it from under an armchair when it had rolled there before. A moment later, the ball went under a low sofa. He could not find it under this sofa, so he came back to the other part of the room and looked for it under the armchair, where this course of action had already been successful.

For the scheme[1] of a permanent object that does not depend on the subject's own actions to become established, a new structure has to be constructed. This is the structure of the "group of translations" in the geometrical sense: *(a)* the translation $AB + BC = AC$; *(b)* the translations $AB + BA = O$; *(c)* $AB + O = AB$; *(d)* $AC + CD = AB + BD$. The psychological equivalent of this group is the possibility of behaviors that involve returning to an initial position, or detouring around an obstacle *(a* and *d)*. As soon as this organization is achieved—and it is not at all given at the beginning of development, but must be constructed by a succession of new coordinations—an objective structuration of the movements of the object and of those of the subject's own body becomes possible. The object becomes an independent entity, whose position can be traced as a function of its translations and successive positions. At this juncture the subject's body, instead of being considered the center of the world, becomes an object like any other, the translations and positions of which are correlative to those of the objects themselves.

The group of translations is an instance of the construction of a structure, attributable simultaneously to progressive coordination of the subject's actions and to information provided by physical experience, which finally constitutes a fundamental instrument for the organization of the external world. It is also a cognitive instrument so important that it contributes to the veritable "Copernican revolution" babies accomplish in 12 to 18 months. Whereas before he had evolved this new structure the child would consider himself (unconsciously) the motionless center of the universe, he becomes, because of this organization of permanent objects and space (which entails moreover a parallel organization of temporal sequences and causality), only one particular member of the set of the other mobile objects which compose his universe.

[1]Throughout this paper the term *scheme* (plural, *schemes*) is used to refer to *operational* activities, whereas *schema* (plural, *schemata*) refers to the figurative aspects of thought—attempts to represent reality without attempting to transform it (imagery, perception and memory). Later in this paper the author says, ". . . images . . . however schematic, are not schemes. We shall therefore use the term schemata to designate them. A schema is a simplified image (e.g., the map of a town), whereas a scheme represents what can be repeated and generalized in an action (for example, the scheme is what is common in the actions of 'pushing' an object with a stick or any other instrument)."

3. We can now see that even in the study of the infant at sensorimotor levels it is not possible to follow a psychogenetic line of research without evolving an implicit epistemology, which is also genetic, but which raises all the main issues in the theory of knowledge. Thus the construction of the group of translations obviously involves physical experience and empirical information. But it also involves more, since it also depends on the coordinations of the subject's action. These coordinations are not a product of experience only, but are also controlled by factors such as maturation and voluntary exercise, and, what is more important, by continuous and active autoregulation. The main point in a theory of development is not to neglect the activities of the subject, in the epistemological sense of the term. This is even more essential in this latter sense because the epistemological sense has a deep biological significance. The living organism itself is not a mere mirror image of the properties of its environment. It evolves a *structure* which is constructed step by step in the course of epigenesis, and which is not entirely preformed.

What is already true for the sensorimotor stage appears again in all stages of development and in scientific thought itself but at levels in which the primitive actions have been transformed into *operations*. These operations are interiorized actions (e.g., addition, which can be performed either physically or mentally) that are reversible (addition acquires an inverse in subtraction) and constitute set-theoretical structures (such as the logical additive ''grouping'' or algebraic groups).

A striking instance of these operational structurations dependent on the subject's activity, which often occurs even before an experimental method has been evolved, is *atomism,* invented by the Greeks long before it could be justified experimentally. The same process can be observed in the child between 4 to 5 and 11 to 12 years of age in a situation where it is obvious that experience is not sufficient to explain the emergence of the structure and that its construction implies an additive composition dependent on the activities of the subject. The experiment involves the dissolution of lumps of sugar in a glass of water. The child can be questioned about the conservation of the matter dissolved and about the conservation of its weight and volume. Before age 7 to 8 the dissolved sugar is presumed destroyed and its taste vanished. Around this age sugar is considered as preserving its substance in the form of very small and invisible grains, but it has neither weight nor volume. At age 9 to 10 each grain keeps its weight and the sum of all these elementary weights is equivalent to the weight of the sugar itself before dissolution. At age 11 to 12 this applies to volume (the child predicts that after the sugar has melted, the level of the water in the container will remain at its same initial height).

We can now see that this spontaneous atomism, although it is suggested by the visible grains becoming gradually smaller during their dissolution, goes far beyond what can be seen by the subject and involves a step-by-step construction correlative to that of additive operations. We thus have a new instance of the origin of knowledge lying neither in the object alone nor in the subject, but rather in an inextricable interaction between both of them, such that what is given physically is integrated in a logicomathematical structure involving the coordination of the subject's actions. The decomposition of a whole into its parts (invisible here) and the recomposition of these parts into a whole are in fact the result of logical or logicomathematical constructions and not only of physical experiments. The whole considered here is not a perceptual ''Gestalt'' (whose character is precisely that of *non*additive composition, as Kohler rightly insisted) but a sum (additive), and as such it is produced by operations and not by observations.

4. There can be no theoretical discontinuity between thought as it appears in children and adult scientific thinking; this is the reason for our extension of developmental psychology to genetic epistemology. This is particularly clear in the field of logicomathematical structures considered in themselves and not (as in ¶ 2 and ¶ 3) as instruments for the structuration of physical data. These structures essentially involve relations of inclusion, order, and correspondence. Such relations are certainly of biological origin, for they already exist in the genetic (DNA) programming of embryological development as well as in the physiological organization of the mature organism before they appear and are reconstructed at the different levels of behavior itself. They then become fundamental structures of behavior and of intelligence in its very early development before they appear in the field of spontaneous thought and later of reflection. They provide the foundations of these progressively more abstract axiomatizations we call logic and mathematics. Indeed, if logic and mathematics are so-called ''abstract'' sciences, the psychologist must ask: Abstracted from what? We have seen their origin is not in objects alone. It lies, in small part only, in language, but language itself is a construct of intelligence. Chomsky even ascribes it to innate intellectual structures. Therefore the origin of these logicomathematical structures should be sought in the activities of the subject, that is, in the most general forms of coordinations of his actions, and, finally, in his organic structures themselves. This is the reason why there are fundamental relations among the biological theory of adaptation by self-regulation, developmental psychology, and genetic epistemology. This relation is so fundamental that if it is overlooked, no general theory of the development of intelligence can be established.

II. Assimilation and Accommodation

5. The psychological meaning of our previous points (¶ 1 to 4) is that the fundamental psychogenetic connections generated in the course of development cannot be considered as reducible to empirical "associations"; rather, they consist of *assimilations,* both in the biological and intellectual sense.

From a biological point of view, assimilation is the integration of external elements into evolving or completed structures of an organism. In its usual connotation, the assimilation of food consists of a chemical transformation that incorporates it into the substance of the organism. Chlorophyllian assimilation consists of the integration of radiation energy in the metabolic cycle of a plant. Waddington's "genetic assimilation" consists of a hereditary fixation by selection on phenotypes (phenotypic variations being regarded, in this case, as the genetic system's "answer" to stresses produced by the environment). Thus all the organism's reactions involve an assimilation process which can be represented in symbolic form as follows:

$$(T + I) \rightarrow AT + E \qquad (1)$$

where T is a structure, I the integrated substances or energies, E the eliminated substances or energies, and A a coefficient > 1 expressing the strengthening of this structure in the form of an increase of material or of efficiency in operation.[2] Put in this form it becomes obvious that the general concept of assimilation also applies to behavior and not only to organic life. Indeed, no behavior, even if it is new to the individual, constitutes an absolute beginning. It is always grafted onto previous

[2]For example, take T to be an already established classification on a set of objects, O, which divides it into two distinct subclasses. I is a set of new objects that are added to the original ones and to which the classification T must be extended. When this is done (I has been assimilated to T), it turns out that there are say two new subclasses (the whole structure is now AT) and some properties of the new objects I (e.g., the number of elements I, or their shape, size or color) have been neglected in the process. We now have $T + I \rightarrow AT + E$, where T = the two original subclasses, and E = the irrelevant properties of the new elements, that is, the properties which are not used as criteria for classifying in this specific instance.

schemes and therefore amounts to assimilating new elements to already constructed structures (innate, as reflexes are, or previously acquired). Even Harlow's "stimulus hunger" cannot be reduced simply to subordination to the environment but must rather be interpreted as a search for "functional input" ("éléments fonctionnels") that can be assimilated to the schemes of structures actually providing the responses.

At this point it is appropriate to note how inadequate the well-known "stimulus-response" theory appears in this context, as a general formulation of behavior. It is obvious that a stimulus can elicit a response only if the organism is first sensitized to this stimulus (or possesses the necessary reactive "competence" as Waddington characterizes genetic sensitization to specific inducers).

When we say an organism or a subject is sensitized to a stimulus and able to make a response to it, we imply it already possesses a scheme or a structure to which this stimulus is assimilated (in the sense of incorporated or integrated, as defined previously). This scheme consists precisely of a capacity to respond. Hence the original stimulus-response scheme should not have been written in the unilateral S $\rightarrow$ R form, but in the form:

$$S \rightleftarrows R \text{ or } S \rightarrow (AT) \rightarrow R \qquad (2)$$

where AT is the assimilation of the stimulus S to the structure T.

We thus return to the equation $T + I \rightarrow AT + E$ where, in this case, T is the structure, I the stimulus, AT the result of the assimilation of I to T, that is, the response to the stimulus, and E is whatever in the stimulus situation is excluded in the structure.

6. If assimilation alone were involved in development, there would be no variations in the child's structures. Therefore he would not acquire new content and would not develop further. Assimilation is necessary in that it assures the continuity of structures and the integration of new elements to these structures. Without it an organism would be in a similar situation to that of chemical compounds, A, B, which, in interaction, give rise to new compounds C and D. (The equation would then be $A + B \rightarrow C + D$ and not $T \rightarrow AT$).

Biological assimilation itself, however, is never present without its counterpart, accommodation. During its embryological development, for instance, a phenotype assimilates the substances necessary to the conservation of its structures as specified by its genotype. But, depending on whether these substances are plentiful or rare or whether the usual substances are replaced by other slightly different ones, nonhereditary variations (often called ''accommodates'') such as changes in shape or height may occur. These variations are specific to some external conditions. Similarly, in the field of behavior we shall call accommodation any modification of an assimilatory scheme or structure by the elements it assimilates. For example, the infant who assimilates his thumb to the sucking schema will, when sucking his thumb, make different movements from those he uses in suckling his mother's breast. Similarly, an 8-year-old who is assimilating the dissolution of sugar in water to the notion that substance is conserved must make accommodations to invisible particles different from those he would make if they were still visible.

Hence cognitive adaptation, like its biological counterpart, consists of an equilibrium between assimilation and accommodation. As has just been shown, there is no assimilation without accommodation. But we must strongly emphasize the fact that accommodation does not exist without simultaneous assimilation either. From a biological point of view, this fact is verified by the existence of what modern geneticists call ''reaction norms''—a genotype may offer a more or less broad range of possible accommodations, but all of them are within a certain statistically defined ''norm.'' In the same way, cognitively speaking, the subject is capable of various accommodations, but only within certain limits imposed by the necessity of preserving the corresponding assimilatory structure. In Eq. 1 the term A in AT specifies precisely this limitation on accommodations.

The concept of ''association,'' which the various forms of associationism from Hume to Pavlov and Hull have used and abused, has thus only been obtained by artificially isolating one part of the general process defined by the equilibrium between assimilation and accommodation. Pavlov's dog is said to associate a sound to food, which elicits its salivation reflex. If, however, the sound is never again followed by food, the conditioned response, or temporary link, will disappear; it has no intrinsic stability. The conditioning persists as a function of the need for food, that is, it persists only if it is part of an assimilatory scheme and its satisfaction, hence of a certain accommodation to the situation. In fact, an ''association'' is always accompanied by an assimilation to previous structures, and this is a first factor that must not be overlooked. On the other hand, insofar as the ''association'' incorporates some new information, this represents an active accommodation and not a mere passive recording. This accommodatory activity, which is dependent on the assimilation scheme, is a second necessary factor that must not be neglected.

7. If accommodation and assimilation are present in all activity, their ratio may vary, and only the more or less stable equilibrium which may exist between them (though it is always mobile) characterizes a complete act of intelligence.

When assimilation *outweighs* accommodation (i.e., when the characteristics of the object are not taken into account except insofar as they are consistent with the subject's momentary interests) thought evolves in an egocentric or even autistic direction. The most common form of this situation in the play of the child is the "symbolic games" or fiction games, in which objects at his command are used only to represent what is imagined.[3] This form of game which is most frequent at the beginning of representation (between 1½ and 3 years of age), then evolves toward constructive games in which accommodation to objects becomes more and more precise until there is no longer any difference between play and spontaneous cognitive or instrumental activities.

Conversely, when accommodation prevails over assimilation to the point where it faithfully reproduces the forms and movements of the objects or persons which are its models at that time, representation (and the sensorimotor behaviors which are its precursors and which also give rise to exercise games that develop much earlier than symbolic games) evolves in the direction of imitation. Imitation through action, an accommodation to models that are present, gradually extends to deferred imitation and finally to interiorized imitation. In this last form it constitutes the origin of mental imagery and of the figurative as opposed to the operative aspects of thought.

But as long as assimilation and accommodation are in equilibrium (i.e., insofar as assimilation is still subordinate to the properties of the

[3]The categories of play defined by Piaget (in *Play, Dreams and Imitation,* 1951, for example) are the following:

a. Exercise Games. These consist of any behavior without new structuration but with a new functional finality. For example, the repetition of an action such as swinging an object, if its aim is to understand or to practice the movement, is *not* a game. But the same behavior, if its aim is functional pleasure, pleasure in the activity in itself, or the pleasure of "causing" some phenomenon, becomes a game. Examples of this are the vocalizations of infants and the games of adults with a new car, radio, etc.

b. Symbolic Games. These consist of behaviors with a new structuration, that of representing realities that are out of the present perceptual field. Examples are the fiction games where the child enacts a meal with pebbles standing for bread, grass for vegetables, etc. The symbols used here are individual and specific to each child.

c. Rule Games. These are behaviors with a new structuration involving the intervention of more than one person. The rules of this new structure are defined by social interaction. This type of game ranges over the whole scale of activities, starting with simple sensorimotor games with set rules (the many varieties of marble games, for instance) and ending with abstract games like chess. The symbols here are stabilized by convention and can become purely arbitrary in the more abstract games. That is, they bear no relation (analogy) with what they represent. (Translator's note) objects, or, in other words, subordinate to the situation with the accommodations it entails; and accommodation itself is subordinate to the already existing structures to which the situation must be assimilated) we can speak of cognitive behavior as opposed to play, imitation, or mental imagery, and we are back in the proper domain of intelligence. But this fundamental equilibrium between assimilation and accommodation is more or less difficult to attain and to maintain depending on the level of intellectual development and the new problems encountered. However, such an equilibrium exists at all levels, in the early development of intelligence in the child as well as in scientific thought.

It is obvious that any physical or biological theory assimilates objective phenomena to a restricted number of models which are not drawn exclusively from these phenomena. These models involve in addition a certain number of logicomathematical coordinations that are the operational activities of the subject himself. It would be very superficial to reduce these coordinations to a mere "language" (though this is the position of logical positivism) because, properly speaking, they are an instrument for structuration. For example, Poincaré narrowly missed discovering relativity because he thought there was no difference between expressing (or translating) phenomena in the "language" of Euclidian or of Riemanian geometry. Einstein was able to construct his theory by using Riemanian space as an instrument of *structuration,* to "understand" the relations between space, speed, and time. If physics proceeds by assimilating reality to logicomathematical models, then it must unceasingly accommodate them to new experimental results. It cannot dispense with accommodation because its models would then remain subjective and arbitrary. However, every new accommodation is conditioned by existing assimilations. The significance of an experiment does not derive from a mere perceptive recording (the "*Protokollsätze*" of the first "logical empiricists"); it cannot be dissociated from an *interpretation*.

8. In the development of intelligence in the child, there are many types of equilibrium between assimilation and accommodation that vary with the levels of development and the problems to be solved. At sensorimotor levels (before 1½ to 2 years of age) these are only practical problems involving immediate space, and as early as the second year, sensorimotor intelligence reaches a remarkable state of equilibrium (e.g., instrumental behaviors, group of displacements; see ¶ 2). But this equilibrium is difficult to attain, because during the first months, the infant's universe is centered on his own body and actions, and because of distortions due to assimilation not yet balanced by adequate accommodations.

The beginning of thought creates multiple problems of representation (which must extend to distant space and can no longer be restricted to near space) as well as the problem of adaptation no longer measured by practical success alone; thus intelligence goes through a new phase of assimilatory distortion. This is because objects and events are assimilated to the subject's own action and viewpoint and possible accommodations still consist only of fixations on figural aspects of reality (hence on states as opposed to transformations). For these two reasons—egocentric assimilation and incomplete accommodation—equilibrium is not reached. On the other hand, from the age of 7 to 8 the emergence of reversible operations ensures a stable harmony between assimilation and accommodation since both can now act on transformations as well as on states.

Generally speaking, this progressive equilibrium between assimilation and accommodation is an instance of a fundamental process in cognitive development which can be expressed in terms of centration and decentration. The systematically distorting assimilations of sensorimotor or initial representative stages, which distort because they are not accompanied by adequate accommodations, mean that the subject remains centered on his own actions and his own viewpoint. On the other hand, the gradually emerging equilibrium between assimilation and accommodation is the result of successive decentrations, which make it possible for the subject to take the points of view of other subjects or objects themselves. We formerly described this process merely in terms of egocentrism and socialization. But it is far more general and more fundamental to knowledge in all its forms. For cognitive progress is not only assimilation of information; it entails a systematic decentration process which is a necessary condition of objectivity itself.

III. The Theory of Stages

9. We have seen that there exist structures which belong only to the subject (¶ 1), that they are built (¶ 2), and that this is a step-by-step process (¶ 7). We must therefore conclude there exist stages of development. Even authors who agree with this idea may use different criteria and interpretations of stage development. It therefore becomes a problem that requires discussion in its own right. The Freudian stages, for instance, are only distinct from each other in that they differ in one dominant character (oral, anal, etc.) but this character is also present in the previous—or following—stages, so that its "dominance" may well remain arbitrary. Gesell's stages are based on the hypothesis of the quasi-exclusive role of maturation, so that they guarantee a constant order of succession but may neglect the factor of progressive construction. To characterize the stages of cognitive development we therefore need to integrate two necessary conditions without introducing any contradictions. These conditions for stages are (a) that they must be defined to guarantee a constant order of succession, and (b) that the definition allow for progressive construction without entailing total preformation. These two conditions are necessary because knowledge obviously involves learning by experience, which means an external contribution in addition to that involving internal structures, and the structures seem to evolve in a way that is not entirely predetermined.

The problem of stages in developmental psychology is analogous to that of stages in embryogenesis. The question that arises in this field is also that of making allowance for both genetic preformation and an eventual "epigenesis" in the sense of construction by interactions between the genome and the environment. It is for this reason that Waddington introduces the concept of "epigenetic system" and also a distinction between the genotype and the "epigenotype." The main characteristics of such an epigenetic development are not only the well-known and obvious ones of succession in sequential order and of progressive integration (segmentation followed by determination controlled by specific "competence" and finally "reintegration") but also some less obvious ones pointed out by Waddington. These are the existence of "creodes," or necessary developmental sequences, each with its own "time tally," or schedule, and the intervention of a sort of evolutionary regulation, or "homeorhesis." Homeorhesis acts in such a way that if an external influence causes the developing organism to deviate from one of its creodes, there ensues a homeorhetical reaction, which tends to channel it back to the normal sequence or, if this fails, switches it to a new creode as similar as possible to the original one.

Each of the preceding characteristics can be observed in cognitive development if we carefully differentiate the construction of the structures themselves and the acquisition of specific procedures through learning (e.g., learning to read at one age rather than another). The question will naturally be whether development can be reduced to an addition of procedures learned one by one or whether learning itself depends on developmental laws which are autonomous. This question can only be answered experimentally, but we shall discuss it further in Section IV. Whatever the answer is, it remains possible to distinguish between major structures, such as the operational "grouping," and particular acquisitions. It then becomes proper to inquire whether the construction of these major structures can be defined in terms of stages. If this were so, it would then become possible to determine their relations to developmental laws of learning.

10. If we restrict ourselves to major structures, it is strikingly obvious that cognitive stages have a sequential property, that is, they appear in a fixed order of succession because each one of them is necessary for the formation of the following one.

If we now consider only the principal periods of development, one can enumerate three of them:

a. A sensorimotor period lasts until approximately 1½ years of age with a first subperiod of centration on the subject's own body (lasting about 7 to 9 months) followed by a second one of objectivization and spatialization of the schemes of practical intelligence.

b. A period of representative intelligence leads to concrete operations (classes, relations, and numbers bound to objects) with a first preoperational subperiod (there is no reversibility or conservation, but the beginnings of directional functions and qualitative identities), which begins around 1½ to 2 years of age with the formation of semiotic processes such as language and mental imagery. This is followed by a second subperiod (at about 7 to 8 years) characterized by the beginnings of operational groupings in their various concrete forms and with their various types of conservation.

c. Finally, there is the period of propositional or formal operations. This also begins with a subperiod of organization (11 to 13 years old) and is followed by a subperiod of achievement of the general combinatory and the group INRC of the two kinds of reversibilities. (See ¶ 28 and fn. 7.)

If we now consider the preceding sequence, it is easy to observe that each one of these periods or subperiods is necessary to the constitution of its successor. As a first example, why do language and the semiotic function emerge only at the end of a long sensorimotor period where the only significates are indexes and signals, and where there are no symbols or signs? (If the acquisition of language were only dependent on an accumulation of associations, as is sometimes claimed, then it could occur much earlier.[4]) It has been shown that the acquisition of language requires that at least two conditions be satisfied. First, there must exist a general context of imitation allowing for interpersonal exchange, and second, the diverse structural characters which constitute the one basic unit of Chomsky's (1957) transformational grammars must be present. For the first of these conditions to be met means that in addition to the motor techniques of imitation (and this is by no means an easy task) the object, spatiotemporal, and causal decentrations of the second sensorimotor subperiod must have been mastered. For the second requirement, our collaborator H. Sinclair, who specializes in psycholinguistics, has shown (in her recent work which will shortly be published) that Chomsky's transformational structures are facilitated by the previous operation of the sensorimotor schemes, and thus that their origin is neither in an innate neurophysiological program (as Chomsky himself would have it) nor in an operant or other conditioning "learning" process [as Chomsky (1959) has shown conclusively].

A second example of the sequential character of our periods and subperiods is the subperiod of ages 2 to 7, which itself results from the sensorimotor schemes elaborated in the ninth and tenth months and which prepares the concrete operations of ages 7 to 10. This subperiod is characterized by some negative aspects (lack of reversibility and absence of the concept of conservation), but it also evolves some positive achievements such as the directional functions [*fonctions orientées*—mappings where $y = f(x)$ with unity of the value $f(x)$ for any (x) and the qualitative identity $a = a$]. In fact, these functions already play an extensive role in preoperational thought. Their one-way orientation explains the general primacy of the concept of order at this level, with its adequate aspects, but this also is the source of systematic distortions (e.g., "longer" understood as "going farther"; estimation of a quantity of water by taking only its level into account). The elementary functions are nothing other than the connections inherent in the schemes of action (which, before

[4]The contention is that there already exists symbol manipulation, that is, storage and computation, on indexes and signals during the sensorimotor stage. Therefore the absence of language cannot be attributed to the lack of such functions, and conditioning (classical or operant) should be possible at least on the input side. At this stage the child can discriminate between sounds and he should be able to respond selectively, verbally or otherwise, to phonetic inputs on a purely associative basis. It is claimed that this is impossible for more than a finite (and very limited) set of inputs because of the absence of the most essential linguistic structure (monoid) which would permit the generation and storage of rules allowing for the analysis and recognition of an unlimited set of organized sequences of sounds. (Translator's note)

they become operational, are always oriented toward a goal) and therefore originate in the sensorimotor schemes themselves. Qualitative identity (the type of identity expressed by the child when he says: "It is the same water," even if the quantity of water changes) has its origin in the concept of permanent object, and in the notion that the subject's own body (as well as those of other subjects) maintains its identity both in time and in space; and these are three achievements of the sensorimotor stage. On the other hand, the one-way, directional functions and the identities they involve constitute the necessary condition for future operations. Thus we can see that the stages between 2 and 7 years are simultaneously an extension of the sensorimotor stages and the basis of the future concrete operations.

The propositional operations that appear between ages 11 and 15 with the INRC group and general combinatorial structures, all consist of applying operations to operations and transformations to transformations. It is therefore obvious that the existence of this last stage necessarily involves the acquisitions of the previous one (concrete operations, or operations to the first power).

11. Thus defined, the stages always appear in the same order of succession. This might lead us to assume that some biological factor such as maturation is at work. But it is certainly not comparable to the hereditary neurophysiological programming of instincts. Biological maturation does nothing more than open the way to possible constructions (or explain transient impossibilities). It remains for the subject to actualize them. This actualization, when it is regular, obeys the law of creodes, that is, of constant and necessary progress such that the endogenous reactions find support in the environment and in experience. It would therefore be a mistake to consider the succession of these stages as the result of an innate predetermination, because there is a continual construction of novelty during the whole sequence.

The two best proofs of this last point are the possibilities of deviations from the norm (with regulation by homeorhesis) and of variations in the time tally with the possibility of accelerations or delays. Deviations may be brought about by unforeseen experiences encountered by the activity of the child himself as well as by adult pedagogical interventions. Some pedagogical interventions can, of course, accelerate and complete spontaneous development; but they cannot change the order of the constructions. For example, educational programs rightly introduce the concept of metric proportions a long time after the elementary arithmetical operations, although a proportion seems to consist only of an equivalence between two divisions, as in 4:2 = 6:3. But there also exist untimely pedagogical interventions, such as those of parents who teach their children to count up to 20 or 50 before they can have any concept of number. In many cases, such premature acquisitions in no way affect the creode specific to the construction of integers. For instance, when two lines of m and n elements $(m = n)$, respectively, are first put into visual one-to-one correspondence and their lengths changed by changing the spacing of the elements, the fact that the child of a certain age can count will not prevent him from saying that the longer line has more elements. On the other hand, when a pedagogical intervention has been successful or when the child obtains by himself a partial conquest in a specific operatory domain, the problem of the interactions between the various creodes remains still unsolved. In the case of classes or relations, for example, are the additive and multiplicative operations always synchronic—as they often seem to be—or can one follow the other, and in that event does the final synthesis remain unchanged (as is probably the case)?

12. In considering the problem of duration or rate of succession of the stages, we can readily observe that accelerations or delays in the average chronological age of performance depend on specific environments (e.g., abundance or scarcity of possible activities and spontaneous experiences, educational or cultural environment), but the order of succession will remain constant. Some authors even believe unbounded acceleration would be possible and desirable. Bruner (1960) went so far as to assert that if one tackles it the right way, one can teach anything to children of any age, but he does not seem to believe this any longer. On this point, however, we can quote two situations investigated by Gruber. The first is that of developing kittens. It has been shown that they go through the same stages as infants in acquiring the "concept" of permanent object, and further that they achieve in 3 months what the infant does in 9. However, they do not progress any further and one may wonder whether the child's slower rate of development does not, in this case, make for greater progress ultimately. The second study by Gruber concerns the remarkable tardiness with which some of Darwin's main concepts appeared to him, although they were logical consequences of his previous ideas. Is this remarkably slow speed of invention one of the conditions of fruitfulness or only a deplorable accident? These are major problems in cognitive psychology that are not yet solved. Nevertheless, we would like to put forward a plausible hypothesis. For a specific subject the speed of transition from one stage to the following one has an *optimal rate*. That is, the stability and even the fruitfulness of a new organization (or structurization) depends on connections which cannot be instantaneous but cannot be indefinitely postponed either since they would then lose their power of internal combination.

IV. The Relations Between Development and Learning

13. If we give the name *learning* to every form of cognitive acquisition, it is obvious that development only consists of a sum or a succession of learning situations. Generally, though, the term is restricted to denote essentially exogenous acquisitions, where either the subject repeats responses, parallel to the repetition of external sequences (as in conditioning), or the subject discovers a repeatable response by using the regular sequences generated by some device, without having to structure or reorganize them himself through a constructive step-by-step activity (instrumental learning). If we accept this definition of learning, the question arises whether development is merely a succession of learned acquisitions (which would imply a systematic dependency of the subject on the objects), or whether learning and development constitute two distinct and separate sources of knowledge. Finally, there is, of course, the possibility that every acquisition through learning in fact represents only a sector or a phase of development itself, arbitrarily provided by the environment (which entails the possibility of a local deviation from the "normal" creodes) but remaining subject to the general constraints of the current developmental stage.

Before we examine the experimental facts, we would like to mention a talented behaviorist's attempt to reduce our theory to Hull's theory of learning. To effect this reduction, however, Berlyne (1960) was obliged to introduce two new concepts into Hull's theory. The first is stimulus-response generalization, which Hull foresaw but did not use. The second and more fundamental is the concept of "transformational responses," which are not restricted to repetitions but are amenable to reversible transformations in the same way as "operations." In discussing equilibration and regulation, Berlyne extends the concept of external reinforcements, introducing the possibility of "internal reinforcements" such as feelings of surprise, incoherence or coherence. Though these modifications of Hull's theory change its structure fundamentally, it is not certain that they are sufficient. The main question remains, indeed, whether the "transformational reponses" are simple copies of observable external transformations of the objects or whether the subject himself transforms the objects by acting on them. The main point of our theory is that knowledge results from *interactions* between the subject and the object, which are *richer* than what the objects can provide by themselves. Learning theories like Hull's, on the other hand, reduce knowledge to direct "functional copies" which do not enrich reality. The problem we must solve, in order to explain cognitive development, is that of *invention* and not of mere copying. And neither stimulus-response generalization nor the introduction of transformational responses can explain novelty or invention. By contrast, the concepts of assimilation and accommodation and of operational structures (which are created, not merely discovered, as a result of the subject's activities), are oriented toward this inventive construction which characterizes all living thought.

To close this theoretical introduction to the problem of learning and development we would like to point out how peculiar it is that so many American and Soviet psychologists, citizens of great nations, which intend to change the world, have produced learning theories that reduce knowledge to a passive copy of external reality (Hull, Pavlov, etc.), whereas human thought always transforms and transcends reality. Outstanding sectors of mathematics (e.g., those that involve the continuum hypothesis) have no counterpart in physical reality, and all mathematical techniques result in new combinations which enrich reality. To present an adequate notion of learning one first must explain how the subject manages to construct and invent, not merely how he repeats and copies.

14. A few years ago the International Center of Genetic Epistemology investigated two problems:

a. Under what conditions can logical structures be learned, and are these conditions identical to those for learning empirical sequences?

b. And, even in this last case (probabilistic or even arbitrary sequences), does learning imply a logic analogous, for example, to the logic of the coordinators of action, the existence of which can be observed as early as during the organization of sensorimotor schemes?

On the first point, studies such as those of Greco, Morf, and Smedslund (1959) have shown that in order to learn how to construct and master a logical structure, the subject must start from another, more elementary logical structure which he will differentiate and complete. In other words, learning is no more than a sector of cognitive development which is facilitated or accelerated by experience. By contrast, learning under external reinforcement (e.g., permitting the subject to observe the results of the deduction he should have made or informing him verbally) produces either very little change in logical thinking or a striking momentary change with no real comprehension.

For example, Smedslund found that it was easy to make children learn the conservation of weight with pieces of clay whose shape was modified and whose constant weight could be read by the child on a pair of scales, because in this case, mere repetition of these observations facilitates generalization. The same processes of reinforcement by observation are not at all sufficient to induce the acquisition of transitivity in the weight equivalences: $A = C$ if $A = B$ and $B = C$. In other words, the logical structure of conservation (and Smedslund has checked the correlation between transitivity and operational conservation) is not acquired in the same way as the physical contents of this conservation.

Morf observed the same phenomenon in the learning of the quantification of inclusion: $A < B$ if $B = A + A'$. The spontaneous tendency of the child is to compare part A to the complementary part A' whenever his attention is called to the parts of the whole B and B ceases to be preserved as a whole.

By contrast, previous training on the intersection of classes facilitates learning of inclusion. It is true that the Dutch psychologist Kohnstamm (1956) has tried to show that it is possible to teach young subjects the quantitative dominance of the whole over the part $(B > A)$ by purely didactic and verbal methods. Hence educational psychologists who believe that educational methods make it possible to teach anything at any age are considered optimistic and the psychologists of the Geneva school who assert that only an adequate spontaneous development makes understanding possible under any circumstances are considered pessimistic. However, the checks on Kohnstamm's experiment now being made in Montreal by Laurendeau and Pinard show that things are not as simple as they appear (verbally trained children make a great many mistakes on the relations between A and A'). One can easily understand that teachers of the traditional school will call anyone who believes in their methods an optimist, but, in our opinion, genuine optimism would consist of believing in the child's capacities for invention. Remember also that each time one prematurely teaches a child something he could have discovered for himself, that child is kept from inventing it and consequently from understanding it completely. This obviously does not mean the teacher should not devise experimental situations to facilitate the pupil's invention.

To turn to the second problem we mentioned, Matalon and Apostel have shown that all learning, even empiricist learning, involves logic. This is true in the sense of an organization of the subject's action as opposed to immediate perception of the external data; moreover, Apostel has started to analyze the algebra of the learning process and its necessary basic operations.

15. Following these investigations at the International Center of Genetic Epistemology, Inhelder in Geneva, with her colleagues Bovet and Sinclair (1967), and later Laurendeau (1966) in Montreal, with her colleagues Fournier-Choninard and Carbonneau, have carried out more detailed experiments. The aim of their inquiries was to isolate the various factors which may facilitate an operational acquisition, and to establish the possible relations with the factors involved in the "natural" constructions of the same concepts (e.g., conservation in the course of spontaneous development).

As an example, one of Inhelder, Bovet, and Sinclair's experiments (with Fot) is performed by showing the child transparent jars filled with the same quantities of liquid. Instead of pouring in the usual manner, these jars empty through taps in their bases into glass jars of various shapes, which in turn empty into more jars on other levels. The heights and widths of

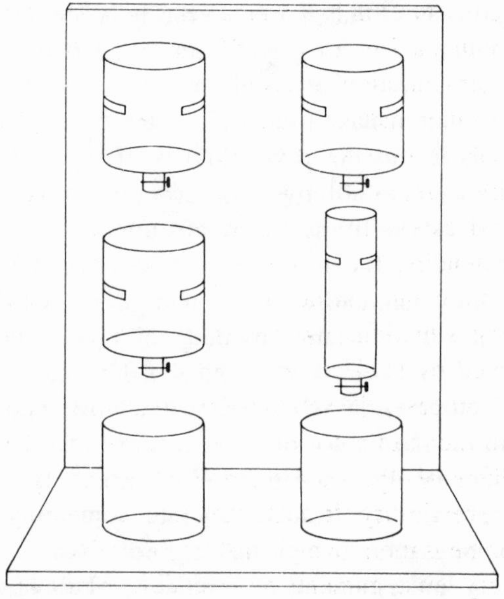

Figure 1. Experimental apparatus for learning the concept of conservation of quantity.

successive jars vary at each level, but at the bottom of the sequence are jars identical to the ones at the top. This arrangement should lead the child to perform both dimensional and quantitative comparisons and eventually to understand the reason for the equality of the quantities at the starting point and at the end point.

It was discovered in this experiment that the results vary very significantly as a function of the initial cognitive levels of the children, which were classified according to the available schemes of assimilation. No child starting at a preoperational level succeeded in learning the logical operations underlying the elementary concepts of the conservation of physical quantities. The great majority (87.5%) did not even show any real progress, while a minority (12.5%) moved up to an intermediate level characterized by frequent oscillations where conservation would be alternatively asserted or denied. This uncertainty is ascribable to the fact that the coordination of the centrations or successive isolated states or their variations were still partial and transient. Clearly, it is one thing to observe that in a closed system of physical transformations nothing is created and nothing destroyed, and quite another to infer from this a principle of conservation. The situation is different with children who initially were already at this intermediate level. In this case only 23% did not achieve conservation, while 77% benefited in various degrees from the exercise and achieved a conservation based on a genuinely operatory structure. It is true that for about half of them (38.5%), this result involved only an extension of a structuration already started at the time of the pretest, whereas for the other half the gradual construction of the conservation principle was easy to observe during the experiment. Subsequently their reasoning acquired a real stability (there were no regressions in the first and the second posttests). In addition, they were able to generalize conservation, extending the concept to include the transformations of a plasticene ball in a context which outwardly only remotely resembled the previous learning situation. However, in comparing the arguments for conservation given by subjects who had acquired it by the much slower "spontaneous" process, it was observed that they were not entirely identical. The former had constructed a structure that did not make use of all the possibilities of operational mobility, which in its complete form entails general reversibility. In fact, they gave a majority of arguments by identity and compensation, which had been evolved in the experimental situation, and very few arguments by reversibility based on cancellation.

On the other hand, progress in the experimental situation was more general and complete in the cases of children who were initially at an elementary operational level (characterized by the acquisition of conservation of quantity during the experiment) but who had not yet acquired the more complex concept of conservation of weight, which, during spontaneous development, generally appears 2 or 3 years later. In this case progress is genuine when the experimental situation does not restrict the child to passive observation but involves a series of operational exercises (e.g., establishing equality of weight for objects of different sizes, and regardless of position on the scales, and, more essentially, comparing the weights of collections of different objects and establishing their equivalence or nonequivalence). After being subjected to this type of training sequence, 86% of the subjects achieved conservation (in three sessions). Among them, 64% were able to use the transitive properties of order or equality in weight and, using arguments based on total reversibility, showed that they felt these properties were logically evident. These kinds of acquisition are therefore clearly distinct from the pragmatic solution given by children who at a preoperational level were subjected (as in Smedslund's experiment) only to empirical evidence.

Essentially what this experiment shows is that learning is subordinate to the subjects' levels of development. If they are close to the operational level, that is, if they are able to understand quantitative relations, the comparisons they make during the experiment are enough to lead them to compensation and conservation. But the farther they are from the possibility of operational quantification, the less they are likely to use the learning sequence to arrive at a concept of conservation.

An experiment carried out by Laurendeau consists of trying to induce progressive decentration and equilibration, and comparing the results thus obtained to those obtained by Skinner-type operant learning with external reinforcement. One group of subjects is asked to predict the level a liquid will reach when it is poured from one container to another of a different shape. The subjects are then shown the level reached when the liquid is actually poured so that they may see whether their prediction was correct. The subjects are then questioned about conservation, and when they deny it they are asked to add the quantity necessary to make the levels equal. This is repeated with containers whose shape is more and more different, until one is very wide and low and the other very high and thin, and it becomes obvious that equal levels do not produce equal quantities of liquid. In this third part of the experiment 12 gradually higher and thinner containers are used, the median ones (6 and 7) being equal; these are filled by the subject with quantities of liquid he judges to be equal. They are then poured into containers 5 and 8, respectively; the operation is then repeated and 6 and 7 are poured into 4 and 9, etc. With children between 5 and 6 a definite improvement in performance can be observed, and this is corroborated by the posttests given 1 week and 3 months later.

Subjects in a second group are asked to make the same prediction, but then they are asked only questions (some 20 in all) about conservation; correct answers are suitably rewarded. In fact, the child is very quickly able to give only correct answers and can still do this 2 or 3 days later, but posttests show that his learning is much more limited and less stable.

To summarize, learning appears to depend on the mechanisms of development and to become stable only insofar as it utilizes certain aspects of these mechanisms, the instruments of quantification themselves, which would have evolved in the course of spontaneous development.

V. The Operative and Figurative Aspects of Cognitive Functions

16. The stages described in Section III are only those concerning the development of intelligence, and the aspects of learning considered in Section IV are only relevant to these stages.

If we wish to obtain a complete picture of mental development, we must not only consider the operative aspect of the cognitive functions, but also their figurative aspect. We will call *operative* the activities of the subject that attempt to transform reality: *(a)* the set of all actions (except those which, like imitation or drawing, are purely accommodatory in intent) and *(b)* the operations themselves. "Operative" is thus a broader term than "operational," which is only related to the operators. In contrast, we shall call *figurative* the activities which attempt only to represent reality as it appears, without seeking to transform it: *(a)* perception, *(b)* imitation, in a broad sense (including graphic imitation or drawing), and *(c)* pictorial representations in mental imagery.

Before discussing these figurative aspects and their relations with the operative aspects of knowledge, we must briefly analyze their relations with the semiotic function (generally called symbolic function). In considering semiotic functions, Pierce introduced a distinction between "indexes" (perceptions), "icons" (images), and symbols, in which he included language. We prefer de Saussure's terminology, which is more widely used in linguistics, and which is characterized psychologically in the following way:

a. *Indexes* are signifiers that are not differentiated from their significants since they are part of them or a causal result, for example for an infant, hearing a voice is an index of someone's presence.

b. *Symbols* are signifiers that are differentiated from their significants, but they retain a measure of similarity with them, for example in a symbolic game representing bread by a white stone and vegetables by grass.

c. *Signs* are signifiers that are also differentiated from their signifiers but are conventional and thus more or less "arbitrary": the sign is always social, whereas the symbol can have a purely individual origin as in symbolic games or in dreams.

We shall thus call the semiotic function (or symbolic function, but semiotic has a broader meaning) the ability, acquired by the child in the course of his second year, to represent an object which is absent or an event which is not perceived, by means of symbols or signs, that is, of signifiers differentiated from their significants. Thus the semiotic function includes, in addition to language, symbolic games, mental and graphic images (drawings), and deferred imitation (beginning in the absence of its model), which appears nearly at the same time (except for drawing, which appears slightly later), whereas indexes (including the "signals" involved in conditioning, already play a role during the first weeks. The transition from indexes to symbols and signs—in other words, the beginning of the differentiation which characterizes the semiotic function—is definitely related to the progress of imitation, which at the sensorimotor level, is a sort of representation through actual actions. As imitation becomes differentiated and interiorized in images, it also becomes the source of symbols and the instrument of communicative exchange which makes possible the acquisition of language.

Thus defined, the semiotic function partially includes the figurative activities of knowledge, which in their turn partially include the semiotic function. There thus exists an intersection between their respective domains but not equivalence or inclusion. In effect, perception is a figurative activity, but it does not belong to the semiotic function since it uses only indexes and no representative signifiers. Language belongs to the semiotic function, but it is only partly figurative (mainly when the child is young, or less so with increased age, especially with the onset of formal operations). In contrast, imitation, mental imagery, and drawing are both figurative and semiotic.

17. The discussion of perception here is very brief; Seagrim's excellent translation of the author's *Perceptual Mechanisms* (1961) will be published in the near future. However, it is relevant to note here that, during our study of the development of perception in the child, we have been led to distinguish between "field effects" (field being understood here as field of visual motor centration, *not* as field in the sense of Gestalt theory) and the perceptual activities of exploration such as visual transports, relating, and visually placing in reference (as far as position or direction are concerned).

Field effects quantitatively decrease with age (this is the case for the primary optico-geometrical illustrations such as Müller Lyer's), but they retain their qualitative characteristics. Consequently, their evolution with age does not yield a succession of stages. For instance, based on the concept of visual centrations (studied with Vinh Bang in ocular movements) we have been able to construct a probabilistic model of "encounters" and "couplings" (through successive centrations) which gives a general law for the plane primary illusions and can be used to compute for each one its theoretical positive and negative maximum point. These points have been checked experimentally and remain the same at every age, though the quantitative amount of the illusion decreases.

In contrast, perceptual activities are modified with age and roughly approximate stages can be distinguished. For example, if one exposes the same subject to 20 or 30 presentations of the Müller Lyer or lozenge illusion (underestimation of the main diagonal), one observes an effect of learning which increases with age after 7 years. Noelting and Gonheim were able to show that it did not appear before 7. This perceptual learning (which is dependent on autoregulations or spontaneous equilibrations) is not reinforced, since the subject does not know the error in his estimate, it is the result of perceptual activities which become more efficient with age.

Moreover, while studying the way in which children perceptually estimate the horizontality of a line (e.g., in a tilted triangle), we found (with Dadsetan) a real improvement toward 9 to 10 years, which is in direct correlation with the corresponding spatial operations. Here, as in all the cases in which we could study the relations between perception and intelligence, it is intelligence which directs the movements—naturally not by experimenting with the perceptual mechanisms but by indicating what must be looked at and which indexes are useful in making a good perceptual estimate.

18. We have studied mental images extensively with Inhelder (1966) and many other colleagues, especially considering their relations to intelligence (e.g., by asking subjects to imagine the result of pouring a liquid into a different container in a conservation experiment, before they have actually seen the result). Our first conclusion is that the image does not come from perception (it only appears at approximately 1½ years together with the semiotic function) and that it obeys completely different laws. It is probably the result of an interiorization of imitation. This hypothesis seems corroborated in the domain of symbolic games in their initial stages (fiction or imagination games, which show all the transitions between imitative symbols by gestures and actions and interiorized imitation or images).

Further, if one distinguishes "reproductive" images (to imagine an object or an event which is known but is not actually perceived at the time) and "anticipatory" images (to imagine the result of a new combination), our results have shown the following:

a. Before 7 years, one can find only reproductive images, and all of them are quite static. For example, the subjects experience systematic difficulty in imagining the intermediate positions between the initial vertical and final horizontal position of a falling stick.

b. After 7 to 8 years, anticipatory images appear, but they are not only applied to new combinations. They also seem to be necessary for the representation of any transformation even if it is known, as if such representations always entailed a new anticipation.

But this research has shown above all the strict interdependency between the evolution of mental images and the evolution of operations. Anticipatory images are possible only when the corresponding operations exist. In our experiments concerning conservation of liquids the younger subjects go through a stage of "pseudo-conservation" where they imagine that in a narrow container the level of the liquid would be the same as in a wide one (and it is only when they see that it is not the same level that they deny conservation). About 23% of the subjects know the level will rise, but this knowledge is contained in a reproductive image (founded on experience) and they conclude that there will be no conservation (when asked to pour the "same quantity" in the two containers, they pour liquid up to the same levels).

In short, while mental images can sometimes facilitate operations, they do not constitute their origin. On the contrary, mental imagery is generally controlled by the operations gradually as they appear (and one can follow their construction stage by stage).

19. The study of mental imagery led us to investigate the development of memory. Memory has two very different aspects. On the one hand, it is cognitive (entailing knowledge of the past), and in this respect it uses the schemes of intelligence, as we shall show shortly in an example. On the other hand, imagery is not abstract knowledge and bears a particular and concrete relation to objects or events. In this respect such symbols as mental images and, more specifically, "memory images" are necessary to its operation. Images themselves can be schematized, but in an entirely different sense, for images in themselves, however schematic, are not schemes. We shall therefore use the term schemata to designate them. A schema is a simplified image (for example, the map of a town), whereas a scheme represents what can be repeated and generalized in an action (e.g., the scheme is what is common in the actions of "pushing" an object with a stick or any other instrument).

The main result of our research has been, in this context, to show not the generality but the possibility that progress in memory is influenced by improvements in the operational schemes of intelligence. For example, we showed (with Sinclair and others) 3- to 8-year-old children an array of 10 wooden bars varying in length between 9 and 16 cm arranged according to their length, and we merely asked the subjects to look at the array. A week, and then a month later they were asked to draw the array from memory.

The first interesting result is that, after 1 week, the younger children do not remember the sequence of well-ordered elements, but reconstruct it by assimilating it to the schemes corresponding to their operational level: (a) a few equal elements, (b) short ones and long ones, (c) groups of short, medium, and long ones, (d) a correct sequence, but too short, (e) a complete seriation. The second remarkable result is that after 6 months without any new presentation, memory was improved in 75% of the cases. Those who were at level *a* moved up to *b*. Many at level *b* moved up to *c* or even *d*. The *c*'s moved up to *d* or *e*, etc. The results, naturally, are not as spectacular in other experiments, and there is less progress as the model is less schematizable (in the sense of being made schematic, and not being assimilated to a scheme). The existence of such facts shows that the structure of memory appears to be partly dependent on the structure of the operations.

VI. The Classical Factors of Development

20. We have seen that there exist laws of development and that development follows a sequential order such that each of its stages is necessary to the construction of the next. But this fundamental fact remains to be explained. The three classical factors of development are maturation, experience of the physical environment, and the action of the social environment. The two last cannot account for the sequential character of development, and the first one is not sufficient by itself because the development of intelligence does not include a hereditary programming factor like the ones underlying instincts. We shall therefore have to add a fourth factor (which is in fact necessary to the coordination of the three others—equilibration, or self-regulation [*auto régulation*].

It is clear that maturation must have a part in the development of intelligence, although we know very little about the relations between the intellectual operations and the brain. In particular, the sequential character of the stages is an important clue to their partly biological nature and thus argues in favor of the constant role of the genotype and epigenesis. But this does not mean we can assume there exists a hereditary program underlying the development of human intelligence: there are no "innate ideas" (in spite of what Lorenz maintained about the a priori nature of human thought). Even logic is not innate and only gives rise to a progressive epigenetic construction. Thus the effects of maturation consist essentially of opening new possibilities for development, that is, giving access to structures which could not be evolved before these possibilities were offered. But between possibility and actualization, there must intervene a set of other factors such as exercise, experience, and social interaction.

A good example of the gap that exists between the hereditary possibilities and their actualization in an intellectual structure can be provided by an inspection of the Boolean and logical structures discovered by McCulloch and Pitts (1947) in the neural connections. In this context the neurons appear as operators which process information according to rules analogous to those of the logic of propositions. But the logic of propositions only appears on the level of thought at around 12 to 15 years of age. Thus there is no direct relation between the "logic of the neurons" and that of thought. In this particular case, as in many others, the process must be conceived of not as progressive maturation, but as a sequence of constructions, each of which partly repeats its immediate predecessor but at a very different level and on a scope that goes far beyond it. What makes possible the logic of neurons is initially exclusively a nervous activity. But this activity makes possible in its turn a sensorimotor organization at the level of behavior. However, this organization, while retaining certain structures of the nervous activity, and consequently being partially isomorphic to it, results at first in a set of connections between behaviors which is much simpler than that of the nervous activity itself because these behaviors have to correlate actions and objects and are no longer limited to exclusively internal transmissions. Further, the sensorimotor organization makes possible the constitution of thought and its symbolic instruments, which imply the construction of a new logic, partially isomorphic to the previous ones, but which is confronted with new problems, and the cycle repeats. The propositional logic which is constructed between 12 and 15 years is thus by no means the immediate consequence of the logic of neurons, but it is the result of a sequence of successive constructions that are not preformed in the hereditary nervous structure but are made possible by this initial structure. So we are now very far from a model of continuous maturation which would explain everything by preformed mechanisms. For this purely endogenous model, there must be substituted a series of actual constructions, the sequential order of which does not imply a simple predetermination but involves much more than this.

21. A second factor traditionally invoked to explain cognitive development is *experience* acquired through contact with the external physical environment. This factor is essentially heterogeneous, and there are at least three categories and meanings of experience, among which we shall distinguish two opposite poles.

a. The first is simple *exercise,* which naturally involves the presence of objects on which action is exerted but does not necessarily imply that any knowledge will be extracted from these objects. In fact, it has been observed that exercise has a positive effect in the consolidation of a reflex or of a group of complex reflexes such as sucking, which noticeably improves with repetition during the first days of life. This is also true of the exercise of intellectual operations which can be applied to objects, although these operations are not derived from the objects. In contrast, the exercise of an exploratory perceptual activity or of an experiment can provide new exogenous information while consolidating the subject's activity. We can thus distinguish two opposite poles of activity in exercise itself: a pole of accommodation to the object, which is then the only source of the acquisitions based on the object's properties; and a pole of functional assimilation, that is, of consolidation by active repetition. In this second perspective, exercise is predominantly a factor of equilibration or autoregulation, that is, it has to do with structurations dependent on the subject's activity more than with an increase in the knowledge of the external environment.

As regards experience proper in the sense of acquisition of new knowledge through manipulations of objects (and no longer through simple exercise), we must again distinguish two opposite poles, which will correspond to categories *(b)* and *(c).*

b. There is what we call *physical experience,* which consists of extracting information from the objects themselves through a simple process of abstraction. This abstraction reduces to dissociating one newly discovered property from the others and disregarding the latter. Thus it is physical experience that allows the child to discover weight while disregarding an object's color, etc., or to discover that with objects of the same nature, their weight is greater as their volume increases, etc.

c. In addition to physical experience *(b)* and to simple exercise *(a),* there is a third fundamental category, which strangely practically never has been mentioned in this context. This is what we call *logicomathematical experience*. It plays an important part at all levels of cognitive development where logical deduction or computation are still impossible, and it also appears whenever the subject is confronted with problems in which he has to discover new deductive instruments. This type of experience also involves acting upon objects, for there can be no experience without action at its source, whether real or imagined, because its absence would mean there would be no contact with the external world. However, the knowledge derived from it is not based on the physical properties of these objects but on properties of the actions that are exerted on them, which is not at all the same thing. This knowledge seems to be derived from the objects because it consists of discovering by manipulating objects, properties introduced by action which did not belong to the objects before these actions. For example, if a child, when he is counting pebbles, happens to put them in a row and to make the astonishing discovery that when he counts them from the right to the left he finds the same number as when he counts them from the left to the right, and again the same when he puts them in a circle, etc., he has thus discovered experimentally that the sum is independent of order. But this is a logicomathematical experiment and not a physical one, because neither the order nor even the sum was in the pebbles before he arranged them in a certain manner (i.e., ordered them) and joined them together in a whole. What he has discovered is a relation, new to him, between the action of putting in order and the action of joining together (hence, between the two future operations), and not, or *not only,* a property belonging to pebbles.

Thus we see that the factor of acquired experience is, in fact, complex and always involves two poles: acquisitions derived from the objects and constructive activities of the subject. Even physical experience *(b)* is never pure, since it always implies a logicomathematical setting, however elementary (as in the geometrical Gestalts of perception). This amounts to saying that any particular action such as "weighing" that results in physical knowledge is never independent of more general coordinations of action (such as ordering, joining together, etc.) which are a source of logicomathematical knowledge.

22. The third classical factor of development is the influence of the social environment. Its importance is immediately verified if we consider the fact that the stages we mentioned in Section III are accelerated or retarded in their average chronological ages according to the child's cultural and educational environment. But the very fact that the stages follow the same sequential order in *any* environment is enough to show that the social environment cannot account for everything. This constant order of succession cannot be ascribed to the environment.

In fact, both social or educational influences and physical experience are on the same footing in this respect, they can have some effect on the subject only if he is capable of assimilating them, and he can do this only if he already possesses the adequate instruments or structures (or their primitive forms). In fact, what is taught, for instance, is effectively assimilated only when it gives rise to an active reconstruction or even reinvention by the child.

An excellent example of this complex situation is provided by the difficult problem of the relations between language and thought. Many authors have maintained that language is not only the essential factor in the constitution of representation or thought, which raises a first question, but also that language is the origin of the logical operations themselves (e.g., classification, order, propositional operations), which raises a second question.

With respect to the first question, it is doubtless true that language plays a major part in the interiorization of action into representation and thought. But this linguistic factor is not the only one at work. We must refer to the symbolic or semiotic function as a whole—and language is only a part of this. The other instruments of representation are deferred imitation, mental imagery (which is an interiorized imitation and not a mere extension of perception), symbolic games (or games of imagination), drawing (or graphical imitation), etc.; and it is certainly imitation in the general sense which constitutes the transition between the sensorimotor and semiotic functions. Thus it is in the general context of the semiotic function that language must be considered, however important its part may be. The study of deaf-mutes, for example, shows how far the other symbolic instruments can reach when the development of articulate language is disturbed.

Turning to the question of the relations between language and logical operations, we have always maintained that the origin of logical operations is both deeper than and genetically prior to language; that is, it lies in the laws of the general coordinations of action, which control all activities including language itself.

An elementary logic already exists in the coordination of the sensorimotor schemes (cf. Section I: the group of translations, the conservation of the objects, etc.) It exists in a form of intelligence which is yet neither verbal nor symbolic. But there still remains to establish more precisely the relations between language and the logical operations on the level of interiorized thought.

This has recently been done by Sinclair in a set of experiments at the psychological and linguistic level, which are most instructive. She studied two groups of 5- to 7-year-old children, one clearly at a preoperational stage and unable to attain the concept of conservation, whereas the other possessed all the instruments that lead to conservation. She was then able to show that their language is on the average noticeably different when one examines them on subjects other than conservation; for instance, when one asks them to compare two or more objects such as a long, thin pencil and a short, thick one. The preoperational group uses mainly the nonrelational terms of a scale: "this one is long, this one is short, this one is thick, this one is thin." The operational group, in contrast, uses mainly "vectors": "this one is smaller and thicker," etc. There is thus a clear relation between linguistic and operational level (and this is also true in other situations). But in which direction? To establish this, Sinclair then taught a group of younger subjects to use the verbal forms used by the older ones. Once this was done she again investigated their operational level and discovered that only approximately 10% had improved; this very small proportion could even represent intermediate cases, or cases who were already very near the operational threshold. We can thus observe that language does not seem to be the motor of operational evolution but rather an instrument in the service of intelligence itself (see Sinclair and Zwart, 1967).

To conclude ¶ 20, 21, and 22, it appears that the traditional factors (maturation, experience, social environment) are not sufficient to explain development. We must therefore appeal to a fourth factor, *equilibration,* and we must do this for two reasons. The first is that these three heterogeneous factors cannot explain a sequential development if they are not in some relation of mutual equilibrium, and that there must therefore exist a fourth organizing factor to coordinate them in a consistent, noncontradictory totality. The second reason is that any biological development is, as we now know, self-regulatory, and that self-regulating processes are even more common at the level of behavior and the constitution of the cognitive functions. We must thus consider this factor separately.

VII. Equilibration and Cognitive Structures

23. The main aim of a theory of development is to explain the constitution *of the operational* structures of the integrated whole or totality *(structure opératoire d'ensemble)* and we believe only the hypothesis of progressive equilibration can account for it. To understand this we must first briefly consider the operational structures themselves.

The concept of structure became classical in psychology when it was introduced by Gestalt theory to combat association and its atomistic habits of thought. But the Gestaltists conceived of only one type of structure as applicable to the whole of psychology, from perception to intelligence. They did not distinguish two characters, which in reality are quite different. The first is common to all structures; they all possess holistic laws derived from the fact that they form a system, and these laws are distinct from the properties of the elements in the totality. The second character is nonadditive composition, that is, the whole is quantitatively different from the sum of the parts (as in Oppel's perceptual illusion). But in the field of intelligence, there exist structures which verify the first characteristic and not the second; the set of integers, for instance, has holistic properties as such ("group," "ring," etc.) but composition in it is strictly additive— $2+2=4$, no more, no less.

We have therefore attempted to define and analyze the structures specific to intelligence, and they are structures involving operations, that is, involving interiorized and reversible actions such as addition, set-theoretic union, logical multiplication, or, in other words, composition of a multiplicity of classes or relations "considered simultaneously." These structures have a very natural and spontaneous development in the child's thought: to seriate, for instance (i.e., to order objects according to their increasing size), to classify, to put into one-to-one or one-to-many correspondence, to establish the multiplicative matrix, are all structures that appear between ages 7 and 11, at the level of what we call "concrete operations" which deal directly with objects. After 11 to 12 other structures appear, such as the four-group and combinatorial processes, which we shall describe later.

To investigate the properties of these concrete operational structures, and to establish their laws, we need to use the language of the logic of classes and relations, but this does not mean we are leaving the field of psychology. When a psychologist computes the variance of a sample or uses the formulas of factor analysis, it does not mean his field has become

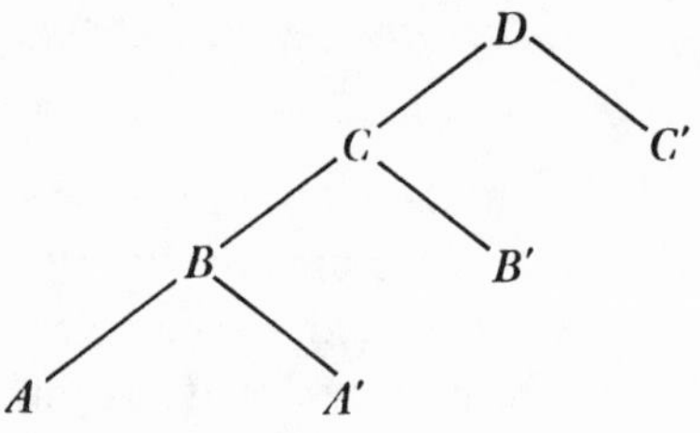

*Figure F7*a.

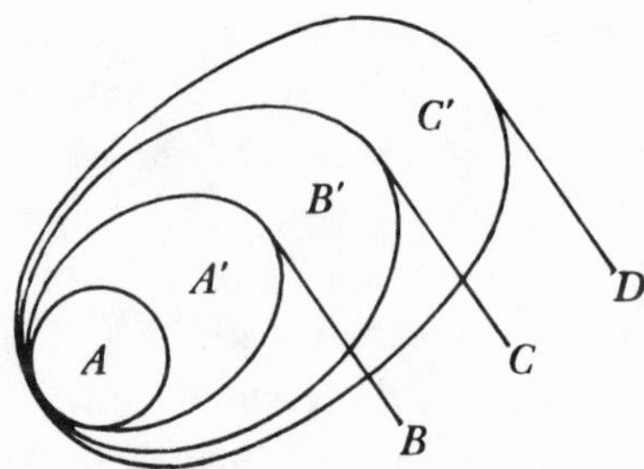

*Figure F7*b.

statistics and not psychology. To analyze structures we must do the same, but, since we are not dealing with quantities, we must simply resort to more general mathematical instruments such as abstract algebra or logic. But they are only instruments which will allow us to reach genuinely psychological entities such as operations, considered as interiorized actions or general coordinations of actions.

A totality structure such as a classification has the following properties, which characterize, simply, the operations that are actually present in the subject's action.

a. He can combine one class A with another A', to obtain class B, denoted $A + A' = B$ (he can then go on to perform $B + B' = C$, etc.).

b. He can dissociate A or A' from B, denoted $B - A' = A$, which constitutes the inverse operation. Notice this reversibility is necessary to the understanding of the relation $A < B$, and we know that until 7 or 8, the child does not grasp easily the idea that if he is given 10 primroses A, and 10 other flowers A', then there are more flowers B than primroses A, because to be able to compare the whole B to the part A, one must be able to combine the two operations $A + A' = B$ and $A = B - A'$, otherwise the whole B is not preserved, and A is then only compared to A'.

c. He will understand that $A - A = O$, and $A + O = A$.

d. Finally, he will be able to associate $(A + A') + B' = A + (A' + B') = C$, while $(A + A) - A = O$ is not equal to $A + (A - A) = A$.

We have called *groupements* these elementary groupings[5] *(structures de groupoïdes),* which are more primitive than mathematical groups, but which are also much more limited structures and less elegant ones, in that composition is defined only between neighboring elements without general combinatorial properties and shows restricted associativity.[6] We have often been criticized for having thus only constructed structures that have no psychological reality. But such structures actually exist, primarily because they describe simply what happens in a classification, a seriation, etc., all of which are quite contemporaneous behaviors. Moreover, they can be recognized on the psychological level by the more general characters that reveal the existence of a totality structure, such as transitivity (for instance, in a seriation $A < C$ if $A < B$ and $B < C$) and the constitution of conservation concepts (conservation of a whole B when the arrangement of its parts A and A' is modified, conservation of length, quantity, etc.).

24. The problem then becomes that of understanding how the fundamental structures of intelligence can appear and evolve with all those that later derive from them. Since they are not innate, they cannot be explained by maturation alone. Logical structures are not a simple product of physical experience; in seriation, classification, one-to-one correspondence, the subject's activities add new relations such as order and totality to the objects. Logicomathematical experience derives its information from the subject's own actions (as we saw in ¶ 21), which

[5]A grouping can be considered as a lattice that has been made reversible. In a lattice, if $A + A' = B$, where B is an upper bound of A and A', A can be recovered by operating on B: $B - A' = A$. But the more general case is where C is an upper bound of A and C', for example, and $A \pm D - C'$. In other words, the operation $A + A'$ can only be "reversed" between contiguous elements such as A and A', in the sense that in the 3-tuple A, A', B any two elements uniquely determine the third (Fig. F7*a*).

This is not the case for A, C', D, where $A + C' = D - D' - B' - A'$. Here we consider a grouping as a group where composition is restricted to contiguous elements only ($A + C'$, for example, is not defined without special conditions) and by the special identities $A + A = A$, $A + B = B$. A grouping is therefore only defined as a sequence of nested elements, such as a classification (Fig. F7*b*). It consists of *(a)* a direct operation: *(b)* an inverse operation: *(c)* an identity operation O: and *(d)* special identities:

$$A + A' = B$$
$$B - A' = A$$
$$A + O = A; \qquad A - A = O$$
$$A + A = A; \qquad -A - A = -A;$$
$$A + B = B$$

[6]Associativity is limited by the fact that the grouping only combines contiguous elements. $A + C'$ can only be constructed by operating step-by-step on the nearest contiguous classes A, A', B', up to D, the first class containing both A and C', then $A + C' = D - B' - A'$. Similarly, $A - C'$ only gives rise to the tautology $A - C' = (D - C' - B' - A') - C'$ where $(D - C' - B' - A') = A$. The consequence of these restrictions is that associativity is not verified before the elements in brackets have first been "reduced": $(A + A') + B' = B + B' = C$, but $A + (A' + B')$ has no meaning since $(A' + B')$ and is not defined as such. (For further details of the reduction rules, cf. Piaget, 1959.) In contrast, on the group of the integers under addition, any number can be immediately added to or subtracted from any other because an integer can be completely freed from its successors that "contain" it. (Translator's note)

implies an autoregulation of these actions. It could be alleged that these structures are the result of social or educational transmission. But as we saw (¶ 22), the child must still understand what is transmitted, and to do this structures are necessary. Moreover, the social explanation only displaces the problem: how did the members of the social group acquire the structures in the first place?

But on all levels of development actions are coordinated in ways that already involve some properties of order, inclusion, and correspondence, and also foreshadow such structures (e.g., seriation for order, classification for inclusion, multiplicative structures for correspondence). What is more important, though, is that coordination of actions involves correction and self-regulation; in fact, we know regulatory mechanisms characterize all levels of organic life (this is true for the genetic pool as well as for behavior). But regulation is a process of retroaction (negative feedback), which implies a beginning of reversibility; and the relationship between regulation (which is correction of error with semireversibility in the retroaction) and operation, whose full reversibility allows for precorrection of errors (i.e., for "perfect" regulation in the cybernetic sense) becomes apparent.

Thus it seems highly probable that the construction of structures is mainly the work of equilibration, defined not by balance between opposite forces but by self-regulation; that is, equilibration is a set of active reactions of the subject to external disturbances, which can be effective, or anticipated, to varying degrees. Equilibrium thus becomes identical with reversibility, but when one objects (as Bruner does, for example) that equilibrium therefore becomes superfluous, because reversibility is sufficient in itself, one forgets that it is not only the final state of equilibrium that must be considered, but that *equilibration* is essential as the self-regulating process leading to this final state and thus to the reversibility that characterizes the structures that must be explained.

25. Equilibration has explanatory value because it is founded on a process with increasing sequential probabilities. We can understand this better through an example. How can we explain the fact that when a spherical lump of clay is changed into the shape of a sausage in front of him, a child will begin by denying that the quantity of clay is preserved under this transformation, and end by asserting the logical necessity of this conservation? To do this we must define four stages, each of which *becomes more probable,* not a priori, but as a function of the present situation or of the one immediately preceding it.

a. Initially the child considers only one dimension, for instance, length (say 8 times out of 10). He then says the sausage contains more matter because it is longer. Sometimes (say 2 times out of 10) he says it is thinner, but forgetting its greater length, he concludes the quantity of matter has decreased. Why does he reason thus? Simply because the probability of considering one dimension only is greater. If the probability for length is .8 and that for width is .2, that for length *and* width is .16, because they are independent occurrences as long as compensation is not understood.

b. If the sausage is made longer and longer, or if the child becomes weary of repeating the same argument, the probability of his noticing the other dimension *becomes* greater (though it was not initially) and he will fluctuate between the two.

c. If there is oscillation, the probability of the subject's noticing some correlation between the two variations (when the sausage becomes longer it becomes thinner) *becomes* greater (third stage). But as soon as this feeling of the solidarity existing between variables appears, his reasoning has acquired a new property: it does not rest solely on *configurations* any more but begins to be concerned with *transformations:* the sausage is not simply "long"; it can "lengthen," etc.

d. As soon as the subject's thought takes transformations into account, the next stage *becomes* more probable in which he understands (alternately or simultaneously) that a transformation can be reversed, or that the two simultaneous transformations of length and width compensate, because of the solidarity he has glimpsed [see stage *(c)*].

We can thus see that progressive equilibration has effective explanatory value. Stage *(a)* (which all those who checked our research have found) is not an equilibrium point because the child has noticed only one dimension: in this case the algebraic sum of the virtual components of work (to quote d'Alembert's principle on physical systems) is not zero since one of them, which consists of noticing the other dimension, has not been completed yet and will be sooner or later. The transition from one stage to another is therefore an equilibration in the most classical sense of the word. But since these displacements of the system are activities of the subject, and since each of these activities consists of correcting the one immediately preceding it, equilibration becomes a sequence of self-regulations whose retroactive processes finally result in operational reversibility. The latter then goes beyond simple probability to attain logical necessity.

What we have just said about an instance of operational conservation could be repeated about the construction of every operational structure. Seriation $A < B < C$, for example, when it becomes operational, is the result of coordinating the relations $<$ and $>$ (each new element in E in the ordered sequence having the property of being both $> D, C, B, A$, and $< F, G, H, \ldots$ and this coordination is again the result of an equilibration process of increasing sequential probabilities of the kind we have described. Similarly for inclusion of classes, $A < B$ if $B = A + A'$ and $A' > O$ is obtained by an equilibration of the same type.

It is not therefore an exaggeration to say that equilibration is the fundamental factor of development, and that it is even necessary for the coordination of the three other factors.

VIII. The Logicomathematical Aspects of Structures

26. The "concrete" operational structures we have just mentioned all presuppose the construction of certain quantities: extension of classes for classification (which explains the difficulty of quantifying the inclusion of classes), size of the differences for seriation, quantitative conservations, etc. But even before these quantitative structures are constructed, some partial and qualitative structures may be observed at the preoperational levels which are of great interest, because they constitute the first half, so to speak, of the logic of reversible operations. These are the directional functions (one-way functions that do not have inverses, which would imply reversibility) and the qualitative identities (see ¶ 10).

The functions, we remember, are "mappings" in the mathematical sense, which have no inverses because, as we saw, they are psychologically related to the schemes of action, which are goal-directed. Suppose, for instance, we have a piece of string b, part a of which is at right angles to the rest (a') and can slide on a nail when a weight is connected with a' and a is held back by a spring. All children between 4 and 7 understand that if one pulls b, a grows shorter as a' grows longer. But they do not yet have conservation of the length of the whole b $(b = a + a')$, and what they perform is not a quantified operation but simply a qualitative or ordinal equation (longer = farther).

Similarly for identity, all children (or nearly all) agree, as we saw, that when a ball of clay is changed into a sausage, it is the "same" lump of clay even if quantity is not preserved. These identities are acquired early and the scheme of permanent objects we mentioned in ¶ 2 is one of them. In a recent book, Bruner considers them the origin of quantitative conservations. This is true in a sense (they are a necessary condition, but not a sufficient one), but a central difference remains: qualities (on which qualitative identity is founded) can be established perceptually, whereas quantity involves a lengthy structural elaboration whose complexity we have just seen (¶ 23 to 26).

In fact, functions and qualitative identity constitute only that half of a logic which is both preoperational and qualitative and leads to the logic of reversible and quantitative operations but is not powerful enough to account for it.

27. This quantification of concrete operations, as opposed to the qualitative nature of preoperational functions and identities, is revealed in particular by the construction, around 7 or 8, of the operations related to number and measure, which are partly isomorphic to one another but have very different content. The construction of cardinal numbers cannot be explained, as was believed by Russell and Whitehead, simply by one-to-one correspondence between equivalent classes, because the correspondence they used, by abstraction of qualities (in contrast with qualified correspondence between individual objects with the same properties) implicitly introduced unity and therefore number, which made their reasoning circular. In fact, when we deal with finite sets cardinal numbers cannot be dissociated from ordinal numbers and are subject to the three following conditions:

a. Abstraction from qualities, which makes all singular objects equivalent and therefore $1 = 1 = 1$.

b. The intervention of order: $1 \rightarrow 1 \rightarrow 1 \ldots$, which is necessary to distinguish the objects from one another—otherwise $1 + 1 = 1$ would be true.

c. An inclusion of (1) in $(1 + 1)$, then of $(1 + 1)$ in $(1 + 1 + 1)$, etc.

The integers thus result from synthesis of order (seriation) and inclusion or nested sets (classification), which is made necessary by the abstraction from qualities. Hence the integers are built up from purely logical elements (seriation and classification), but they are rearranged in a new synthesis which allows for their quantification by an iterative process: $1 + 1 = 2$, etc.

Similarly, measurement in a continuum (e.g., a line, a surface) implies *(a)* its partition into segments, one of which is then chosen as unity and made equivalent to others by congruence $a = a = a \ldots$, *(b)* its translation in a certain order, $a \rightarrow a \rightarrow a$, etc., to make it congruent to others, and *(c)* the units settling into its additive compositions, thus *a* into $(a + a)$ and $(a + a)$ into $(a + a + a)$. This synthesis of partition with nested segments and order in the translations of unity is thus isomorphic to the synthesis of order and inclusion which characterizes number, and this makes it possible to apply number to measurement.

It is thus clear that without having recourse to anything other than the synthesis of elementary "groupings" of inclusion or order relations, the subject attains a numerical or metrical quantification whose power by far surpasses the elementary quantification (relations from part to whole) of the extension of classes or of seriation based on differences evaluated simply by "more" or "less."

28. After the concrete operational structures mentioned in ¶ 23, two other new structures are constructed between ages 11 and 15 which make possible the manipulation of such propositional operations as implications $(p > q)$, incompatibilities $(p \mid q)$, and disjunctions $(p \vee q)$, etc. These two new structures are the four-group and combinatorial operations. Combinatorial activity at this stage consists of classifying all possible classifications (just as permutations are a seriation of seriations) *aa, ab, ac, bc, bb, cc,* etc., and this does not therefore constitute an entirely new operation but an operation on other operations. Similarly, the four-group *INRC*[7] results from connecting in a whole the inversions *N* and

[7]The *INRC* group is a set of operations that act on the operations or elements of some other algebraic structure which has an involutive operation (an operation which is in its own inverse: $N^2 = I$). An example of an involutive operation is the duality (de Morgan) law of Boolean algebra: $\overline{p \cup q} = \bar{p} \wedge \bar{q}$, which we can write $N(p \vee q) = \bar{p} \wedge \bar{q}$ (*N* for negative). If we define *C* (correlative) to be the rule that acts on the connectives, changing $\wedge$ into $\vee$ and conversely, and *R* (reciprocal) to be the rule that acts on the sign of the variables, changing *p* into *p* and conversely, then by using *C* and *R* in succession [on, say $(p \cup q)$], we get the same result as by using *N*. The following "state diagram" shows the relations between N, R, and C acting on $(p \vee q)$.

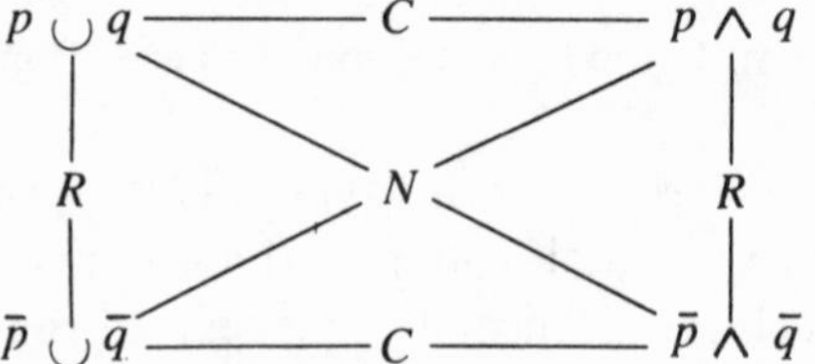

Identity *I* can now be defined as the rule that changes any formula into itself, and the following properties can easily be verified by "chasing around the diagram."

a. $RC = N$, $RN = C$, $CN = R$, and all couples are commutative—$RC = CR$, etc.

b. $C^2 = N^2 = R^2 = I$ (all transformations are involutive, i.e., each element has an inverse).

c. $RNC = I$.

From this we can show the set $[I, N, R, C]$ together with the operation of composition (in the usual reciprocities R (thus the inverse of the reciprocal $NR = C$ appears, as well as the identity operation $I = NCR$). But inversion already exists in the groupements of classes, under the form $A - A = O$, and reciprocity exists under the form $A = B$ therefore $B = A$ in the groupements of relations. The *INRC* group is thus again an operational structure bearing on prior operations. As for the propositional operations, $p > q$, etc., which involve both combinatorial activity and the *INRC* group, they are new in their form, but in their content they deal with connections between classes, relations, or numbers, etc., and are therefore again operations on operations.

In general, the operations belonging to the third period of development (see ¶ 10, period *c* for ages 11 to 12) have their roots in concrete operations (subperiod *b II*, between 7 and 11) and enrich them, just as the source of concrete operations is in the sensorimotor schemes (period *a*, until about 2) which they also considerably modify and enrich. The sequential character of the stages (which we sufficiently stressed in ¶ 10) thus corresponds from the point of view of the construction of structures to a mechanism which we must now analyze, because it is too important for us to merely call it a sequential or progressive equilibration process. We must still understand how the constructions that bring about novelty occur, and this is a well-known problem in the development of mathematical structures.

29. We saw (¶ 21*c*) that before the level at which logicomathematical operations are constructed and thus become a deductive system we can speak of logicomathematical experiments, which extract information from

sense of applying one transformation on the result of another) forms a noncyclic group of four elements (known as the Klien four-group).

The *INRC* group can also be defined on physical systems that have the proper structure (i.e., an involutive transformation that can be "decomposed" into two other involutive transformations). In one of his experiments on double reference-systems Piaget uses a snail, which can move from left to right and conversely on a small board, which can itself be moved both ways on a table. We can define C to be the rule that reverses the movement of the snail: $C\ (L, L) = (R, L)$, for example [where (R, L) means the snail (first coordinate) is moving right, and the board moving left]. Then we can define R to be the rule that reverses the second coordinate, for example, $R\ (L, L) = (L, R)$ (this reverses the movement of the board). The "state diagram" has the same structure as before, and N (N reverses both movements) is the product of R and C.

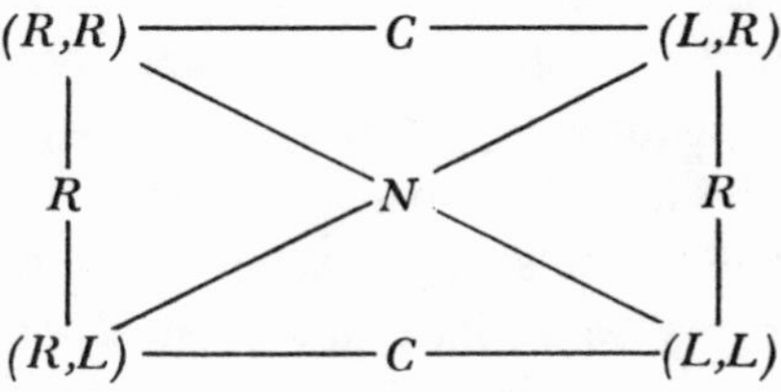

(Translator's note)

the properties of actions applied to objects, and not from the objects themselves, which is quite another matter. We thus have, in contrast with abstraction proper, a new type of abstraction which we shall call *reflective abstraction* and which is the key to our problem. To abstract a property from an action or an operation, it is not enough to dissociate it from those that will be disregarded (e.g., a dissociation between the "form" to be retained and the "content" to be disregarded); the property or form thus retained must in addition be transferred somewhere, that is, on a different plane of action or operation. In the case of abstraction proper this question does not appear since we are dealing with a property of an object, which is assimilated by the subject. In the case of reflective abstraction, however, when the subject extracts a property or a form from actions or operations on a plane P_1, he must then transfer it to a higher plane P_2, and this is thus a reflection in a quasi-physical sense (as in the reflection of a light beam). But for this form or property to be assimilated on this new plane P_2, it must be reconstructed on this new plane and therefore subjected to a new thought process which will this time mean "reflection" in a cognitive sense. Thus it is in both senses of the word that we must understand "reflective abstraction."

But if a new cognitive processing is necessary on plane P_2 to assimilate the properties or forms abstracted from plane P_1, this means new operations or actions on plane P_2, will be added to those of plane P_1 from which the required information was abstracted. Consequently, reflective abstraction is necessarily *constructive* and *enriches* with new elements the structures drawn from plane P_1, which amounts to saying it constructs new structures. This explains why the concrete operations based on sensorimotor schemes are richer than they were and why the same is true of propositional or formal operations, which are themselves based on concrete operations. As operations *on* operations, they add new modes of composition (combinatorial ones, etc.).

But reflective abstraction is the general constructive process of mathematics: it has served, for example, to evolve algebra out of arithmetic, as a set of operations on operations. Cantor constructed transfinite arithmetic in the same manner; he put into one-to-one correspondence the sequence 1, 2, 3, 4, . . . , with the sequence 2, 4, 6, 8. . . . This generates a new number ($\aleph_0$) which expresses the "power (a number) of the denumbrable," but is an element of neither sequence. Present function theory constructs "morphisms" and "categories," etc., in the same manner, and this is also true for the Bourbaki with the "mother structures" and their derivatives.

It is thus a remarkable fact that the process of the construction of structures we observe in the sequential stages of development in children and in the mechanisms of equilibration through self-regulation (which result in this self-regulation through feedback of a higher order, which is a reversible operation) coincides with the constant constructive process used by mathematics in their indefinitely fruitful development. This is a solution to the problem of development which reduces to neither an empirical process of discovery of a "ready-made" external reality nor to a process of preformation or predetermination (a priori), which would also mean believing that everything is ready-made from the beginning. We believe truth lies between these two extremes, that is, in a constructivism which expresses the manner in which new structures are constantly being elaborated.

IX. Conclusion: From Psychology to Genetic Epistemology

30. The theory we have outlined is necessarily interdisciplinary, and it involves, in addition to psychological elements, components belonging to biology, sociology, linguistics, logic, and epistemology. The relations with biology are obvious since the development of cognitive functions is a part of the epigenesis that leads from the first embryological stages to the adult state. From biology we essentially retain the three following points:

a. There can be no transformation of the organism or of behavior without endogeneous organizational factors, because the phenotype, although it is constructed in interaction with the environment, is the genome's "response" (or a response of the entire population's genetic pool, the individual genome being a cross section of the gene pool) to environmental "stresses."

b. Conversely, there is no epigenetic or phenotypic transformation independent of interaction with environmental influences.

c. These interactions involve continuous processes of equilibration or self-regulation, of which the equilibrium between assimilation and accommodation is an early instance. This also appears in sensorimotor, representative, and preoperational self-regulations, and even in operations themselves since they are anticipatory self-regulations and corrections of error which do not rely any more on the feedback from an error which has already happened.

The relations with sociology are also self-evident, because even if the origin of cognitive structures is in the general coordinations of action, they are also interpersonal or social as well as individual, since the coordination of the actions of individuals obeys the same laws as intra-individual coordination. This is not true of social processes involving constraint or authority, which lead to a sociocentrism closely akin to egocentrism, but it is true in situations of cooperation, which are in reality "co-operations." One of the fundamental processes of cognition is that of decentration relative to subjective illusion (see ¶ 8) and this process has dimensions that are social or interpersonal as well as rational.

The relations with linguistics would have very little meaning if linguistics were still defending positions like Bloomfield's, with its naive antimentalism. But we can adopt, in G. A. Miller's words, a position of "subjective behaviorism," and in linguistics proper, the contemporary work of Chomsky and his group on transformational grammars is not very far from our own operational perspectives and psychogenetic constructivism. But Chomsky believes in the hereditary basis of his linguistic structures, whereas it will probably be possible to show that the necessary and sufficient conditions for the construction of the basic units on which are founded the linguistic structures are satisfied by the development of sensorimotor schemes, and this is what Sinclair is working on at the present time.

The relations with logic are more complex. Modern symbolic logic is a "logic without a subject," whereas psychologically there exists no "subject without a logic." The subject's logic is undeniably poor and the groupement structures in particular are of little algebraic interest, except for the fact that related elementary structures do seem to arouse the mathematician's interest. But we must note that in studying the subject's logic we were able to formulate the laws of the four-group of propositional transformations *INRC* in 1949, that is even before logicians themselves began to look into it. On the other hand, present work on the limits of formalization, initiated with Gödel's proof, will, more or less necessarily, orient logic toward a kind of constructivism, and in this light the parallel with psychogenetic construction has some interest. Generally speaking, logic is an axiomatic system, and in our context we must ask: An axiomatization of what? It is certainly not an axiomatization of the subject's conscious thought processes, because they are inconsistent and incomplete. But behind conscious thought are the "natural" operatory structures, and it is obvious that, even though it can indefinitely surpass them (because the productivity of axiomatics has no formal limit), they became the basis of logical axiomatization through a process of "reflective abstraction."

31. Finally, there remains the great problem of the relations between the theory of the development of cognitive functions and epistemology. When one adopts a static rather than a psychogenetic point of view and when one studies, for example, the intelligence of an adult or of subjects considered at a single level, it is easy to distinguish psychological problems (how intelligence functions or what are its performances) from epistemological problems (what are the relations between the subject and the objects, and whether or not knowledge of the former adequately attains the latter). But when one adopts a psychogenetic point of view, the situation is completely different because one is then concerned with the formation or the development of knowledge, and it is essential to consider the roles of objects or of the activities of the subject, those issues which necessarily raise all the epistemological problems. In fact, those who attribute the formation of knowledge exclusively to experience, in the sense of physical experience, and those who introduce the activities of the subject in the sense of necessary organization will orient toward different epistemologies. To distinguish, as we have done (¶ 21), between two types of experience—one physical with abstraction beginning from objects and the other logicomathematical with reflective abstraction—is to make a psychological analysis, but one whose epistemological consequences are clear.

There are authors who fail to appreciate the interconnections between genetic psychology and epistemology, but this only indicates that they are choosing one epistemology among other possible ones, and that they believe their own epistemology is evident. For example, when Bruner tries to explain conservations by means of identities and symbolization based upon language and imagery, believing himself able to avoid operations and all epistemology, he is actually taking the point of view of empirical epistemology. At the same time he invokes an operation of identity without noticing that it implies others. In giving conservations a more operational explanation, and in supposing that quantities call for a complex construction and not simply a perceptual activity, we *de facto* remove ourselves from empiricism in the direction of a constructivism, which is another epistemology; moreover, it is much closer to present biological trends, which underscore the necessity of constructive autoregulations.

If we turn now to the epistemological side, we discover that *its* trends also differ noticeably, according to whether it adopts a static or a historical and genetical point of view as is its natural internal tendency. When epistemology simply asks itself what knowledge is in general, it believes itself able to make abstractions without recourse to psychology, because, in fact, when knowledge is achieved, the subject retires from the scene. But, in reality, this is a great illusion, for all epistemology, even when it tries to bring down to *a minimum* the activities of the subject, makes implicit appeal to psychological interpretations. For example, logical empiricism attempts to reduce physical knowledge to perceptual states and logicomathematical knowledge to laws of an ideal language (with its syntax, its semantics, and its pragmatics, but without reference to transformational actions). Now, these are two highly conflicting hypotheses, first, because physical experience rests on actions and not only on perceptions and always supposes a logicomathematical framework drawn from the general coordination of actions (of such kind that the operationalism of Bridgman must be completed by that of Piaget!). Second, logicomathematical knowledge is not tautological but constitutes a structural organization drawn from reflective abstraction of the general coordination between our actions and our operations.

But, most importantly, it is impossible that epistemology is static in point of view, because all scientific knowledge is in perpetual evolution, including mathematics and logic itself [of which the constructivist aspect has become evident since the theorems of Gödel have shown the impossibility of a theory to be self-sufficient (complete)—therefore, the necessity of always constructing "stronger" ones; from whence finally the inevitable limits of formalization!] As Natorp said in 1910: ". . . science evolves continually. The progression, the method is everything . . . a consequence, the *fact* of science can only be understood as *fieri*. Only the fieri is the fact. All being (or object) that science attempts to fix must again dissolve in the current of becoming. It is in the furthest removes of this becoming, and there only, that one has the right to say, It is (fact). Therefore, that which can and must be sought is 'the law of this process' " (p. 15).

32. These uncontestable declarations are tantamount to stating the principle of our "genetic epistemology," that in order to resolve the problem of what is knowledge (or its diversity of forms) it is necessary to formulate it in the following terms: How does knowledge grow? by what process does one pass from knowledge judged to be ultimately insufficient to knowledge judged to be better (considered from the point of view of science)? It is this that the proponents of the historicocritical method have well understood (see among others the works of Koyré and Kuhn). These critics, to understand the epistemological nature of a notion or a structure, look to see first how they were formed themselves.

If one takes a dynamic rather than a static point of view, it is impossible to maintain the traditional barriers between epistemology and the psychogenesis of cognitive functions. If epistemology is defined as the study of the formation of valid knowledge, it presupposes questions of validity, which are dependent on logic and on particular sciences, but also questions of fact, for the problem is not only formal but equally real: How, in *reality,* is science possible? In fact, all epistemology is therefore obliged to invoke psychological presuppositions, and this is true of logical positivism (perception and language) as well as of Plato (reminiscence) or of Husserl (intuition, intentions, significations, etc.). The only question is to know if it is better to content oneself with a speculative psychology or whether it is more useful to have recourse to a verifiable psychology!

This is why, as all our efforts lead to epistemological conclusions (this was moreover their initial goal), we have founded an International Center for Genetic Epistemology, so that psychologists, logicians, cyberneticists, epistemologists, linguists, mathematicians, physicists, etc., may collaborate there, depending on the problems being considered. This center, which has already published 22 volumes (and several others are in press), has therefore had as its goal, from the beginning, to study a certain number of epistemological problems seeking to analyze experimentally the psychological data necessary for the other aspects of the problem.

We have thus studied the interrelations of logical structures from the double point of view of their psychological genesis and their formal genealogy (with Grize, Papert, Apostel, etc.), which has permitted us to find a certain convergence between the two methods. We have examined the problem with what the great logician Quine ironically called the "dogma" of logical empiricism, that is to say, the absolute distinction between the analytic and the synthetic: after having declared that all these authors, being occupied with that question, have had recourse to *factual* data, we have put them under experimental control and have declared that numerous intermediaries exist between these two sorts of relationships incorrectly judged as irreducible.

We have also studied the problems of the development of the notions of number, space, time, speed, function, identity, etc., and have been able to bring to all these questions new psychogenetic data, while completely removing from their regard epistemological conclusions, which are as far removed from the a priori as from the empirical, and suggesting a systematic constructivism. With regard to empiricism, we have above all analyzed the conditions for an adequate interpretation of experience, and have added to this result what a mathematician-philosopher has summed up in these terms: "Empirical study of experience refutes empiricism!" We have seen previously (¶ 14) several of our studies on the role of learning.

In a word, the psychological theory of the development of cognitive functions seems to us to establish a direct, and even quite intimate, relationship between the biological notions of interactions between endogenous factors and the environment, and epistemological notions of necessary interaction between the subject and the objects. The synthesis of the notions of structure and of genesis that determines psychogenetic study finds its justification in the biological ideas of auto-regulation and organization, and touches on an epistemological constructivism which seems to be in line with all contemporary scientific work; in particular, with that which concerns the agreement between logicomathematical constructions and physical experience.

REFERENCES

Apostel, L. *Etudes d'Epistémologie Génétique II: Logique et équilibre*. Paris: Presses Universitaires de France, 1957.

Berlyne, D., and J. Piaget, *Etudes d'Epistémologie Génétique XII: Théorie du comportement et opérations*. Paris: Presses Universitaires de France, 1960.

Bruner, J. *The Process of Education*. Cambridge, Mass.: Harvard University Press, 1960.

Chomsky, N. Review of B. F. Skinner, *Verbal Behavior in Language*, 1959, 35, (1), 26-58.

Chomsky, N. *Syntactic Structures*. The Hague: Mouton, 1957.

Greco: *Etudes d'Epistémologie Génétique VII: Apprentissage et connaissance, Ier et II parties*. Paris: Presses Universitaires de France, 1959.

Inhelder, B., M. Bovet, and H. Sinclair, in *Revue suisse de psychologie*, 1967.

Kohnstamm, G. A. "La méthode génétique en psychologie," *Psychologie française*, No. 10, 1956.

Laurendeau, M., and A. Pinard, in *Psychologie et épistémologie génétique*. Dunod, 1966.

Morf, A., J. Smedslund, Vinh Bang, J. Wohlwill, *Etudes d'Epistémologie Génétique IX: L'Apprentissage des structures logiques*. Paris: Presses Universitaires de France, 1959.

Natorp, P. *Die logischen Grundlagen des exacten Wissenschaften*. Berlin, 1910.

Piaget, J. *Traité de logique*. Colin, 1959.

Piaget, J. *Les mécanismes perceptifs*. Paris: Presses Universitaires de France, 1961. (Contains contributions of Vinh Bang, Gonheim, Noelting, Dadsetan.)

Piaget, J., and B. Inhelder, *L'image mental chez l'enfant*. Paris: Presses Universitaires de France, 1966.

Pitts, W., and W. S. McCulloch, "How We Know Universals: The Perception of Auditory and Visual Forms," *Bull. Math. Biophys.*, 1947, 9, 127-147.

Sinclair, H., and Zwart, *Acquisition du langage et développement de la pensée*. Dunod, 1967.

Waddington, C. H. *The Strategy of the Genes*.

III. CLINICAL ISSUES

In this section papers are collected which we consider to be clinical in nature because they are primarily based on the direct observation of children in their natural settings and because the inferences drawn from them do not lead to important theoretical formulations. A good example of this is the first presentation by Margaret Mahler, "Rapprochement Subphase of the Separation-Individuation Process." Dr. Mahler is one of the most important contributors to the field of child development. From direct observation of children over many years and experience in the psychoanalysis of children, she has chosen to investigate an area of signal significance, the study of the dyadic relationship between infant and mother and the central significance of this relationship for the understanding of developmental processes. Mahler's previous investigation of the early symbiotic and autistic dispositions of the child were forerunners of her careful outline of the steps which lead to both the child's ability to separate from the mother in order to achieve relative independence and the steps which lead toward the establishment of individuation and of a beginning stable sense of self. These "lines of development" led to new insight which has contributed to the theory of development and equally to the understanding of psychopathology in children and adults. In this paper, Mahler focuses on the "rapprochement subphase." Her approach exemplifies the interrelationship between clinical observational data and Mahler's ability to extract detailed developmental sequences from these data.

The next co-authors, Alexander Thomas and Stella Chess, present findings in an area in which they have made numerous contributions. Today we see as much emphasis on the earliest years as on adolescence. This paper on middle childhood is the more important because it fills a gap. Over the years, Thomas and Chess have studied the developmental characteristics of a large number of children and have proposed categories which outline "temperamental characteristics." These longitudinal studies of children allowed for the formulation of various developmental tasks and their achievement or inhibition. Here, too, we see the close interrelationship between clinical data and theoretical formulations. Moreover, the paper postulates a phase in development which the authors refer to as "middle childhood" and discuss in the context of overall development.

It will be of great interest to read the comprehensive study by Annemarie Weil based on infant observations. Here, too, there is a close interplay between clinical observational findings and theory formation, particularly at a time of increased need to understand the earliest period of development, in order to see its influence on further progression and from this to find more appropriate social and health services for the very young child. In order to gain this understanding, one must study the first year of life. Dr. Weil uses psychoanalytic propositions to explain findings which she places here in the context of contributions from investigators from different schools of developmental theory. This paper gives evidence of the attention paid to details in early development and of the productiveness of such an approach. It exemplifies the possibility of integrating observational developmental and clinical findings with theory formation and clinical implications.

10. Rapprochement Subphase of the Separation-Individuation Process*

Margaret S. Mahler, M.D.
Clinical Professor of Psychiatry, A.E.C.O.M. Emeritus
Visiting Professor of Child Analysis
Medical College of Pennsylvania

From our studies of infantile psychosis, as well as from observations in well-baby clinics, we have already learned that the human infant's physiological birth by no means coincides with his psychological birth. The former is a dramatic, readily observable, and well-defined event; the latter is a slowly unfolding intrapsychic process.

For the more or less normal adult, the experience of being both fully 'in' and at the same time basically separate from the world 'out there' is one of the givens of life that is taken for granted. Consciousness of self and absorption without awareness of self are the two poles between which we move with varying degrees of ease and with varying alternation or simultaneity. This, too, is the result of a slowly unfolding process. In particular, this development takes place in relation to (a) one's own body; and (b) the principal representative of the world as the infant experiences it (the primary love object). As is the case with any intrapsychic process, this one continues to reverberate throughout the life cycle. It is never finished; it can always be reactivated; new phases of the life cycle witness later derivatives of the earliest process still at work (*cf.*, Erikson, 1959). However, as we see it, the principal psychological achievements in this process take place in the period from about the fourth or fifth to the thirtieth or thirty-sixth month of age, a period that we refer to, in accordance with Annemarie Weil's (1954) helpful suggestion, as the separation-individuation phase.

During the course of a rather unsystematic, naturalistic pilot study, we

*The work described here was partially supported in 1970 and 1971 by the FFRP, New Haven, Connecticut. Presented at a meeting of the Washington Psychoanalytic Society, April 21, 1972, and at a meeting of the Philadelphia Psychoanalytic Society, May 12, 1972. This paper is one part of a forthcoming book, *On Human Symbiosis and the Vicissitudes of Individuation, Vol. II. The Separation-Individuation Process and Its Minor Deviations*, by the author with Fred Pine, Ph.D. and Anni Bergman, M.A., to be published by the International Universities Press, Inc., in 1973.

could not help taking note of certain clusters of variables, at certain crossroads of the individuation process, insofar as they repeated themselves at certain points of the maturational timetable. This strongly suggested to us that it would be to our advantage to subdivide the data that we were collecting on the intrapsychic separation and individuation process in accordance with the behavioral and other surface referents of that process that we had found to be repeatedly observable (*cf.*, Mahler, 1963, 1965). Our subdivision was into four subphases: *differentiation, practicing, rapprochement,* and a fourth subphase, occurring during the third year, which, the longer we studied it, the more cautiously did we have to designate it as "*the child on the way to object constancy.*" And according to my definition, it should be regarded as the stage in which a unified representation of the object becomes intrapsychically available, as the love object had been available to the child in the outside world during his complete and later partial need-satisfying object relationship stage.

When inner pleasure prevails as the result of the child's being safely anchored within the symbiotic orbit (which is mainly proprioceptive and contact perceptual) and when pleasure in the maturationally widening outer sensory perception (as, for example, vision) stimulates outward directed attention cathexis, these two forms of attention cathexis can oscillate freely (*cf.*, Spiegel, 1959; Rose, 1964). The result is an optimal symbiotic state out of which expansion beyond the symbiotic orbit and smooth differentiation from the mother's body can take place. This process, to which I gave the name "hatching out," may be looked upon as a gradual ontogenetic evolution of the sensorium—the perceptual conscious system—a "tuning in" process that leads to the infant's having a more permanently alert sensorium when he is awake (*cf.* also, Wolff, 1959).

It is during the first subphase of separation-individuation that all normal infants achieve, through maturation of apparatuses, their first tentative steps of breaking away, in a bodily sense, from their hitherto completely passive lap-babyhood—the stage of dual unity with the mother. They push themselves with arms, trunk, and legs against the holding mother, as if to have a better look at her, as well as the surroundings. One is able to see their individually different inclinations and patterns, as well as the general characteristics of the stage of differentiation itself. All five-to-six-month-old infants like to venture and stay just a bit of a distance away from the enveloping arms of the mother; as soon as their motor function permits, they like to slide down from mother's lap, but they tend to remain as near as possible to her and to play at her feet.

Once the infant has become sufficiently individuated to recognize the mother, visually and tactilely, as not just part of the symbiotic dyad but as his partner in it, the fact that he is ready to take this step is indicated by his preferential, specific smiling response to and for mother. At about the same time, or perhaps within an interval of a few weeks, he then turns, with greater or less wonderment and apprehension (commonly called "stranger reaction"), to a prolonged visual and tactile exploration and study of the faces of others, from afar or at close range. He appears to be comparing and checking the features—appearance, feel, contour, and texture—of the stranger's face with his mother's face, as well as with whatever inner image he may have of her. He also seems to check back, apparently to compare all other interesting new experiences with the mother's gestalt, her face, in particular.

It should be emphasized that we view separation and individuation as intertwined developmental processes, rather than as a single process. And they may proceed divergently, as the result of a developmental lag of one or the other. We have observed that children who achieve premature locomotor development, and are therefore able and prompted to separate physically from their mothers, may become prematurely aware of their own separateness much before their individuation (reality testing, cognition, etc.) has given them the means with which to cope with this awareness. On the other hand, we have found that in infants with overprotective and infantilizing mothers, individuation may develop well ahead, and may result in a lag of boundary formation and a lag in readiness to function as a separate individual without undue anxiety.

The period of differentiation is followed or, we might better say, is overlapped by a practicing period. This takes place usually from about seven to ten months, and continues to fifteen or sixteen months of age. In the course of processing our data, we found it useful to think of the practicing period in two parts: (a) the early practicing subphase, which overlaps with differentiation and is ushered in by the infant's earliest ability to physically move away from mother through crawling, climbing, and righting himself, yet still holding on; and (b) the practicing period proper, phenomenologically characterized by free upright locomotion.

During the early practicing subphase, throughout which crawling, paddling, pivoting, climbing, and righting himself are practiced by the infant, usually with much glee, these functions widen the child's world. Not only can he take a more active role in determining closeness and distance to mother, but the perceptual modalities that had up till then been used to explore the relatively familiar environment are suddenly exposed to a wider world; the sensorimotor intelligence, in Piaget's sense, takes a big step forward.

The optimal psychological distance in this early practicing subphase would seem to be one that allows the infant, whose movements are mostly quadrupedal, freedom and opportunity for exploration at some physical distance from mother. It should be noted, however, that during the entire practicing subphase mother continues to be needed as a stable point, a 'home base' to fulfil the need for refueling through physical contact. We have seen seven-to-ten-month-old infants crawling or rapidly paddling to their mother, righting themselves on her leg, touching her in other ways, or just leaning against her. This phenomenon was termed by Furer (1959/1960) "emotional refueling." It is easy to observe how the wilting and fatigued infant "perks up" in the shortest time, following such contact, after which he quickly goes on with his explorations, once again absorbed in pleasure in his own functioning.

The Practicing Subphase Proper

With the spurt in autonomous functions, such as cognition, but especially upright locomotion, the "love affair with the world" (Greenacre, 1957) begins. The toddler takes the greatest step in human individuation. He walks freely with upright posture. Thus, the plane of his vision changes; from an entirely new vantage point he finds unexpected and changing perspectives, pleasures, and frustrations (*cf.*, Greenacre). At this new visual level there is more to see, more to hear, more to touch, and all this is experienced in the upright bipedal position. How this new world is experienced seems to be subtly related to the mother, who is the center of the child's universe from which he gradually moves out into ever-widening perimeters.

During this precious six-to-eight-month period, for the junior toddler (ten-twelve to sixteen-eighteen months) the world is his oyster. Libidinal cathexis shifts substantially into the service of the rapidly growing autonomous ego and its functions, and the child seems to be intoxicated with his own faculties and with the greatness of his world. It is after the child has taken his first upright independent steps (which, by the way, more often than not he takes in a direction away from mother, or even during her absence) that one is able to mark the onset of the practicing period par excellence and of reality testing. Now, there begins a steadily increasing libidinal investment in practicing motor skills and in exploring the expanding environment, both human and inanimate. The chief characteristic of this practicing period is the child's great narcissistic investment in his own functions, his own body, as well as in the objects and objectives of his expanding 'reality'. Along with this, we see a relatively great imperviousness to knocks and falls and to other frustrations, such as a toy being grabbed away by another child. Substitute adults in the familiar setup of our nursery are easily accepted (in contrast to what occurs during the next subphase of separation-individuation).

As the child, through the maturation of his locomotor apparatus, begins to venture farther away from the mother's feet, he is often so absorbed in his own activities that for long periods of time he appears to be oblivious to the mother's presence. However, he returns periodically to the mother, seeming to need her physical proximity from time to time.

The smoothly separating and individuating toddler finds solace for the minimal threats of object loss that are probably entailed in each new stage of progressive development in his rapidly developing ego functions. The child concentrates on practicing the mastery of his own skills and autonomous capacities. He is exhilarated by his own capacities, continually delighted with the discoveries he is making in his expanding world, quasi-enamored with the world and with his own omnipotence. We might consider the possibility that the elation of this subphase has to do not only with the exercise of the ego apparatuses, but also with the infant's delighted escape from re-engulfment by the still-existing symbiotic pull from the mother.

Just as the infant's peekaboo games seem to turn at this juncture from passive to active, to the active losing and regaining of the need-gratifying love object, so too does the toddler's constant running off (until he is swooped up by his mother) turn from passive to active the fear of being re-engulfed by, or fused with, mother. It turns into an active distancing and reuniting game with her. This behavior reassures the toddler that mother will want to catch him and take him up in her arms. We need not assume that this behavior is intended to serve such functions when it first emerges, but quite clearly it produces these effects and can then be intentionally repeated.

Most children, during the practicing subphase proper, appear to have major periods of exhilaration, or at least of relative elation. They are impervious to knocks and falls. They are low-keyed only when they become aware that mother is absent from the room, at which times their gestural and performance motility slows down, interest in their surroundings diminishes, and they appear to be preoccupied with inwardly concentrated attention and with what Rubinfine (1961) calls "imaging." During this period, the toddler's sensorimotor intelligence imperceptibly develops into representational intelligence and into concomitant emotional growth that characterizes the third subphase of the separation-individuation process—the period of rapprochement.

The Period of Rapprochement

The rapprochement subphase (from about fifteen to twenty-two months, and very often far beyond the second birthday) begins hypothetically with the mastery of upright locomotion and the consequent diminishing absorption in locomotion and other autonomous functioning.

By the middle of the second year of life, the infant has become a toddler. He now becomes more and more aware of and makes greater and greater use of his physical separateness. Side by side with the growth of his cognitive faculties and the increasing differentiation of his emotional life, there is also, however, a noticeable waning of his previous imperviousness to frustration, as well as of his relative obliviousness to the mother's presence. Increased separation anxiety can be observed—a fear of object loss that can be inferred from many behaviors; for example, from the fact that when the child hurts himself, he visibly discovers to his perplexity that his mother is not automatically at hand. The relative lack of concern about the mother's presence that was characteristic of the practicing subphase is now replaced by active approach behavior, and by a seeming constant concern with the mother's whereabouts. As the toddler's awareness of separateness grows, stimulated by his maturationally acquired ability physically to move away from his mother and by his cognitive growth, he now seems to have an increased need and wish for his mother to share with him his every new acquisition of skill and experience. These are the reasons for which I called this subphase of separation-individuation the period of rapprochement.

Now after mastery of free walking and beginning internalization, the toddler begins to experience, more or less gradually and more or less keenly, the obstacles that lie in the way of what was, at the height of his "practicing," an omnipotent exhilaration, a quite evidently anticipated "conquest of the world." Side by side with the acquisition of primitive skills and perceptual cognitive faculties, there has been an increasingly clear differentiation, a separation, between the intrapsychic representation of the object and the self-representation. At the very height of mastery, toward the end of the practicing period, however, it has already begun to dawn on the junior toddler that the world is *not* his oyster; that he must cope with it more or less "on his own," very often as a relatively helpless, small, and separate individual, unable to command relief or assistance merely by feeling the need for them or giving voice to that need.

The quality and measure of the *wooing* behavior of the toddler toward his mother during this subphase provide important clues to the assessment of the normality of the individuation process. We believe that it is during this rapprochement subphase that the foundation for subsequent relatively stable mental health or borderline pathology is laid.

Incompatibilities and misunderstandings between mother and child can be observed at this period even in the case of the normal mother and her normal toddler, these being in part specific to certain seeming contradictions of this subphase. Thus, in the subphase of renewed, active wooing, the toddler's demands for his mother's constant participation seem contradictory to the mother: while the toddler is now not as dependent and helpless as he was half a year before, and seems eager to become less and less so, he even more insistently expects the mother to share every aspect of his life. During this subphase, some mothers are not able to accept the child's demanding behavior; others cannot tolerate gradual separation—they cannot face the fact that the child is becoming increasingly independent of and separate from them, and is no longer a part of them.

In this third subphase, while individuation proceeds very rapidly and the child exercises it to the limit, he is also becoming more and more aware of his separateness and is beginning to employ all kinds of partly internalized, partly still outwardly directed and acted-out coping mechanisms in order to resist separation from the mother. No matter how insistently the toddler tries to coerce the mother, however, she and he no longer function effectively as a dual unit; that is to say, he can no longer get her to participate with him in his still maintained delusion of parental omnipotence. Likewise, as the other pole of the erstwhile dual unity, the mother must recognize a separate individual, her child, in his own autonomous right. Verbal communication has now become more and more necessary; gestural coercion on the part of the toddler, or mutual preverbal empathy between mother and child, will no longer suffice to attain the child's goal of satisfaction, of well-being (*cf.*, Joffe and Sandler, 1965).

Similarly, the mother can no longer make the child subservient to her own predilections and wishes.

The junior toddler gradually realizes that his love objects (his parents) are separate individuals with their own individual interests. He must gradually and painfully give up his delusion of his own grandeur, often through dramatic fights with mother, less so it seemed to us, with father. This is a crossroad that we have termed the 'rapprochement crisis.'

Depending upon her own adjustment, the mother may react either by continued emotional availability and playful participation in the toddler's world or by a gamut of less desirable attitudes. From the data we have accumulated so far, we would state strongly that the mother's continued emotional availability is essential if the child's autonomous ego is to attain optimal functional capacity. If the mother is "quietly available" with a ready supply of object libido, if she shares the toddling adventurer's exploits, playfully reciprocates and thus helps his attempts at imitation, at externalization and internalization, then the relationship between mother and toddler is able to progress to the point where verbal communication takes over, even though vivid gestural behavior, that is, affectomotility, still predominates. By the end of the second or the beginning of the third year, the predictable emotional participation of the mother seems to facilitate the rich unfolding that is taking place in the toddler's thought processes, reality testing, and coping behavior.

The toddler's so-called "shadowing" of the mother at fifteen to twenty months of age (an often encountered phenomenon that is characteristic of this subphase) seems obligatory, except in the cases of those mothers who by their protracted doting and intrusiveness, which spring from their own symbiotic-parasitic needs, become themselves the "shadowers" of the child. In normal cases, a slight shadowing by the toddler after the hatching process gives way to some degree of object constancy in the course of the third year. However, the less emotionally available the mother has become at the time of rapprochement, the more insistently and even desperately does the toddler attempt to woo her. In some cases, this process drains so much of the child's available developmental energy that, as a result, not enough may be left for the evolution of the many ascending functions of his ego. We shall illustrate the characteristics and certain typical conflicts of the rapprochement subphase with a few vignettes.

During the period of rapprochement Barney behaved with particular poignancy. He had gone through a typical, although precocious, "love affair with the world" in which he would often fall and hurt himself and always react with great imperviousness. Gradually he became perplexed to find that his mother was not on hand to rescue him, and he then began to cry when he fell. As he became aware of his separateness from his mother, his previous calm acceptance of knocks and falls began to give way to increased separation anxiety.

Early maturation of Barney's locomotor function had confronted him with the fact of physical separateness from his mother, before he was fully ready for it at nine to ten months of age. For this reason, we believe, he displayed to an exaggerated degree during his period of rapprochement the opposite of "shadowing." He would challenge mother by darting away from her, confidently and correctly expecting her to run after him and sweep him into her arms; at least momentarily he had undone the physical separateness from her. The mother's own increasingly frantic response to the dangerous darting made Barney, in turn, intensify and prolong this behavior so that his mother for a while despaired of being able to cope with Barney's "recklessness." We see this behavior as the result of the precocious maturation of the child's locomotor functions coupled with the relative lag in maturation of his emotional and intellectual functions. Hence, he could not properly evaluate, or gauge, the potential dangers of his locomotor feats.

The imbalance between the developmental line of separation and that of individuation, causing a jumbled intermeshing of factors of the second, the practicing, and the third, the rapprochement subphases, appeared to have set an overdetermined pattern of accident proneness in this child (*cf.*, Frankl, 1963). Barney's reckless behavior had introjective qualities as well. It was, as every symptomatic behavior is, overdetermined. It no doubt also derived from identification with, or better stated, from introjection of his father's sports-loving nature. (The children were permitted to watch and admire, and, at times, to participate in their father's highly risky athletic feats.)

Barney's mother, whom we observed as the ideal mother during Barney's early practicing subphase, now at his chronological age of the rapprochement subphase would alternately restrict Barney or, from sheer exhaustion, give up altogether her usual alertness to his needs and her previous high level of attunement to his cues. She would either rush to him in any situation, whether or not his need was real, or she would find herself keeping away from him at a time when she was really needed; in other words, her immediate availability became unpredictable to her, no less than to him.

The disturbance of the relationship between Barney and his mother during this period was not a total one, however, nor did it, we believe, inflict permanent damage on Barney's personality development. Neither hostility, splitting, nor increased and more permanent ambivalence resulted. Barney continued to bring everything within reach to his mother to share, filling her lap. He would have periods in which he sat quietly and did jigsaw puzzles or looked at picture books with his mother, while remaining full of confidence and basic trust toward the world beyond the mother.

This mother-child relationship became mutually satisfactory again with the advent of the fourth subphase, as a result of which Barney in the third year became a patient, well-functioning, and, within normal limits, more sedentary child. I believe that Barney's very satisfactory symbiotic, differentiation, and early practicing subphases, as well as the fact that his father (with whom he roughhoused and whom he hero worshipped), became an important part of his world during his second year of life, were all favorable factors in his development.

A different manifestation of the crisis of the third subphase was observable in Anna. Her mother's marked emotional unavailability made Anna's practicing and exploratory period brief and subdued. Never certain of her mother's availability, and therefore always preoccupied with it, Anna found it difficult to invest libido in her surroundings and in her own functioning. After a brief spurt of practicing, she would return to her mother and try to engage her with greater intensity by all possible means. From such relatively direct expressions of the need for her mother as bringing her a book to read to her, or hitting at the mother's ever-present book in which she was engrossed, Anna turned to more desperate measures, such as falling or spilling cookies on the floor and stamping on them, always with an eye to gaining her mother's attention, if not involvement with her.

Anna's mother was observed to be greatly absorbed in her own interests which were anything but child-centered. She emphasized with seeming satisfaction and with some mock self-depreciation that both her older children seemed to have preferred their father, who had apparently shared the mother's task in diapering and bottle-feeding the babies.

We observed in Anna, as early as the ninth and tenth month, an increased clamoring for closeness to mother, a refusal to accept any substitutes in the mother's presence, let alone in her absence, and a greatly reduced pleasure in and diminution of activity. She had far too little investment of libido in practicing the autonomous partial functions of her individuating ego; approaching, even beseeching, behavior toward mother far outweighed any involvement in activity away from mother. Hence there was a complete overlapping and intermingling of characteristics of both the practicing and rapprochement subphases.

Whereas all the landmarks of individuation—the development of partial motor skills, of communication, of imitation and identification, and of defenses—appeared at appropriate times, there was a minimal progress toward object constancy (in Hartmann's sense).

Concomitant with Anna's inability to let mother out of sight, her activities and movements were low-keyed: they lacked the vivacity and luster that was characteristic of the behavior of her practicing contemporaries. Her happier moods and greater vivacity, which coincided with the achievement of free walking, were fleeting. On the other hand, her language development was even precocious.

Anna's chronic frustration in her attempt to win her mother's love had noticeably impaired the amalgamation of libido and aggression. Her ambivalence visibly affected her mood, which was characterized by ready smiles when her mother or a father substitute approached her, but which quite readily switched to the opposite—moroseness, unhappiness, and even despair. This reminded us of the mood swings and fluctuations of self-esteem that we observe so conspicuously in borderline phenomena in the psychoanalytic situation.

In our study we had a fairly good setup, we feel, for gauging the junior and later the senior toddler's capacity to function in the mother's presence, and to compare it with his functioning during the brief periods of her physical absence. The latter situation varies from the mother's just being in the adjacent nursery, or in the nearby interviewing room, to being out of the building. The toddler stays within a familiar setting, with familiar adults and contemporaries.

It may be of interest for me to relate a few details of Anna's personality development in the fateful "second eighteen-month period of her life." It had already been observed by us that Anna's play had a quality of early reaction-formation. The mother reported that Anna had shown disgust when she gave her a portion of her older brother's clay to play with, and this had been as early as eighteen or nineteen months. Anna's toilet training started at about twenty months, seemingly without pressure. Anna was already saying the word "do-do" at that age and at first her mother was quite well attuned to cues from her concerning her toilet needs. She praised Anna whenever the latter produced either urine or feces. From her twentieth month on, Anna was repeatedly heard saying, "Bye-bye, wee

wee,'' as she pulled the chain to flush the toilet. Soon, however, many observers noted that Anna was beginning to request bathroom trips whenever she wanted her mother's attention, or whenever she wanted to prevent mother from leaving the room for an interview—in any event, more frequently than she could actually have had a bowel or urinary urge.

Anna was bowel trained by twenty-two months, and at that age she went for days without wetting. At the beginning of toilet training (particularly bowel training), we saw that Anna was willing and able to oblige her mother so that both mother and daughter found in the toileting an emotionally and positively charged meeting ground. But within two months, toileting had been drawn into the conflictual sphere of this mother-child interaction. At around twenty-three months of age, Anna used wetting all across the room as a weapon. Her mother was then pregnant and, as time went on, her pregnancy caused her to become narcissistically self-absorbed. She had fewer and fewer positive reactions to Anna's demands to accompany her to the upstairs bathroom at home. In fact, she told us that she asked her then four-year-old son to substitute for her in taking Anna to the toilet. The boy, we later learned, did not miss the opportunity to provocatively and aggressively display his manly prowess, his penis, to his little sister. Anna's penis envy thus gained momentum, as did her defiance of mother.

A battle around toilet training ensued between Anna and her mother. At around two years of age, twenty-four to twenty-seven months to be exact, Anna started to use her sphincter control to defy her mother. From twenty-two months on, severe constipation developed in the wake of Anna's deliberate withholding of her feces.

We did not see Anna for about three months (from her twenty-fifth to her twenty-eighth month) during which time a sister was born.

Anna returned at twenty-nine months of age. Her mother carried the baby sister, Susie, with Anna following close behind. The mother looked harassed and tired as she entered the room, and, with a tight smile, exclaimed, ''I feel filthy dirty, and so mad, mad, mad!'' She complained that Anna ''is driving me crazy.'' Anna had indeed been very difficult, whining, and demanding, but, in addition, for the past two or three days had been withholding her feces and had not had a bowel movement. The mother mimicked Anna as she held her thighs tightly together and stamped her feet. She also said that Anna was in pain most of the time and actually very uncomfortable. The pediatrician, she reported, had assured her that this was a normal occurrence after the birth of a new baby and that she should take it calmly and pay no attention to Anna's toileting at this time. Making a hopeless gesture, ''But I simply can't do it; I just get so mad.''

Anna was observed in the toddler's room playing with water. This, however, is not the kind of play that children her age usually enjoy, and it appeared to us to be of a more "compulsive" nature. She began to scrub a bowl to which flour had stuck and was very determined to scrub it clean, becoming annoyed when she could not do so. She looked up at the observer and said, "bowl not clean." All this while Anna seemed most uncomfortable. She obviously needed to defecate and was under continual bowel pressure. Beads of perspiration appeared on her forehead and the color would come and go from her face. Twice she ran to the toilet. She sat on the toilet and urinated; then she got up and became preoccupied with flushing the toilet. She went back to the toddler room and listlessly played with dough, but again, and all during her play, Anna was in discomfort and kept jiggling and jumping, with the color repeatedly draining from her face. Finally, she jumped up and ran to the toilet, sat down on it, and said to the observer, "Get me a book." Sitting and straining, she looked up at the observer with a rather painful expression on her face, and said, "Don't let Mommy in, keep Mommy out, keep Mommy out." The observer encouraged her to talk about this some more, and she said, "Mommy would hurt me." She then looked at the book, at the pictures of the baby cats and baby horses, and as the observer was showing the pictures of the baby farm animals, Anna began to look as though she was particularly uncomfortable. She looked down at her panties, which had become stained, and said she wanted clean ones. Finally, in extreme discomfort, she seemed unable to hold back the feces any longer, and called out, "Get me my Mommy, get me my Mommy." Her mother came quickly, sat down beside her, and Anna requested that she read to her.

A participant observer watched from the booth, and noted that the mother was reading the same book about farm animals that the first observer had previously read to Anna. Pointing to the animals, the toddler was heard to say, "My Poppy has a piggy in his tummy." Her mother looked perplexed and asked Anna, "What?" Anna repeated the sentence. The mother seemed distraught as her daughter was now talking gibberish. She felt Anna's forehead to see whether she was feverish, but the child smiled, pointed to the book again, and said, "No, it's a baby horse." At this point, with a blissful expression on her face, Anna defecated. After her bowel movement, Anna was more relaxed; she played peekaboo with the door, asking the observer to stand behind it.

In this episode, the sequence of behaviors and verbalizations enabled us to draw conclusions, to reconstruct, as it were, the development of Anna's early infantile neurosis in statu nascendi. With her deficient emotional supplies from maternal support, the development of autonomy had not been enough to gradually replace the obligatory early infantile symbiotic omnipotence. In spite of her excellent endowment, Anna was unable to ward off the onslaught of separation anxiety and the collapse of self-esteem. Her anger at mother for not having given her a penis was unmistakable in her verbal material. She coveted those gifts that mother received from father, among which was a porcelain thimble which she was allowed to keep. Anna turned in her disappointment to father, and, when mother became pregnant, in a perplexed way she obviously equated gift with baby, with feces, and with penis. She showed great confusion about the contents of the body: her own pregnancy fantasies were quite evident, but she was unclear as to who had what in his or her belly. She seemed to expect a baby in the belly of her father, as well as in her mother's. The equation of feces = baby = phallus was explicitly expressed in her behavior.

The mother-toddler relationship was such that Anna had to defend the good mother against her destructive rage. This she did by splitting the object world into good and bad. The good was always the absent part-object, never the present object. To clarify this, let me describe another sequence of events and verbalizations in Anna's third year. Whenever her mother left, she had temper tantrums and would cling to her beloved and familiar play teacher, but not without verbally abusing her while still keeping her arms around her neck. When they read a book together, Anna found fault with every picture and every sentence that the playroom teacher offered; she scolded the teacher, everything was the opposite of what the teacher said, and she was "Bad, Bad, Bad."

I watched this behavior from the observation booth and ventured quietly into the playroom where I sat at the farthest corner from Anna and her loved-and-hated teacher. Anna immediately caught sight of me and angrily ordered me out. I softly interpreted to Anna that I understood: Anna really wanted nobody else but her Mommy to come back in through that door and that was why she was very angry. She was also very angry because not Mommy but the observer was reading to her. I said that she knew that Mommy would soon come back. With my quasi interpretation, some libidinal channels seemed to have been tapped; the child put her head on the observer's shoulder and began to cry softly. Soon, the mother came back. It was most instructive to see, however, that not a flicker of radiance or happiness was noticeable in Anna at that reunion. Her very first words were "What did you bring me?" and the whining and discontent started all over again. For quite a while Anna did not succeed in attaining a unified object representation or in reconciling the synthesized good and bad qualities of the love-object. At the same time, her own self-representation and self-esteem suffered.

By contrast, what we saw in Barney's case was merely a transitional developmental deviation in the form of a rapprochement crisis. In Anna we observed a truly neurotic symptom-formation, developing on the basis of a rather unsatisfactory mother-child relationship yet activated and, to a great extent, produced by accumulated traumata.

Till way beyond the fourth subphase, Anna's relationship to her mother remained full of ambivalence. Her school performance was excellent, however. Constipation continued as a symptom for several years. Her social development was good. Our follow-up study will tell us more about the fate of her infantile neurosis.[1]

Summary

In our observation of two toddlers, we saw why the rapprochement crisis occurs and why in some instances it becomes and may remain an unresolved intrapsychic conflict. It may set an unfavorable fixation point interfering with later oedipal development, or at best add to the difficulty of the resolution of the oedipus complex.

The developmental task at the very height of the separation-individuation struggle in the rapprochement subphase is a tremendous one. Oral, anal, and early genital pressures and conflicts meet and accumulate at this important landmark in personality development. There is a need to renounce symbiotic onmipotence, and there is also heightened awareness of the body image and pressure in the body, especially at the points of zonal libidinization.

Three great anxieties of childhood meet at this developmental stage. (1) While the fear of object loss and abandonment is partly relieved, it is also greatly complicated by the internalization of parental demands that indicate beginning superego development. In consequence, we observe an intensified vulnerability on the part of the rapprochement toddler. (2) Fear in terms of loss of the love of the object results in an extra-sensitive reaction to approval and disapproval by the parent. (3) There is greater awareness of bodily feelings and pressures, in

[1]The follow-up study is being conducted by John B. McDevitt, M.D. with Anni Bergman, Emmagene Kamaiko, and Laura Salchow, the author of this paper serving as consultant. It is sponsored by the Board of the Masters Children's Center.

Greenacre's sense. This is augmented by awareness of bowel and urinary sensations during the toilet training process, even in quite normal development. There is often displayed, and in some instances quite dramatically, a reaction to the discovery of the anatomical sex difference with prematurely precipitated castration anxiety.

REFERENCES

Erikson, Erik H. (1959). *Identity and the Life Cycle. Selected Papers.* Psychological Issues, Vol. I., No. 1, Monograph 1. New York: International Universities Press, Inc.

Frankl, Liselotte (1963). "Self-Preservation and the Development of Accident Proneness in Children and Adolescents," in *The Psychoanalytic Study of the Child, Vol. XVIII.* New York: International Universities Press, Inc., pp. 464-483.

Furer, Manuel (1959/1960). Personal communications.

Greenacre, Phyllis (1957). "The Childhood of the Artist: Libidinal Phase Development and Giftedness," in *The Psychoanalytic Study of the Child, Vol. XII.* New York: International Universities Press, Inc., pp. 47-72.

Joffe, W. G., and J. Sandler (1965). "Notes on Pain, Depression, and Individuation," in *The Psychoanalytic Study of the Child, Vol. XX.* New York: International Universities Press, Inc., pp. 394-424.

Mahler, Margaret S. (1963). "Thoughts about Development and Individuation," in *The Psychoanalytic Study of the Child, Vol. XVIII.* New York: International Universities Press, Inc., pp. 307-324.

——— (1965). "On the Significance of the Normal Separation-Individuation Phase, in *Drives, Affects, Behavior, Vol. II,* ed. Max Schur. New York: International Universities Press, Inc., pp. 161-169.

Rose, Gilbert J. (1964). *Creative Imagination in Terms of Ego "Core" and Boundaries. Int. J. Psa.,* XLV, 75-84.

Rubinfine, David L. (1961). "Perception, Reality Testing, and Symbolism," in *The Psychoanalytic Study of the Child, Vol. XVI.* New York: International Universities Press, Inc., pp. 73-89.

Spiegel, Leo A. (1959). "The Self, The Sense of Self, and Perception," in *The Psychoanalytic Study of the Child, Vol. XIV.* New York: International Universities Press, Inc., pp. 81-109.

Weil, Annemarie (1954). Personal communication.

Wolff, Peter H. (1959). *Observations on Newborn Infants. Psychosomatic Med.,* XXI, 110-118.

11. Development in Middle Childhood*

Alexander Thomas, M.D.
PROFESSOR OF PSYCHIATRY
NEW YORK UNIVERSITY SCHOOL OF MEDICINE

Stella Chess, M.D.
PROFESSOR OF CHILD PSYCHOLOGY
NEW YORK UNIVERSITY SCHOOL OF MEDICINE

Much attention has been paid to many of the general adaptational issues confronting children between the ages of 6 and 12. To Freud this was a period of "latency" between the passing of the Oedipal stage and the beginning of adolescence. During this period, the energy of infantile sexuality is turned away either wholly or partially from sexual utilization and directed toward other aims (7). More specifically in psychoanalytic thinking, the latency child "transfer[s] libido to contemporaries, community groups, teachers, leaders, impersonal ideals and aim-inhibited, sublimated interests" (6).

While the Freudian use of latency implies a kind of "psychosexual moratorium in human development" (5), it "does not mean that changes do not occur during this period. In the psychoanalytic view, it is primarily a period of acquisition of culturally valued skills, values and roles" (1). However, latency has sometimes been used in the literature as an all-encompassing concept denoting the absence of change during this age period without recognition that Freud restricted its meaning to issues of sexuality. As a result, Shaw calls it "an unfortunate term since it suggests that nothing really important is happening and that the child is simply waiting for puberty to begin" (21).

The concept of latency arising from the emphasis of classical Freudian theory on the vicissitudes of sexual development has led even some writers with a psychoanalytic orientation to question the usefulness of this theory

*From *Seminars in Psychiatry*, 4:4 (November) 1972, pp. 331-341. Reprinted by permission of Grune & Stratton, Inc. and the authors.

for understanding the 6-12-year age period. Thus, Lidz states that "psychoanalytic psychology has relatively little to offer concerning the critical aspects of the period" (14). Even the concept of latency in sex is open to question. Jersild, a leading student of child development, states that "when viewed in the light of empirical studies of children's interest and actions during this period, 'latency' cannot be taken literally. For many children, interest in sex during this period is not latent or inactive or held in abeyance but is distinctly manifest and active. In normal development, sex never takes a holiday" (8).

Erikson calls this age period the "age of industry." Having "mastered the ambulatory field and the organ modes [and having] experienced a sense of finality regarding the fact that there is no workable future within the womb of his family, the child becomes ready to apply himself to given skills and tasks. . . . To bring a productive situation to completion is an aim which gradually supersedes the whims and wishes of his autonomous organism" (4). For the child, "this is socially a most decisive stage," during which the dangers to identity development are a sense of inadequacy and inferiority. These may arise if the child's family life has not "prepared him for school life, or when school life . . . fail[s] to sustain the promises of earlier stages" (4).

Sullivan considers these years in terms of a child's interpersonal relationships. He refers to a "juvenile era" that follows childhood and precedes preadolescence which he puts at 8½ or 9½ to 12 years of age (25). The juvenile is marked by the "maturation of a need for compeers," even an "urgent need for compeers with whom to have one's existence." School becomes "the great new arena for experience," and the "talents for cooperation, competition and compromise" are developed. For this author, a child's developing a relationship to a social environment and peer groups is crucial in that stage. It is the beginning of the end of a youngster's "egocentristic" outlook and the start of the true social orientation he develops in preadolescence.

While these investigators have focused on the motivational and psychodynamic aspects of personality development, Piaget has highlighted factors of cognitive functioning that are crucial in the middle years of childhood (18). He has found that 6-11-year-olds are in the stage of concrete operations, during which they develop the concept of conservation and the notion of invariance upon which rest the later acquisition of complex reasoning.

Lidz has presented a thoughtful summary of the work of these investigators and has, in addition, suggested "other character traits that appear to have their roots in this period of life'' (14). These are a ''sense of belonging'' and a ''sense of responsibility'' both of which are basic to the trait of ''leadership.'' He notes, too, that ''adapting to . . . new environments and finding his place in them has required a substantial reorganization of the personality'' of the school-age child.

The above authors have made major contributions to our understanding of the general developmental tasks facing youngsters in middle childhood. However, they have, for the most part, not paid as much attention to how individual children characteristically meet these specific new demands. They have also focused on broad theoretical issues rather than on the particular dynamics of specific interactive processes.

The New York Longitudinal Study

The New York Longitudinal Study, in which the behavioral development of 136 children has been followed from the first months of infancy onward, has provided data on a number of features of development during the 6-12-year age period. These have included the specific nature of behavioral attributes that characterize this stage of development, the frequency of new behavior disorders and symptoms as compared to earlier ages, the follow-up of behavior disorders first manifested in the preschool and early school periods, and the dynamics of the child-environment interactional process.

In our longitudinal study, data has been gathered anterospectively at sequential age levels on the nature of each child's individual characteristics of functioning at home, in school, and in standard test situations; on special environmental events and the child's reactions to them; and on parental attitudes and child-care practice (5). Parent and teacher interviews, as well as direct observation of the youngsters, have been the source of most data. In addition, each child has been tested by a staff psychologist at 3 and 6 years and at some time during his middle childhood years. The staff child psychiatrist has done a psychiatric evaluation of each child presenting symptoms. Wherever necessary, neurologic examination or special testing (such as perceptual tests) have been done.

A major focus of the longitudinal study has been on the delineation of temperamental characteristics in the early years of life and their relationship to later functioning, to the development of behavior disorders and to academic achievement and school functioning. The definition of temperamental characteristics, methods of data collection and analysis, and findings have been reported extensively in the literature (2, 3, 26-28).

Our theoretical framework from the beginning has involved an interactionist approach that views development as a constantly evolving process of interaction between the child and his environment from the very first days of life onward (and even prenatally). We have attempted to avoid simplistic environmentalist or constitutional approaches and any adherence to a "heredity" versus "environment" dichotomy. The concept of a continuous evolving organism-environment interaction has been formulated in various ways in the work of Pavlov (17), Stern (24), and Lewin (13), among others, and has been precisely stated by Schneirla and Rosenblatt (20):

> Behavior is typified by reciprocal stimulative relationships . . . Behavioral development[,] because it centers on and depends upon reciprocal stimulative processes between female and young, is essentially social from the start. Mammalian behavioral development is best conceived as a unitary system of processes changing progressively under the influence of an intimate interrelationship of factors of maturation and of experience—with maturation defined as the developmental contributions of tissue growth and differentiation and their secondary processes, experience as the effects of stimulation and its organic traces on behavior.

An interactionist approach to individual development, therefore, involves the simultaneous scrutiny and analysis of responses of the organism and of the objective circumstances in which these responses occur. Individual differences in the degree and even quality of response to stimuli and demands must be considered as well as the specific nature of these environmental influences. Furthermore, the crucial factors in this dynamic interplay will vary both from one child to another and in the same child at different age periods. New behavioral attributes and abilities emerge as the child grows older, and fresh environmental demands and expectations replace or supplant those of earlier years. At the same time, previous patterns of interaction may persist and continue to influence the child's reactions to what is new.

Behavioral Characteristics

As indicated above, Erikson, Sullivan, and Lidz, among others, have defined in general terms some of the behaviors that characterize the middle childhood period. The specific traits through which industriousness, peer relations, and a sense of belonging are manifested have, however, not been spelled out by these authors.

We have started to examine the protocols of our study population in the 6-12-year age period to identify specific behavioral characteristics that appear ubiquitous and prominent and capable of differentiating the children from each other. Our initial effort has been in the 6-8-year period, for which we have parent reports, teacher reports, and school observations. (Also available are detailed descriptions of each child's behavior during IQ testing at 6 years, but these data have not as yet been utilized for the present analysis.) The protocols of ten children were selected at random, and an inductive content analysis of the behavioral data was done. Fifteen categories were defined, each of which could be rated on a three-point scale. These categories are: (1) Spontaneity (high vs. low): the child's initiation of an activity or the injection of his own ideas without overt instructions to do so. (2) Autonomy vs. interdependence: the child's requests for or rejection of help when unable to perform on his own. (3) Degree of organized activity (high vs. low). (4) Frequency of interaction with other children (high vs. low): the frequency with which a child interacts with others and the number of children he prefers. (5) Social assertiveness, positive (high vs. low): refers to whether or not the child stands up for his own rights and has leadership abilities. (6) Social assertiveness, negative (high vs. low): refers to the degree to which the child is disruptive, abusive, or domineering. (7) Popularity (high vs. low): how other youngsters respond to the child. (8) Frequency of initiation of interaction with others (high vs. low): how frequently the child initiates interactions with others. (9) Coping ability in disagreements with other children (high vs. low): how the child settles disagreements. (10). Independence vs. Dependency: absence or presence of demands for help when the child is capable of performing on his own. (11) Cooperation with rules, regulations, and routines (high vs. low). (12) Degree of participation and interest in various activities (high vs. low). (13) Decisiveness vs. indecisiveness: the child's ability to make up his own mind and stick to his decisions. (14) People vs. tasks: refers to the child's preference for activities (tasks) or people. (15) Emotional expressiveness (clear vs. unclear): can an observer tell what the child is feeling by his expression or verbalization?

Categories 1, 2, and 3 appear to relate primarily to the way in which a child undertakes activities and may be related to Erikson's overall category of industriousness. Categories 4 through 9 relate to the character of the child's social relationships. Categories 10 through 14 relate to both issues inasmuch as each describes both how the child goes about an activity and the way he relates to people. Category 15, the clarity of the youngster's emotional expressiveness, does not appear related to either his industry or his social relations, although it may indirectly affect the reactions of others to him.

The scoring of the protocols of the study sample as a whole is currently in progress. While the results are as yet incomplete, they appear to indicate that these categories can reliably differentiate these children in the 6-8-year period. When this analysis is completed, we plan to extend it to the older age periods, to determine the correlations between these behavioral traits and temperamental characteristics in the first 5 years of life, and to examine their relationship to the development and course of behavior disorders.

A number of these 15 behavioral characteristics can be identified in some of the children at ages earlier than 6 years. It is in the school-age period, however, that these traits appear to become prominent and ubiquitous.

These characteristics, of course, are not the only ways to describe school-age children. Other important aspects of their functioning—temperament, cognitive level, perceptual abilities, special talents—remain influential in determining the child-environment interaction, as was the case in the preschool period.

An additional new factor in psychologic development in the middle childhood years has been the transition from action to ideation that characterizes the course of development from infancy to adulthood. This transition was clearly evident in the sequential analysis of the characteristics of symptom expression and evolution in some of the children who developed behavior disorders in the preschool period that continued into the middle childhood years. In the earlier period, their symptoms were expressed primarily on an overt behavioral level. As they grew older, the symptoms became more and more ideational in character and reflected complex subjective states, attitudes, distorted self-images, and psychodynamic patterns of defense.

A typical example of this shift in symptom expression was found in a child, Diana, who as an infant had organic bowel symptoms, the result of a defect in anal structure. These symptoms did not respond satisfactorily to either physical or pharmacologic treatment. Her difficulties in evacuation became over time a source of tension and stress because of marked inconsistency in the mother's approach. The child also met disapproval in nursery school when teachers complained about having to clean up her intermittently huge and odorous evacuations. An avoidance mechanism developed in the 3-4-year age period, which Diana expressed primarily in behavioral terms: she withheld bowel movements, hid in corners to evacuate, and refused to use the toilet. As Diana grew older, her mother continued to be inconsistent in handling the issue and began to exhibit an overall tendency to minimize the extent of the problem. Diana herself also began to use this denial mechanism and tried to avoid acknowledging the existence of a problem. By 8½ years of age, she developed a neurotic denial mechanism in which she insisted that she had not soiled herself even when it was evident that she had and denied having to evacuate while wiggling to hold back a bowel movement. Although she persisted in denying having a bowel problem, she showed no overt or indirect manifestations of anxiety extending to other areas of functioning. However, at age 9 years, the reactions of disapproval by others in her environment became so sharp and frequent that her denial mechanism became ineffective. Diana became aware that her disguise was not perfect and finally requested help for her bowel problem.

Another example is a child with explosive tantrum-type behavior that led repeatedly to disapproval, condemnation, and punishment. As he grew older, he began to conceptualize the meaning of his behavior in terms of a derogatory self-image that was fated to endure forever and then developed the defense mechanism of avoidance. Another boy with quick adaptability as a prominent temperamental characteristic showed two periods of disturbance, at 4 and 8 years, with markedly different symptoms at each age. In both instances, the disturbance resulted primarily from inappropriate imitation of selected aspects of his father's behavior and attitudes. At age 4, the symptoms were basically behavioral, and, at age 8, ideational in character.

These three cases, among others, illustrate the shift in psychologic organization from action to ideation that becomes increasingly evident in the middle childhood years, both in normal development and in symptom formation.

Behavior Disorders

It is possible to divide the children in the longitudinal sample in the 6-12-year age period into five groups with regard to behavior disorder. First, there were those youngsters who had coped successfully with the demands of previous age periods and continued to do so in their school years. These children, a majority of those in the study, maintained a steady course of healthy development.

Second were those children who had behavior difficulties in earlier age periods, which now were resolved, either because the stress on the child was diminished or eliminated or the child's maturation gradually enabled him to cope successfully with previous excessive stresses. This change occurred spontaneously in some cases, in others through therapeutic intervention. In these cases, the original excessive stress had not produced any structural psychologic changes in the child, such as fixed neurotic personality characteristics, so that the youngster could begin to cope successfully with his environment and develop in a healthy direction with no significant neurotic residue.

Third, there were children whose behavioral difficulties in earlier age periods had been resolved, either spontaneously or following therapy, but who later developed new maladaptive behavior patterns or were confronted by a recurrent or new environmental demand or expectation that was excessively stressful for their capacities. In these cases, there was a recurrence of behavior disturbance. When this happened, the symptoms shown by a child might be similar to those found earlier, or they might be quite different, due to the youngster's higher level of psychologic functioning.

Fourth, there were those children whose behavior disorders at earlier age periods continued into their school years, either because there had been no lessening of the excessive stress with which they were confronted, or because structural psychologic changes had developed, or both.

Finally, there were a few youngsters, whose earlier development had been normal, who developed problems de novo during middle childhood. In these instances the new demands and expectations of this period were not consonant with the child's capacities even though there had been no such dissonances earlier.

In this last group the analysis of the anterospective longitudinal data, as well as the clinical psychiatric evaluation, indicated that the behavior disorder did not reflect the repetition of conflicts of earlier age periods with new symptoms or symbolic representation but rather new conflicts, excessive stresses, and maladaptation arising in the middle childhood period.

The children who have developed normally from early childhood onward are not drawn from any special group regarding temperament, intellectual ability, sociocultural background of the family or hierarchal position (firstborn vs. second, third or fourth child). Thus, even though the children with the "difficult child" temperamental constellation—slow adaptability, initial negative responses to many new situations, intense and frequently negative reactions to stimuli, and irregularity of sleep and feeding patterns—show a significantly higher percentage of behavior problem development than do children with other temperamental patterns (28), some difficult children did cope successfully with the demands of each stage of development without developing symptoms. Furthermore, the children with normal development included some with special environmental stresses in their lives, such as divorce of the parents, death of a parent, hospitalization in early childhood, etc. Whether the mother worked outside the home or not also seemed irrelevant as such. The basic issue determining normal development appeared to be the existence of a consonance or "goodness of fit" between the child with his individual characteristics and the demands and expectation of the intra- and extrafamilial environments.

An example of a child with earlier behavior disorder and complete resolution in the school-age period—of whom we have seen a number—is a girl with the difficult child temperamental pattern, which made her care in the early years stressful to the parents. The mother responded with uncertainty and inconsistency in handling, the father with antagonism, hostility and punitiveness. The youngster developed multiple symptoms at 5 years of age, including explosive anger, fear of the dark, difficulty in relating to groups of children, and an insatiable desire for attention. At psychiatric evaluation 3 months later, the diagnosis of neurotic behavior disorder was made. Psychotherapy for the child was recommended and instituted. In the following few years her symptoms improved gradually. Also she blossomed out with artistic talents in a number of directions, was intellectually bright and did well in school. These combinations of talents and success in school so impressed her father that his attitude toward her changed dramatically and radically. His hostility changed to affection and his criticism to praise and admiration. The change in child and father gave the mother increasing confidence in her handling of the girl, which was positively reinforced by her progressive improvement. This combination of the help provided by psychotherapy, the success in school and the increasingly positive interaction with both parents resulted in progressive improvement to the point where psychiatric evaluation at age 10 years showed no evidence of psychopathology. Follow-up over the next 5 years showed continued normal development.

The sequence of a behavior disorder in the preschool period that was resolved and then recurred in the school years is illustrated by the two boys cited above, the one with explosive tantrum-type behavior in a frustrating school situation at age 5, and the other with inappropriate imitation of selected aspects of his father's behavior at age 4. The first youngster's symptoms disappeared after a change more appropriate to his needs, and the second after a change in parental attitudes and behavior. Both boys experienced a recurrence of disturbance in the middle childhood years, due to child-environment interactions similar to those of the earlier age period. The new symptoms were different, however, and reflected the new age-stage level of development.

Diana, the girl with bowel symptoms cited previously, illustrates the sequence of behavior disorder starting in the preschool years and continuing into the school years.

The youngsters with the development of a behavior problem *de novo* in middle childhood showed variations on two themes: (1) excessive stress resulting from new or altered demands or traumatic situations, leading to symptom formation, or (2) stress that had been present earlier, due to a dissonant child-environment interaction, but which did not crystallize in the form of a behavior disorder until this age. These two sequences are illustrated by two cases.

During early childhood, Margie had a habitual pattern of ritualizing routines. For example, before she would go to bed each night she had to have a special story, a snack, some water, a certain song, a kiss on her nose, be tucked in just so and then given a special doll. Each of these had been gradually added into the routine, which was now the ritual of getting to sleep. However, with this situation, as with others with similar rituals, she would easily give up specific aspects when requested to do so by her parents. This tendency, therefore, to organize routine activities in a compulsive manner, was not a pathologic defense, nor was it a problem for the parents, as she would give up her rituals following suggestions that she do so. Furthermore, she showed no other indications of tension or maladaptive functioning.

At age 10, Margie was confronted by a series of traumatic experiences. She had to have warts removed from her feet, and this became an extremely painful procedure, since the local anesthetic did not work despite multiple injections. Following this surgery, there were frequent dressing changes and her physician insisted that she be "super clean" to prevent the recurrence of the warts. Then, a few months later, she developed a severe sore throat that necessitated medication. However, Margie went into shock following the penicillin injection and required emergency treatment; for several days afterwards there was considerable apprehension about her condition.

In the wake of these experiences, Margie developed a series of fears with regard to the dangers of wastes (cat droppings) and poisons (lead paint) that she picked up from the passing comments of others and warnings on television. She included menstruation among the things she considered poisonous. In addition, she showed a number of symptoms related to the need to be clean—excessive handwashing, fear of dirt and animal excretions—and developed rituals around these as well as a general state of tension.

Margie was seen by the staff psychiatrist, who diagnosed her as having a reactive behavior disorder. It was felt that her obsessional behavior was situationally determined and that in the absence of further trauma she could be talked out of these new rituals as she had been talked out of others in the past. On the psychiatrist's recommendation, the parents brought each set of behavioral compulsions and obsessive ruminations into the open and discussed them with Margie clearly and compassionately. In this way, her grave fears were reduced to nonproblem issues, and her rituals were easily ended.

In Tina's case, by contrast, the behavioral disorder was not precipitated suddenly but crystallized slowly, after several years of a negative child-parent interaction. Tina was a slow-to-warm-up and persistent child, who reacted negatively to her initial exposures to new people or new situations. She had a twin sister, an easily adaptable child, with whom her mother frequently compared Tina—and the latter always came out on the bottom. Tina came to see herself as less loved than her sister, and this was a realistic reaction in view of her mother's obvious favoritism for her twin.

Over the years, this negative interaction between mother and child continued to build up. When she was 7, symptoms of disturbance began and finally, at age 9, the parents brought her for evaluation. Their major concern was what they saw as her learning problem: she often did things wrong, "avoided" using her mind, and had poor achievement grades. In addition, she frequently showed negative mood, behaved immaturely and was easily frustrated if her wishes were not immediately granted. The parents' concern at this time was the result not of her problems (as all had been present for quite some time) but of their worries about her academic achievement. By this stage, Tina was in third grade and often had homework assignments. The parents felt they had to help her, but her reaction was to dawdle, not to work quickly and to stick to what she was doing when they wanted to move on to something else. This additional negative interaction between child and mother, over and above the latter's obvious favoritism for and special attention to her other daughter, was sufficiently stressful to result in Tina's developing a behavior disorder.

The initial therapeutic recommendation was for parent guidance, and the mother, especially, was advised as to specific ways in which to modify her approach with Tina. At this writing, too little time has elapsed for a follow-up study.

Incidence and Symptomatology

Table 1 shows the distribution in our study population of age of onset of behavior disorder as well as age at which symptoms became severe enough for the child to be referred for psychiatric evaluation.

As can be seen from Table 1, the great majority of cases, 34 out of 47, had the onset of their behavior disorders before the age of 6. Only one new case developed between the ages of 9 and 12 years.

TABLE 1.
Age at Onset and Referral of Behavior Disorder

	0-3 Yr	3-6 Yr	6-9 Yr	9-12 Yr
Onset, males	4	16	7	0
Onset, females	4	10	5	1
Onset, total	8	26	12	1
Referral, males	0	16	11	0
Referral, females	1	10	6	3
Referral, total	1	26	17	3

The total number of cases, 47, is a cumulative number. At any one time the actual number was less because of recovery in some cases. The great majority of the cases were milder disturbances, diagnosed as reactive behavior disorders (28), and this was true for all the age periods of onset covered in this report. The high incidence of mild disorders in children has been reported by others (10, 11, 19). Some authors have emphasized the transient nature of the behavior disorder and the tendency to spontaneous improvement in many children (22), others have advocated the need for professional help for school-age children with behavioral difficulties (23). Our own follow-up of the first 42 cases in the longitudinal sample, with onset ranging from 2 years to 8½ years of age, showed that eventually (4-11 years after initial evaluation) 14 children had recovered and 19 others displayed either marked or moderate improvement (29). There was therapeutic intervention in all cases—simple parent guidance in all cases, supplemented by psychotherapy in seven children—so that we cannot estimate the possibilities of spontaneous recovery in the sample.

The low incidence of behavior disorder onset in the middle childhood years has also been reported by MacFarlane et al. in the Berkeley Study (15). Lapouse and Monk in their extensive epidemiologic study (9-12) confirmed the finding that "increased age is associated with a decreased prevalence of behavior disorder in school-age children." This finding is most likely related to the lesser number of new environmental demands and expectations in this age period, at least for middle class children. The demands for routinization and socialization—toilet-training, regular sleep and feeding patterns, adaptation to rules and regulations, etc.—had been made in the preschool years. Most of the children attended nursery school, so that the demands for adaptation to a new structured extrafamilial situation, for adaptation to a peer group, and for working with educational materials all came early in life.

By contrast, the incidence of behavior disorders in a population of working class Puerto Rican children was relatively higher during the school years as compared to the preschool years than in the middle-class children in the New York Longitudinal Study. The difference in age period occurrence of behavior disorders in the two groups appears related to the fact that the Puerto Rican parents were very permissive and nondemanding with their preschool children. They did not pressure them to modify sleep or feeding irregularities or other types of mild behavioral deviations. Their typical attitude was "he's a baby—he'll outgrow it."

With the start of school, however, there was a sudden increase in the number of new demands made of the Puerto Rican children. And whereas the preschool years presented more stresses to the middle class children, the school years were more stressful for the Puerto Rican youngsters. The latter did not have the experience of going to nursery school and it was only at age 5 or 6 that demands for regularity of sleep, discipline, learning, and obedience to safety regulations began to be made (29).

A review of the kinds of presenting symptoms in the 47 middle class children with behavior disorders showed that, in the younger children, sleep disturbances, temper tantrums, and maladaptation to the rules of social living were predominant. During the school years, symptoms associated with peer relations and learning came to the fore. This age-related distribution of symptoms corresponds in general to the findings of other studies (11, 15, 16, 30).

Masturbation was observed and reported by many parents in their preschool and school-age children, but with the statement that, since they knew it was "harmless and normal," they did not interfere with it. Many parents also reported increasing sexual interest and curiosity in their school-age children, and this, too, they said, did not worry them and was not considered a problem. It was the impression of the staff interviewers that some parents were not fully at ease with this stated attitude toward their child's masturbation, and that they might have intervened were it not for the influence of child-care authorities. However, independent evaluation of the children by the staff indicated that neither the masturbation nor sexual curiosity of these children were problems indicative of psychopathology in any case.

Conclusions

The findings of our longitudinal study indicate that the middle childhood period is one of continued development and psychologic change. New behavioral characteristics emerge and become influential in determining the nature of the child-environment interaction. Of those children earlier diagnosed as having behavior problems, some showed improvement or recovery where others showed worsening. Several children who were without problems earlier first developed disorders at school age. In the vast majority of the school-age children, sexual interest and activity were evident throughout the age period but were without any pathologic significance.

The term "latency," therefore, would appear to be a confusing and inappropriate way to designate and characterize children between the ages of 6 and 12. We would suggest that this term be abandoned and that simple descriptive designations, such as middle childhood and elementary school age, which imply no a priori assumptions or theories about the dynamics and course of psychologic development, be used in its place.

REFERENCES

1. Baldwin, A. L. *Theories of Child Development*. New York: Wiley & Sons, 1967.
2. Chess, S. "Temperament and Learning Ability in School Children," *Amer. J. Public Health,* 58:2231, 1968.
3. ———, and A. Thomas. "Differences in Outcome with Early Intervention in Children with Behavior Disorders," in M. Roff, L. N. Robins, and M. Pollack, eds., *Life History Research in Psychopathology,* Vol. II. Minneapolis: University of Minnesota Press, 1972.
4. Erikson, E. *Childhood and Society*. New York: Norton, 1950.
5. ———. *Identity: Youth and Crisis*. New York: Norton, 1968.
6. Freud, A. *Normality and Pathology in Childhood: Assessments of Development*. New York: International Universities Press, 1965.

7. Freud, S. *Collected Papers,* II. London: Hogarth, 1924.
8. Jersild, A. T. *Child Psychology*. Englewood Cliffs, N.J.: Prentice-Hall, 1968.
9. Lapouse, R. "The Relationship of Behavior to Adjustment in a Representative Sample of Children," *Amer. J. Public Health* 55:1130, 1965.
10. ———, and M. A. Monk. "An Epidemiologic Study of Behavior Characteristics in Children," *Amer. J. Public Health* 48:1134, 1958.
11. ———, and ———. "Fears and Worries in a Representative Sample of Children," *Amer. J. Orthopsychiat*. 29:803, 1959.
12. ———, and ———. "Behavior Deviations in a Representative Sample of Children: Variation by Sex, Age, Race, Social Class and Family Size," *Amer. J. Orthopsychiat.* 34:436, 1964.
13. Lewin, K. *Dynamic Theory of Personality*. New York: McGraw Hill, 1935.
14. Lidz, T. *The Person*. New York: Basic Books, 1968.
15. MacFarlane, J. W., L. Allen, and M. P. Honzik. *A Developmental Study of the Behavior Problems of Normal Children Between Twenty-one Months and Fourteen Years.* Berkeley: University of California Press, 1962.
16. Mensh, I. N., M. B. Kantor, W. R. Domek, M. C.-L. Gildea, and J. C. Glidewell. "Children's Behavior Symptoms and Their Relationships to School Adjustment, Sex and Social Class," *J. Social Issues* 15:8, 1959.
17. Pavlov, I. P. *Conditioned Reflexes,* G. V. Anrep, ed. & transl. London: Oxford University Press, 1927.
18. Piaget, J. *The Origins of Intelligence in Children*. New York: International Universities Press, 1952.
19. Rutter, M., J. Tizard, and K. Whitmore. *Education, Health and Behavior*. New York: Wiley & Sons, 1970.
20. Schneirla, T. C., and J. S. Rosenblatt. "Behavioral Organization and Genesis of the Social Bond in Insects and Mammals," *Amer. J. Orthopsychiat*. 31:223, 1961.
21. Shaw, C. R. *The Psychiatric Disorders of Childhood*. New York: Appleton-Century-Crofts, 1966.
22. Shepherd, M., A. N. Oppenheim, and S. Mitchell. "Childhood Behavior Disorders and the Child Guidance Clinic: An Epidemiological Study," *J. Child Psychol. Psychiat.* 7:39, 1966.
23. Stennet, R. G. "Emotional Handicap in the Elementary Years: Phase or Disease, *Amer. J..Orthopsychiat*. 36: 444, 1966.
24. Stern, W. *Psychologie der frühen kindheit, biz zum sechsten lebensjahre*. Leipzig: Quelle and Meyer, 1927.
25. Sullivan, H. S. *Conceptions of Modern Psychiatry: The First William Alanson White Memorial Lectures*. Reprinted from *Psychiatry: Journal of the Biology and Pathology of Interpersonal Relations,* Volume 3, February, 1940 and Volume 8, May 1945.
26. Thomas, A. "Significance of Temperamental Individuality for School Functioning," in J. Hellmuth, ed., *Learning Disorders*. Seattle: Special Child Publications, 1968.
27. ———, H. G. Birch, S. Chess, M. E. Hertzig, and S. Korn. *Behavioral Individuality in Early Childhood*. New York: New York University Press, 1963.
28. ———, S. Chess, and H. G. Birch. *Temperament and Behavior Disorders in Children*. New York: New York University Press, 1968.
29. ———, ———, J. Sillen, and O. Mendez. *Cross-cultural Study of Behavior in Children with Special Vulnerabilities to Stress,* in M. Roff and M. Pollack, eds., *Life History Research in Psychopathology,* Vol. III. Minneapolis: University of Minnesota Press. In press.
30. Werry, J. S., and H. C. Quay. "The Prevalence of Behavior Symptoms in Younger Elementary School Children," *Amer. J. Orthopsychiat*. 41:136,1971.

12. The First Year: Metapsychological Inferences of Infant Observation*

Annemarie P. Weil, M.D.

SUPERVISING PSYCHIATRIST
CHILD DEVELOPMENT CENTER, JEWISH BOARD OF GUARDIANS
FACULTY, NEW YORK PSYCHOANALYTIC INSTITUTE

This is a short survey of the infant's development during the first year, an attempt to schematize and conceptualize metapsychologically which facets of personality development and which interactions we can observe, and what we can infer from these observations. It is an attempt to show how behavioral manifestations gradually point toward the evolving underlying psychological structures.

Examples of such inferences are the following: When a baby sucks his fist, we can draw some inferences about the state of the apparatus serving motility; and about his drives—the libidinal ones as expressed in his oral needs and the aggressive energies as expressed in forcefulness. We can also draw inferences about his choice of tension discharge (sucking versus, e.g., general activity) and the success of tension discharge (he stops fretting). Another example: When a baby smiles at a person, we can draw inferences about the apparatus underlying motility, perception, and memory; the development of these autonomous ego functions, as well as about the precursor of another ego function—the dawning relatedness to the human being.

Such an approach helps to highlight the quantitative and qualitative changes in a specific child. Moreover, it points to individual differences as well as individual deviations. And such considerations have relevance to our clinical work.

*A shorter version of this paper was presented at the Meeting of the Association for Child Psychoanalysis, March 24, 1974, New Orleans.

Different Facets of the Developing Personality That Interact with Each Other and with Experiential Factors

The first factor concerns the libidinal and aggressive drives in which we can discern variations in endowment (Alpert, Neubauer, and Weil, 1956) that in turn will influence development. Secondly, there is the ego. Here, too, one needs to distinguish between two parts (Hartmann, 1939): the preconflict autonomous endowment—the apparatus[1] underlying such ego functions as perception, motility, memory, and speech; and the ego as an evolving structure, characterized by a variety of functions, among which are the beginning integrative function, reality testing, dawning object relatedness, acceptance of the reality principle, defenses, and the incipient capacity for neutralization (Hartmann, 1955). Following Hartmann (1952) and Hartmann, Kris, and Loewenstein (1946), I assume that in the beginning there is an undifferentiated stage, an undifferentiated ego-id nucleus from which gradually ego and id evolve. I also consider as part of the autonomous endowment the autonomic reactivity as described by Lustman (1956) and habituation as elaborated on by Bridger (1962).[2]

There exist innumerable possibilities for interaction *between* the apparatus, the ego-id nucleus and experiential factors—as well as *within* each sphere. An example of the latter, interaction within the experiential sphere, was described by Lustman (1957) as imperceptivity: a child overwhelmed by inner stimuli (colic) does not perceive outer stimuli (bottle).

Some examples of interaction between spheres, between the apparatus

[1]The apparatus are considered independent variables which in the course of maturation come under the control of the ego and, on their part, influence ego development (Hartmann, 1950, 1952). See Hartmann and Kris (1945) for the distinction between maturation and development.

[2]Lustman and Bridger demonstrated that babies are born with different reactivity and habituation responses. Infants react differently in different body spheres to various stimuli. Lustman found important differences between different infants and between different zones in the same infant. He argued that these originally autonomous differences, e.g., in lip sensitivities, may have far-reaching effects considering different consequences of indulgence and deprivation. "There is a reaction to stimulation which indicates that sensations of some degree of differentiation exist. We think that such sensations precede and mold the first rudimentary perceptions."

Bridger investigated the earliest differences in habituation (the decline in responsiveness as the same stimulus is repeated—namely, decrease of startle reaction and cardiac response to the repeated same sound or air puff). Bridger relates this to inborn autonomous, subcortical threshold differences. "Differences in organismic characteristics may also help explain why certain environmental stresses can apparently produce severe damage in some individuals but not in others."

Subsequent investigators experimenting with a variety of stimuli have further delineated the individual differences and deviations in various spheres (Birns, 1965; Engen and Lipsett, 1965; Friedman et al., 1970).

In later months, with increasing psychological awareness and functioning, habituation relates to the infant's disattending—becoming bored—once a stimulus is familiar. It proves the infant's preference for new stimulation and implies the importance of this aspect in the early mother-infant interaction.

and the ego's use of them, would be the following. An infant, observed in an anaclytic depression, has the apparatus to make sounds, to grasp, but he does not do so or only rarely does so. It is as if the evolving ego does not make use of the apparatus, i.e., does not invest them with drive energies. Or, the reverse process, an infant starting to stand will do so over and over again until he has mastered this new capacity. Here it is as if the budding ego invests a great deal, especially in the service of mastery.

The following example shows the interaction between the maturation of the motor apparatus, the use of motility by the developing ego, and experiential factors: a crawling child, in comparison with a sitting one, will have a wider range of experiences and therefore more possibilities for reality testing—a function of the budding ego. He will also be able to crawl toward the mother or away from her; this has a bearing on separation-individuation and object relatedness. He can also crawl away from certain unpleasant stimuli—an ability that relates to adaptation and defense.

Since each stage of development affords us different opportunities for observation, I shall proceed by describing the predominant features of each stage and the inferences we can draw from them.

The Newborn

The newborn's main task is to survive and to maintain a precarious equilibrium. In order to do this he needs to be shielded from strong, intrusive stimuli. Most of the time his high threshold provides protection, especially from the outside. Moreover, his mother, functioning as an auxiliary ego, provides protection and relief from distressing stimuli of both kinds.

Whereas only fifteen years ago the neonate was usually described in terms of diffuse reactions and a few specific reflexes, recent investigations have taught us that the neonate shows what Wolff (1973) calls a "remarkable competence." Wolff himself set a proliferating research interest in motion after he (1959, 1965a, Wolff and White, 1965) had shown that during short periods of lowered thresholds, newborns have states of so-called "alert inactivity" during which they can give more focused attention to and visually follow an object. Fantz (1961) and others then demonstrated that during such states of alert inactivity neonates can discriminately see and show visual preferences. (For example, they prefer the picture of a realistic face to one with jumbled features.)

A host of subsequent experimental studies elucidated the functioning and the world of the neonate and very young infant. For example, not only does he attend and disattend, but he can discriminate, and seems to prefer moderately complex to plain stimuli (Fantz, 1961, Hershenson et al., 1965) as well as unfamiliar to familiar or very unfamiliar ones (Friedman et al., 1970). (As this continues, it will help in the construction and revision of schemata.) Not only does exposure to stimuli of the ''right'' novelty, intensity, and complexity create or maintain a state of mild arousal, but the neonate or young infant himself will seek stimulation. For instance, given contingency experiences in an experimental situation in the first month, he will engage in more intense (nonnutritive) sucking in order to see a picture more clearly or hear music (Siqueland and de Lucia, 1969). Bower (1971) demonstrated that the neonate shows evidence of spatial orientation (he will perform defensive head and hand movements toward an approaching object) and of a visual-touch intercoordination (startling and showing upset when touching a virtual object). Bower feels that the neonate prefers the inherent task given in new situations to the stimulus itself.

Many of these experiments demonstrate that the neonate exhibits from the very beginning a certain activeness that involves seeking, preferring, avoiding. These reactions show individual differences and, in association with different responses by individual mothers, will color various mother-infant interactions.

Neonates differ with respect to other characteristics that are directly observable. Among these are:[3] the turgor of the body; the activity type (Fries, 1944), which includes the degree of general motor activity and the startle response, Korner (1974) feels that the amplitude of the child's motions, the reliance on small, medium or large movements might be even more typical for the individual child. Escalona and Heider (1959) have modified activity type to ''availability of energies,'' in which they include, in addition to activity level, zest and energy reserves under stress. Other differences occur in: the strength of the cry; the activeness of the rooting response; the strength of the sucking and grasping reflexes; the degree of wakefulness and alertness as well as the distinctness of state. Furthermore, we can observe different perceptual sensitivities in different types of stimulation (reactions to sound, touch, and visual stimuli; to feeding and bodily care). We can note the infant's behavior when he is without stimulation. We can observe what quiets the baby (rocking, sucking, rhythmical sound), his soothability as well as his capacity for self-soothing (Korner and Grobstein, 1967).

[3]Some of the items are in accordance with a list of Easton and Blau (1963).

Naturally we also observe what the mother offers, her reactions, her ability to understand cues, and her handling of the infant. Above all, we note how mother and infant match, how soon they achieve synchrony, what Sander (1969, 1970) calls "regulatory stability," a first level of temporal fitting together.

Inferences

These observable differences allow us to draw inferences about: the state of the apparatus of perception and motility;[4] the energy level and activity pattern; the autonomous reactivity, e.g., of lips and face, determining oral needs; drive quantities expressed in oral needs (libidinal drive) and in activity patterns (aggressive drive). Especially if we follow the neonate a week or so longer, we already find a repertoire of budding ego functions: a varying rudimentary organizing function that regulates the balance between threshold and tension discharge, thereby permitting a more or less harmonious integration of stimuli.

We can draw conclusions about the preferred modes of tension release by observing: increased general activity, sucking, listening, and being rocked—also as related to mother's handling, comforting. We see the first indication of outward directedness: rooting, scanning, and ceasing to cry when he hears a voice.

Following Wolff (1965a) and Wolff and White (1965), we can discern indications of the earliest capacity for attention cathexis, concentration; and there are already individually varying reactions to frustration: withdrawal or increased activity, possible forerunners of later ego characteristics (Fries and Woolf, 1953), as well as avoidance, another forerunner of defense.

From Birth to Three Months

Much of the further development depends on the interaction of each infant's special endowment with his special environment, an interaction that starts at birth. In fact, interaction started before birth, with mother's reaction to pregnancy and the fetal movement, and with the fetus's experience of the maternal rhythms (cardiac and respiratory) (Greene,

[4]I agree with Bower (1971) that the newborn's reactions to space and solidity are based on inborn structural properties that are part of the autonomous perceptual apparatus equipment which helps adaptation. Hartmann (1939) distinguishes between adaptation and the prior state of adaptedness.

1958). It then continues in such intangibles as the matching of body turgors, mutual rhythms, and thresholds which, if all goes well, lead to regulatory synchrony (Sander, 1969).

There is no doubt that the environment shapes the infant—but the infant also shapes the environment. Each infant calls forth special potentials in his mother, and each mother influences the special potentials in her infant.

In the first few months, in line with the infant's complete dependence, mother and child function ideally as a "dual unit" (Mahler, 1967), the mother being the "external executive ego" (Spitz, 1965) for the infant's needs. Mahler calls this period the symbiotic phase. In this period we observe increasing perceptivity and reactions to the environment. There is change of threshold and lessened interference from proprioceptive stimuli. Hence, increasing energies can be directed to the outside. There is an increase in attentive stages, in states of "alert inactivity," and better functioning even in states of "alert activity"—hence increasing readiness for attention and arousal. The baby can hold his head better and focus better and longer. There are two consequences to this: first, by one month, the infant can look and maintain a longer gaze into the mother's eyes and a blissful interplay ensues (Robson, 1967); second, with better distance perception, visual investigation of the environment expands.

This increased acquaintance with the outside world—beginning reality testing—is not only fostered by the maturation of apparatus of perception, motility, and a beginning memory, but also depends on the degree of stimulus hunger the infant has shown and has had satisfied by his mother. There are great individual differences in the degree to which new stimuli are welcomed or even demanded.

Many investigators feel that in early infancy one can already find distinct differences in reaction tendencies to new stimuli. (Considering the more recent research investigations, we should qualify: stimuli that are relatively strong, complex, and unfamiliar.) Bayley (1956) refers to these reactions as "active-extroverted against inactive-introverted"; Chess et al. (1959) speak of "approach or withdrawal behavior"; Meili (1959) distinguishes between "positive and negative attitudes to new experiences." Meili maintains that infants react in characteristic ways to new and strong stimuli. Some will quickly deal with the stimulus excitation, then turn to the object motorically and show changes in their facial expression; others cannot deal with the stimulus excitation and remain inhibited in expression and motorically. He believes that this reaction to the world of new things and experiences remains constant.[5]

A sensitive mother will adjust her approach, her stimulation, to her infant's needs and tolerance. The better she is able to respond to his sensitivity, the more she can produce stimulation acceptable to him—contingency experiences which are interesting or pleasurable to just the right degree. The more the infant can be alert and attentive, the more he will become motivated to orient himself toward stimulation, to explore, to assimilate information (similar thoughts were expressed by Lewis and Goldberg, 1969).

Another example of how the maturation of apparatus feeds ego formation would be the following. Gradually, gestalt complexes of pleasure-pain stimuli (contingency experiences) are taken in and vaguely remembered, and with this, anticipation begins. For instance, in the second month, the baby will suck when put into the feeding position; in the third month, the infant usually is able to wait when he hears the refrigerator door or the running water that warms the bottle. The sequence is: conditioned reflex, primitive memory, and with it anticipation; and this is associated with the capacity to delay, i.e., development toward acceptance of the reality principle.

Benedek (1938) related this capacity to anticipate and to wait to "confidence"—a stage of object relationship which is on the one hand connected with primary narcissism, on the other hand it already reaches out for the object. Mahler (1967) phrases it: "When the infant is able to wait for and confidently expect satisfaction, only then is it possible to speak of the beginning of an ego and of a symbiotic object as well." Hartmann (1939) considered anticipation a most important aspect of early ego development.

We assume that with increasing alertness and apparatus skills and with the regularly repeated experience of need satisfaction (that often follows the infant's crying), the "new ability to distinguish between the perception of reality . . . and inner mental images [will come about], one of the most significant advances in the infant's mental development" (Anna Freud, 1953).

With the beginning capacity to make this distinction, and with greater specificity of reactions, definite responses to the other human being

[5]Escalona (1959) found this characteristic to be less constant. The differences are probably due to the impact of the separation-individuation process in different children.

It is of clinical interest that this same innate neurophysiologically determined inhibition, not welcoming new stimuli, may later fuse with a much more complex inhibition of curiosity based on experience, fantasies, conflicts.

become distinct: the smile, the first high point of outward directedness. This relates to the predictable social smile which is increasingly endowed with psychological meaning and which Spitz (1965) considers the first organizer of mental development.[6]

The smile was preceded by other behavior manifestations indicating various degrees of outward directedness, such as molding, turning head to breast and rooting, quieting, ceasing to cry on hearing a voice, capacity for discrete communication,[7] scanning, capacity for synchrony, eye-to-eye contact, reaction to the general climate. All of these create or add to mother's bliss and foster motherliness; hence, they add to the cyclic interaction between infant and mother.

Clinically, the smile is associated with, or in subsequent months followed by, such specific reactions as: anticipatory gesture (heralding beginning differentiation); holding on; a discriminate smile for mother (six months); imitation; eventual back-and-forth play. We find considerable individual differences in these reactions.

Within this period of the smile, the third month, affects become more visible and communication more distinct. The cycle tension-quiescence (or disequilibrium-equilibrium) changes to displeasure-relief-pleasure. In the same way as the infant's smiling and cooing appear to communicate ease and pleasure, his crying gradually becomes not just an expression of unease, but an increasingly distinct signal of displeasure and, as time goes on, a more definite request.[8]

In the third month, another, almost universal behavior pattern contributes to dawning ego development: the infant's looking at his own hands, seeing a part of himself and watching his own movements. Some greater visual self-experience gains momentum. Greenacre (1960) believes that touch and vision—taking in the various body parts with the eyes—help draw the body together into a central image beyond the level of immediate sensory awareness. "It differs from the reciprocal contacts between body parts by cutaneous touch alone and may offer a nuclear beginning to an ego development at a mental level."[9]

During this period, we also find that preferential reactions become

[6]The exogenous, social, predictable smile replaces the endogenous smile, which is related to tension discharge and rhythmic processes, as well as the unpredictable exogenous smile, which is a reaction to stimuli from various modalities (Spitz et al., 1970).

[7]"Congenitally given differentiation of expressive movements" (Wolff, 1959), which makes cuing easier.

[8]I am thinking of K. Bühler's (1929) description of the stages of language development: expression, appeal, and representation.

[9]Fraiberg (1968) has shown that in blind children the development of self-awareness is delayed.

much more marked, all of which give a rather typical individual coloring to each baby at three months. One baby may prefer to look, another to listen; one seems to be beaming, another appears more solemn.

I was very impressed when I observed a three-month-old baby (who sometimes did smile) fascinatedly staring at his mother's colorfully designed sweater, rather than responding to her friendly talk with a smile. It was as if the baby's rudimentary ego had already made the choice between investing the autonomous ego function of looking and the budding ego function of relating to the object, i.e., the mother.

Inferences

With regard to instinctual development, we can infer the nature of oral needs. Zone stimulations can of course be induced by a mother who, for example, constantly offers the bottle or who uses the thermometer or suppositories to prevent constipation. This, particularly if associated with special zonal sensitivities, may pave the way for later fixations. Moreover, we find an individually varying increase of the aggressive drive admixture in the general forcefulness and in the baby's increased alertness and activity, in his motivation for (orientation toward) learning—a beginning neutralization.

With regard to the apparatus, as neuromuscular maturation progresses, cooing and babbling are added to crying as forerunners of speech. Possibilities of interaction are increased: Maturation of motility enhances perception, and both enhance memory imprints.

Subsequently, the many new achievements influence ego formation and foreshadow the budding ego's potential. As mentioned, there is the beginning of reality testing, the beginning acceptance of the reality principle, the dawn of object relatedness (the smile). We can add more visible affects with more expressiveness. Spitz (1966) states that to make such expression of affect possible, there must be at least some rudimentary form of ego. There are already visible differences in moods, which are ego modalities (Jacobson, 1957). Some babies are beaming; others serious and "scrutinizing," even somber. Also, the resilience will start to show conspicuous individual differences, typical for each baby's budding ego.

As I described in my Basic Core paper (1970), all of this lends definite individual characteristics to each infant at this time, and sometimes foreshadows pathology, although the separation-individuation process will add significant structural and contextual imprints.

Such differences or deviations are especially related to the social-emotional sphere, the dawn of object relatedness (i.e., to ego development), and to the libido-aggression balance.

From the Fourth to the Eighth Month

The fourth month is a period of transition. The infant has now reached a certain level of achievement in the sphere of perception and visual-motor skills, in his capacity to investigate, seek, create, and respond to stimulation, and in his ability to interact socially with the environment. But these only foreshadow the manipulatory skills which will appear in the months to come.

That a certain higher plateau, a first climax of psychological awakening within the symbiotic period, is reached is probably also borne out by the fact that the EEG changes attained in the third month—with the smile—show a greater maturity and organization (Spitz et al., 1970), with REMs disappearing from nonsleep periods and spindles becoming more defined, and probably indicating increased cortex functioning.

Increased and more advanced social reactions, seeking, maintaining, responding—but also avoiding—are illustrated by the many typical, playful interactions which a well-functioning infant of this age has with a well-attuned mother—interactions which are so characteristic for this period. As Stern (1974) puts it: "Several major lines of social behavior developments converge—gaze, smiling, vocalizing—and are integrated into the performance of play activity . . . the early visual motor control representing an important ego mechanism to accomplish coping and defensive operations in an interpersonal situation."

As mentioned, the infant is now on the way toward developing manipulatory skills. There is better arm-hand motility, but the infant still can explore only with his fingers and hold something put into his hand, he cannot yet reach and grasp. There is better discriminatory perception and more reaction to what he perceives. Yet sometimes the unfamiliarity or familiarity of the total gestalt may supersede recognition of finer details. For example, he will no longer smile to a mask, but reserve this response to the human face; yet he may scream when his mother has her hair up in rollers. He will start to suck when a doll is moved toward his face and not suck when a bottle is held still (Rubinow and Frankl, 1934).

After the transitional period of the fourth month, the stage from the fifth through the eighth month is characterized primarily by the change from predominantly perceptual acquaintance with the environment to activity—manipulation, exploration, grasping—and action on the environment by hand and mouth.

I want to describe this stage mainly from the following viewpoint: what do the new skills of trunk, arm, hands imply for the baby's development, and what inferences can be drawn? Escalona (1968) describes the integration of grasping and looking: "The child experiences the visual consequences of his motoric actions. All this brings about a more distinct awareness of the object, more than was possible before through looking alone." This indicates that the integrative capacity gains momentum. We will observe whether grasping and looking are integrated; and, very important, somewhat later, once the infant is able to grasp two objects, whether he brings them into relation with each other. Provence and Ritvo (1961) have taught us that failure to do so can be the first indication of matters out of kilter.

Arm motility and grasping serve differentiation, need satisfaction, learning and adaptation, as well as defense. The infant can grasp: mother, himself, and objects. Grasping therefore serves individuation and reality testing. This new skill of grasping is, of course, fed by and feeds perception and memory imprints. As in other areas, the specific characteristics of individual infants interact with the specific features of different mothers' handling. There is grasping and taking objects to the mouth and biting them (it is the period of teething, weaning). Hoffer (1949, 1950) states, "the mouth ego begins, . . . finger sucking [is] a lesson in self-discovery, . . . the infant fingers his fingers," i.e., he experiences his body actively and passively; and this, in association with visual perception, helps establish the body ego.

The role of differentiation is clear: the abilities to observe mother with improved distance perception; to sit more often and face her directly; to grasp and explore her face, hair, and mouth; to press actively against her body—all these enhance awareness of the other person, the mother, an accomplishment which is characteristic for this period of differentiation (Mahler et al., 1975).

With more precise memory traces, the infant no longer smiles indiscriminately, but smiles easiest and most often to mother.

By grasping and letting go ("geographic experimentation" Piaget, 1937) the infant investigates space—an important learning experience, a potential for neutralization. Neutralization, or forerunners of neutralization, can be observed very early (Hartmann, 1955) in an infant's persistent investment of energy in learning, e.g., in the third month, in the repetition of his own chance vocalizations until he can ease them into his repertoire (Wolff, 1965b). However, at this period of grasping and manipulation such persistence in learning—grasping, releasing, exploring, imitating—becomes much more conspicuous. The intensity of an infant's looking after the dropped toy leaves no doubt that Piaget's keen observation is correct; the infant is fascinated with space and wants to explore it.[10]

Moreover, grasping and better arm control allow the infant to steer toward and to avoid unpleasant stimuli. No doubt there are individual variations in the use of these modalities. It is significant whether and how much the potential for action is used primarily in the service of adaptation and learning or as a defense for avoiding unpleasant stimuli.[11] Benjamin (1962) calls this "a difference in ego attitudes: active mastery versus passive acceptance."

Gradually, with increasing memory, there is a shift of cathexis from the function to the object, from just grasping anything to grasping the desired object. Hence, volition, intentionality, motivation, persistence begin to come into play. Again, there are considerable individual differences in infants as well as in the mothers' handling.

Better awareness leads to increasing social interaction. The infant begins to imitate little movements, which is often fostered by the mother.[12] He now understands the other person's gestures and the implication of a situation; e.g., some infants cry when mother, or a familiar person, leaves the room.

The greater physical skills have an impact on the mother-child relationship in that they alter the infant's feelings of dependence and independence. In the falling-asleep pattern of infants who can hold the bottle themselves, there is now a range of possibilities. One may take over while another may still want mother to hold the bottle for falling asleep and soothing tension relief. Various needs of infants and mothers will interact.

[10]It is therefore especially regrettable when a mother interferes with this learning intention—an interference that sometimes may initiate a sadomasochistic interaction.

[11]In the diaper test (Buehler & Hetzer, 1932), in which a diaper is placed on the head of a sitting child, some infants just freeze or cry, even though they would be able to grasp and pull the diaper away.

[12]While imitation has been observed very early, especially vocal imitation, the imitation of this period seems to have acquired more psychological meaning in the service of, and as an indication of, ongoing self-object differentiation. It is "acting in turn" or, if a little more advanced, represents "attempts to approximate the model" (Uzgiris, 1972).

The role of the environment takes on new facets. Mother's pleasure in the infant's functioning adds to his pleasure in functioning and mastery, thus enhancing trends toward neutralization. On the other hand, with the infant's increasing volition and intentionality and more diversified wishes, it becomes a harder task for a mother to follow cues and to guide toward good development.

Mahler and Furer (1963) talk of possible chronic misinterpretations. Some mothers will respond indiscriminately to all cues with a bottle, or with a toy, or by putting the infant on the floor; others will involve themselves more directly with the infant through play or bodily contact.

Inferences

I have already mentioned the implications of the maturing apparatus skills. With regard to the instinctual strivings, sensitivities from all three psychosexual zones may play a role. The oral zone: it is the time of teething, sometimes weaning. The anal zone: if stimulated by the mother in the described way, but also if we consider kinesthetic pleasure as somehow associated with anality, anal concerns may come to the fore, e.g., the infant of this period often likes to smear the food drippings on the table; or the reverse, he shows signs of fastidiousness (beyond mother's influence), a possible forerunner of later reaction formation. The genital zone: with better arm and hand control, the child discovers his genitals and infantile masturbation may begin.

With regard to the ego: there is now aim directedness; there is definite cathexis of specific goals. First there is cathexis of a function, with pleasure in functioning (K. Bühler, 1929); then there is increased cathexis of the object.

Motivation, intentionality, and the beginning of neutralization come conspicuously intc play. There is increasing awareness of the other human being and primitive identification—imitation of the gestural type—as well as increased anticipatory awareness of the affective implication of a situation. The active-passive modality may become distinct. Moreover, one can recognize marked changes of resilience with individual differences.

Leitch and Escalona (1949) describe the different conditions that create tension in different infants—what creates stress; how each individual infant expresses increased tension; what he needs for tension relief; and how quickly he recovers.

In addition to these ego characteristics, the way in which each child channels the aggressive energies becomes conspicuous and typical during this period. This characteristic allows inferences to be drawn with regard to energy level, activity, forcefulness, assertiveness, different moods such as anger and angry expressions; goal directedness, insistence, persistence, and neutralization.

From the Ninth Through the Twelfth Month

The last three months of the first year represent a high point in ego development. The ongoing separation-individuation process is enhanced by locomotion—moving to and away from mother or objects. Gradually, with increasing locomotor skills and exploratory needs, the infant enters the practicing period. The ongoing separation-individuation and the increasing capacity to test reality also are enhanced by speech development and speech understanding. The child begins to understand names, his own name, simple phrases, and prohibitions. Mother's reassurances may facilitate waiting, which is essential for the acceptance of the reality principle. The words that mother supplies strengthen reality testing. Beginning speech is situational and global: father's jacket may also be "Daddy"; "hot" may become everything that hurts—the hot plate as well as the freshly cut field not to be stepped on with bare feet.

Better and more precise memory imprints become strengthened by more definite cathectic investment and culminate in the discovery of the permanence of the object (Piaget, 1937), and the stranger reactions (Spitz, 1965).

In what follows, some of the developmental steps leading to this stage will be reviewed.[13]

First, the infant's reaction to inanimate objects. In the fifth month, he reaches for and grasps anything; the function is invested. In the sixth and seventh months, he will hold on fast and show displeasure when the rattle is taken away; the object is invested. He will look briefly for a lost toy; this shows improved object memory. He will pull a rattle away that is held fast. He will pull out a rattle that partly sticks out from the observer's pocket. These last examples show the considerable degree of recognition and investment of the object, even if it is only partly in the infant's field of vision.

[13]The examples are taken from the Buehler-Hetzer tests (1935).

At eight months, the infant does not forget the object when it is no longer visible; he will pull the diaper away that hides the rattle. And with that, he has discovered the permanence of the object.[14] The object, i.e., an inner image of the object, is now established and cathected—a beginning evocative memory—at least in times of need or following an outer stimulus (Fraiberg, 1969).

In line with this development, the infant shows increasingly discriminatory cathexis of objects, e.g., if offered two different toys simultaneously, he will always grasp the same rattle or cube.

The discovery of the human object is preceded by several achievements. In the beginning, the infant will root, mold, scan, turn to the breast. At two months, the infant starts to smile and coo at a human face. At three and four months, he shows displeasure when contact is broken. (Interestingly, this is two months before he shows displeasure when a toy disappears.) With increased distance perception, he will follow the moving adult with his eyes. His interest is widening, probably in association with special memory imprints, connected with the adult. At five months, he will reflect the expression of a smiling or frowning adult. This is reflecting, "mirroring" (Greenacre, 1941), rather than imitation. At six and seven months, he will no longer smile at everybody. Yet, in spite of greater discrimination and selectiveness, there is a need for human company. He may cry if an adult who played with him turns away. He will also create contact by smiling and cooing when looked at passively. When the adult stops a peekaboo game, he will expect continuation, and he starts to imitate when shown a simple movement, like hitting a rattle at the table.

Somewhere around eight months, the stranger is recognized as different from the now more precise and cathected memory imprints of the mother. (At this time, he will always grasp the same toy when offered two.) Abruptly approached by a stranger, he will react in some conspicuous way, and often with varying degrees of distress.[15]

[14]This is Piaget's "object permanence," which has sometimes been confused with the analytic concept of "object constancy" as defined by Hartmann (1952), Anna Freud (1952), and Hoffer (1952) and elaborated on by Mahler (1972), who calls the end phase of separation-individuation "on the way to object constancy." See also Fraiberg (1969).

[15]In 1950, Spitz states: "if the stranger does not present his face *actively*"; and in his modified Buehler-Hetzer test (from Xeroxed copies) this item reads: "Approach the baby at the beginning of the test *aggressively*." The significance of active impinging (Schaffer, 1966), and of the mode of approach (Décarie, 1973), has been confirmed by later studies. Other investigators point out the individual differences in timing, quantity, and quality of this reaction (Mahler et al., 1975) or the variations and deviations (Weil, 1956) or the associated circumstances (Bretherton and Ainsworth, 1974). Benjamin (1961) believed that the strength of the stranger anxiety is related to a preceding fear of the strange (changed gestalts in fourth month) and the aggressive investment of the mother which increases fear of object loss.

At the same time, a certain need for contact with human beings continues. When the strange adult is not abrupt but turns his back, the infant will initiate contact by tugging on his clothing—as he did before by smiling and cooing.

Stranger anxiety is preceded, associated with, and usually followed, in the second year, by separation anxiety in individual variations (rapprochement period, Mahler, 1972).

As the biological mutuality between mother and infant decreases (the infant can do more things by himself now), his psychological needs apparently increase at times. Moreover, he regularly returns to mother for "emotional refueling" as his increased locomotor skills and exploratory needs induce him to stray farther from her (Mahler et al., 1975).

There is ever-increasing social interaction. Gradually, there is more differentiation between persons: family members, especially the father, take on more distinct roles which are anticipated and demanded.

There is ever-increasing imitation, which often occurs spontaneously after mother has gone away. The imitation of facial expressions possibly initiates a vague rudimentary feeling for the other person. The infant now can also engage in simple reciprocity in games (bringing and taking of little things), which signifies that the other person's expectations are acted upon.

The increasing memory and cathexis of objects, however, also bring more possibilities of frustration. The infant's and the mother's intentions may not be completely opposite. The "no" becomes established or gains momentum. In unfortunate situations, an angry interaction may be cathected by mother and child. Maternal handling may vary greatly and foster similar mechanisms in the child—from instinctual gratification to distracting—i.e., displacement.

The variety of possible interplays with mother is known. Her mechanisms of dealing with his displeasure will be taken over by the infant into his defense formations. Her investment of him will be reflected in his own self-feeling, and her cathexis of the animate and inanimate world will influence his relatedness. Her cathexis of his functioning, achievement, and mastery will influence his capacity for neutralization, her moods will influence his moods and affective reactions.

Inferences

With the achievement of the upright posture, locomotion, speech development, increasing memory (a system of engrams, "*ein*

Spurensystem," Piaget, 1937), and intellectual development, the scope of experience and the knowledge of the world widen—if the environment tolerates or even stimulates these accomplishments.

As previously described, the libidinal drives may be influenced by all three zones, depending on the particular interaction of anlage and maternal handling. There are already possibilities of fixations as a consequence of traumatic experiences.

Increasing ego achievements have been mentioned: growing awareness of mother and self interacts with the other evolving ego functions. The infant's greater awareness of himself is also borne out by his response to being called by name. "A sense of individual entity and identity" begins (Mahler, 1958).

During this first year, the mother has changed from being experienced as one with the infant; from a vague, need-satisfying part object; from a gestalt complex of contours, colors, smells, and sounds; from one that creates a specific climate and (usually) secures well-being—to *the other,* very specific person who is most cathected; "from a predominantly need-satisfying object to a psychological catalyst" (Spitz, 1965).

In the area of ego development we can follow the steps from the undifferentiated phase, the ego-id nucleus, to the development of many specific functions. Among them are: the beginning of object relatedness, individuation, reality testing, the acceptance of the reality principle, defense formation, neutralization, moods, and the beginning of experienced, already quite differentiated, affects. In the third month, quiescence turns into pleasure, and tension becomes displeasure. In the course of further development, displeasure becomes pain, anger, disappointment; and pleasure becomes joy, attachment, zeal. All this proceeds via the interaction of the many innate and experiential variables.

To develop from a newborn to a one-year-old means to develop from a predominantly reactive biological organism to a little person with a definite psychological individuality. It means developing from helplessness and complete dependence to increasing intentionality and volition. It means developing from undifferentiation to a high point in the individuation process, the discovery of self and mother.

BIBLIOGRAPHY

Alpert, A., P. B. Neubauer, & A. P. Weil (1956). "Unusual Variations in Drive Endowment," *The Psychoanalytic Study of the Child,* 11:125-163.

Bayley, N. (1956). "Individual Patterns of Development," *Child Develpm.*, 27:45-74.

Benedek, T. (1938). "Adaptation to Reality in Early Infancy." *Psychoanal. Quart.*, 7:200-215.

Benjamin, J. D. (1961). "Some Developmental Observations Relating to the Theory of Anxiety," *J. Amer. Psychoanal. Assn.*, 9:652-668.

——— (1962). Panel discussion, *J. Amer. Acad. Child Psychiat.*, 1:59-66.

Birns, B. (1965). "Individual Differences in Human Neonates' Responses to Stimulation," *Child Develpm.*, 36:249-256.

Bower, T. G. R. (1971). "The Object in the World of the Infant," *Sci. American*, 225(4):30-38.

Bretherton, L., & M. Ainsworth (1974). "Responses of One-Year-Olds to a Stranger in a Strange Situation," in M. Lewis & L. Rosenblum, eds., *Origins of Fear*. New York: J. Wiley.

Bridger, W. H. (1962). "Sensory Discrimination and Autonomic Function in the Neonate," *J. Amer. Acad. Child Psychiat.*, 1:67-82.

Buehler, C., & H. Hetzer (1932). *Testing Children's Development from Birth to School Age*, tr. H. Beaumont. New York: Farrar & Rinehart, 1935.

Bühler, K. (1929). *Die Krise der Psychologie*. Jena: Fischer.

——— (1934). *Sprachtheorie*. Jena: Fischer.

Chess, S., A. Thomas, & H. Birch (1959). "Characteristics of the Individual Child's Behavioral Responses to the Environment," *Amer. J. Orthopsychiat.*, 29:791-802.

Décarie, T. et al. (1974). *The Infant's Reaction to Strangers*. New York: International Universities Press.

Easton, K., & A. Blau (1963). "Neonatal and Mother-Infant Observations in Child Psychiatry Training," *J. Amer. Acad. Child Psychiat.*, 2:176-186.

Engen, T., & L. P. Lipsett (1965). "Decrement and Recovery of Response to Olfactory Stimuli in the Human Neonate," *J. Comp. Physiol. Psychol.*, 59:312-316.

Escalona, S. K. (1968). *The Roots of Individuality*. Chicago: Aldine Publishing Co.

———, & G. M. Heider (1959). *Prediction and Outcome*. New York: Basic Books.

Fantz, R. L. (1961). "The Origin of Form Perception," *Sci. American*, 204:66-84.

Fraiberg, S. (1968). "Parallel and Divergent Patterns in Blind and Sighted Infants," *The Psychoanalytic Study of the Child*, 23:264-300.

——— (1969). "Libidinal Object Constancy and Mental Representation," *The Psychoanalytic Study of the Child*, 24:9-45.

Freud, A. (1952). "The Mutual Influences in the Development of Ego and Id: Introduction to the Discussion," *The Psychoanalytic Study of the Child*, 7:42-50.

——— (1953). "Some Remarks on Infant Observation," *The Psychoanalytic Study of the Child*, 8:9-19.

Friedman, S., A. N. Nagy, & G. Carpenter (1970). "Newborn Attention: Differential Response Decrement to Visual Stimuli," *J. Exp. Child Psychol.*, 10:44-51.

Fries, M. S. (1944). "Psychosomatic Relationships between Mother and Infant," *Psychosom. Med.*, 6:159-161.

———, & P. J. Woolf (1953). "Some Hypotheses on the Role of the Congenital Activity Type in Personality Development," *The Psychoanalytic Study of the Child*, 8:48-62.

Greenacre, P. (1941). "The Predisposition to Anxiety," *Trauma, Growth and Personality*. New York: W. W. Norton, 1952, pp. 27-82.

——— (1960). "Considerations Regarding the Parent-Infant Relationship," *Int. J. Psycho-Anal.*, 41:572-595.

Greene, W. A. (1958). "Early Object Relations, Somatic, Affective and Personal," *J. Nerv. Ment. Dis.*, 126:225-253.

Hartmann, H. (1939). *Ego Psychology and the Problem of Adaptation*, tr. D. Rapaport. New York: International Universities Press, 1958.

——— (1952). "The Mutual Influences in the Development of Ego and Id," *The Psychoanalytic Study of the Child,* 7:9-30.

——— (1955). "Notes on the Theory of Sublimation," *The Psychoanalytic Study of the Child,* 10:9-29.

———, & E. Kris (1945). "The Genetic Approach in Psychoanalysis," *The Psychoanalytic Study of the Child,* 1:11-30.

———, ———, & R. M. Loewenstein (1946). "Comments on the Formation of Psychic Structure," *The Psychoanalytic Study of the Child,* 2:11-38.

Hershenson, M., H. Munsinger, & W. Kessen (1965). "Preference for Shapes of Intermediate Variability in the Newborn Human," *Science,* 147:630-631.

Hoffer, W. (1949). "Mouth, Hand and Ego-Integration," *The Psychoanalytic Study of the Child,* 3/4:39-56.

——— (1950). "Development of the Body Ego," *The Psychoanalytic Study of the Child,* 5:18-24.

——— (1952). "The Mutual Influences in the Development of Ego and Id: Earliest Stages," *The Psychoanalytic Study of the Child,* 7:31-41.

Jacobson, E. (1957). "On Normal and Pathological Moods: Their Nature and Functions," *The Psychoanalytic Study of the Child,* 12:73-113.

Kalnins, I., & J. Bruner (1973). "Infant Sucking Used to Change the Clarity of a Visual Display," in J. L. Stone, H. T. Smith, & L. B. Murphy, eds., *The Competent Infant.* New York: Basic Books, pp. 707-713.

Korner, A. F., & R. Grobstein (1967). "Individual Differences at Birth: Implications for Mother-Infant Relationship and Later Development," *J. Amer. Acad. Child Psychiat.,* 6:676-690.

———, E. B. Thoman, & J. H. Glick (1974). "A System of Monitoring Crying and Noncrying Large, Medium and Small Neonatal Movements," *Child Develpm.,* 45:946-952.

Leitch, M., & S. K. Escalona (1949). "The Reaction of Infants to Stress: A Report of Clinical Findings," *The Psychoanalytic Study of the Child,* 3/4:121-140.

Lewis, M., & S. Goldberg (1969). "Perceptual Cognitive Development in Infancy: A Generalized Expectancy Model as a Function in the Mother-Infant Interaction," *Merrill-Palmer Quart.,* 15:81-100.

Lustman, S. L. (1956). "Rudiments of the Ego," *The Psychoanalytic Study of the Child,* 11:89-98.

——— (1957). "Psychic Energy and Mechanisms of Defense," *The Psychoanalytic Study of the Child,* 12:151-165.

Mahler, M. S. (1958). "Autism and Symbiosis: Two Extreme Disturbances of Identity," *Int. J. Psycho-Anal.,* 36:1-7.

——— (1965). "On the Significance of the Normal Separation-Individuation Phase," in M. Schur, ed., *Drives, Affects, Behavior,* Vol. 2. New York: International Universities Press, pp. 161-169.

——— (1967). "On Human Symbiosis and the Vicissitudes of Individuation," *J. Amer. Psychoanal. Assn.,* 15:740-763.

——— (1972). "On the First Three Sub-Phases of the Separation-Individuation Process," *Int. J. Psycho-Anal.,* 53:333-338.

———, & M. Furer (1963). "Certain Aspects of the Separation-Individuation Phase," *Psychoanal. Quart.,* 32:1-14.

———, & ——— (1968). *On Human Symbiosis and the Vicissitudes of Individuation.* New York: International Universities Press.

———, F. Pine, & A. Bergmann (1975). *The Psychological Birth of the Human Infant.* New York: Basic Books.

Meili, R. (1959). "A Longitudinal Study of Personality Development," in L. Jessner & E. Pavenstedt, eds., *Dynamic Psychopathology in Childhood.* New York & London: Grune & Stratton, pp. 106-123.

Piaget, J. (1937). *The Construction of Reality in the Child*. New York: Basic Books, 1954.

Provence, S., & S. Ritvo (1961). "Effects of Deprivation on Institutionalized Infants," *The Psychoanalytic Study of the Child,* 16:189-205.

Robson, K. S. (1967). "The Role of Eye-to-Eye Contact in Maternal Infant Attachment," *J. Child Psychol. Psychiat.,* 8:13-25.

Rubinow, O., & L. Frankl (1934). "Die erste Dingauffassung beim Säugling: Reaktionen auf Wahrnehmung der Flasche," *Z. Psychol.,* 133.

Sander, L. W. (1969). "The Longitudinal Course of Early Mother-Child Interaction: Cross-Case Comparison in a Sample of Mother-Child Pairs," in H. M. Foss, ed., *Determinants of Infant Behavior,* 4. London: Methuen, pp. 189-227.

———, G. Stechler, P. Burns, & H. Julia (1970). "Early Mother-Infant Interaction and 24-Hour Patterns of Activity and Sleep," *J. Amer. Acad. Child Psychiat.,* 9:103-123.

Schaffer, H. R. (1966). "The Onset of Fear of Stranger and the Incongruity Hypothesis," *J. Child Psychol. Psychiat.,* 7:95-106.

Siqueland, E. R., & C. A. de Lucia (1969). "Visual Reinforcement of Nonnutritive Sucking in Human Infants," *Science,* 165:1144-1146.

Spitz, R. A. (1950). "Anxiety in Infancy," *Int. J. Psycho-Anal.,* 31:138-143.

——— (1965). *The First Year of Life*. In collaboration with W. Godfrey Cobliner. New York: International Universities Press.

——— (1966). "Metapsychology and Direct Infant Observation," in *Psychoanalysis–A General Psychology,* ed. R. M. Loewenstein, L. M. Newman, M. Schur, & A. J. Solnits. New York: International Universities Press, pp. 123-151.

——— Emde, R. N., & D. R. Metcalf (1970). "Further Prototypes of Ego Formation: A Working Paper from a Research Project on Early Development," *The Psychoanalytic Study of the Child,* 25:417-441.

Stern, D. N. (1971). "A Micro-Analysis of Mother-Infant Interaction," *J. Amer. Acad. Child Psychiat.,* 10:501-517.

——— (1974). "The Goal and Structure of Mother-Infant Play," *J. Amer. Acad. Child Psychiat.,* 13:402-421.

Stone, L. J., H. T. Smith, & L. B. Murphy, eds. (1973). *The Competent Infant*. New York: Basic Books.

Uzgiris, I. C. (1972). "Patterns of Vocal and Gestural Imitation in Infants," in *Proceedings of the Symposium on Genetic and Social Influences on Psychological Development*. Basel: Karger.

Weil, A. P. (1956). "Some Evidences of Deviational Development in Infancy and Early Childhood," *The Psychoanalytic Study of the Child,* 11:292-299.

——— (1970). "The Basic Core," *The Psychoanalytic Study of the Child,* 25:442-460.

Wolff, P. H. (1959). "Observations on Newborn Infants," *Psychosom. Med.,* 21:111-118.

——— (1965a). "The Development of Attention in Young Infants," *Ann. NY Acad. Sci.,* 118:815-830.

——— (1965b). "The Natural History of Crying and Other Vocalizations in Early Infancy," in B. M. Foss, ed., *Determinants of Infant Behavior,* 4 London: Methuen, pp. 81-109.

——— (1973). "Organization of Behavior in the First Three Months of Life," in *Biological and Environmental Determinants of Early Development,* ed. J. Numberger. Baltimore: Williams & Williams.

———, & B. L. White (1965). "Visual Pursuit and Attention in Young Infants," *J. Amer. Acad. Child Psychiat.,* 4:473-484.

IV. SPECIAL ISSUES

The heading "Special Issues" refers to a variety of interests which have sufficient importance to be included in this volume, but which defy categorization under any of the previous section headings. In contrast to those by authors in the other chapters, many of the papers in this section address themselves to microscopic studies of human nature.

A good example of this is Corinne Hutt's "Sex Differences in Human Development." This paper is an overview; it brings together findings which indicate that gender differences can be observed in the first weeks of life, and that these differences, like other aspects of development, continue to be molded by the differentiating developmental process which leads to sex identity and social role designation. In recent years, new investigations have added to the rapidly increasing knowledge in this area. These investigations will aid us to better understand the social and clinical issues which are linked to male-female function.

The next paper, by Charlotte Bühler, belongs either in the section on concepts or in the one on clinical issues. Certainly her interest in the total life cycle is reminiscent of Erik Erikson's contribution and of the wish to follow the developmental processes beyond childhood. In opposition to the assumption that development spans childhood only and that what follows is not influenced by similar processes or changes, Bühler and others propose that developmental stages should also be outlined for adult life. Bühler thus attempts to delineate periods or stages characterized by specific psychic organization with their own conflicts and achievements superseded by further stages of adult life. Bühler's paper summarizes her extensive studies which began in Vienna and the data and criteria which can be used to understand developmental stages of adult "development."

The next paper in this section is one which summarizes the work of an important Russian psychologist, "Vygotsgy's View About the Age Periodization of Child Development," translated by Zender and Zender. In this paper Vygotsgy expands Pavlovian theory and attempts to apply

Marxist dialectical materialism to the study of developmental processes. The translators review a particular interest of Vygotsgy's, namely, age periodization, and thereby focus on a specific factor which is central to any theory of development. There is a good review of the theories which influenced Vygotsgy. You will find references to educational processes and contributions to the concept of critical periods. This study permits us to compare these formulations with those offered by psychoanalysis and by Piaget, both of which offer a rationale for the existence of stages and stress the significance of critical periods.

The next paper, by Louis Sander and collaborators, is "Primary Prevention and Some Aspects of Temporal Organization in Early Infant-Caretaker Interaction." This paper, as the title indicates, combines stringent methodology of infant observation with clinical considerations and draws inferences for the understanding of early development. The authors have contributed, over the years, significant new findings on early development. They have emphasized the dyadic interplay between mother or caretaker and child as it affects adaptation and the regulatory processes. This paper continues the thread of interest of Vygotsgy's concept of periodization, and it is also linked to the next paper, by Peter Wolff, who assesses the pattern of sucking. Sander's paper is an example of the special ways early infant behavior can be studied and of the significance of these findings for the evolvement of a theory of early development.

As the title indicates, Peter Wolff's paper on the role of biological rhythms in early psychic development exemplifies what is characteristic for him in his latest work—the focus on a specific behavior in early development which he then studies in great detail. It is possible to compare the concept of rhythmicity to periodicity, and furthermore, this paper can be seen in connection with Dr. Sander's studies of vision, sucking and sleep activity. Dr. Wolff explores, in his methodologically precise way, the rhythmicity of sucking, and he presents his findings in tables and statistical assessments. Furthermore, he relates these findings to normal as well as pathological development. He draws conclusions as to the early establishment of biological rhythms, thus revealing a view of the evolvement of rhythmic stability, a criterion which aids in the measurement of health or pathology. Moreover, we can see here the link between biologically anchored functions and the emergence of psychological meaning in the child.

13. Sex Differences in Human Development*

Corinne Hutt
Senior Research Fellow
Department of Psychology
University of Keele, England

During the past two decades there has been a regrettable silence on the subject of sex differences in human development in the psychological literature. What reports there were, clearly influenced by the 'Psychosexual-neutrality-at-birth' theory (Diamond, 1965), dealt mainly with questions of sex-role identification, sex-role adoption, learning of appropriate sex-role behaviours, and so on.

Two timely rebukes were administered recently by Garai and Scheinfeld (1968) and Carlson and Carlson (1960). Each pair of authors was lamenting the lack of attention paid to sex differences in their own field—the former in developmental psychology and the latter in social psychology. They noted that in each area a large number of studies failed to look for sex differences; others used single-sex samples, and some were even unaware of the sex of their subjects. Since these two areas account for a substantial proportion of psychological research undertaken, the neglect of sex differences seems to have been particularly regrettable.

A turning-point in this trend was the publication in 1966 of the book 'The development of sex differences' edited by Eleanor Maccoby. Although still reflecting a predominantly 'psychosexual-neutrality-at-birth' orientation, it nevertheless brought to light a large amount of incriminating evidence. Then followed the third edition of 'The psychology of human differences' (Tyler, 1965) which contained a cogent review of cognitive sex differences, and more recently, the impressive monograph by Garai and Scheinfeld (1968). Since then, and given an ironic fillip by the Women's Liberation Movement no doubt, many reports acknowledging the presence of sex differences, have once again appeared in the literature.

*Based, in part, on a paper read to the Annual Conference of the British Psychological Society, Exeter, 1971, in a symposium on 'The biological bases of psychological sex differences' convened by the author.

It is notable that, since its inception two years ago, the journal 'Developmental Psychology' has contained one or more reports on sex differences in nearly every issue.

In many ways, however, psychological sex differences are the tip of the iceberg. By the time differences in behaviour and performance manifest themselves, so much differentiation has already taken place. As contributors to the symposium on 'The biological bases of psychological sex differences' made only too clear, many of these differences are determined from the moment an ovum is fertilised by a sperm carrying an X or a Y chromosome. Possession of a Y chromosome, for example, confers a particular flavour on the development of the male zygote and embryo—an effect more pervasive than would result from simply the determination of masculinity (Ounsted and Taylor, 1972). Subsequently, the gonadal hormones exert their organisational influence on reproductive structures and, more significantly, on the central nervous system (Harris, 1964, 1970; Levine, 1966; Whalen, 1968; Hutt, 1972a; Michael, 1971).

In this paper, therefore, I would like to discuss some empirical results of behavioural and intellectual sex differences in early human development in the context of what is known about the biological determination of such differences.

Embryological Development

As Garai and Scheinfeld (1968) point out, from the moment of conception males and females exhibit radically different patterns of development. The neuroendocrinological processes and their influence on early development are essentially the same in all placental mammals and these have been adequately described elsewhere (Harris, 1964, 1970; Gorski and Wagner, 1965; Whalen, 1968; Hutt, 1972a).

The most notable feature of mammalian development is that there is no *neuter* sex. In the presence of a Y chromosome, the male gonad differentiates and then produces the androgenic evocator substance which exerts its action upon hypothalamic centres to produce the acyclic pattern of gonadotrophic hormone release characteristic of the male. In the absence of a Y chromosome, or more specifically, early androgenic influence, the natural propensity of mammalian creatures is to differentiate as *females*. This is so even in the case of a genetic male in whom, due to early castration or some disorder, the testicular hormone is absent or ineffective.

Such an instance occurs in humans in the syndrome of testicular feminisation, where, due to a recessive disorder, the testes of the genetic male often develop in an inguinal hernia and the gonadal hormone, if produced at all, is without effect (Federman, 1967). This individual differentiates as a female. Conversely, in the presence of androgens during the critical period, even the genetic female will differentiate as a male, as happens in the case of the adrenogenital syndrome (Wilkins, 1962; Bongiovanni and Root, 1963; Federman, 1967). Curiously, in the absence of *any* gonadal hormone, the development might be described as excessively ''feminine'': this happens in the case of Turner's syndrome, where one sex chromosome is lacking, the karyotype being XO, and there is gonadal dysgenesis. The comparison of behavioural and psychological features in androgenised females and in cases of Turner's syndrome made by Money and Erhardt (1968) is most instructive.

The particular interest of the processes and determinants of sexual differentiation to psychologists lies in the fact that it is not merely the reproductive structures which are organised in a typically male or female pattern, but higher neural centres as well. Characteristic differences appear, therefore, in patterns of sexual behaviour as well as in non-sexual behaviour. The behavioural differences are particularly striking in the higher mammals, namely, the primates (see Hamburg and Lunde, 1966; Goy, 1966, 1968, for informative review.

Physical Growth, Maturation and Susceptibility

From very early in uterine life males show their characteristic vulnerability: on average 120 males are conceived for every 100 females and by term this ratio has decreased to 110:100 (Glenister, 1956). The majority of spontaneous abortions (miscarriages), therefore, are of male foetuses (Stevenson and McClarin, 1957). In terms of live births the ratio is only 106: 100, which indicates a greater male susceptibility to perinatal complications such as anoxia (Stevenson, 1966; Stevenson and Bobrow, 1967). Throughout life males remain more vulnerable to a variety of disorders, e.g., cerebral palsy, viral infections, ulcers, coronary thrombosis and some forms of mental illness (Taylor and Ounsted, 1972; Garai, 1970). In fact the male's longevity is so curtailed that by the 6th and 7th decades of life the sex ratio is reversed in favour of the females. The sex-linked recessive disorders like haemophilia and colour-blindness predominantly affect the males; the recessive genes being carried on the X chromosome, males manifest the disorder even in the heterozygotic condition, whereas females are protected, other than in the homozygous condition, by the normal allele on the other X chromosome. The adage of the male being the stronger sex requires a very literal interpretation indeed.

At birth, males are heavier and longer than females (Ounsted, 1972). From infancy on boys have a consistently higher basal metabolism and greater vital capacity, develop proportionately larger hearts and lungs, and have a higher concentration of haemoglobin, notably after puberty (Hutt, 1972). Moreover, the male hormone facilitates protein synthesis whereas the female hormones have no such direct action. All these features characterise the male for a more active and strenuous life.

In sharp contrast to his physical advantages, however, is the male's developmental retardation: growth velocity lags nearly 2 years behind the female's (Tanner, 1970), bone ossification is completed much later (see Hutt, 1972b) and puberty is attained about 2½ years after the girl (Nicholson and Hanley, 1953). The onset of walking and talking, as well as aspects of dentition occur earlier in girls than in boys. In terms of maturity the newborn girl is equivalent to a 4- to 6-week-old boy (Garai and Scheinfeld, 1968).

Behaviour Differences in Infancy

Motor activity and sensory capacities. In general, male newborn infants exhibit more spontaneous motor activity and this consists predominantly of gross movements, whereas the activity of the female infants consists typically of finer movements, largely of the facial area, e.g., mouthing, smiling or sucking (Korner, 1969). Female neonates have lower tactual and pain thresholds (Lipsitt and Levy, 1959) and this sex difference very probably obtains throughout the lifespan since Galton observed it in adults and specifically commented upon it as early as 1894. Female infants also react more irritably to tactual stimulation (Bell and Costello, 1964).

There is now substantial evidence that the visual acuity of males is superior to that of females, at least from adolescence on (Burg and Hulbert, 1961), whereas females have better auditory discrimination and localisation (Corso, 1959; Schaie et al., 1964). The results obtained by Lewis suggest that such sensory proficiency and preferences may be evident even in early infancy: he found that male infants showed greater interest in visual patterns generally, while female infants attended more to auditory sequences (Kagan and Lewis, 1965); of visual patterns female infants found *facial* configurations most interesting and at 3, 6 and 9 months of age they were able to differentiate between such patterns more effectively than the males (Lewis, 1969).

On the basis of results obtained from 3-month-old infants, Moss and Robson (1970) concluded that, whereas social experience and learning appeared to have a strong influence upon the visual behaviour of females, that of the males was more a function of endogenous attributes like state. These several results illustrate not merely the sex-dependent sensory capacities but also the differences in those influences to which they are amenable. Such differences, however, are not peculiar to the human species—very similar behaviour is shown by monkeys (Mitchell and Brandt, 1970).

The early dependence on particular sensory modalities has the consequence that auditory and visual stimuli have different reinforcing properties, depending on the sex of the subject. For instance, Watson (1969) found that visual fixation on a target could be operantly conditioned in 14-week-old infants, the effective reinforcers being visual for males and auditory for females. Moreover, the boys failed to learn under conditions of auditory reinforcement. This reliance of males and females on visual and auditory channels, respectively, is observable throughout childhood and adolescence (Stevenson et al., 1963) and persists in adulthood (Miller, 1963; Pishkin and Shurley, 1965).

Mother-infant interaction. The earliest social behaviour displayed by the human infant is in the context of the mother-infant interaction. Many studies reporting differences in the way mothers handle their male and female infants, or for that matter, any sex differences in human behaviour, tend to account for such differences in terms of the mothers' expectations of a son or a daughter, of her greater affinity for the same-sex infant, or else in terms of the reinforcement of sex-appropriate behaviours. A study by Moss (1967) is notable, therefore, for the demonstration that considerable differences in the behaviour of male and female infants exist at the age of 3 weeks. The differential reactions of the mother are very probably contingent upon these behaviours and not contrariwise, as commonly supposed. Two of Moss' findings seem particularly significant, especially since they were also apparent at the age of 3 months: mothers stimulated their infant sons more, and imitated the vocalisations of their daughters more. The first of these raises the interesting possibility that we may have here the human analogue of the "early-handled" animals described by Levine (1960), Denenberg (1964) and others. If such findings are replicated, we may seriously have to inquire whether the early experience of male infants in any way contributes to their subsequent lower emotionality (Gray, 1971a; Gray and Buffery, 1971; Buffery and Gray, 1972). Secondly, the fact that mothers imitated, and thereby very probably reinforced, their daughters' vocalisations is surprising, since the actual amounts of vocalisation by boys and by girls were almost identical. Since a similar finding was also reported by Goldberg and Lewis (1969), it immediately raises the question as to what parameters of infants vocal behaviour the mothers were responding. May this fact also explain, in part, the earlier acquisition of speech in girls?

Goldberg and Lewis (1969) were able to demonstrate striking sex differences in infants of 13 months, both in their behaviour towards their mothers as well as in the character of their play. Girls were more reluctant than boys to leave their mothers, tended to stay near them when playing and sought physical reassurance more frequently.

Fear. Analysing data from the Berkeley Growth Study, Bronson (1969) found sex-differences in the onset of the fear-of-stranger reaction: fear at 10-15 months was positively correlated with fear and shyness at a later age in *boys* but not in girls. This was chiefly due to a sub-group of boys who showed a precocious onset of fear (4-6 months) and remained so throughout childhood. Thus, an early onset of fear-of-novelty in male infants was predictive of fearfulness during the entire pre-school period.

Behavioural Differences in Childhood

Social interactions. In an investigation of the types of activity boys and girls generally engaged in (Brindley et al., 1972), it was found that girls engaged in social interactions much more frequently than boys—a dramatic illustration of the early differentiation of masculine and feminine interests, boys being interested in objects or 'things' and girls in people (Little, 1968). Honzik (1951) and Hattwick (1937) observed very similar differences in older children, as did Farrell (1957).

More specifically, *aggression* is an aspect of social behaviour that has interested many students of child behaviour and a number of studies have shown boys to be more aggressive than girls (Green, 1933; Dawe, 1934; Jersild and Markey, 1935; Hattwick, 1937; Walters et al., 1957; Jegard and

Walters, 1960; Bandura et al., 1963; Digman, 1963; Pederson and Bell, 1970). Many of these results, however, were interpreted in terms of sex-role expectations and conventions, with no reference made to the fact that the males of most mammalian species are more aggressive than the females, nor was surprise expressed at the apparent universality of male aggression—despite differences in culture-patterns, conventions and social norms. In our own study of nursery school children (Brindley et al., 1972), we found that two thirds of all aggressive acts were initiated by boys. Moreover, not only did boys *display* more aggression, but they also *elicited* aggression. Many of such disputes arose over the possession of toys, equipment or territory. Girls, whose aggression generally found verbal expression, were equally aggressive to other girls, boys, teachers or objects. Boys retaliated more and hence prolonged such encounters whereas the girls usually submitted or else employed more devious strategies to secure their objectives (McCandless et al., 1961). These sex-dependent features of aggression are observable in older children as well as in adults. In experiments which allowed subjects to mete out punishment to a mock opponent, adult males gave bigger shocks when they thought their opponent was a male than when they thought it was a female (Buss, 1963; Taylor and Epstein, 1967). In a similar experiment 10- and 11-year-olds, using noise as punishment, behaved exactly as the adults had done (Shortell and Biller, 1970).

Male monkeys engage in threat displays while the females show fear grimaces, and in a male monkey group the dominance hierarchy is established by the aggressive behaviour and threat displays of the ascendant male while in female groups the hierarchy is established and maintained by the submissive behaviours of the non-dominant females (Angermeier et al., 1968). Thus, when the human results are considered in the general context of primate social behaviour, any purely cultural or environmental sex-role theory of sexual differentiation becomes difficult to countenance. Elsewhere (Hutt, 1972a, b), I have also presented the experimental evidence for regarding aggressive behaviour as primarily a function of the early sexual differentiation of the brain, and secondarily as an effect of circulating hormone levels.

Another aspect of early social behaviour that we studied was cooperative or mutual behaviour (Brindley et al., 1972), where children joined each other, either spontaneously or at the request of one of them, to engage in some mutual activity. Girls initiated such acts much more than boys, and directed their attention in this respect predominantly towards *younger* children (chiefly girls), thus manifesting their proclivities for fulfilling a nurturant and protective role (Mischel, 1970). This is evident in many ways: readiness to help younger ones carry things, to button pinafores or tie aprons, and to comfort a hurt or distressed child. The boys appear to show a remarkable indifference to a peer's discomfort or distress. McGrew (1972) has also described the characteristic tendency of the girls to shepherd and care for a new entrant to the nursery group, whereas boys manifest their customary indifference to such a newcomer. The boys in our study tended to direct their cooperative acts primarily towards other *older* boys, usually attempting to join a game or excursion already in progress. Similar sex-typical behaviours have been described in many infra-human primate groups too (de Vore and Jay, 1963; Harlow, 1962; Goodall, 1968).

In general, there is a marked tendency in humans—children and adults alike (Hutt, 1972; Tiger, 1969)—to interact with others of their own sex. The men's club, the officers' mess, the women's institute, all clearly have their ontogenetic origins in the kindergartens and their phylogenetic origins in diverse primate groups.

Exploration and play. In the study of 13-month-old infants by Goldberg and Lewis (1969), boys were active, frequently banged toys, and showed an interest in manipulating the fixtures; girls were more sedentary, interested in combining toys and showed a preference for the toys with faces. Results essentially similar were obtained in our study of nursery school children in Reading (Brindley et al., 1972): girls chiefly engaged in sedentary activities like crayonning, cutting-out or plasticene work; boys were much more active—running, jumping and showing a marked preference for push/pull toys. Many of these sex-dependent differences were also observed by Clark et al. (1969) in Cambridge nursery schools.

In studies of the exploratory behaviour of nearly 200 nursery school children, a striking finding that emerged was that boys and girls, after investigating a new toy, went on to use it in very different ways (Hutt, 1970a, b). Boys more frequently engaged in inventive or creative play with this toy, whereas more girls than boys failed to explore at all. Objections regarding the neutrality of the toy were shown to be invalid on several grounds (Hutt, 1970b, 1972). To a certain extent these differences are comprehensible in the context of early sexual differentiation in psychological and cognitive faculties. Girls, being advanced developmentally in many respects, at the age of 3 and 4 years are becoming increasingly proficient in verbal and social skills while boys are still actively manipulating and exploring their environment. Nevertheless, there was one other question that concerned us: were we witnessing in this situation some characteristic expression of the originality of the future creative artist or scientist? A follow-up study of these children with tests of creativity was thus indicated. Prior to this study, however, a pilot investigation was carried out, with a view to seeing how children of 7-9 years of age in British primary schools performed on such tests.

Creativity and divergent thinking. On creativity tests like those described by Wallach and Kogan (1965), two measures can be derived: (1) the *total* number of responses given to any item, i.e. fluency; and (2) the number of *unique* responses offered for any item, i.e. originality. On testing 60 boys and 60 girls between the ages of 7 and 10 years, girls were found to score unequivocally higher than boys on the fluency measure (Bhavnani and Hutt, 1972; Hutt, 1972a). When, however, the unique responses alone were considered there were no differences between the sexes. This was surprising in view of the fact that the number of unique responses is dependent to some extent on the total number of responses, since the former tend to be given when the more conventional responses have been exhausted (Wallach and Kogan, 1965). Wallach and Kogan themselves make no mention of sex differences despite the fact that they obtained a significant difference in favour of the boys on one of the uniqueness measures. Hudson (1968), on the other hand, found that sixth form boys (16 years) were more fluent than girls, but he omits any mention of the results on the originality measure. Thus, the evidence for sex-typical performances on both the fluency and originality measures is equivocal. But certainly no study has demonstrated greater originality or uniqueness in the responses of girls.

This conclusion, moreover, is concordant with other evidence, both empirical and circumstantial, which shows adult males to be considerably more divergent and creative than females. Shouksmith (1970) for instance, carried out an extensive factorial study of intelligence, reasoning, problem solving and creativity, and on the basis of his results concluded that:

> . . . males and females do not think alike. Factorially the female group is more complex than the male . . . For females a much greater range of behaviour patterns appear to be mutually exclusive categories . . . for example, we see that "creative associating" is opposed to "deductive reasoning" in women, whereas it is not so clearly opposed in men . . . true creativity depends on an ability to switch from the one to the other of these as and when necessary. On this argument, one would expect to find fewer women among the ranks of truly inventive geniuses or scientific discoverers. (pp. 188, 189.)

Again, Maccoby (1966) reported a study of Radcliffe College academics who, though of equal professional status with their male colleagues, were nevertheless considerably less productive. More circumstantially, Hudson (1966) noted that the proportion of men to women in the Royal Society (Britain's select and august scientific body) was 40 to 1. Klein (1966) found that in the physical and applied sciences the male:female ratio was considerably in excess of 50 to 1. In the aesthetic fields too, despite several decades of relative feminine liberation, it is a lamentable fact that women have not figured more prominently among the creative artists. The domestic bondage of women cannot eternally be proffered as an excuse—after all, even in less auspicious times women contributed to the literary fields.

Intellectual functions. The performance of the 8- and 9-year-olds on the tests of creativity also indicated that, despite their greater verbal fluency, girls were not necessarily more original than boys. Other studies suggest that verbal fluency is an aspect of language function that is dissociated from other more conceptual aspects like reasoning and comprehension. Garai and Scheinfeld (1968) for instance, provocatively concluded that though girls may acquire language earlier than boys—chiefly due to their maturational advancement—and are superior in terms of verbal fluency as well as in reading, writing and spelling, they are certainly inferior in matters of verbal comprehension, verbal reasoning, and even vocabulary. In general agreement with this conclusion, the relevant evidence was documented in an earlier review (Hutt, 1972a). Thus, although girls are indubitably superior in the *executive* aspects of language, they seem to be less adequate in manipulating and relating verbal concepts. Very striking evidence for such a conclusion is readily obtained from the norms for verbal reasoning, spelling, and sentence length, on the differential aptitude test (Bennett et al., 1959) given in Table I.

Although the position is rather more ambiguous with respect to

TABLE I.
Norms for 3 sub-tests of the differential aptitude test for boys and girls of 2 age-groups

Age	Sex	Verbal reasoning	Language usage I, spelling	Language usage II, sentences
13	Boys	15.8	25.9	20.2
	Girls	14.6	37.9	28.6
17	Boys	29.3	59.1	40.9
	Girls	25.2	72.1	45.8

intellectual capacities, once again the available evidence suggests that males achieve a higher verbal IQ on the WAIS and WISC than females, whereas females obtain a higher performance IQ than males. Tyler's (1965) summary statement is even more affirmative:

> Most of the available evidence seems to indicate . . . that it is in the verbal *fluency* (what Thurstone has called W) rather than in the grasp of verbal meanings (V) that females are superior . . . Comparisons of various groups of males and females on various tests, however, has also made it fairly clear that girls and women do *not* have larger vocabularies than boys and men do. (p. 244.)

Results very similar to those noted above were also observed in younger children (Heilman, 1933; Hobson, 1947). Even Wechsler (1941) who originally maintained that there were no sex differences, having discarded those items which differentiated between the sexes, eventually (Wechsler, 1958) conceded that:

> Our findings do confirm what poets and novelists have often asserted, and the average layman long believed, that men not only behave but *think* differently from women.

The similarity of Shouksmith's (1970) conclusion, almost 13 years later and based on very different performances, to Wechsler's is indeed striking.

Determinants of IQ. On the basis of data obtained from 26 boys and 27 girls in the Berkeley Growth Study, Bayley and Schaefer (1964) concluded that, whereas the intellectual capacities of boys were susceptible to environmental influences, those of girls were more genetically determined. This conclusion was based on the finding that the IQ of girls showed a higher correlation with those of their parents than boys with their parents, as well as a correlation between early maternal behaviour and child's IQ for boys but not for girls. Bayley (1966) subsequently reported other studies which had also demonstrated higher parent-daughter than parent-son correlations in intellectual capacities. Maccoby (1966) regarded the Bayley and Schaefer (1964) conclusion circumspectly in the absence of other supportive evidence. From a follow-up study of 231 boys and 254 girls born in Hawaii, Werner (1969) concluded that her data did not support the Bayley-Schaefer hypothesis, but indicated a sex difference in rate of maturation in favour of the girls as well as 'a greater responsiveness of the girls to achievement demands and educational stimulation in the home in middle childhood'.

It seems to me, however, that the emphases of both Bayley and Schaefer (1964) and Werner (1969) are misplaced for the following reasons. First, the earlier maturation of the girls would determine that a polygenic ability as IQ will be fully manifested earlier in girls than in boys, thereby yielding a higher daughter-parent correlation at any age prior to adolescence. Secondly, much evidence indicates that girls lateralise many cerebral functions earlier and more effectively than males (Taylor, 1969; Buffery, 1971) and hence acquire greater proficiency in them initially. Werner's (1969) data, in fact, corroborates both these points: the discrepancy in parent-child correlations at 20 months and at 10 years was far greater for boys than for girls. Moreover, at 10 years girls showed a significant correlation on all 11 of the parental and environmental variables and boys on 10 of the 11 variables. Thirdly, evidence from longitudinal studies like those of Moore (1967) have demonstrated that in the first 8 years girls are more constrained and more predictable in their intellectual development, which takes place primarily through linguistic channels. Since the principal environmental factor associated with the IQ of the girls in Werner's (1969) study was educational stimulation, a characteristic property of which was 'enlargement of vocabulary', the higher parent-daughter correlation is predictable. The boys in Moore's study, on the other hand, showed an almost haphazard course of development—no earlier score reliably predicted any later one. There was evidence too that non-verbal experiences and skills contributed more to the IQ of boys than to that of girls. In view of all these considerations there seems little need to postulate a different genetic contribution to the IQ of girls and boys, or a differential responsiveness of boys and girls to environmental influences. It is sufficient to state the empirical observations that: (1) the IQ of girls and boys are differently constituted; (2) that the girls' IQ is manifested largely in terms of verbal skills and is, therefore, sensitive to linguistic influences; (3) that since girls mature earlier, the several genes contributing to intelligence are all expressed by an earlier age—this being evident in a more stable IQ—thus yielding a higher parent-daughter correlation during childhood than the comparable parent-son correlation.

There are many other respects in which males and females are characteristically different, but since these have been adequately outlined or discussed elsewhere (Tyler, 1965; Maccoby, 1966; Garai and Scheinfeld, 1968; Hutt, 1972a, b), enumeration of them here seems superfluous.

Concluding Discussion

The foregoing discussion of the process of sexual differentiation and the phenomena of sex differences has been an attempt to reiterate the many biological and psychological differences that characteristically differentiate males and females in our species. These particular properties have clearly been selected in accordance with, on the one hand, certain morphological features, and on the other, with the particular roles human males and females fulfil. That these morphological and functional requirements are not unique to a particular society, nor even to the human species, is evident in the fact that very similar differences are demonstrable in infra-human primate species. This fact alone makes an exclusively environmental theory of sex differences difficult to countenance. Moreover, as Buffery and Gray (1972) point out, such similarities behove us to seek a more appropriately biological explanation for the phenomena. Gray himself has discussed the endocrinological, neural and adaptive bases for sex differences in mammals generally (Gray, 1971a, b; Gray and Buffery, 1971; Buffery and Gray, 1972). The evidence reviewed by both Gray and myself (Hutt, 1972) shows that not only is behaviour affected by circulating hormones, but that these hormones have an important formative and organisational influence on brain function and structure.

It is a common, but nonetheless fallacious, assumption that the recognition of individual differences, be they sex- or personality-dependent, is to commit oneself to a psychological or behavioural determinism. On the contrary, the recognition of such differences and their possible determinants enables individuals to modify and/or exploit environmental circumstances to profitable advantage.

The conformity and consistency of the female's behaviour in fulfilling a predominantly nurturant role, makes her a stable and reliable support for the dependent infant. Even her distractability (Garai and Scheinfeld, 1968) appears to be adaptive. In her intellectual faculties too the human female seems to have exploited those facets that ensure the optimal execution of her primary role—the maternal role. For more effective communication increasing reliance is placed on linguistic skills, and it is noteworthy that in verbal functions as in non-verbal ones, it is in *execution* that the female excels. The male on the other hand, and necessarily, excels in spatial and numerical abilities, is divergent in thought and action, and is generally superior in *conceptualisation*. The fact that such functional dimorphism exists may be unacceptable to many, but it is a dimorphism that has been uniquely successful.

REFERENCES

Angermeier, W. F., J. B. Phelps, S. Murray, and J. Howanstine. "Dominance in Monkeys: Sex Differences", *Psychon. Sci. 12:* 344 (1968).

Bandura, A., D. Ross, and S. A. Ross. "Transmission of Aggression Through Imitation of Aggressive Models," *J. abnorm. soc. Psychol. 63:* 575-582 (1961).

Bayley, N. "Developmental Problems of the mentally retarded child," in Philips, *Prevention and Treatment of Mental Retardation,* New York: Basic Books, 1966.

———, and E. S. Schaefer. "Correlations of Maternal and Child Behaviours with the Development of Mental Abilities: Data from the Berkeley Growth Study," *Monogr. Soc. Res. Child Develop. 29:* 1-80 (1964).

Bell, R. Q., and N. S. Costello. "Three Tests for Sex Differences in Tactile Sensitivity in the Newborn," *Biol. Neonat. 7:* 335-347 (1964).

Bennett, G. K., H. G. Seashore, and A. G. Wesman. *Differential Aptitude Tests.* Manual, 3rd ed. New York: Psychological Corporation, 1959.

Bhavnani, R., and C. Hutt. "Divergent Thinking in Boys and Girls," *J. child Psychol. Psychiat.* (1972, in press).

Bongiovanni, A. M., and A. W. Root. "The Adrenogenital Syndrome," *New Engl. J. Med. 268:* 1283 (1963).

Brindley, C., P. Clarke, C. Hutt, I. Robinson, and E. Wethli. "Sex Differences in the Activities and Social Interactions of Nursery School Children," in Michael and Crook, *Comparative Ecology and Behaviour of Primates.* London: Academic Press, 1972.

Bronson, G. W. "Fear of Visual Novelty: Developmental Patterns in Males and Females," *Develop. Psychol. 1:* 33-40 (1969).

Buffery, A. W. H. "Sex Differences in Cognitive Skills." Paper Ann. Conf. Brit. Psychol. Soc., Exeter; in Symp. on Biological bases of psychological sex differences (1971).

———, and J. A. Gray. "Sex Differences in the Development of Perceptual and Linguistic Skills," in Ounsted and Taylor, *Gender Differences–Their Ontogeny and Significance.* London: Churchill, 1972.

Burg, A., and S. Hulbert. "Dynamic Visual Acuity as Related to Age, Sex and Static Acuity," *J. appl. Psychol. 45:* 111-116 (1961).

Buss, A. H. "Physical Aggression in Relation to Different Frustrations," *J. abnorm. soc. Psychol. 67:* 1-7 (1963).

Carlson, E. R., and R. Carlson. "Male and Female Subjects in Personality Research," *J. abnorm. soc. Psychol. 61:* 482-483 (1960).

Clark, A. H., S. M. Wyon, and M. P. Richards. "Free-Play in Nursery School Children," *J. child Psychol. Psychiat. 10:* 205-216 (1969).

Corso, J. F. "Age and Sex Differences in Pure-Tone Thresholds," *J. acoust. Soc. Amer. 31:* 489-507 (1959).

Dawe, H. C. "An Analysis of 200 Quarrels of Preschool Children," *Child Develop. 5:* 139-156 (1934).

Denenberg, V. H. "Animal Studies on Developmental Determinants of Behavioural Adaptability," in Harvey, *Experience, Structure and Adaptability,* pp. 123-147. New York: Springer, 1966.

de Vore, I., and P. Jay. "Mother-Infant Relations in Baboons and Langurs," in Rheingold, *Maternal Behaviour in Mammals.* New York: Wiley & Sons, 1963.

Diamond, M. "A Critical Evaluation of the Ontogeny of Human Sexual Behaviour," *Quart. Rev. Biol. 40:* 147-175 (1965).

Digman, J. M. "Principal Dimensions of Child Personality as Inferred from Teachers' Judgments," *Child Develop. 34:* 43-60 (1963).

Farrell, M. "Sex Differences in Block Play in Early Childhood Education," *J. educ. Res. 51:* 279-284 (1957).

Federman, M. D. *Abnormal Sexual Development*. Philadelphia: Saunders, 1967.

Galton, F. "The Relative Sensitivity of Men and Women at the Nape of the Neck by Webster's Test," *Nature*, Lond. *50:* 40-42 (1894).

Garai, J. E. "Sex Differences in Mental Health," *Genet. Psychol. Monogr. 81:* 123-142 (1970).

———, and A. Scheinfeld. "Sex Differences in Mental and Behavioural Traits," *Genet. Psychol. Monogr. 77:* 169-299 (1968).

Glenister, T. W. "Determination of Sex in Early Human Embryos," *Nature*, Lond. *177:* 1135 (1956).

Goldberg, S., and M. Lewis. "Play Behaviour in the Year-Old Infant: Early Sex Differences," *Child Develop. 40:* 21-31 (1969).

Goodall, J. L. van. "The Behaviour of Free-Living Chimpanzees in the Gombi Stream Reserve," *Anim. Behav. Monogr, 1:* 161-311 (1968).

Gorski, R. A., and J. W. Wagner. "Gonadal Activity and Sexual Differentiation of the Hypothalamus," *Endocrinology 76:* 226-239 (1965).

Goy, R. W. "Role of Androgens in the Establishment and Regulation of Behavioural Sex Differences in Mammals," *J. anim. Sci. 25:* suppl., pp. 21-35 (1966).

———. "Organising Effects of Androgen on the Behaviour of Rhesus Monkeys," in Michael, *Endocrinology and Human Behaviour*. London: Oxford University Press, 1968.

Gray, J. A. "Sex Differences in Emotional Behaviour in Mammals Including Man: Endocrine Bases," *Acta psychol.*, Amst. *35:* 29-46 (1971a).

———. *The Psychology of Fear and Stress*. London: Weidenfeld and Nicolson, 1971b.

———, and A. W. H. Buffery. "Sex Differences in Emotional and Cognitive Behaviour in Mammals Including Man: Adaptive and Neural Bases," *Acta psychol.*, Amst. *35:* 89-111 (1971).

Green, E. H. "Friendships and Quarrels Among Preschool Children," *Child Develop. 4:* 236-252 (1933).

Hamburg, D. A., and D. T. Lunde. "Sex Hormones in the Development of Sex Differences in Human Behaviour," in Maccoby, *The Development of Sex Differences*. London: Tavistock, 1966.

Harlow, H. F. "Development of Affection in Primates," in Bliss, *Roots of Behaviour*. New York: Harper, 1962.

Harris, G. W. "Sex Hormones, Brain Development and Brain Function," *Endocrinology 75:* 627-648 (1964).

———. "Hormonal Differentiation of the Developing Central Nervous System with Respect to Patterns of Endocrine Function," *Philos. Trans.* B *259:* 165-177 (1970).

Hattwick, L. A. "Sex Differences in Behavior of Nursery School Children," *Child Develop. 8:* 343-355 (1937).

Heilman, J. D. "Sex Differences in Intellectual Abilities," *J. educ. Psychol. 24:* 47-62 (1933).

Hobson, J. R. "Sex Differences in Primary Mental Abilities," *J. educ. Res. 41:* 126-132 (1947).

Honzik, M. P. "Sex Differences in the Occurrence of Materials in the Play Constructions of Pre-Adolescents," *Child Develop. 22:* 15-35 (1951).

Hudson, L. *Contrary Imaginations*. London: Methuen, 1966.

———. *Frames of Mind*. London: Methuen, 1968.

Hutt, C. "Specific and Diversive Explorations," in Reese and Lipsitt, *Advances in Child Development and Behaviour*, Vol. 5. London: Academic Press, 1970a.

———. "Curiosity in Young Children," *Sci. J. 6:* 68-72 (1970b).

———. "Neuroendocrinological, Behavioural and Intellectual Aspects of Sexual Differentiation in Human Development," in Ounsted and Taylor, *Gender Differences–Their Ontogeny and Significance*. London: Churchill, 1972a.

———. Males and females. Penguin Books (1972b, in press).

Jegard, S., and R. H. Walters. "A Study of Some Determinants of Aggression in Young Children," *Child Develop. 31:* 739-747 (1960).

Jersild, A. T., and F. V. Markey. *Conflicts Between Preschool Children.* Child Develop. Monogr. 21 (1935).

Kagan, J., and M. Lewis. "Studies of Attention in the Human Infant," *Behav. Develop. 11:* 95-127 (1965).

Klein, V. "The Demand for Professional Woman I Power," *Brit. J. Sociol. 17:* 183 (1966).

Korner, A. F. "Neonatal Startles, Smiles, Erections, and Reflex Sucks as Related to State, Sex and Individuality," *Child Develop. 40:* 1039-1053 (1969).

Levine, S. "Stimulation in Infancy," *Sci. Amer. 202:* 80-86 (1960).

———. "Sex Differences in the Brain," *Sci. Amer. 214:* 84-90 (1966).

Lewis, M. "Infants' Responses to Facial Stimuli During the First Year of Life," *Dev. Psychol. I:* 75-86 (1969).

Lipsitt, L. P., and N. Levy. "Electrotactual Threshold in the Neonate," *Child Develop. 30:* 547-554 (1959).

Little, B. "Psychospecialisation: Functions of Differential Interest in Persons and Things," *Bull. Brit. psychol. Soc. 21:* 113A (1968).

Maccoby, E. E., ed. *The Development of Sex Differences.* London: Tavistock, 1966.

McCandless, B. R., B. Bilous, and H. L. Bennett. "Peer Popularity and Dependence on Adults in Preschool Age Socialisation," *Child Develop. 32:* 511-518 (1961).

McGrew, W. C. "Aspects of Social Development in Nursery School Children with Emphasis on Introduction to the Group," in Blurton-Jones, *Ethological Studies of Child Behaviour.* London: Cambridge University Press, 1972.

Michael, R. P. "The Endocrinological Bases of Sex Differences." Paper Ann. Conf. Brit. Psychol. Soc., Exeter, in Symp. Biological Bases of Psychological Sex Differences (1971).

Miller, A. "Sex Differences Related to the Effect of Auditory Stimulation on the Stability of Visually Fixed Forms," *Percept. Mot. Skills 16:* 589-594 (1963).

Mischel, W. "Sex-Typing and Socialisation," in Mussen, *Carmichael's Manual of Child Psychology,* Vol. 2. London: Wiley, 1970.

Mitchell, G., and E. M. Brandt. "Behavioural Differences Related to Experience of Mother and Sex of Infant in the Rhesus Monkey," *Develop. Psychol. 3:* 149 (1970).

Money, J., and A. A. Ehrhardt. "Prenatal Hormonal Exposure: Possible Effects on Behaviour in Man," in Michael, *Endocrinology and Human Behaviour.* London: Oxford University Press, 1968.

Moore, T. "Language and Intelligence: A Longitudinal Study of the First 8 Years. I. Patterns of Development in Boys and Girls," *Human Develop. 10:* 88-106 (1967).

Moss, H. "Sex, Age and State as Determinants of Mother-Infant Interaction," *Merrill-Palmer Quart. 13:* 19-36 (1967).

Moss, H. A., and K. S. Robson. "The Relation Between the Amount of Time Infants Spend at Various States and the Development of Visual Behaviour," *Child Develop. 41:* 509-517 (1970).

Nicolson, A. B., and C. Hanley. "Indices of Physiological Maturity: Derivation and Interrelationships," *Child Develop. 24:* 3-38 (1953).

Ounsted, C., and D. C. Taylor. "The Y Chromosome Message: A Point of View," in Ounsted and Taylor, *Gender Differences–Their Ontogeny and Significance.* London: Churchill, 1972.

Ounsted, M. "Sex Differences in Intrauterine Growth," in Ounsted and Taylor, *Gender Differences–Their Ontogeny and Significance.* London: Churchill, 1972.

Pedersen, F. A., and R. Q. Bell, "Sex Differences in Preschool Children Without Histories of Complications of Pregnancy and Delinquency," *Develop. Psychol. 3:* 10-15 (1970).

Pishkin, V., and J. T. Shurley. "Auditory Dimensions and Irrelevant Information in Concept Identification of Males and Females," *Percept. Mot. Skills 20:* 673-683 (1965).

Schaie, K. W., P. Baltes, and C. R. Strother. "A Study of Auditory Sensitivity in Advanced Age," *J. Geront. 19:* 453-457 (1964).

Shortell, J. R., and H. B. Biller. "Aggression in Children as a Function of Sex of Subject and Sex of Opponent," *Develop. Psychol. 3:* 143-144 (1970).

Shouksmith, G. *Intelligence, Creativity and Cognitive Style*. London: Batsford, 1970.

Stevenson, A. C. "Sex Chromatin and the Sex Ratio in Man," in Moore, *The Sex Chromatin*. Philadelphia: Saunders, 1966.

———, and M. Bobrow. "Determinants of Sex Proportions in Man, with Consideration of the Evidence Concerning a Contribution from X-Linked Mutations to Intrauterine Death," *J. med. Genet. 4:* 190-221 (1967).

———, and R. H. McClarin. "Determination of the Sex of Human Abortions by Nuclear Sexing the Cells of the Chorionic," *Nature*, Lond. *180:* 198 (1957).

Stevenson, H. W., R. Keen, and R. W. Knights. "Parents and Strangers as Reinforcing Agents for Children's Performance," *J. abnorm. Soc. Psychol. 67:* 183-186 (1963).

Tanner, J. M. "Physical Growth," in Mussen, *Carmichael's Manual of Child Psychology*, 3rd ed. New York: Wiley, 1970.

Taylor, D. C. "Differential Rates of Cerebral Maturation Between Sexes and Between Hemispheres," *Lancet iii:* 140-142 (1969).

———, and C. Ounsted. "The Nature of Gender Differences Explored Through Ontogenetic Analyses of Sex Ratios in Disease," in Ounsted and Taylor, *Gender Differences–Their Ontogeny and Significance*. London: Churchill, 1972.

Taylor, S. P., and S. Epstein. "Aggression as a Function of the Interaction of the Sex of the Aggressor and Sex of the Victim," *J. Personality 35:* 474-486 (1967).

Tiger, L. *Men in Groups*. London: Nelson, 1969.

Tyler, L. *The Psychology of Human Differences*, 3rd ed. New York: Appleton-Century-Crofts, 1965.

Wallach, M. A., and N. Kogan. *Modes of Thinking in Young Children*. New York: Holt, Rinehart & Winston, 1965.

Walters, J., D. Pearce, and L. Dahms. "Affectional and Aggressive Behaviour of Pre-School Children," *Child Develop. 28:* 15-26 (1957).

Watson, T. S. "Operant Conditioning of Visual Fixation in Infants Under Visual and Auditory Reinforcement," *Develop. Psychol. 1:* 508-516 (1969).

Wechsler, D. *The Measurement of Adult Intelligence*. Baltimore: Williams & Wilkins, 1941.

———. *The Measurement and Appraisal of Adult Intelligence*, 4th ed. Baltimore: Williams & Wilkins, 1958.

Werner, E. E. "Sex Differences in Correlations Between Children's IQ and Measures of Parental Ability, and Environmental Ratings," *Develop. Psychol. 1:* 280-285 (1969).

Whalen, R. E. "Differentiation of the Neural Mechanisms Which Control Gonadotropin Secretion and Sexual Behaviour," in Diamond, *Reproduction and Sexual Behaviour*. Bloomington: Indiana University Press, 1968.

Wilkins, L. "Adrenal Disorders. II. Congenital Virilizing Adrenal Hyperplasia," *Arch. Dis. Childh. 37:* 231 (1962).

14. The Course of Human Life as a Psychological Problem

Charlotte Bühler

PROFESSOR OF PSYCHOLOGY
UNIVERSITY OF SOUTHERN CALIFORNIA MEDICAL SCHOOL
CLINICAL PROFESSOR OF PSYCHIATRY
UNIVERSITY OF VIENNA

1. A model of human development through the life cycle. This paper restates a theory of human development set forth in a much earlier publication (Bühler, 1933) and evaluates the applicability of this theory to more recent data and thinking.

The model was originally developed from analysis of 202 biographical studies and some additional statistical and interview material. The biographies were assembled under the direction of E. Frenkel and E. Brunswik in Vienna and were selected for completeness and reliability of the sources, particularly statements regarding motives, attitudes and other inner experiences.

The majority of published biographies concern themselves with the lives of personalities who for one reason or another have become outstanding. An impressive fact was that most of these lives seemed to have an inner coherence which appeared due to some unifying or integrating principle. This integrating principle seemed to evolve from certain expectations which permeated these people's lives; it suggested that human life was lived under certain directives. I called this principle intentionality.

2. Evidence of intentionality. In the majority of the biographies, the individual's intentionality became repeatedly apparent. Only those lives in which failure predominated seemed to lack this unifying principle.

Some anamnestic interview studies of lives of average middle class and working class people, as carried out by Marie Jahoda and Gertrud Wagner in Vienna, seemed to confirm the view that healthy persons experience their lives as a unit. A more recent study of the life of Bill Roberts (Bühler, 1961) also confirmed this view.

Yet studies of a great many younger people do not seem to justify this assumption. When asked about life goals, younger people often cannot point them out clearly and there is no evidence of consistent pursuits.

Intentionality becomes quite apparent in interview and clinical studies of individuals over 50 or 55 years old. When asked to tell the story of their lives, they usually end up with a summarizing statement: "All in all it was a good life," or "There were so many disappointments," or "It all came to nothing."

Such summary statements do not necessarily always indicate complete or appropriate evaluations. Some neurotic individuals evaluate their lives unrealistically. Thus a woman who died at age 66 after a period of depression said a short time before her death: "I have lived as good a life as anyone." This was actually untrue, because her main interests in life, her marriage and her relationship with her children, had been mostly unhappy and unsuccessful.

While in many cases no distinct intents could be established for the earlier periods of life, study of later phases revealed that practically always there had been expectations which had either been fulfilled or disappointed.

Sometimes the expectations a person has held all through the years become clear only late in life. Thus a man of age 55 discovered after two years of psychotherapy what it was he always had hoped for.

> "All I ever wanted was recognition and attention . . ." "If I had the assurance of getting it I would make a supreme effort." Then he said: "I feel I am through. In a few weeks I am 55—I have no incentive—just hope to die." And some time later: "I feel like I am dead. I don't seem to want to come to life any more. . ." "I am unhappy about my whole life . . ."

The fact that toward their end, if not before, people feel their expectations were fulfilled or disappointed points to the occurrence of earlier, even if unconscious, directives regarding the whole of their lives. Thus my original hypothesis seemed confirmed that a person's life is permeated by some kind of intentionality, an intentionality directed toward fulfillment. Fulfillment is defined as a closure experience of an overall feeling of satisfaction, accomplishment and success, which in different individuals is anticipated and visualized differently. This anticipation helps in varying degrees to direct and to unify a person's endeavors.

The next question was to see in what way intentionality was put into effect. In the detailed study of 53 of the 202 available biographies, a general structure of the lives became apparent. This structure applied to the great majority of the biographies, especially to outstanding persons.

Although it did not apply in the same manner to disrupted and disorganized lives, this normal structure could be thought of as a normative developmental structure.

The overall picture seemed to reveal five phases of self-determination to certain results of life, results which promised some kind of personal fulfillment. These results were to be achieved by means of the successful pursuit of certain goals. The latter were called life goals, in distinction to other intermediate goals. According to this theory and to the findings, the unification and integration of a life takes place by means of the fulfillment of certain long-range goals.

The phases were seen as: (1) before self-determination of life goals sets in (to about age 15); (2) a tentative and preparatory self-determination of life goals (from age 15 to about age 25); (3) self-determination of life goals becomes more specified and definitive (from age 25 to about age 45 or 50); (4) assessment of the foregoing life and the attained or failed fulfillment (from age 45 or 50 to age 60 or 65); (5) a phase in which either more or less complete fulfillment is acknowledged, and a post-self-determination life sets in with rest and memories, sometimes illness and decline; or elsewhere partial fulfillment and partial failure motivate the individual to return to previous forms of striving, sometimes also to resignation; or elsewhere the feeling of more or less complete failure ends in depression or despair.

In all these phases there are, in addition to the normative patterns, various deviations of problematic and neurotic personalities.

3. Areas of fulfillment. When this theory of intentionality and self-determination was conceived, studies of goals were only sporadic. Ach's "determining tendencies" and Lewin's "aspiration level" were early predecessors of a line of inquiry that is only now coming to the fore in psychology. Neither then or now have there been any lists of goals available, nor any empirical studies of the hierarchy of goals. The question of how far goals represent *values* is only a recent subject of discussion. Allport (1937) was a forerunner in this area.

My hypothesis of what kind of goals were designated as life goals, and the model of the progressive phases in the pursuit of life goals, were both based on an interpretative study of the aforementioned biographies. In the biographies, three areas of life seem to stand out as significant: One is the area of activities. In the fully developed adult life, the range of activities seem to yield fulfillment under a number of varying conditions. Fulfillment seems to depend on the appropriateness of activities in terms of an individual's activity needs and preferences, his aptitudes and potentialities, the achievement and acknowledgement he attained, and his beliefs and values. Thus overall fulfillment depends, to varying degrees, on fulfillments in the direction of four basic tendencies, *Need-Satisfaction, Creative Expansion, Self-Limiting Adaptation* and *Upholding the Internal Order* (Bühler, 1959).

A person wants to enjoy activities functionally, wants to achieve and find acknowledgement of his achievements, wants to use his best potentialities and aptitudes and wants to believe that what he is doing is valuable. This can be seen with respect to occupational as well as avocational activities. For most people, however, the occupational area seems to be the most decisive.

A second area of life goals is personal relationships. Here, too, fulfillment depends on conditions which can be analyzed in terms of the four basic tendencies. The most important are the finding of love, the satisfactory development of a marital relationship, and the relationship with children who are developing well. Important also are relationships with other people—friends and acquaintances, co-workers, neighbors and others.

A third area of life goals, that of the development of the self, comes less often into awareness. Often without being conscious of it, people have certain expectations regarding their own selves. Again corresponding to the four basic tendencies, they want to feel good about themselves and to like themselves (Need-Satisfaction); they want to be able to accept themselves and feel they belong (Self-Limiting Adaptation); they want to feel they grow and develop as persons (Creative Expansion); and they want to believe in themselves and to feel they have worth (Upholding the Internal Order).

Self-fulfillment is usually experienced as incidental to fulfillment in work or in personal relationships, but even simple people are able to abstract the notion that they "let themselves down" or that they are "content with themselves" with respect to how they have lived their lives.[1]

4. The beginnings of self-determination in the first two phases of life. As already mentioned, the first phase of childhood (until approximately 15 years of age) was originally conceived as a period in which there is not yet an awareness of life as a whole. This observation must however be qualified. In more recent clinical studies (Bühler, 1962), as well as in nursery-school studies to which Nancy Dilworth (1968) contributed, it was found that sometimes even three- to five-year-old children concern themselves with long-range plans regarding what they want to do or to be.

[1]Development throughout the life cycle is not sufficiently characterized by the development of the self alone, as Erikson (1959) suggests. Self-development seems to this author to be only one aspect of an individual's maturation.

Of course, the future into which they project these ideas is only vaguely perceived, but even so, the thoughtful child's reflections about himself must not be considered altogether futureless.

Thus it is only generally speaking that we may call childhood the period before self-determination of life goals. Childhood is primarily a period in which different types of behavior develop which are preparatory to long-range goal-setting. These categories, described in detail in another context (Bühler, 1966), are: (1) "spontaneous" activity with which the newborn takes hold of the world around him; (2) selective perception, with which even the young infant begins to build his own world; (3) contact which the individual establishes, from infancy on, with those who take care of him; (4) the beginning of will, identity formation and conscience with which the two- to four-year-old child begins to find direction of his own; (5) experiences of "I can" and "I cannot," which give even the baby his first inklings of mastery; (6) more complex reactions to the experiences with the outside world, an attitude of predominant constructiveness or destructiveness which the older school child decides upon in going along with or going against his environment; (7) a gradually consistent attitude toward achievement as a goal; (8) an increasingly established set of beliefs and values which allows the older school child to handle matters on the basis of opinions and convictions; (9) the adolescent's first commitments in love, friendship and other more permanent relationships; (10) the adolescent's struggles to integrate all he knows and wants in a first *"Weltanschauung";* (11) the adolescent's first attempts to find *direction, purpose and meaning* for his life as a whole; (12) the adolescent's first concepts of the different fulfillments life might offer. These last three categories mark the arrival of the second phase of life.

This list includes all those behavioral categories which indicate an inner-determined directiveness. Early child psychologists, from Preyer (1882) on, spoke in this connection of "spontaneous" behavior. American developmental psychologists, those oriented toward behaviorism as well as those oriented toward psychoanalysis, have only recently accepted the idea that activity is not solely a reaction to environmental stimuli. Only very recently has the individual's own initiative been acknowledged as a factor that determines a selective and directive thrust into the world, as it were.

From the present author's point of view, the briefly enumerated behavioral advances of the first phase of life are in part an expression of the underlying intentionality, the self's active contribution to the individual's developing self-determination.

In the *"second phase,"* the period from about 15 to 25 years, life goals are conceived of tentatively and experimentally. There is a first grasp of the idea that one's own life belongs to oneself and represents a time unit with a beginning and an end. He becomes interested in how it all began. A thoughtful person may write his first autobiography during this phase.

The production of autobiographies are just as phase-characteristic of adolescents as the autobiographies of older people who see their lives in retrospect. Often the adolescent autobiography represents the beginning of a diary and gives evidence that this youth has begun to see himself in a historical perspective. After World War I, in the years between 1921 and 1934, the author analyzed and published a considerable number of diaries. Several other authors, among them particularly Bernfeld, Kupky and Stern, followed with publications of further diary material which they considered eye-openers to the inner life of adolescents.

While admittedly most of these diaries brought out the thinking and feeling of rather introverted youths, they were the first documentary material to reveal certain general adolescent trends. Most important, they revealed that kind of longing with which the young person starts out his life, and begins to search for partly undefinable goals.

Among these goals may be the search for fulfilling encounters with a partner to love or with a God to believe in. But beyond that, vaguer concerns are opened up: the questions regarding the purpose and meaning of life and the "quests," as Darion (1966) calls them in "The Man of La Mancha," this man who "dreams the impossible dream" and "reaches for the unreachable stars."

While a great many youths are too realistic and even too materialistic to go out for causes or to "right the unrightable wrongs," I have found in clinical work that these sober attitudes reflect often more a manufactured detachment than the reality of these adolescents' feelings. Often all this hardness proves to be a facade, which eventually is relinquished.

Küppers (1964) who recently published a post-World War II collection of diaries of German adolescents, expresses a similar view. She denies that present-day youth are skeptical and without ideals. They may be more reticent in the expression of feelings, but she does not find a great difference between them and the previous generation.

This may of course be different in American culture. One new trend is the emphasis on the *immediate experience,* through which adolescents try to find themselves. They have a problem with the future in that they feel rebellious regarding the goals and values of their elders. Some choose to turn away even from thinking about the future. Others, however, concern themselves with values and attempts at re-evaluations.

5. *Healthy, problematic and neurotic patterns of self-determination.* Unfortunately there is not as yet any comprehensive study of people's

procedures in life-goal planning nor of how they handle success and failure at various stages of their lives.

In my original life-cycle model, the adolescent period was seen as one in which life goals are set tentatively and experimentally, while in the following adult period (about 23 to 45 or 50 years) life goals were seen as set in a more specified and definitive way. Between 45-50 and 60-65 years, people were assumed to concern themselves with assessments of their fulfillments and failures. These *normative* motivational stages occur in different patterns. The different patterns appear to be more or less favorable for progress to the next phase, depending on how problematic or even neurotic the development of a person. I would like to forward a further hypothesis about these developments and patterns.

The hypothesis is twofold. One part concerns how the present is experienced; the other concerns how past and future are handled. The two problems are interrelated. The manner in which a person experiences the present depends greatly on what type of past he had. His outlook on the future, on the other hand, is greatly determined by the way he experiences the present.

As we know from psychoanalysis the past is apt to intrude on a person's present life to the degree that it was emotionally disturbing and damaging. Certain neurotics are so preoccupied with their past that they handle their present lives poorly and are prevented from a healthy self-realizing existence.

The healthy, self-realizing person lives predominantly in the present. He sees his future as tied to his present life in a meaningful continuity (Shostrom, 1964).

On close inspection, one might distinguish an immediate, an intermediate and a distant future. The immediate future is closely intertwined with a person's present in that it requires immediate preparation. The intermediate and the distant futures may be planned more or less tentatively, clearly, definitely, flexibly or rigidly. Hope or fear may prevail depending on successes and failures of the present and past.

The manner in which a person experiences the present is hypothesized to occur in five different directions:

1. A person may experience a phase maturely, which means that his self-determination is phase-characteristic. If the person is immature, his goal behavior will be that of the foregoing phase. If he is premature he will rush to the goal behavior of the next phase.

2. A person may experience satisfaction or disappointment in the self-determination he gave himself, because he feels he pursued the right or

the wrong goal, right or wrong in the sense of appropriateness to his tastes and talents, his intentionality and his potentialities.

3. A person may experience himself as capable or incapable of handling the problems and conflicts which he encounters in pursuing his goals.

4. A person may register successes or failures with respect to the results of his pursuits, which give him feelings of victory or defeat.

5. A person may experience fulfillment or unfulfillment, even despair, in an existential awareness of the totality of his life. This may be a momentary feeling of fulfillment or despair, or a feeling about one's life as a whole, as related to one's intentionality and to the world-at-large and the universe.

The following cases illustrate these five modes of experience in the different phases of life.

> David, 22, is an example of a person who lives his second phase adequately. He is a science student who plans to become a college professor. His occupation is preparatory as is his engagement to a girl he intends to marry. He is satisfied with his plans and feels he will be developing his best potentials: he is on the whole quite capable of coping with various problems and conflicts; he can register more successes than failures, and he looks hopefully to a fulfillment of his goals and his life as a whole.
>
> David's past has not been happy. His early-divorced and enormously harassed mother was not up to this brilliant boy, her only child, and she tried to control him with excessive demands and harsh, punitive discipline. David grew up defending himself against his mother. He conceived early in life of a future in which he would live on his own and work toward a scholarship in a distant university. He managed to fulfill this hope and to succeed relatively well in not letting memories of his unhappy childhood detract him. Inasmuch as he was disturbed, he sought out psychotherapy to work them through.
>
> David has a schematically outlined program for the future. He is more definite about it than many other young people. He might even become quite disturbed if the program did not work out; that is to say, he is probably not quite flexible enough about it. But it seems a reasonable enough plan to become realized.
>
> His program for his immediate future is to study for his college degree and to earn enough money to support himself. In the intermediate future he plans to become a college teacher and to marry. His fiancée agrees to this plan. On his distant future, David visualizes himself ambitiously in an outstanding college position. He also expects to be a happy husband and father and a truly satisfied person.

This tripartite division of expectations and planning would apply to almost any age; however, in adolescence the more immediate plans are likely to be more predominant than at a later age. And often they are not as yet successfully tied to further plans. David has an unusually specified program as compared with many young people. He is helped in his self-determination by his early awareness of his potentials as well as his needs.

Emotional immaturity prevents a great many young people from committing themselves even tentatively in occupations or personal relationships. As Otto (1964) established in questionnaire studies, astonishingly few people analyze and consider their own potentialities in choosing a direction for themselves. Many young people also fail to clarify the values they believe in and want to live for. They make tentative choices of certain life patterns and are disappointed because they do not seem to yield what they really want.

A third point in the development of self-determination is connected with the individual's ability or inability to handle intervening problems and conflicts. A 28-year-old woman, for example, overwhelmed by guilt feelings she experienced after leaving a convent was subsequently unable to achieve a new self-determination.

A fourth point in the development of self-determination is the experience of success and failure which may validate or invalidate the choice. One adolescent, whose father had nourished in him from childhood the idea that he would become a doctor, came close to a breakdown when he found his undergraduate courses to go far beyond his capacities.

A fifth point is found in the experience of fulfillment or unfulfillment, even despair, which a person may feel with regard to his whole existence. Fulfillment or unfulfillment, as used here, refers to an inclusive feeling about one's life, or occasionally an episode or a period related as a whole to one's intentionality. It is what leads people to say that their "life was good," or "it all came to nothing," or "there were so many disappointments" or similar summarizing statements. David represents the feeling of a young adult on the way to fulfillment.

> Wayne, age 21, whose ambition was to become an actor, represents complete relinquishment and withdrawal. Wayne had been a great success as an actor in high school and he assumed that the world was open and waiting for him. He experienced severe disappointment when he did not find any access to any theater. Refusing to compromise his plans in any way, he withdrew and returned to his divorced mother, who doted on her only son. Wayne excused himself with various psychosomatic illnesses requiring care and rest and left the question of his future completely unresolved. He felt hopeless and as if he were at the end.

Wayne's relinquishing of effort toward his self-determination resulted not only from the failure of his attempts, but also from his inability to handle the problems he encountered on the way. Refusing detour solutions, he insisted on his goal inflexibly.

His rigid self-determination in the area of a career was, furthermore, *premature,* since he could not ascertain his chances of realizing it.

All premature self-determinations in the second phase create definitive situations without sufficient preparation. Frequent examples are the many very young marriages of our time, on which young girls more often than boys insist, fearing they might not find again a partner who would want them or simply impatient for a life of their own. These premature self-determinations often end in failure.

> A healthy person moving from a second to a third phase self-determination proceeds gradually from tentative to more specified and more definite goals. This process takes place from about 25-30 years of age to about 45-50 years of age. The case of Bill Roberts is a good example.[2]
>
> Bill had worked at a variety of unskilled jobs since he was 14 years old. At age 26 he married. A year in the army at the end of World War I interrupted his career plans—upon his return, however, he obtained a job as an employee of a big trucking company. After three years of special training, he advanced to an excellent position in this firm, which he held until the depression when he was forced to switch to other jobs. Most of the time, however, he was able to stick to the occupation he was trained for. At age 46, a severe illness as well as his firm's bankruptcy stopped his established way of life.

Similar to the many variations of preliminary planning in adolescence, a variety of normative patterns of self-determination are found in the third phase of life. In the ideal case, this is the time of life in which a person's potentials have evolved more or less fully and in which many aptitudes are culminating. Also an individual's personal life normally reaches a certain peak during this period, a marital bond is established, sexual capacity is at its best, family life is developing and increasing the scope of the individual's life and a circle of friends is being acquired within the settled circumstances of a stable career and an established domicile.

The middle of life might then be expected to be the period in which an individual could settle down to live within the frame of reference of the present in pursuing many immediate objectives; he also might be expected to acquire a clearer outlook on the intermediate and even distant future. But

[2]Case presented originally in Bühler, *Values in Psychotherapy* (1962).

the many conditions of a settled third phase are of course seldom fulfilled. A satisfactory third phase pattern is probably more the exception than the rule. Clinical material reveals the many hindrances people encounter in their effort to settle down. A few of the most frequent problem patterns are indicated here.

Again we find first an *immaturity* pattern, that is the inability to settle down into definite circumstances.

> At 34 years old, Myron has not as yet been able to establish himself in any career or to marry. Extremely dependent on his domineering mother, he allowed himself to be employed in the family business, although he disliked it intensely. He had not married because his mother disapproved of whatever girl he brought home.
>
> Sex fears prevented Diane, age 33, from accepting as marriage partners any suitors she had had. She was also unable to place herself appropriately in her career.

While immature middle-age persons persist in tentative and preparatory pursuits, others are handicapped by disappointments and conflicts or are forced to regress because of failures.

Corresponding to the disappointed group of adolescents, individuals in the third phase also experience disappointments over what seem to be wrong choices of goals.

> Bob, who in his second phase experienced failure in his self-determination to become a doctor, suffered a breakdown in the third phase over the disappointment he felt in the career he finally chose.
>
> When Bob found himself unable to meet the requirements of medical studies, he chose to leave college and to become a salesman. This activity distressed him to such a degree that he took to alcohol and later even to drugs to escape his feelings of failure and disappointment.
>
> In psychotherapy he gradually realized that in both his occupational choices he had failed to inquire into his own potentialities and that both his choices were not related to what he could do best and would have liked to do. What he really felt he could do well was to advise, guide and help people. While this was what appealed to him in the doctor's role, he could have planned for this kind of functioning just as well in any kind of counselor's role. He decided that while it was too late for him to start over at age 33, he could use his free time to study for a degree in business and to get managerial training for an executive position.

Very frequently, disappointments of this third phase occur from the wrong choice of marital partners.

> Ethel, age 41, had married a man with whom she was deeply in love. While he soon proved to be unreliable and irresponsible in many respects, Ethel could for years not reconcile herself to a divorce. She went on hoping things would change for the better and when, during psychotherapy, she finally decided to free herself from the bondage, she suffered a breakdown.

Emotionally disabling conflicts unsettle the third phase for some. This is parallel to the disablement in self-determination found in the previous phase.

> Georgia, age 35,[3] needed psychotherapy to resolve her conflict over caring for her demanding mother at the risk of dissolving her otherwise happy marriage.
>
> Frances, age 29, was also emotionally disabled. After an unsatisfactory marriage she had started to live in a homosexual relationship and was in inner conflict about her way of life.

Success or failure experiences may also modify the third phase. Both Bob and Ethel, who were disappointed over their wrong choices, perceived themselves as failures. Both regressed to indetermination. Bob escaped from his unresolved conflicts into alcohol and later to drugs. Ethel was unable to hold a job. She had to fall back on accepting help from her parents.

The third phase may also generate premature self-determinations in anticipation of the critical self-assessment of the fourth phase. As mentioned earlier, self-assessments take place repeatedly. To different degrees people are motivated repeatedly to evaluate their lives and themselves. But they are particularly stringent in the fourth phase which, like the second phase, represents a crisis period of life.

The fourth phase self-assessment, occurring in the climacteric years from about 45-50 to about 60-65, is normally a more comprehensive survey of a person's whole life in retrospect. It comes in a critical period in which many people have to reorient themselves for a number of reasons. In many occupations a person in this age group is no longer employable; retirement looms ahead for the majority. This means for the most the potentiality of a drastic reduction of income. It also means for many the end of a career that offers an effective means to interact with the world outside themselves. In many cases, reduced abilities or the beginning of severe illnesses testify to the beginning of decline.

In the healthy person, the fourth phase self-assessment includes a

[3] Case described originally in Bühler, *Values in Psychotherapy* (1962).

stock-taking of the past and leads to revised planning for the future in light of necessary limitations. There may also be some anticipatory thinking about the last years of life.

> Bill Roberts is again a good example. At 46, Bill had to accept a settlement from his firm, which had gone bankrupt. He decided to take his family on a three-month tour of the United States. When interviewed at 67, Bill spoke of this trip as the highlight of his life, a "peak experience" (Maslow, 1962).
>
> Upon return, he found a good job, but ill health soon forced him to look for a new occupation. He bought a grocery store which he ran with the help of his wife until age 64, when he retired from this occupation also.

Bill is an example of an average healthy person, who in his fourth phase twice assesses his situation and makes two important decisions on the strength of the evaluation. Forced to interrupt a successful career, he considers this a good moment at which to rest and to reach out for a unique treat. On returning, he feels lucky to find a good job. When severe illness forces him to seek reduced activity, he chooses a new occupation with appropriate consideration of what might happen when later he is forced to retire more and more completely from work. His decision to retire at 64 marks his retreat from competitive gainful occupations as he enters the fifth phase of life.

As in the foregoing phases, different patterns are observable in the fourth phase in the attitude toward self-assessment. The first is again an immaturity pattern seen in those who try to avoid the issue of self-assessment, even though circumstances almost enforce it on them.

> One example is Richard, age 50, a contractor whose business went bankrupt. If he had assessed himself and his past life sincerely, he would have had to admit to himself that the same personality defects which were destroying his family life were responsible for his business failure. In both situations he was dishonest and exploited people, and a summarizing self-appraisal would at this point have been very much in order. But Richard refused to face himself and insisted that he knew remedies for all his troubles.
>
> Gary, age 48, whose third marriage failed because of his repeated extramarital involvements, also demonstrates immaturity. Deeply hurt because he truly loved his third wife, he was nevertheless unable to see himself and the repetitious pattern in his life.

A second group reflects *disappointment* over hoped-for fulfillments in life.

George, age 50, felt that he should have accomplished more in life than he had. This was true of his marriage to a woman who had never quite responded to his love. It was also true of his career as a teacher, where he never had been as successful as he had wanted to be. He found it difficult to resign himself to it being unlikely that he would get a full measure of satisfaction out of life.

A third group encounters insoluble *problems* in their chosen careers or with their partners. In the fourth phase, the insoluble problems enforce job changes, often with losses or marital separations and divorces.

Randolph, now 63, had to give up a political career which was highly meaningful to him because he lost the confidence of his supporters. Forced to switch to a business career, he experienced considerable bitterness.

As in the earlier phase of life, the experience of failure may be the mode of an individual's fourth phase.

Flora, a woman of 65, had divorced her husband some twelve years before. Her attitude toward her marriage had been ambivalent, and when after prolonged suffering over her conflict, she decided on divorce, her action did not bring her the hoped-for relief. She mourned for what she had lost and resented her fate. Flora also had problems with her only daughter and in her career as a public school teacher. She experienced what many others would interpret as almost all-round failure. She tried to sustain herself with what she could save out of a tenuous relationship with her daughter and later her grandchildren. She ended her teaching career early and took up church activities in its place. Defensively, she thought of the outcome of her life rather in terms of unfortunate developments than of failure on her part.

Finally, feelings of fulfillment or unfulfillment are generated in the fourth phase. As mentioned earlier, this phase represents a crisis period in which fulfillment becomes often problematic.

Ben, age 51, a twice-divorced and childless salesman, entered psychotherapy at fifty because of impotence, various psychosomatic complaints and depression. He explained his depression as owing to his guilt over his empty, meaningless life. He felt he had wasted his life in the pursuit of goals in which he did not believe.

He had started this way in opposition to a father he hated because he had tried to push the gifted boy in a harsh and unloving manner. Ben quit school, left home and got a clerical job in order to be independent. Only after his father's death, when he was in his twenties, did he finish high school, go to college and get a degree in law. He practiced law for some time, but he was restless and was unsuccessful in this and in later managerial positions.

> At heart, Ben was a writer and a scholar, and he grieved forever that he had never gotten beyond haphazard attempts at pursuing his real interests and his true potentialities. Now he was too restless and too disturbed to settle down to anything like that. He did not believe in anything he did. His bad feelings about himself were reinforced by the failure of two meaningless marriages which ended after short durations.
>
> Psychotherapy enabled Ben to experience meaningful love for the first time in his life, but his attempts to write failed tragically. He realized that his life history had led to a tragic reduction of his original potentialities, but he could not resign himself to this insight. His early death in an accident was perhaps not quite as accidental as it seemed.

When convinced he was a hopeless failure, Ben hastened prematurely into his fifth phase of life in resigning himself to the end of his life.

The *fifth phase* of life, beginning around 65 to 70 years, is one in which most people rest and retire from the self-determination to goals of life. In doing so, they may regress to the need-satisfaction or self-limiting living patterns of the pre-self-determined childhood period. If in good physical and mental condition, they may enjoy leisure activities like travel, games or collecting, or they may put themselves at the disposal of some welfare, church or political cause.

If ill, they may of course have to resign themselves to an inactive end, almost a waiting for death to come. If unusually strong and productive, they may go on with previous expansive pursuits.

Important, however, in the fifth phase experience is the gradually evolving awareness of the past life as a whole resulting essentially in fulfillment or unfulfillment and even despair. Not infrequent, also, is a kind of closure experience of resignation. Case material indicates that people who hardly ever before thought of their life as a whole, do so in the fifth phase.

A healthy fifth phase attitude can be exemplified again with the case of Bill Roberts.

Bill Roberts, interviewed at age 67, volunteered some statements summarizing his life as a whole. He says he lived what he calls a "decent and religious life without being a fanatic." He says he had a good wife, and normal children who gave them wonderful grandchildren. He has always been able to provide for his family. His life was worthwhile to him throughout, and he is lucky to have no major regrets. His one big decision to move to California proved to be a very good one. He described his present activities in terms of "interests," emphasizing that he always had many interests and knew what to do with his free time.

In comparison with this mature and fulfilled final phase, other fifth phase structures are more problematic or even desperate.

> Lowell, age 62, looks at his life immaturely. A man who worked himself up from the poorest beginnings to moderate riches, he does not find anything worthwhile he can do any more. Having reached his goal he feels empty. In continuous work, he has lost the ability to enjoy himself. He has never thought about his life as a whole, nor its meaning. Uncertain about what to do with himself, his attitude is one of disgust and boredom.

The same case could also be cited with reference to the experience of disappointment, instead of fulfillment, when the goal was reached and there seemed nothing more to do.

Other people take unresolved problems and conflicts into the last stages of their lives.

> Norman, age 70, an immigrant, had been a German military officer whose partly Jewish ancestry cost him his career during the Nazi regime. With only a military education and no interest or aptitude in business, he had been unable to establish himself in the new world and ended up playing small military roles in the movies. He responded with great bitterness and hostility which he expressed even to those who tried to help him. He was sarcastic and hardly close to anyone. He never married and lived alone.

This man's life ended in inner rebellion against the world and his own fate to which he never realized he contributed. Thus it must also be looked at as a failure, resulting in unfulfillment if not despair.

While there are not as yet any statistical data available, the impression gained from a survey of cases is that relatively few people enjoy the feeling of essential or even relative fulfillment in the last stages of their lives. On the other hand the incidence of actual despair also seems small. The majority of aging persons whose cases were studied, showed a closure pattern that might best be termed as resignation. The resigned ending may be caused by very different kinds and degrees of disappointments, which either prevent the feeling of fulfillment or come close to unfulfillment and despair.

The pattern found in the case of Amelia seems to appear frequently.

> Amelia, age 72, had lived alone for about twenty years, after a late divorce from a husband who had shown little interest in her or their two children. The family atmosphere was one of unhappiness and both children left home early in life.
>
> As time went on, Amelia felt that she had failed herself and the children. After her divorce, she tried to get closer to her children. Psychotherapy enabled her to see her own lack of understanding which she tried to remedy to a degree.

In talking about her life, she expressed feelings of regret regarding her past life, but had resigned herself to having found a somewhat belated satisfaction in her recent relationship with her children and grandchildren.

Summary

The process of human life is discussed in relation to life goals. Human life is seen as a process characterized by an intentionality, generated in the core-self system, and directed toward a fulfillment at the end. The intentionality materializes in phases of self-determination towards goals which in the ideal case bring the individual's best potentials to realization. The five phases are one in which self-determination is prepared and built up; one in which life goals are set experimentally and programmatically; one in which life goals become specific and definite; one in which success and failure are being assessed; and one in which rest or continuation of striving occur with a closure experience of fulfillment or unfulfillment, resignation, sometimes despair.

REFERENCES

Allport, G. *Personality*. 2nd ed., 1961. New York: Holt & Co., 1937.

Bühler, C. *Der menschliche Lebenslauf als psychologisches Problem* ("The course of human life as a psychological problem") *Verlag für Psychologie,* Gottingen, 2nd. ed., 1959; 1st ed. Leipzig: S. Hirzel, 1933.

———. "Theoretical Observations About Life's Basic Tendencies," *Amer. J. Psychother.* XIII, *3*:561-581 (1959).

———. "Meaningful Living in the Mature Years," in R. W. Kleemeier, ed., *Aging and Leisure*. Oxford Univ. Press, 1961.

———. *Values in Psychotherapy*. New York: Free Press of Glencoe, 1962.

———. "Human Life Goals in the Humanistic Perspective." AAHP Presidential Address, New York, 1966. *Amer. J. Hum. Psychol.* 6 (1967).

———, and F. Massarik, eds., *The Course of Life. A Study of Goals in the Humanistic Perspective*. New York: B. Springer, 1968.

Darion, J., in D. Wasserman, J. Darion, and M. Leigh, *Man of La Mancha*. New York: Random House, 1966.

Erikson, E. *Identity and the Life Cycle*. New York: International Press, 1959.

Küppers, W. *Mädchentagebücher der Nachkriegszeit* ("Girls' diaries of the post-war period"). Stuttgart: E. Klett, 1964.

Maslow, A. "Lessons from the Peak-Experiences," *Amer. J. hum. Psychol.* *2*:9-18 (1962).

Otto, H. "The Personal Resources Development Research—the Multiple Strength Perception Effect," *Proceedings of the Utah Academy of Science, Arts and Letters* *38*:182-186 (1961-62).

Preyer, W.: *Die Seele des Kindes* ("The soul of the child"). Leipzig: Grieben, 1882.

Shorstrom, E. L. "Personal Orientation Inventory, San Diego." Educational and Industrial Testing Service (1962).

15. Vygotsky's View About the Age Periodization of Child Development

Mary A. Zender and B. F. Zender
PROFESSORS OF PSYCHOLOGY
WESTERN MICHIGAN UNIVERSITY, KALAMAZOO

The study of the central mediating processes between the stimulus and response has not been a matter of urgent concern for American psychologists until the last decade or so. Since that time, the more recent investigations about the neural processes in the brain have uncovered new insights about its information functions, and this knowledge has turned the attention of investigators to some neglected domains. Subsequently, items like consciousness, attention, personality and meaning have started to reappear in the research literature. Likewise, arguments about the propriety of these terms have once again made their appearances.

While returning to the old, American psychologists have also begun simultaneously to rely more and more on the new with their use of the digital computer as a basic research tool. This shift has permitted a choice of theoretical models that is epitomized by the selection of either a stimulus-response connection or a feedback loop for the experiment. In turn, the new reliance upon the computer, instead of animals, for simulating human behavior has also caused psychologists to conceive of the brain as a very complex information system with central mediating processes.

About the same time that American psychologists started to free themselves from the oversimplification of early behaviorism, their counterparts in the Soviet Union were throwing off the shackles of Stalin's ideological tyranny and restoring many of his victims to their rightful place in the history of Soviet science. It was no surprise that among the ranks of "resurrected" scientists was one of the Soviet Union's most brilliant psychologists, Vygotsky (1896-1934). Ironically, he had established his reputation as a scholar by resurrecting the formerly discredited idea that the study of consciousness was a function of psychology.

Even though official attempts were made to suppress Vygotsky's findings about the mediation between the stimulus and response, while sanctioning ideologically those of the reflexologists, his views still influenced a generation of Soviet psychologists. Besides elaborating Pavlov's conception of a second system of signals that allows man to process symbols, Vygotsky made original contributions in perception, cognition, mental retardation, psychopathology, and child development (Pavlov, 1954, p. 412).[1]

What is even more remarkable about his tremendous output is that he began his psychological studies relatively late in his life and they were terminated rather abruptly a decade later with his untimely death at 38. Thus he had achieved in a span of ten years what most other psychologists had not even attained in a lifetime.

Nevertheless, it would be a great mistake to limit Vygotsky's contributions to the field of psychology. His research, according to Ivanov, has played a major role in the Soviet development of such contemporary branches of knowledge as cybernetics (the science of communication, control, and information) and semiotics (the science of signs) (Vygotsky, 1971, p. 266). Consequently, his work has implications for the psychologist, cybernetician and semiotician.

After the publication of an English translation of *Language and Thought* in 1962, a number of Western scholars realized at last the far-reaching implications of Vygotsky's research about the intellectual and linguistic development of children. Such a realization led Bruner to express the following view: ''But looking at Vygotsky's place in world psychology, his position transcends either the usual functionalism of the Dewey-James variety or the conventional historical materialism of Marxist ideology. Vygotsky is an original'' (Vygotsky, 1965, p. vi). Another significant appraisal was offered by the English scholar, Bernstein, who wrote that ''Vygotsky's studies opened the way to a unification of the biological and social sciences, and that their continuation may have at least as great significance for science as the deciphering of the genetic code'' (Vygotsky, 1971, p. 289).

Another even more significant Western appraisal was offered by Piaget, whose early works were critically examined by Vygotsky. Upon reading his criticism in the English translation of *Language and Thought*, Piaget (1962, p. 1) paid tribute to his Soviet counterpart by acknowledging the import of his views: ''It is not without sadness that an author discovers twenty-five years after its publication, the work of a colleague who has died in the meantime, when that work contains so many points of immediate interest to him which should have been discussed personally and

[1]As a result of his later research, Pavlov criticized the views of American behaviorists for their oversimplified views about the higher nervous activity and their attempts to explain such processes as learning only within the framework of conditioning.

in detail.'' Thus, the Western world's foremost authority on the central mediating processes of children realized almost a quarter of a century later that the findings of his Soviet colleague were still as significant in the sixties as they were in the thirties.

Meanwhile, in the Soviet Union, two of the Soviet Union's outstanding psychologists, Leontiev and Luria, edited and prepared for publication other materials by Vygotsky that were somewhat controversial in the thirties. In 1960, the resulting manuscript was published as a book, *The Evolution of Higher Mental Processes*. The response of Soviet scholars to this publication in the early sixties and their reaction in the late fifties to the publication of *Language and Thought* caused Soviet historians to reconsider some of their views about Vygotsky and his work. At the end of the last decade, for example, an official historian for Soviet psychology listed Vygotsky's research in the thirties as one of the outstanding events in the history of Soviet psychology (Petrovsky, 1967, p. 355). Moreover, he apologized for the past neglect of Vygotsky's work and predicted in the future more concern about his research: ''In our narrative, we do not have the needed space to devote to a detailed treatment of Vygotsky's work which still awaits thorough investigation by the historians. However, we are convinced that many future historical and psychological studies will be made of his work'' (Petrovsky, 1967, p. 246).

Briefly, then, Soviet behavioral scientists, just like their American counterparts, discovered that they could not continue to ignore the fact that consciousness with all its psychological functions and physiological processes plays a crucial role in determining behavior. Cyberneticians, psychologists, semioticians, economists, and others involved with data processing in both countries found the brain's mediating processes central in their investigations. This fact was clearly reflected in how both groups began to use electronic computers for simulating the information processes of the brain and to rediscover the findings of Vygotsky, Piaget, and others like them who were concerned with the processes of cognition.

Consequently, the main purpose of this article is to make available for American readers some of Vygotsky's theories about child development and his views of Western notions about it. Instead of ''speaking'' for him, the aim here is to let him ''speak'' for himself. To achieve these ends, the authors selected and translated an article that appeared in a recent issue of *Voprosi Psikhologii*, one of the Soviet Union's leading psychological journals.

In this previously unpublished paper, Vygotsky traces the major ways of dividing child development into periods and evaluates these approaches to periodization. After describing and analyzing them, he proceeds to elaborate his own approach to this fundamental psychological problem. What is particularly impressive about his method is that he shifts from an investigation of mere externals, like the appearance of milk teeth, to the unfolding of the child's very personality. In his description and analysis, he attempts to state some of the general laws and fill in some of the details concerning the development of personality.

Leontiev, one of the Soviet Union's foremost psychologists, sums up in the following fashion the reasons for the renewed interest in Vygotsky's view: "Vygotsky's writings retain their scientific urgency to this day, they continue to be printed and attract the attention of readers. Of how many of the studies to which Vygotsky referred can this be said? Very few. This fact alone reveals the lasting value of his ideas in scientific psychology" (Vygotsky, 1971, p. xi).

The Problem of Age Periodization of Child Development[2]

All of the proposals for the periodization of child development can be arranged, according to their theoretical foundations, into three categories.

In the first group, there is an attempt to divide childhood into periods, not according to the breakdown of the child's development, but according to a gradual unfolding of other processes in one way or another related with the development of children. For example, one notes the periodization of childhood based on a biogenetic principle. This theory of biogenesis is based on the assumption that strong parallels exist between the development of the human race and the growth of the child or that in the short and long run ontogenesis repeats phylogenesis. From this theoretical viewpoint, all of natural childhood develops in individual periods corresponding to the basic periods of humanity. Thus, the basis for the periodization of childhood is the periodization of phylogenetic development. In this category, one finds the views of Hutchinson and others like him.

However, not all the efforts to break down child development according to other processes seem as groundless in their basic assumptions as those of the preceding authors. Such is the case of periodization of childhood that is based on the formal processes of education in the educational system of a given country. For example, one notes that there is a period for nursery school, elementary school, etc. Therefore, what really

[2]The following translation is based on an article published in the March-April issue of *Voprosi Psikhologii*, 1972. Vygotsky did not give complete references in his manuscript and thus they are not included in the translation.

emerges in this scheme of periodization is not the division of childhood itself according to its own intrinsic characteristics, but the fragmentation of childhood according to the levels of formal education. More concisely, the resulting periodization is based on levels of schooling and not on stages of development. Nevertheless, the subdivision of childhood according to pedagogical knowledge brings us extraordinarily close to a true division of childhood because the levels of schooling are based on years of experience in educating children. Consequently, the processes of childhood are very closely related to the stages of child development.

In the second category, the periodization of childhood stems from more multifaceted efforts which are directed at finding some kind of common phenomenon as a conditional criteria for dividing childhood into different periods. For example, this category is represented by the research of Blonsky, who divided childhood into periods on the basis of dentition, that is, the cutting and losing of teeth. In the category of a common phenomenon like dentition, the more useful basic determinants for separating one period of child development from another have three important characteristics: (1) a general indice for determining the overall development of the child; (2) easy accessibility for observation, and (3) an objective means for measurement. It should be pointed out that dentition possesses these traits not only singularly but repeatedly throughout the process of development.

Furthermore, dentition is also closely related to other essential traits of the growing organism, particularly the activity of the endocrine glands. Likewise, they are easily accessible for observation and their reliability is without question. According to such data, the postnatal stage is divided into three phases: toothless, milk teeth, and permanent teeth. The toothless period ends when all the milk teeth have erupted. The milk teeth period is marked by the beginning of tooth loss (at the approximate age of 6½ years). Finally, the permanent tooth period ends with the appearance of the first wisdom tooth. In the cutting of milk teeth, one can first divide this process into three stages: (1) without teeth (the first half year); (2) the initial cutting of teeth (second half year), and (3) the cutting of incisors and canine teeth (third year of postnatal life).

An analogous effort at the periodization of childhood, based on some kind of one-sided development, is the scheme of Shtratetz. He stands out in the ranks of those who use sexual development as a single criterion.

In other attempts to find a singular criterion for periodization, some investigators have focused upon psychological criteria. The periodization by Stern is an example of this approach. He conceives of childhood as a stream with three parts: (1) the period of only play activity (up to 6 years of age); (2) the period of cognitive learning with a separation of play and work; and (3) a period of youthful pubescence with the development of individual personality and a plan for the future (from 14 to 18 years).

The efforts at periodization in this category are subjective. Although Stern and others like him advance objective means as their criteria for the delineation of development, these very same data are derived from a very subjective approach, depending upon which process (sexual or dental) is singled out for study by the investigator. Development is an objective phenomena, not a conditional, nor an arbitrarily selected quantity. Thus, the boundaries, differentiating growth, cannot be fixed according to points outside the path of the child, but must be determined exclusively by those objective traits that end one period and begin another.

The second shortcoming of this category is that periodization is based on a single criterion for all ages. This reliance on a single identifying characteristic overlooks the fact that in the course of development, the value, meaning, significance, appearance, and importance of one indicator changes. The trait, that is significant and essential for determining the development of one epoch, loses its meaning in the next, because those characteristics, which earlier stood out in the first phase, are shunted aside in the second phase of development. Thus, the criterion of sexual puberty is significant and essential for the pubescence period, but is nonessential and insignificant in the preceding period. The cutting of teeth during early childhood could be accepted as a significant sign in the general development of the child. But the loss of teeth at age 7 and the appearance of wisdom teeth cannot be equated in significance with the first appearance of teeth in the development of the child.

This approach does not take into consideration the reorganization of the very processes of development—a dynamic force in which its important and significant characteristics are continually changing during the transition from one period to another. All of this excludes the possibility of dividing childhood into separate periods by using a single indicator for all ages. Child development is such a complex process that no one of its stages can be delineated according to one kind of identifying characteristic.

The third shortcoming of this category is its major reliance upon the study of external phenomena and its neglect of the internal essentials of development. More specifically, the very essence of things and their manifestations are not congruent. As Marx stated, "If the manifestations and the essence of things directly coincided, then all science would be unnecessary." Scientific research, therefore, presents us with the necessary means for knowing reality, the incongruity between the manifestation and essence of things. At the present time, psychology is going through a clearly descriptive, empirical, and phenomenological study of phenomena towards the discovery of their very essence. Until only recently, the main problem in the investigation of child development consisted of studying the symptomatic complexities, that is the aggregate of external manifestations which differentiated the various periods, stages, and phases of child development. Its symptoms were signified by the phenomena. Thus, to say that psychology has been mainly concerned with the symptomatic complexities of each period, stage, and phase means that psychology has been the study of externals. The real problem of psychology is now to begin the investigation of that which undergo the obvious characteristics and causes them. Quite simply, it means focusing on the very process of child development and its internal dynamic. Scientifically speaking, all of this means that we should turn away from the classification of symptoms and move on, as it was done in the other sciences, to a classification based on the internal dynamics of the studied process.

The third category of periodization consists of attempts to move from clearly symptomatic and descriptive investigations to the study of the more essential traits of child development. However, it is evident throughout these studies that it is much easier to pose the problem properly than to solve it correctly. These efforts were simply halfway measures falling always short of the mark and displaying their methodological shortcomings. Their fatal flaw stems from their methodological approach, flowing from an anti-dialectic and dualistic conception of child development, not allowing them to envisage it as a single process of development itself.

For example, Gesell attempts to delineate childhood into periods by noting the changes in the internal rhythm and tempo of development and determining the general flow of the process. On the basis of mainly direct observations of changes according to age and rhythm of development, he divides all of childhood into different periods or waves, unified within themselves by a constant tempo that lasts for the duration of a given period and bounded from the other periods by a clear change in its tempo. Gesell views the dynamic of child development as a process of gradual deceleration. He is affiliated with that group of contemporary theorists who, according to his very own expression, view early childhood as the crucial moment for interpreting personality. The most important phase in the development of the child ends, according to Gesell, in the first year during the first months of the infant's life. On the whole, the subsequent development does not equal the first act of this drama with its maximally saturated content.

What is the basis for such an error? By necessity, it stems from an evolutionary conception of development which is the basis for Gesell's conception. This viewpoint cannot explain the emergence of the new nor the appearance of qualitative changes in development. It is only the growth and expansion of that which was present at the very beginning. Such an explanation of ''more to less'' requires special measures at all times and is obviously characterized by the presence of qualitatively new growth that are subordinate to its rhythm. It does not encompass the process of development. It is true that we observe the maximal tempo in early growth that influences the rest of the child's development. The elementary organs and functions mature earlier than the higher ones. But it seems questionable to assume that all of development is exhausted by the growth of these basic, elementary functions which are only the preconditions for the highest parts of the personality. If we examine them the results will be the opposite: the tempo and rhythm of personality growth seem very minimal during the first act in the drama of development and maximal in its finale.

We have viewed the theory of Gesell as an example of the third category. These attempts at periodization are the halfway points in the transition from the study of symptoms to the investigation of essentials.

Now, what should be the basic principles underlying the periodization of development? We already know where to begin the search for this base: only the internal changes of development itself, only the bends and turns in its flow can give us the sought-after base for determining the basic epochs in the development of the child's personality, that is what we call growth. All theories of child development can be reduced to two basic conceptions. Notably, one of them is none other than that development is the realization, modification, and combination of advances. Here, we find nothing new, only the accumulation, development, and regrouping of those features which were already present at the very beginning. The other basic conception is that development is an unbroken process of self-activity that is characterized in its first stages by the incessant appearance and formation of the new which was not present in the past levels. This conception envisages development as some kind of process which can be understood in terms of the dialectic. In turn, this viewpoint can be divided into two views: an idealistic theory of personality development and a materialistic one. According to the idealistic viewpoint, development is explained in terms of a theory of creative evolution which stems from an autonomous, internal life force that purposefully develops the personality and which is directed by a will to assert and perfect oneself. On the other hand, the materialistic view advances a theory of development in which it is viewed as a process, characterized by the unity of the psychic and materialistic, social and private phenomena in the child's movement through the various stages of growth.

In this approach, there can be no other criteria for determining the actual epochs of development of growth besides those newly formed traits which characterize the very essence of each age. In regard to these new formations, one needs to understand the new types of structures in the personality and its activities, the psychic and social changes, which first appear at a given age level and which primarily determine the child's cognition, his relationship with his environment, his inner and outer behavior. In other words, the entire path of development during a given period.

Nevertheless, there is still something missing in the new scientific attempt at the periodization of childhood. One still needs to consider its dynamic, the dynamic of transition from one stage to another. The empirical research of the psychologist has focused our attention on this period. For example, Blonsky has stated that the changes during growth "can happen sharply and critically and can occur gradually and smoothly." Furthermore, he explained: "Let us designate those epochs and stages of time in the child's life that separate one from the other during the critical times in an epoch (more critical) and a stage (less critical). Let us also call that period of time separating smoothly one period from another, a phase."

Really, development is characterized by a slow evolutionary or gradual flow at certain times. It is during the age of primarily smooth, frequently unnoticed internal changes in the child's personality that he is completing the course of rather insignificant molecular activity. Here, the entire personality of the child is transformed, without going through some kind of sharp displacement, during an extended period of usually a few years. More or less, these transformations become visible towards the end of a rather extensive hidden molecular process. They come to light and become accessible to direct observations only at the conclusion of a prolonged process of latent development.

In these relatively steady and stable periods, the development of the child perpetuates itself on the whole at the expense of microscopic changes in the personality of the child that follow some known course and then appear spasmodically as some kind of new formation. If one looks at these periods in regards to their context, the largest portion of the time is spent at school. It is only through a comparison of childhood in the beginning and the end of the stable period that the great transformations in personality emerge distinctly because development goes along a subterranean path during such a period.

In the past, these stable cycles were studied more thoroughly than those which characterize the other segments of development—the crises. These phenomena were also discovered and studied in empirical research. Yet, they have not been systematized and included in any general scheme of periodization for child development. Many authors even question the very existence of such an important aspect of development. Others are more inclined to interpret crises as some sort of "sick" development than an inherently important and necessary period in childhood because the cycles of crisis deviate from the so-called normal path of development. Almost none of the bourgeois psychologists can understand the real meaning and theoretical implications of the "deviations." Thus, our experiments at systematizing, interpreting, and including them in the general scheme of child development should be viewed as one of the first attempts of its kind.

Not a single researcher can negate the fact that these distinctive periods exist during childhood. More importantly, the authors, using the dialectical approach, recognize the necessity to hypothesize the presence of crises in the development of children even in their infancy [Stern].

Such periods are characterized on the outside by traits that are in an inverse proportion to those which we described as characteristic for the stable periods. During the periods of crisis that last for a relative short duration of a few months to a year or two at the most, there are sharp displacements and much confusion that mark the changes and transformations in the personality of the child. Generally speaking, the child changes in a very short period of time the basic traits of his personality. Development is exhibited as stormy, impetuous, and sometimes even catastrophic behavior. During this period, development reminds us of a revolutionary course of action in regard to the tempo of happening events and the emergence of a complete transition. It is such turning points in the child's development that become the sharply defined crises.

A primary characteristic of these periods is that their boundaries, dividing the start and finish of a crisis from an adjacent period, appear to be almost indistinct at the higher levels. The critical period emerges almost unnoticeably because of the difficulty in determining the exact moment of its appearance and disappearance. On the other hand, it is a common characteristic that acute conditions appear in the central portion of these growth periods. The presence of such culminations in which the crisis reaches its apogee characterizes all the critical periods and distinguishes them from the stable periods of childhood.

Another important trait of the critical periods is that they have been the subject of much empirical research. These aspects of childhood have been marked by the appearance of problems in school. The children, who follow along the normal path of formal education, seem to lose their interest in those school subjects which captured their attention not so long ago. During the critical periods of childhood, a decrease in academic achievement, a loss of interest in the classroom, and a decline in the ability to work become frequently the patterns of behavior in school children. Moreover, the development of the child during the critical periods generally is characterized also by sharp conflict with his peers. Furthermore, the inner life of the child during these times is marred by conflicts with painful and agonizing experiences.

Truthfully, one does not find these patterns all of the time. Various children have critical periods which unfold in a variety of ways. In the evolvement of crises, even those which occur at similar times and social contexts, much more variation exists among them than in stable periods. In the patterns of behavior of many children, one does not note any kind of moral aberration or decrease in academic achievement. Different children exhibit a wide range of variations in the duration of these periods. The influence of external and internal conditions on the very crisis itself is so significant and important that many investigators have raised this type of question: since the crises of child development are generally the consequences of exceptional external forces, acting unfavorably on the child, should such stages be considered the exception rather than the rule in the history of child development [Boozeman and others].

It stands to reason that external conditions determine the concrete aspects of the appearance and duration of the critical period. The tremendous diversity among children stipulates an extremely variegated and many-sided picture of the diverse variations in the critical periods. Nevertheless, neither the presence nor the absence of some kind of specific external condition, but the internal logic of the very process of development itself stipulates the necessity for critical turning points in the life of the child. A study of related indices convinced us of this view.

Thus, if we go from an absolute valuation of the child's problem behavior to a relative one, based on a comparison of the ease or difficulty in educating the child during the critical periods with similar data from the preceding or following stable periods, then it is impossible not to note that all children during their critical periods become relative problems in comparison with their own behavior in their adjacent stable periods. Likewise, if we move from an absolute to a relative appraisal of academic achievement that is based on the child's tempo of educational progress during various stages of his development, then it becomes obvious that every child achieves comparatively less during the periods of crises than those of stability.

The third dominant characteristic of the critical period, if you please, is its most outstanding yet unnoticed characteristic. It should be added that this trait has caused considerable confusion in the attempts to understand properly the crises of childhood. More specifically, it has been very difficult for investigators to comprehend fully the presence of a negative character in development. Everyone, who writes about these distinctive periods, notes at the outset that development during critical periods differs from the stable ones in that crises seem to be of a negative nature instead of a positive one. The progressive development of personality, that is the uninterrupted appearance of the new which so distinctively identifies the stable periods, is temporarily suspended, as if it were growing dim and even extinguishing itself during the periods of crises. The process of development is marked by the disappearance and curtailment, the breakup and dissolution of that which was combined in the past and characterized the child in a given period of stability. During the period of crises, the child does not acquire so much, but does lose many of his past acquisitions. These periods are not noted for the emergence of new interests, goals, and activities. The children, entering into these stages of development, are more accurately characterized by retrogressive traits. The children lose interest in their past pursuits. Nevertheless, the past is still the controlling influence in their lives. However, those very same activities which not so long ago occupied the greatest part of their time and attention lose their appeal. Now, the formerly developed relationships with their external and inner world are in transition, as if they were dying or being swept away. Leo Tolstoy has figuratively yet accurately designated one of these periods of childhood as a "wilderness of adolescence."

Many investigators have such a view in mind when they describe the negative character of the periods of crises.

Most investigators also have a Tolstoyan idea foremost in their minds when they explain the negative aspects of the critical periods. In their explanations, these researchers want to express the idea that development has changed its positive, constructive aspects during these periods and such a viewpoint forces these investigators to characterize such periods primarily as unfavorable and negative. This conviction is even reinforced by the very way that the critical period is named. (At times, it is called the negative phase and on other occasions, it is designated as the obstinate stage.)

Various conceptions of the critical periods can be traced to empirical research and some chance occurrences. Earlier, some constructs were used to describe and explain the crisis of age seven. (The 7th year in the life of the child is the transition between the preschool and adolescent periods.) The child of 7 or 8 is neither a preschooler nor an adolescent. The 7-year-old is as different from the preschool child as he is from the school boy. As a result of this difference, the 7-year-old is frequently viewed as a problem child in school. The negative content of this period emerges primarily from the interruption of the child's psychic balance, his imperious will, and uncivil mood.

Later, the crisis of the 3-year-old child was noted and described. It was frequently called (by many investigators), the obstinate and stubborn phase. During this span of time that generally lasts for only a short interval, the personality of the child undergoes sharp and even sudden changes. He becomes a problem because he displays obstinate, stubborn, capricious, and selfish behavior. Internal and external conflicts frequently run through this entire period.

Still later, the crisis of the 13-year-old child was studied and described as the negative phase of sexual puberty. As its very name suggests, the negative character of the period had dominated it and perfunctory investigations had seemed to confirm this characterization of the period. The decline in academic achievement, a decrease in work performance, the conflicting personality moods, the loss of old interests, and the protesting character of behavior—all of this allowed some investigators to characterize this period as a stage of such disorientation in the child's external and internal relationships in which the individual and the world are more at odds than at any other time.

Comparatively speaking, it was not so long ago when the transition from infancy to early childhood that ends somewhere near the first year of the child's life was recognized and studied as a prime example of a critical period with all its familiar traits.

In order to point out the remaining link in the chain of critical periods, we turn to the very first link which is the most distinctive of all and is known as the age of the newborn child. This thoroughly studied cycle clearly stands out by itself in the periodic system of crises and its very nature makes it the most obvious crisis in the life of the child. The act of birth itself is a spasmodic change in the child's development. When the newborn child emerges into his completely new environment, this changes all aspects of his life and characterizes the beginning of development.

The crisis of the newborn separates the embryonic period from the infant period in child development. The crisis of one year divides infancy from early childhood. The transition from early childhood to the preschool period is marked by a crisis at age three. The unifying link between the preschool and the school period appears to be the crisis at age seven. Of course, the crisis at age 13 coincides with the break between the school and puberty periods. Thus, the natural picture is uncovered before us. The critical periods alternate with the stable ones. The former are sudden changing and turning points in child development, confirming once more that the development of the child is a dialectic process in which the transition from one stage to another follows not an evolutionary but a revolutionary path.

If empirical research would not uncover the critical periods, a conception of their existence in the scheme of development would result from a theoretical analysis. Now, the theory lags behind and it needs only to catch up with what empircal research has already established.

During the critical periods, the child becomes somewhat of a problem because the changes in the educational system that are applied to the child are not in time with the fast changes in his personality. The pedagogy for the critical periods appears to be the least elaborated in regard to its practical and theoretical relationships. "As for all life, there is a time for death" (Engels). And there is also in child development, one of the most complex forms of life, the processes of curtailment and disappearance. The appearance of the new in development certainly signifies the disappearance of the old. The transition to the new periodal ways marks the decline of the past. These processes of fading and dissolving are concentrated primarily in the critical periods. But it would be the greatest mistake to assume that these traits are the only significant aspects during times of crises. Development is never without its creative parts and, consequently, one can also observe the constructive phases of development in the critical periods. Moreover, the processes of involution, reflected so clearly in these periods and subordinated to the processes of positive personality growth, are directly related to them and ever combined with them into a whole. The destructive aspects of the critical periods bring about such measures as those which are necessary for the development of certain personality traits and characteristics. Factual research shows that the negative content of development during times of crises are only the opposite sides of positive personality change. This is the main theme that runs through all the critical periods.

The positive significance of the crisis at age 3 can be described in terms of the new personality traits that emerge. Subsequently, it has been discovered that if the crisis at age 3, for some kind of reason or another, evolves in a limp or inexpressive fashion, then it will cause a significant delay in the emotional and volitional development in the following period. In regard to the crisis at age 7, all the research has indicated that along with the negative symptoms, there are a number of great achievements. During this period, the child's independence increases and his relationships with other children change significantly.

During the crises at age 13, the decrease in the child's mental productivity can be explained by understanding that there is a shift from object discernment to understanding and deduction. This transition to a higher form of intellectual activity is accompanied by a temporary decrease in classwork. It can be shown for all the remaining negative aspects of crisis that they have positive counterparts which emerge usually in the transition to new and higher form.

Finally, one cannot doubt the presence of the positive in the crisis at one year. Here, the negative aspects are directly and obviously related with such positive achievements as the child standing on its own and mastering speech. Likewise, one could point out similar developments in the crisis for the newborn. In this period, the child retrogresses at the start even in respect to his physical development. During the first few days after birth, one can observe the infant's loss of weight. The adjustment to a new form of life creates such a great demand upon the child's constitution that "a man never stands so close to death as he does at the hour of his birth" (Blonsky). The fact that development is the process of the formation and appearance of the new, becomes more evident during the first crisis than in any of the following ones. All that we note in the child's development during these first days and weeks is one complete new formation. Those aspects of an undesirable nature, making up the negative content of this period, stem from the difficulties caused by the novelty of the new environment and its demands for a higher level of adjustment.

The most essential part of development during the critical period is that it ends in the appearance of new forms. But they have, as research has indicated, a higher degree of distinctiveness and specificity. Their main difference from the new formations of the stable periods is their transitory character. It means that they do not retain as such their forms in which they first appeared during the critical period and that they will not be among the numbers of essential items in the integral structure of the future personality. The emerging formations in the crises extinguish themselves as if they were dissolving the forms into the following stable period and entering into their composition as subordinate parts. They do not have an independent existence, but are absorbed and transformed so much that without a special and deep analysis, their presence is frequently overlooked in the following stable periods. As such, these emerging forms of the critical periods disappear together with the emergence of the following stable periods. Despite their disappearance from view, they continue to exist in a latent form, not living an independent life of their own. Nevertheless, these formations from the critical periods play a partial role in that subterranean development which characterizes the stable periods and leads to the spasmodic appearance of new forms.

Filling in a few details about these general laws that govern the emerging forms in the stable and critical periods will be the subject of the following parts of this work and will be devoted to examining briefly each separate period.

In our scheme, the new forms should serve as the basic criteria for dividing child development into separate periods. The alternation of the stable and critical periods should determine the sequence of the developing periods. The duration of the stable period is marked by very distinctive boundaries at its beginning and end that reveal very accurately its length. In regard to the approximate times for the critical periods, these ages are quickly determined by noting the culmination point or the peak for the crisis and then moving back about a half year from the peak in order to determine its beginning and counting ahead about a half year from the same high point in order to locate its ending.

The stable periods, as empirical research has indicated, consist of two parts which are divided into two stages: the first and second. The critical periods have three parts that come from its transitory phase: the precritical, critical, and postcritical.

One should note the essential differences which distinguish our scheme of child development from the approaches of those whose outlines of periodization closely resemble ours. Besides applying the principle of developing new formations as a criteria for the division into periods, what is new in our scheme is as follows: (1) the introduction of critical periods into the scheme of age periodization, (2) the exclusion of the embryonic period of development from our scheme, (3) the exclusion of the period of youth (from 17 to 18 years up to the appearance of final maturity) from our scheme of periodization, and (4) the inclusion of puberty in the ranks of stable, not critical, growth.

The embryonic development of the child has been excluded for this simple reason. It cannot be examined and studied in the series of external developments of the child as a social being. Embryonic development is conceived as an entirely different type of development that is subordinate to other laws besides those which become operable on the child's personality at the moment of birth. Embryonic development is the subject of the science of embryology which is not a part of psychology. However, the psychologist should take into consideration the findings of the embryologist because his research offers some clues about the postuterine development of the child. Nevertheless, the subject matter of psychology cannot be included in the investigation of the embryo. More specifically, it is necessary for the psychologist to consider the laws of heredity, but not to reduce all of genetics into the rubric of psychology. Furthermore, the psychologist does not study heredity and the uterine development of the child as such, but only the role and influence of both in the processes of social development.

The period of youth has been excluded from our scheme of age periodization of childhood for this reason. The theoretical and empirical in equal measure require us to resist the excessive stretching of child development that spans the first 25 years of the individual's life. According to prevalent views and basic laws of growth, the period from 18 to 25 years is more appropriately explained as the first link in the chain of mature growth than as the final link in the chain of child development. It is difficult for us to conceive that the development of the individual at the beginning of maturity (from 18 to 25 years) could be regulated by the laws of child development.

The inclusion of puberty in the ranks of the stable periods is a logical conclusion of that which is known to us about this growth and which characterizes this period as a great step forward in the life of the child and as the highest synthesis of personality at that time. All of this follows as a necessary logical conclusion of the preceding critique and exposition of the theories in the Soviet science that have thrust puberty into "normal pathology" and described it as a deep inner crisis.

REFERENCES

Pavlov, I. P. *Izbrannye trudy* ("Selected works") Moscow: State Publication, 1954.

Petrovsky, A. V. *Istoriya Sovetskoj psikhologii* ("History of Soviet Psychology"). Moscow: Prosvyeschyenie, 1967.

Piaget, J. *Comments on Vygotsky's Critical Remarks* Cambridge: MIT Press, 1962.

Vygotsky, L. S. *The Psychology of Art*. Cambridge: MIT Press, 1971.

———. *Language and Thought*. Cambridge: MIT Press, 1962.

16. Primary Prevention and Some Aspects of Temporal Organization in Early Infant-Caretaker Interaction

Louis W. Sander, M.D.
PROFESSOR OF PSYCHIATRY
BOSTON UNIVERSITY SCHOOL OF MEDICINE

Gerald Stechler, Ph.D.
CHAIRMAN, DEPARTMENT OF CHILD PSYCHIATRY
BOSTON UNIVERSITY SCHOOL OF MEDICINE

Harry Julia, Ph.D.
CHAIRMAN, DEPARTMENT OF PSYCHOLOGY
FRAMINGHAM STATE COLLEGE

and Padraic Burns, M.D.
ASSOCIATE PROFESSOR OF PSYCHIATRY
BOSTON UNIVERSITY SCHOOL OF MEDICINE

The work described in this paper was carried out with infants who were selected to meet rather stringent criteria for normality, and it was limited to observations within the first two months of life. These two considerations introduce at once the question of the usefulness of this material in a discussion of primary prevention and the high-risk infant. The relevance of further normal developmental data to a discussion of primary prevention can be challenged in the face of the appalling scale on which existing infant-rearing conditions close at home reveal obvious and often abysmal deficiency. There seems little doubt that "intervention" by a wide assortment of individuals in the early developmental situation will be rapidly increasing in the years to come. Whatever action is carried out by these individuals in the name of "primary prevention" will be based on the conceptualizations they happen to have of the process of development going on at that earliest time of life. The long-term effectiveness of their actions will depend on the adequacy of their point of view. It is the contribution which the study of normal development can make to our understanding of the process into which we step in intervening that makes it relevant to an Academy Symposium on Primary Prevention.

Consideration of Organization of Behavior in Early Infancy

Recent infancy research, especially in the areas of early perception and learning, is giving us a new picture of the sensitivities and capabilities of the neonate, and an appreciation of new levels in the early interaction between genomic and experiential factors. Just what these recent findings imply for the subsequent development of the individual or for our comprehension of the early developmental process is not at all clear, however, and reflects a huge gap in our present understanding. The gap in large measure concerns ignorance of the lawful principles which govern postnatal organization of infant functions and the characteristics of the organizing process over ensuing months. The meagerness of substantive empirical data in early infancy has made it well-nigh impossible to consider an attack on the problem of early organization as a suitable or proper research aim. However, the accumulation of empirical research will in time inevitably demand precisely such an approach.

An illustration of the relationship between empirical findings and the problem of organization may be found in the monograph of Bell et al. (1971). The authors there report on the findings of an NIMH project in which 75 infants were studied both as newborns and at the 27-33-month age level. The authors were impressed with the relatively few links which could be established by significant positive correlations between variables measured at one age point and those measured at the other. On the other hand, they were impressed by the finding that variables (e.g., measures of respiratory rate, tactile threshold, reaction to interruption of sucking) which measure overly intense behavior in the newborn period (in terms of frequency, speed, and amplitude) showed significant correlation with variables measuring *low* intensity at the 27-33-month point. (Variables here were interest, participation, assertiveness, gregariousness, and communicativeness.) To quote the authors, "In other words, there was a longitudinal inversion of intensity." How should we understand or account for such an inversion? The answer lies somewhere in the, as yet dimly conceived, machinery of "organization."

It is the lack of correlation between variables measured in early infancy and those measured later which has made the construction of developmental scales in early infancy so difficult, and their usefulness in assessing early development so limited. It is this issue with which Hebb (1949) was concerned when he emphasized that there is something different about the effects of the first learning experiences of the infant organism on his development, in contrast to effects of later experience and later learning. He proposed that the difference was that the initial phase concerned the organization of certain autonomous central processes related to perceptual experience which would then underlie later, more complex learning and problem-solving behavior. However, the effects of first learning or first experience may not be limited to a primary perceptual or sensorimotor development but may be related to the establishing of overall regulatory mechanisms involving the infant as a whole in relation to his environment and basic to any subsequent adaptive functioning. Mechanisms of regulation on the level of "the infant as a whole" appear as highly complex integrations involving many subsystems.

In emphasizing the need for a field of "integrative physiology," Mason (1968) stated that "the distinction between analytic and integrative approaches seems clearly of bedrock fundamental importance" (p. 804). In his discussion he made clear that he regarded the analytic and integrative approaches as complementary rather than antithetical: the study of the relationship between parts is obviously dependent upon prior study and characterization of individual parts. Mason reviewed the enthusiasm during the first third of this century in the study of integrative processes and biological organization and pointed out the difficulty of finding any clear historical continuity of this interest in the past three decades. "While there has been some movement in the direction of more emphasis on regulatory mechanisms, the single system model has usually been employed and there has been very little work on coordinative or integrative mechanisms . . ." (pp. 801*f*.).

In proposing his conceptualization of "overall hormonal balance as a key to endocrine organization," Mason restated an old issue in biology, namely, that comprehension of organization of the organism cannot be grasped at the level of analysis of individual variables alone. He proposed that before the role of a single endocrine system could be defined, its contribution to the balance maintained in the complex interaction of the entire array of endocrine systems must be determined. The role of the single endocrine system might be in one direction (anabolic) in one context, and in another context it might be in an opposite direction (catabolic), synergistic and antagonistic combinations with the other endocrines shifting with the shift in total context. The context in which a variable is measured is thus as important as the measurement itself, if one aims to understand lawful relationships between variables. The identification itself of salient contextual parameters represents a major step in this understanding. We hope that the material presented in this report will evoke discussion of the implications of the issue of "organization" for primary prevention, a concern distinct from the implications of data related to single variables or systems. We shall describe here a study of temporal organization in early infant care interaction and discuss its relevance to primary prevention.

Research Strategy

Our point of departure begins with the notion that a conceptualization of organizing mechanisms cannot be pursued suitably at the level of the individual infant alone, but requires consideration of a next level, namely, the infant plus the caretaking environment—that part of the surround with which he is in exchange. We have assumed that infant-caretaker dyads should be compared, rather than babies; furthermore, that the study of relationships between variables requires repeated measurement of more than one variable over an adequate span of time.

Since organism-environment exchange depends at the biological level on mechanics of regulation, conceptualization of infant and caretaking environment as a regulatory system seemed to promise a good starting point. Infant and caretaker could be visualized as becoming joined in a regulatory system as the behavior of each, through recurrent encounters, is modified toward the establishment of stable (expectable) configurations in the exchanges between the partners. One of the outstanding features of postnatal exchange between infant and caretaker is that the recurrent encounters themselves take place at intervals which begin irregularly, and gradually take place with greater regularity. In the usual instance, postnatal caretaking is a matter of two individuals, disparately organized at many levels, but especially in the temporal distribution of their states of readiness for activity, having to live together around the clock day after day. It is precisely this continuous 24-hour-a-day feature of encounter which makes the time of occurrence of events and their duration all-important issues to both partners. Under such conditions, organization of events into a day and a night time of occurrence becomes a feature of real concern, as does the emergence of a pattern of recurrence of sufficient stability to constitute a comfortably predictable 24-hour frame of reference.

Attention to the time distribution and the various temporal

relationships between events became, then, our second point of departure in this study of organization of an infant-caretaker regulatory system. The method of continuous monitoring of infant and caretaker which was developed in this investigation led directly to the finding of the periodicity characterizing recurrent infant states. This finding required a consideration of the contribution of biological rhythms to the mechanics of organization of exchanges between infant and caretaking environment.

Methodology

The infants, 9 in each group, were taken into the study one at a time, after meeting rather stringent pre- and perinatal criteria of normality based on a detailed newborn examination. The three caretaking conditions, the methods of observation, and some of the variables have been described in previous publications (Sander and Julia, 1966; Sander et al., 1969, 1970, 1972), and need be reviewed only briefly.

The first of the three caretaking conditions was lying-in nursery care with four-hourly scheduled feedings; infants experiencing this caretaking were designated as Group A. This caretaking was limited to the first 10 days of life. The second caretaking condition was foster care with infant-demand feeding provided around the clock by one individual acting as surrogate mother, rooming in with the baby on the hospital maternity floor; infants experiencing this caretaking in the first 10 days of life were designated as Group B. The third caretaking condition was natural mother care provided around the clock by the infants' own mothers, first in a hospital rooming-in facility and then in the home (again infant-demand feeding); these infants were designated as Group C.

Infants for Groups A and B were drawn from a population of infants for whom adoption was being planned, and their availability for the study during the first two months of life depended on the time taken for the completion of agency arrangements. (In the interval since the study took place, these agencies have now reduced this time span.) Groups A and B were matched for prenatal and background factors. Group C consisted of infants of selected multiparous mothers of stable family situations and was not intended as a matched group, although the babies came from similar socioeconomic levels. We wanted a group which represented relatively optimal rearing circumstances, inasmuch as the 24-hour data we were collecting were unique, and there was no way to guess on which side of more optimal caretaking conditions the data collected for Groups A and B might lie. Findings will be reported chiefly for Groups A and B.

There were three time periods in the study, illustrated in Figure 1.

TABLE 1

Group	N		Caretaking Period I (0-10 days)	Caretaking Period II (11-28 days)	Caretaking Period III (29-56 days)
A	9		Nursery	Single Care-taker (X or Y) Rooming-in	Foster Home
B	9		Single Care-taker X or Y Rooming-in	Single Care-taker Y or X Rooming-in	Foster Home
		0-5 days	6-10 days		
C	9	Natural Mother Rooming-in	Natural Mother At home	Natural Mother At home	Natural Mother At home

Figure 1. Design of infant and caretaking groups over the first 56 days of postnatal life.

The design of time periods was intended to provide examination of, first, the effect of first 10-day caretaking on behavior over the remaining days of the month, since, after the 10th day, both Groups A and B received similar caretaking, i.e., between days 11-29. What is the effect of the infant's experience, for even this brief 10-day period, of an environment (lying-in nursery) in which there is no respect for the temporal organization of his recurring states of awake or sleep, and no mutuality of modification in arriving gradually at a stable regularity of daily events?[1] The second aim of the design was to study the effect of substituting one experienced caretaker for another at the end of the first 10 days of life (carried out for Group B only). Does the initial adaptation between infant and caretaker depend on nonspecific factors related to the furnishing of adequate feeding, holding, quieting, or does a stable coordination between infant and caretaker depend upon some quite idiosyncratic pattern of exchange related to individual

[1]The temporal asynchrony between infant activity and that of the nursery caretaking environment has been described (Sander et al., 1969; see also Aldrich et al., 1945); the variable of "delay time," the time elapsing between onset of infant crying and the initiation of an intervention, has been used to study this asynchrony in the nursery situation.

differences in characteristics of regulation in the partners and reached by mutual but specific modifications?

There were five major observational methods employed: (1) a 24-hour-per-day recording bassinet which monitored, automatically and continuously and in real time, infant crying, motility, caretaker approach, caretaker removal of infant from the bassinet and return of infant to the bassinet; (2) a 24-hour record of clock time of observed onset of major sleep and wake periods; (3) daily event-recorded feeding interactions; (4) systematic observations of infant behavior when confronted by visual stimuli, such as the human face; (5) pediatric neurological examination, adapted from an early format of Brazelton's newborn examination method (1973).

Findings

The first finding dealt with the activity of the newborn, that is, a greater *duration* of relatively more active states during the initial postnatal days. This finding became evident only because around-the-clock records could be obtained day after day over the first month of life. The total daily *duration* of more active states of the infant (ones characterized by crying, increased motility, and/or removal of infant from bassinet) was greater over the first days of life than it was again until the end of the first month of life. This held whether the infant was in Group A or B. Until this study, we had supposed that the newborn baby in the first few days of life was recovering from the exhaustion of the delivery and the depressing effects of medication and that as he recovered and grew older, he steadily grew stronger, gradually day by day remaining active for longer periods; in other words, a linear increase in duration of active states over the first month of life. But the picture is more like that shown in Figure 2.

Remember that we are here talking about the *duration* of more active states, not about intensity nor quantity of activity. The Group B infant whose caretaking was relatively unchanged over the first 10 days of life spent less time crying in the second 5 days of life; but the Group A baby also showed reduced crying over the second 5 days of life, even though he was receiving significantly less caretaking time in the second 5 days than in the first 5 days of life. What might be the adaptive significance of the longer time each day in states of relatively greater arousal during the first few days of life? Is there a reason for a relatively greater readiness for interaction with the caretaking environment at the outset?

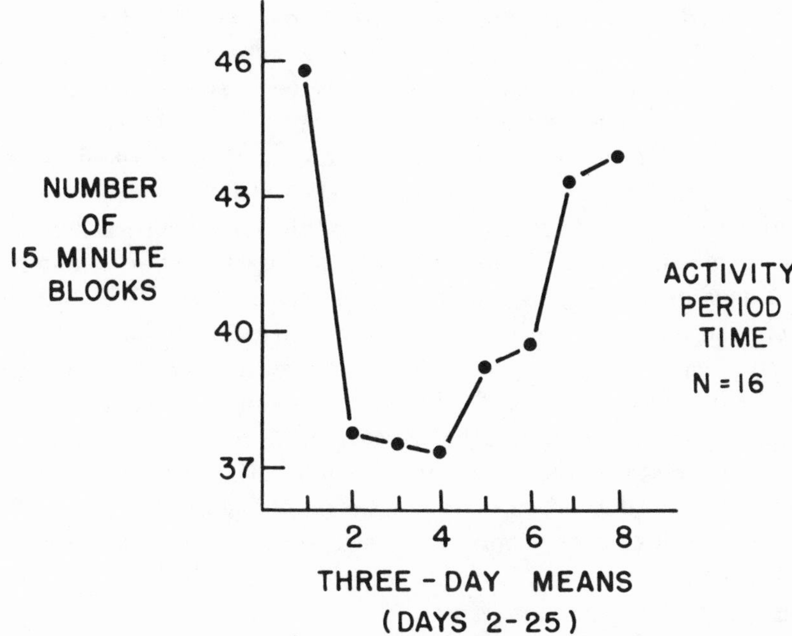

Figure 2. Activity-segment time per 24 hours. Each point represents a mean for 3 days for which the totals for 8 group A and 8 group B infants are combined. Quadratio F = 27.84 df – 1/84 cubic F = 7.36 df 1/84 – Linear F = 1.46 df = 1/84 (Sander et al., 1972).

If each awakening provides an opportunity to experience repetition in specific contingencies between a sequence of infant states and a sequence of particular caretaking activities, the first days of life might be providing an opportunity for establishing certain stable patterns in the infant-caretaker interaction. There are great infant differences in the sequence and in the time course of state changes over an awakening from the end of one sleep phase to the onset of the next sleep phase. The behaviors which an infant characteristically displays with his changing states, especially in the transitional segments, become clues for the experienced caretaker to guide her decisions. They constitute the configurations which identify the unique individual qualities of a particular infant. It is just these individual differences which are being learned by the caretaker and are being modified by the infant as they establish adaptation through mutual coordinations.

A second finding was that the emergence of day-night differences in distribution of relatively more active states was under some environmental control. As long as Group A infants were in the lying-in nursery on the 4-hourly scheduled feedings, they continued to cry more at night, 6 P.M.-6 A.M., than in the daytime, 6 A.M.-6 P.M., and to be in these more active states longer at night than in the daytime. As soon as they were transferred to the care of the surrogate mother on the 11th day, in the first 24 hours in fact, this distribution reversed. As soon as caretaking became contingent to change in infant state, the infant slept in longer epochs.

With demand-feeding caretaking by the infant's own mother, the longest sleep period per 24 hours migrates to the night 12 hours within the first 10 days of life. In the Group B situation, day-night differences in 24-hour distribution of variables, highly correlated with awake states, appeared already in the first 3-day block and became highly significant within the first 10 days of life (see Figure 3). Obviously, once the longest sleep span becomes stabilized in the night segment, the day segment can be occupied only by the briefer sleep periods and the awakenings. This raises the question whether extrinsic environmental factors may, in part, determine the linking of subphases of sleep—the REM and non-REM epochs—into one longest sleep period per 24 hours and, in part, determine its stabilization in the nighttime hours.

Day-night differentiation in distributions of sleep and wake states is one of the earliest indicators to the mother of the progress which her infant is making in settling down and becoming predictable. Our data show wide individual differences in the rate of advance day-night differences for normal infants who have been cared for by the same individual as surrogate mother. One *abnormal* infant we observed showed no significant D-N difference over the entire first 2 months of life. Work which has come from the laboratories of Prechtl (1968), Aschoff (1967, 1969), and Stroebel (1969) has caused us to wonder if there is a connection between the way an infant becomes organized in respect to the 24 hours of the day and the temporal organization or phase-synchrony which exists or can become established intrinsically between his various physiological subsystems. Such intrinsic coordination is usually considered a matter of genomic determination, as are rates of change for the most part. The data we have obtained have suggested the possibility that *extrinsic* determinants may have a significant role in modifying both rates of change and the temporal organization of *intrinsic* infant subsystems, that is, the relationship of the phasic characteristics of one function in respect to another.

A third finding which also surprised us was the persistence of effect of the first 10 days of caretaking. We found that these same Group A infants, who suddenly began sleeping more at night when transferred to the single

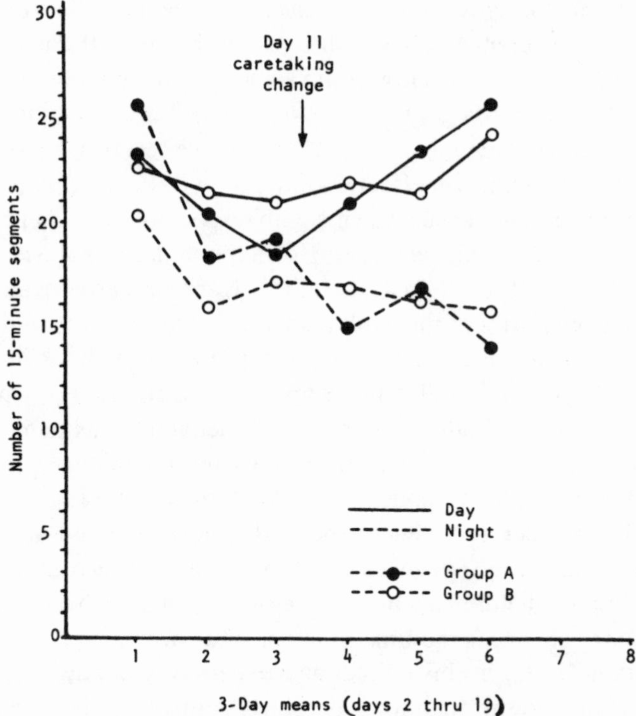

Figure 3. Activity-segment time occurring in daytime days 11-25. Anova for days 11-25 (DN x group x sex) F – 5.99 df = 1/12 p = .05. Females having had nursery caretaking in first 10 days show greater day-night differentiation in days 11-25 than do females who have had rooming-in caretaking in first 10 days. Males show the opposite tendency.

caretaker on day 11, also after day 11 now suddenly began to show a significantly *greater* day-night difference in sleep distribution than did the Group B infants. Recall that during days 11-29, both Group A and Group B infants were receiving similar care on a one-to-one basis in the rooming-in situation. The Group B infants had shown a gradually increasing day-night difference already from the first days of life. There was therefore not only an abrupt change at 11 days for Group A infants in their around-the-clock behavior, but then, an overcompensation, a precocious advance with greater time awake during the day hours and less sleeping.

Was there a possibility that the individual who provided the care between days 11-29 was producing this effect? Fortunately, only two women had provided the care so it was possible by analysis of variance to determine that there was no significant effect on day-night difference being contributed by the individual currently caring for the baby. The only factor which made the difference was whether or not the first 10 days had been spent in the lying-in nursery. How could something or some things that had happened in the first 10 days of life be exerting such a continuing effect on the time in the day of sleeping and waking over the rest of the first month? And possibly some unknown effect on the timing of the fluctuations in the infant's other physiological subsystems with respect to each other?

Some may see a relevance here of reports from animal research concerning the effect of "stress," in the form of early handling, on regulatory characteristics of the adult animal or on appearance of day-night differences in activity. Pre-weaning handling or electric shock in rat pups appears to produce an adult that shows relatively more exploratory behavior and less emotionality (Ader, 1969; Ader and Deitelman, 1970). It has been proposed that in the adult, this represents a regulatory system that is capable of more graded responses in contrast to all-or-nothing responses.

Ader (1969; Ader and Deitelman, 1970), however, also showed that shock or early handling advances the time of appearance of a 24-hour rhythm in output of adrenal cortical steroids, and that handling of the pregnant mother advances the time of appearance in the pups of a 24-hour activity rhythm. Thus, in this animal and under these conditions, rates of development in certain functions or subsystems may be sensitive to environmental inputs.

Obviously, in the human we have no idea as yet what the early or later effects of neonatal "stress" are, or of early stability or instability, or of shifting the developmental rate of change in one function relative to another, on the kind of basic regulatory organization the individual will have, or on the intrinsic coordination between his various physiological subsystems. What may be gained adaptively by the adult for one kind of a later environment may be lost by the same adult for another kind of later environment.

Returning now to our data, we found *a difference between male and female infants in this persistent effect of first 10-day caretaking experience,* which gives further impetus to the task of specifying the interaction of intrinsic and extrinsic factors in rates of advance in 24-hour organization. We found that the precocious advance of Group A babies in day-night difference during days 11-29 was contributed chiefly by the *female* infants. Girls experiencing the less stressful individual caretaking of the Group B condition, by contrast, advanced only in the slowest and most gradual manner. The males, on the other hand, showed their most rapid advance in days 11-29 when they had received the individual care of the surrogate mother during the first 10 days of life. They were retarded or slowed down by a first 10-day lying-in nursery experience (see Figure 4).

This finding seems to add further evidence to the suggestion, already proposed, that we are possibly dealing with a different set of rules from the outset for the organization of little girls and of little boys. Findings of sex differences appear to be ubiquitous in current research reports in early infancy. A further example: in our study, total sleep per 24 hours was significantly greater for girls than for boys. At this point in infancy research, the implications of these findings for "preventive intervention" do not seem nearly as exciting as the implications that by further detailed examination of male-female differences, we may stumble on a better grasp of basic mechanisms of organization of the infant-caretaker system.

A further interesting finding relevant to the temporal characteristics of sleeping and waking emerged from around-the-clock observations of sleep-wake onset, during days 11-29 of life, which were made by the two nurses who carried out the surrogate mothering on most of the infants. The infants cared for by *one* of the two surrogate mothers developed significantly longer first- and second-longest sleep, and first- and second-longest awake periods per day than did infants cared for by the other. This was a finding of which we became aware only with data analysis. Both women were under our daily observations, both were adhering to the rule of not waking the baby for a feeding, both were recording sleep and wake onsets reliably. In contrast to the effect of the Group A or Group B experience on day-night distribution, this time statistical analysis revealed *no* effect of first 10-day caretaking experience on the length of sleep or wake periods during days 11-29. The key determinant appeared to be which of the two women did the caretaking.

There were many differences between the two women. We are unable to specify causative factors, since mechanisms of phase control are too little understood. The babies having the longer epochs showed more total crying and more often cried after being put down in the crib; those with the shorter epochs were more often asleep or nearly so when returned to the bassinet. The mean difference between infants, grouped according to surrogate mother caretaker, in duration of longest sleep epoch was 45.5 minutes, and in duration of longest awake epoch, 26.4 minutes. These durations, together approximating the duration of a basic rest-activity cycle, suggest the possibility that we are encountering here some mechanism by which temporal adaptation is being effected between infant

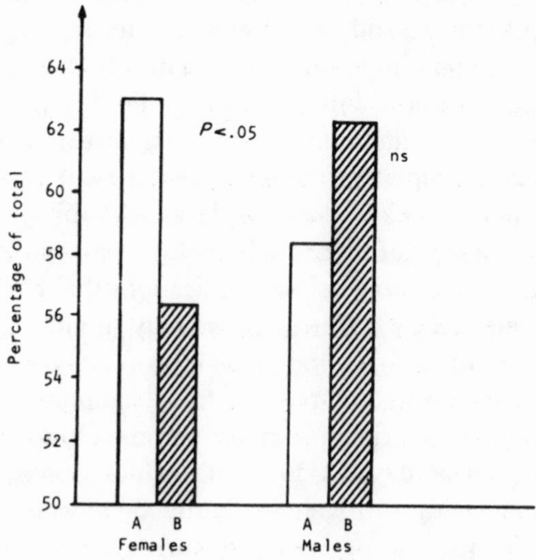

Figure 4. Activity-segments days 2-19. Equal number of days before and after change of caretaker on day 11. Anova, days 2-19 (DN x group x period) $F = 2.80$ $df = 5/60$ $p < .025$. Infants experiencing nursery caretaking do not show day-night differentiation in activity segment time until after removal to surrogate mother situation on day 11.

and caretaker, perhaps by determining the phase relations between the basic rest-activity cycle and the major sleep or wake epochs.

When examined day by day in detail at the level of the variables we have utilized, Groups A, B, and C appear to be clearly following different courses over the first two months. Space does not permit us to take up other variables and the way the three groups differ in respect to each of them, but a number of noteworthy findings should at least be listed:

1. The response to twice-weekly systematic presentations of visual stimuli over the first 2 months of life indicates that the infants of the three groups may be developing their styles of handling visual information quite differently.

2. Burns et al. (1972) presented evidence based on their study of the feeding behavior of Group A and B infants, before and after the change at

11 days, that regulation of feeding behavior may, already in the first 10 days of life, become dependent upon specific adaptation to the one individual caretaker who regularly feeds.

3. The impression gained from Group C indicates that regulation in the natural mother situation is idiosyncratic to a greater degree than in Groups A and B, reflecting rather than modifying unique individual differences.

4. Group A is distinguished from B and C over the first 2 months of life in terms of the greater instability week to week in the rank order of infants with each of the 3 samples when ranked on the basis of values obtained for the variables we have studied.

5. One thing which this greater week-to-week rank order instability indicates is that individual infant differences are not becoming established as consistent individual characteristics of Group A babies. What does this greater instability at the outset of life imply for the coordination between subsystems *within* the individual, or for eventual characteristics of self-regulation in the adult?

6. This may indicate further that initial variability[2] is as important in the description of the dyadic system as of the individual infant.

Not only, then, is the temporal pattern of exchange between infant and caretaker different for Groups A, B, and C, but the course of development of various infant functions shows important differences between the groups as well.

Discussion

The task remains to find some way to bring these findings together as a coherent picture and to focus the question of their relevance to the subject

[2]Our recent work with 24-hour monitoring of infant state indicates that variability may have quite a different meaning when regarded from the standpoint of the individual than when regarded from the perspective of the system. Furthermore, just as within-day variability in the values of variables can be distinguished from across-day variability, so also can within-subject variability be distinguished from between-subject, within-sample variability. Within-day, within-subject variability appears related to the fluctuations of circadian rhythmicity and is greater in the normal than in the infant at-risk. On the other hand, the stability over time, i.e., week to week, of the rank order position an infant holds in relation to his peers appears to be more a characteristic of regulation in the dyadic system. When individual infant differences are playing a significant role in the establishing of interactive regulation in the postnatal dyadic system, regulation becomes based on these unique individual characteristics, so that their consistent expression becomes established also.

of primary prevention. The points reviewed above suggest that it may be possible to establish systematic empirical connections between part and whole; namely, connections linking characteristics of early temporal organization of exchanges between partners in the dyad, and the early course of differentiation of certain of the infants' functions (e.g., feeding or perception). Distribution over the 24 hours of the day of the infant's behavioral states along a sleep-wake continuum is one major determinant of the pattern of exchange in the dyad. This cycling recurrence of states not only constitutes a category of individual differences which affect the pattern of exchange in the dyad in a major way, but provide, also, an avenue by which the characteristics and role of certain cyclic or periodic phenomena in the early developmental picture can be investigated. What is it about infant state that requires our central attention?

The manifest state of the infant, governed by interplay of activating and inhibiting systems, represents a confluence of at least (1) an intrinsically generated time course of phases in a basic rest-activity cycle (Kleitman 1953); (2) a summation of *intrinsic* input parameters arriving from a variety of infant subsystems, e.g., nutritional, excretory, sleep-wake (possibly at the outset of postnatal life, each with a semi-autonomous temporal organization); and (3) *extrinsic* inputs of parameters representing recurrences of periodic events in the caretaking environment. We realize that it is precisely those infant behaviors generated over the course of the periodic fluctuations of infant state which provide behavioral clues by which a mother arrives at her basic caretaking decisions. In the "state" of the infant and in the mutual influence of "state" and "exchange" between infant and caretaker, each acting upon the other, we have a site of adaptive mechanics by which adjustments can be effected between intrinsic subsystems of the infant and between infant as a whole and the extrinsic caretaking environment. Such a site of confluence suggests a kind of analogy of Mason's model (1968) of "overall balance" in which multiple factors, each governed by its temporal structure of phases of maxima and minima, exert influence one on the other, the role of one part at any given time in the interaction between parts influenced by and influencing, in turn, the particular phase of each of the other parts at that moment.

The literature related to investigation of biological rhythms suggests a refinement of such a possibility. It has been reported that over the course of the first 3-6 months of life, circadian rhythmicity is appearing in one physiological function after another, i.e., not across all simultaneously

(Hellbrügge et al., 1964). The possibility later on in life of phase-dissociation, under particular environmental conditions, between various physiological systems which are ordinarily in phase-synchrony, suggests that a primary feature of early postnatal development may be that of establishing and maintaining proper phase-synchrony within the infant between his various physiological components. There may be a particularly sensitive period during which a basic regulatory core can jell. There is considerable support for the view that this turn depends on proper relationship between time structure in infant and time structure in environment.

The literature dealing with biological rhythms indicates a very complex relationship between specific extrinsic signals—*Zeitgeber*—and response curves of a circadian rhythm (Aschoff, 1965). Phase control via inputs from outside world provide an intriguing possibility of a mechanism linking intrinsic infant and extrinsic environmental regularities. It is not possible here to review the adaptive significance of biological rhythms nor the kind of models of organization which they suggest. Data from humans in environments free of time cues indicate that the relationship of the parts to each other within the individual may in some way be governed by the time and schedule structure in the relationship of the individual to his environment (Aschoff, 1969). There is some evidence that, for the human, social contingency is a far more powerful synchronizing factor than is a light-dark schedule (Wever, 1970).

Aschoff (1969) has summarized these relationships as follows:

> Circadian rhythms are examples of an evolutionary adaptation to time structures in the environment. The process resulted in (a) self-sustained oscillations, the periods of which match approximately that of the environment, (b) species-specific phase relationships between the circadian oscillations and the environment warranted by entrainment, and (c) temporal order between a multiplicity of oscillating systems. Maintenance of the temporal order within the organism seems to depend partly on phase-setting effects of the entraining Zeitgeber. Therefore, lack of proper Zeitgebers may have deleterious effects to the organism. (p. 849)

To return to the subject of "primary prevention," one of the problems raised by the recent spate of dramatic new findings in early infancy which are related to single variables or single systems, such as the perceptual, is their impact on the kind of interaction which is focused upon in the infant-caretaker exchange. For those interested in stimulating the generation of early sensorimotor schemata as a means of advancing cognitive development, findings of exquisite sensitivity or responsivity of the infant to visual, auditory, tactile, or kinesthetic inputs can suggest special value in attention to or "training" of the infant in these areas. The general issue of attempting to exploit these capabilities prematurely has been discussed by Wolff (1969), who makes the point that "In all aspects of cognitive and motor acquisition there seems to be a crucial difference between the first qualitative steps—which are relatively independent of controlled environmental input and probably not 'learned' in the usual sense—and the subsequent quantitative refinements" (p. 12). Wolff adds that these first qualitative steps, although relatively independent of "controlled" environmental input, are critically dependent on a certain "background" or "non-specific" stimulus environment.

Some of the summarizing points which Wolff makes in referring to cognitive development and the issue of what can and cannot be taught infants and young children are the following:

> The over-riding problem in cognitive development is revealed in many facets: from a physically heterogeneous environment, the naïve child is able to extract a set of complex rules for categorizing experiences and for generating new rules of action and thought. The origins and development of this ability are at the core of what we must understand before we can decide what we can and cannot teach young children. . . . Children have at their disposal unlearned, or at least unteachable, acquisition devices for creating order out of random events, and for transforming ordered experiences into generative principles (Cognitive Structures). The source of such devices does not conform to our current conceptions of how children learn. (pp. 11, 18)

The fact is that the "physically heterogeneous environment" is not a random one, a realization which nothing makes more clear than the ubiquitous presence of rhythms and cyclic recurrences in biological systems, orchestrated in symphonic coherence to give unity and continuity to organic existence.

The mechanisms which make a nonspecific stimulus environment essential may be built around the redundancies which are constituted in the recurring encounters attending periodic fluctuations of behavioral states of the infant, during which patterns of exchange are becoming stabilized. This essential redundancy may need to be encountered at the outset of postnatal life, perhaps critically, much earlier than heretofore suspected. Regulation for the infant as a whole may be inseparable from a stable regularity or redundancy in key exchanges between infant and caretaker.

An around-the-clock regulation of infant-caretaker interaction in terms of consideration of "the infant as a whole" has fallen largely to the synthesis provided by a mother's intuition. Much of this synthesis, unconscious or only at the borders of consciousness, is utilizing machinery involved in the temporal organization both of intrinsic infant variables and the extrinsic variables related to events in the dyadic exchange. When infant and caretaking environment can be regarded together as an organic system, research in the area of biological rhythm suggests that the nature of this machinery may include mechanisms of phase control, phase synchrony, entrainment, etc. in the establishing and maintaining of basic regulation.

Summary

At this point, we wish to summarize a few of the implications for primary prevention which these data and the experience of collecting them have generated for us. In the first place, we have yet to define precisely what basic mechanisms are involved in the regulation of the cycling infant states, how interaction with the caretaker bears upon these mechanisms, and what relation the particular course of history, through which regulatory processes pass in becoming established, bears to *later* characteristics of regulation, differentiation of function, or organization of behavior. The kind of environment to which the individual may have to adapt later may confer advantage or disadvantage upon the various configurations which are possible.

In the second place, the significance of the first 10 days of life may be much greater than we have realized in the establishing of a basis for temporal organization of infant-caretaker interactions. The nonchalant separation of infant and mother in the first 5 days of life, which we have accepted unquestioningly as part of standard maternity care, needs a thorough reappraisal.

Furthermore, when we consider mechanisms of regulation, day-by-day and around-the-clock data provide a different set of variables by which adaptive processes can be investigated. The information which is available from investigations of biological rhythmicity carried out over the past 40 years cannot be neglected. Characteristics of periodicity, entrainment, phase control, and phase synchrony may play a central role and demand a keener appreciation for the role of time and temporal relationships. Models other than our familiar learning model are becoming available to account, in the immediate postnatal period, for the impact of specific features of extrinsic environment on periodic characteristics of infant states.

In a general way, we have merely been putting our customary language of the infant-mother "relationships" into a new vocabulary. The formulation of more detailed models of "organization" in the infant environment system provides the means of analyzing events at a more detailed level—within a framework that preserves a meaning, a logic connecting them. It is not intended as a substitute for the traditional concept of "relationships" in early development, but as a bridge to underlying processes.

That her infant stops crying when she picks it up is interpreted as "being spoiled" by one mother, and as a sign of her successful mothering by another. The "meaning" this has for us as investigators has customarily been focused upon such alternatives as these maternal interpretations of the events suggest. We pay especial attention to any events we can assimilate into our formulations of maternal character or which suggest predictions in respect to qualities of later "object relations." The event itself—namely, the termination of a cry when the baby is picked up—may also be viewed in terms of more complex models, such as the adaptive-regulatory, which envision the event as an interaction of infant, caretaker, and age effects, requiring a consideration of the history of such interactions and its relations to a context of other influences and events.

As we have pursued our research questions, it appears that we have been left with new questions as the best answers we have been able to find to our old ones. Although we may come to "know" the factors, or the mechanisms, which lie behind "simple" notions about relationships and their importance to the human, the existential demand upon the mother in actuality is that of an integration of all such "mechanisms" in her "relationship" with her new baby. The subtle orchestration which optimally can characterize the experience of a mother and infant in their mutual encounter presents us with as great a problem in understanding integration as confronts the biologist in his efforts to understand integration in the single cell. He seems to see this as a problem in understanding the life process itself.

It appears to us that the rather complex perception by the mother of behaviors identifying infant state, ordered in some temporal framework, may be replacing, in the human infant-caretaker situation, the more stereotyped and fixed action patterns that govern maternal and infant behavior at the infrahuman level. The "state" of the baby represents a manifest configuration depending upon a complex synchrony of intrinsic subsystems and may provide an initial site for synthetic function—a sensitive behavioral indicator, by means of which a next level of phase synchrony can be established between infant "as a whole" and recurrent regularities in the extrinsic world. It is conceivable that as we gain a clearer understanding of infant state regulation, a more meaningful comprehension of the postnatal caretaking adaptation will become available, as will a more meaningful comprehension of the nature of what we are trying to accomplish by interventions carried out in the immediate postnatal period in the name of "primary prevention."

REFERENCES

Ader, R. "Early Experiences Accelerate Maturation of the 14-Hour Adrenocortical Rhythm," *Science,* March 14, 1969, *163:* 1225-1226.

———, & R. Deitelman. "The Effects of Prenatal Maternal Handling on the Maturation of Rhythmic Process," *J. Comp. & Phys. Psychology,* Vol. 71, No. 3 (1970), 492-496.

Aldrich, C., C. Sung, C. Knop, G. Stevens, & M. Burchell. "Crying of Newly Born Babies," *J. Pediatrics,* Vol. 26, p. 313 (1945); Vol. 27, p. 89 (1945); Vol. 17, p. 428 (1945).

Aschoff, J. "Response Curves in Circadian Periodicity," in J. Aschoff, ed., *Circadian Clocks, Proceedings of the Feldafing Summer School.* Amsterdam: North Holland Publishing Co., 1965.

———. "Desynchronization of Human Circadian Rhythms," *Jap. J. Physiology, 17:* 450-457 (1967).

———. "Desynchronization and Resynchronization of Human Circadian Rhythms," *Aerospace Medicine,* 844-849, August 1969.

Bell, R., G. Weller, & M. Waldrop. "Newborn and Preschooler: Organization of Behavior and Relations Between Periods," SRCD Monograph, Serial 142, Vol. 36, #1-2.

Brazelton, T. *The Neonatal Behavioral Assessment Scale.* Spactics International Medical Publications in association with London: William Heineman Medical Books; Philadelphia: J.B. Lippincott Co., 1973.

Burns, P., L. W. Sander, G. Stechler, & H. Julia. "Distress in Feeding: Short-Term Effects of Caretaker Environment of the First 10 Days," *J. Amer. Acad. Child Psychiatry,* Vol. 11, #3 (July 1972).

Hebb, D. *The Organization of Behavior.* New York: John Wiley & Sons, Inc., 1949.

Hellbrügge, T., J. Lange, F. Rtuenfranz, & K. Stehr. "Circadian Periodicitity of Physiological Functions in Different Stages of Infancy and Childhood," *Annals of N. Y. Academy of Sciences,* Vol. 117, 631-73.

Kleitman, N., & T. Engleman. "Sleep Characteristics of Infants," *J. Appl Physiology, 6:* 269-282, 1953.

Mason, J. "Over-All Hormonal Balance as a Key to Endocrine Organization," *Psychosomatic Medicine,* Vol. 30, 791-808.

Prechtl, H. F. R. "Polygraphic Studies of the Full-Term Newborn." II. Computer Analysis of Recorded Data, *Studies in Infancy Clinic in Developmental Medicine 27,* M. Box & K. C. MacKeith, eds., SIMP. London: Heineman, 1968.

Sander, L. W., & H. Julia. "Continuous Interactional Monitoring in the Neonate," *Psychosomatic Medicine,* Vol. 28, #6 (Nov.-Dec. 1966).

Sander, L. W. "Regulation and Organization in the Early Infant-Caretaker System," in R. Robinson, ed., *Brain and Early Behavior.* London: Academic Press, Inc., 1969.

Sander, L. W., G. Stechler, P. Burns, & H. Julia. "Early Mother-Infant Interaction and 24-Hour Patterns of Activity and Sleep," *Journal of the American Academy of Child Psychiatry,* Vol. 9, #1, January 1970.

Sander, L. W., H. Julia, G. Stechler, & P. Burns. "Continuous 24-Hour Interactional Monitoring in Infants Reared in Two Caretaking Environments," *Psychosomatic Medicine,* Vol. 34, *3,* 270-282 (1972).

Stroebel, C. "Biologic Rhythm Correlates of Disturbed Behavior." *Rhesus Circadian Rhythms in Non-Human Primates,* Rohles Basel, ed., N.Y., 1969, #9, 9-105.

Wever, R. "Zur Zeitgeber-Starke eines Licht-Dunkel-Wechsels fur die Circadiane Periodik des Menschen," *Pflugers Arch.* 321, 133-142, Springer-Verlag, 1970.

Wolff, P. "What We Must and Must Not Teach Our Young Children from What We Know About Early Cognitive Development," *Planning for Better Learning.* SIMP/Heineman, 1969.

17. The Role of Biological Rhythms in Early Psychological Development*

Peter H. Wolff, M.D.
PROFESSOR OF PSYCHIATRY
HARVARD MEDICAL SCHOOL

Introduction

In a recent review of biological rhythms research, Sollberger (1) lists over 2,000 references pertaining to the rhythmical features of animal behavior. Even in such an exhaustive survey, however, the empirical relations between intrinsic rhythms and the experience of time (2), the development of a time concept (3-4), and the acquisition of motor syntax and language (5) are barely considered, although such relations imply many of the classical arguments in human psychology. As Sollberger's review indicates, the investigation of periodicities in human behavior has usually focused on cycles of motility, sexual activity, sleep and waking, work proficiency, psychopathology, and the like, and therefore on the analysis of macro-rhythms or temporal sequences with basic frequencies of hours, days, months or seasons. Others have worked out the adaptive significance of macro-rhythms in animals (6-9), and clarified the extent to which these are endogenous, can be entrained on external synchronizers, or are "learned."

Rhythmical repetition, however, is also characteristic for reflex activities of the human neonate, although in this case the cycles have much higher basic frequencies of seconds and fractions of seconds. It has been proposed that such *micro-rhythms* may represent primitive controls for sensorimotor behavior in the human infant (3), but the signficance of this assertion is difficult to assess, since most references to high frequency

*Reprinted from *Bulletin of the Menninger Clinic*, Vol. 31, No. 4 (July 1967) 197-218. An earlier version of this paper was presented at the Menninger Foundation in October 1966, upon the occasion of the 1966 Helen Sargent Memorial Award. Work for this study was carried out while the author was supported by the Career Development Program of the U.S.P.H.S.-N.I.M.H., Grant K-MH-3461.

rhythms in neonatal behavior are of a general descriptive nature without any quantification of their temporal features. The first section of this essay will attempt a formal analysis of two such high frequency rhythms in the human neonate, and will show that even apparently simple motor patterns are organized in complex time sequences.

As a corollary to the proposition that micro-rhythms have a controlling function in early motor activity, it has been assumed that the manifest rhythms are suppressed in development and replaced by qualitatively different regulations (3). An alternative possibility—that the endogenous rhythms of neonatal behavior have their own rules of development, that they persist to give rise to more complex temporal sequences, and that as such they influence the sequential order of cognitive functions, as well as of motor habits, in the adult—has not been seriously explored. The intrinsic regulation of time-sequences in adult human behavior is, however, a question of theoretical interest for the psychology of cognition, language and logic. In his essay on the problem of serial order in behavior, for example, Lashley (5) presents cogent reasons why one must postulate the existence of endogenous high frequency oscillators, and why in the final analysis one cannot account for the serial order of voluntary adult behaviors without assuming their presence at birth. To Lashley's exposition one could only add the suggestion that a developmental study of such rhythms would clarify important aspects of the problem which an investigation of their final forms alone cannot. Clinical examples of motor rhythms in older children, and their possible relevance for the development of micro-rhythms as regulators of adaptive behavior, will be considered in the second part of this essay.

Heart rate, respiration and "brain wave" activity are the instances of micro-rhythms which have been studied most carefully in man. While among these the electroencephalogram is most directly, or at least most obviously related to early psychological development, studies of EEG activity in humans have more often and more persuasively demonstrated the limitations imposed by neural rhythms on perceptual-motor performance than they have shown that neural pulses directly instigate rhythmical motor sequences (10).

Such an inherent relation between central nervous system pulses and rhythmical motor action has been demonstrated for lower species by von Holst (11-12) and Paul Weiss (13-15), who worked with deafferented nonmammalian vertebrates. Using a variety of experimental techniques these investigators showed that motor organs which are essential for locomotion under normal circumstances can also be activated in the absence of any peripheral feedback. From these studies one must conclude that the deafferented central nervous system generates stable high frequency rhythms, and that the corresponding autonomous oscillatory mechanisms interact reciprocally to instigate complex behavior sequences.

The studies mentioned above have been carried out only on the central nervous systems of lower species which have a capacity for extensive "repair" after derangement experiments. Totally deafferented yet viable human organisms do not occur as "experiments in nature," and even nonhuman primates become totally unresponsive when surgically deafferented. It might therefore seem to be only an academic exercise to invoke the adaptive role of high frequency oscillators in human behavior, were it not for Lashley's persuasive demonstration that there is a functional continuum from spontaneous rhythmical motor movements instigated by an isolated nervous system to the simple motor reflexes of human infants, to the violinist's rapid finger movements in playing an arpeggio, to the syntax of spoken language; and that whenever human behavior is arranged in temporal sequences of high frequency, central regulatory mechanisms come into play which cannot be reduced to experience alone, but must originate in intrinsic regulators of serial order (5).

In this essay, I will present an account of only isolated studies and clinical cases, which pertain primarily to the repetition of simple reflexes. While I have not attempted to examine more complex phase interactions in behavior, it is to be expected that their analysis would provide answers of far greater relevance to the problem of serial order in voluntary behavior than any numerical analysis of simple repetitions alone.

Crying

The first instance of high frequency rhythms in behavior to be considered is that of neonatal crying. To visualize the vocalization patterns for a detailed analysis of their form and rhythms, samples of crying were recorded under natural conditions in the nursery, and the recorded samples analyzed by the sound spectrograph (16). Under limited and specifiable conditions, neonatal crying is arranged in patterns of remarkably stable serial order that can be demonstrated visually with the sonogram (Figure 1). This pattern has sometimes been called the "hunger cry" because it is often heard when one might expect an infant to be hungry; but since most crying infants eventually vocalize in this pattern regardless of the offending

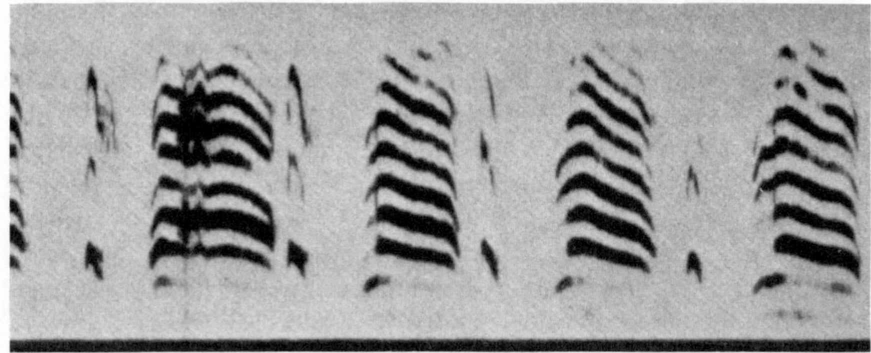

Figure 1. Basic cry of 4-day-old full-term infant. Abscissa-time base (4.8 seconds); ordinate-frequency range (0-8000 cycles per second).

cause unless they fall asleep or get exasperated, it has also been called the "basic cry" (17-18). It is present in all normal four-day-old neonates, in older infants, and in many infants with minor cerebral dysfunction. In Table 1 the distinct features of one string of basic cries from a normal neonate

TABLE 1
Rhythmical Cry—Four-Day-Old Infant

	Cry Expiratory	Rest Period	Inspiratory Whistle	Rest Period
	.63 secs.	.08 secs.	.03 secs.	.17 secs.
	.62	.05	.03	.15
	.70	.06	.04	.26
	.51	.08	.03	.15
	.87	.10	—	—
	.24	.05	—	—
	.64	.02	.04	.17
	—	—	.04	.28
	.57	.04	.04	.17
	.64	.03	.03	.27
	.70	.09	.04	.09
	.64	.16	.04	.14
	.64	(?)	.05	.24
	.61	.24	.04	.24
	.79	.09	.04	.21
	.59	.10	.04	.19
	.56	.09	.05	.19
	—	—	—	—
Mean	.62	.09	.04	.20

were grouped as expiratory cries (mean duration 0.62 seconds), rest periods (mean duration 0.085 seconds), inspiratory whistles (mean duration 0.039 seconds), and rest periods (mean duration 0.195 seconds), to demonstrate the stability of rhythmical features.

A vocalization pattern, which some mothers call the "angry" cry because of its strident character, is quite similar to that of the basic cry except for the greater turbulence which occurs when an excess amount of air is forced through the vocal cord, and which on the sonogram appears as diffuse black areas (see Figure 2) (17). Turbulence does not interfere with the basic rhythm demonstrated below, so that the "mad cry" has

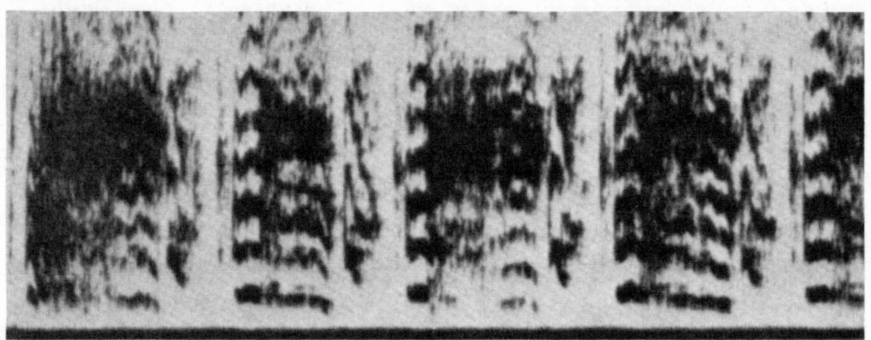

Figure 2. "Mad" cry of a 4-day-old full-term neonate.

approximately the same rhythmical features as the basic cry (mean duration of expiratory cry 0.69 seconds; of rest periods 0.20 seconds; of inspiratory whistles 0.049 seconds; and of second rest periods 0.11 seconds—see Table 2).

Cries in response to other causes are organized in different sequences: The first response to a heel prick, for example, is a long vocal expiration which lasts five to six times as long as the expiratory vocalization of the basic cry, and is followed by a long silence in expiration that may last up to seven seconds. When the tape recording of a pain cry was played to mothers so that they did not know their child was not crying, they responded with great concern. But when the time sequence of the same recorded cry was altered by removing most of the long silent period, mothers uniformly responded with less distress. The temporal arrangement of vocalizations thus served an important signaling function even in the newborn period (18).

A cry of different pattern is provoked by giving the infant a pacifier to suck, removing it, and giving it back, until he is exasperated. Cries recorded just after the pacifier has been removed a number of times are similar in most respects to the pain cry except that the long period of breath holding in expiration is not present (see Table 3). When the tape recordings of such cries are played to a mother who cannot see her baby, she reacts with far less anxiety than to the pain cry, and with about the same concern as to a pain cry from which the long silence in expiration has been removed.

TABLE 2
"Mad" Cry—Three-Day-Old Infant

	Cry Expiratory	Rest Period	Inspiratory Whistle	Rest Period
	.78 secs.	.18 secs.	.04 secs.	.17 secs.
	.69	.15	.04	.15
	.69	.19	.04	.24
	.77	.21	.06	.15
	.74	.23	.04	.14
	.68	.24	.04	.11
	.65	.29	—	—
	.60	.27	.04	.06
	.70	.30	.06	.09
	.62	.23	.06	.11
	.62	.30	.07	.02
	.62	.18	.10	.06
			.06	.09
			.08	.04
	.90	.15	.03	.04
			.04	.12
	.62	.09	.03	.15
	.76	.21	.06	.12
	.67	.06	.03	.15
	.67	.04	.03	.12
	.61	.24	.03	.09
	—	—	—	—
Mean	.69	.20	.05	.11

In a preliminary experiment to observe whether the distortion of auditory feedback would alter the rhythm of crying, masking noise was played into the ears of seven infants while they are crying in the basic pattern. Although the noise itself often stopped the crying completely, the *rhythm* itself was not altered by the masking sound as long as the infants continued to cry. These preliminary findings, when considered in conjunction with the almost universal appearance of stable crying rhythms in healthy neonates (17), were considered a circumstantial evidence that the vocalization rhythms of the neonate are partially controlled by autonomous central mechanisms (22, 23).

Sucking

A second motor rhythm of high frequency can be observed in the neonate's spontaneous mouthing activity and in his response to a pacifier. From an extensive study of pacifier sucking (19), I will summarize here only details relevant to the proposition that central rhythms extrinsic to the motor act itself control the rhythms of non-nutritive sucking. During restful sleep shortly before a meal, many infants make spontaneous rapid movements with the lips, jaw and tongue that can be distinguished without difficulty from the sucking and chomping movements observed during lighter sleep (19, 24). These movements are grouped in bursts of 4-12 distinct events separated by rest periods lasting from 2-10 seconds. The mean duration of bursts and rest periods may vary among infants, but remains the same for any one infant over several days. When the individual movements were counted and timed by stopwatch, and the length of bursts, the duration of rest periods, and the mean frequency of sucks per second in

TABLE 3
Cry in Response to Pain and to Being Teased

	Cry in Response to Pain (Mean Value for 5 Infants at 4 Days)			
	Cry Proper	Rest	Inspiratory Whistle	Rest
First Sequence After Pain Stimulus	3.83 secs.	3.99	0.18	0.16
Mean of Subsequent Sequences	0.78	0.25	0.08	0.25
	Cry in Response to Being Teased (Mean Value for 7 Infants, 3-4 Days Old)			
	Cry Proper	Rest	Inspiratory Whistle	Rest
First Sequence After Pacifier Removed	2.67	0.07	0.13	0.13
Mean of Subsequent Cry Sequences	0.59	0.02	0.07	0.12

a burst were calculated, they constituted a regular pattern that was quite stable over time for each infnat. For technical reasons, the method of direct observation, however, was not reliable, and it could not capture the finer details of the moment to moment changes in sucking. To obtain more precise measures, the infant's mouthing activity was therefore recorded from a pacifier attached to a pressure transducer and polygraph writer, so that the changes of positive pressure in the pacifier could be recorded as the infant pressed on the pacifier with his lips and tongue. Since the sensorimotor components of pacifier sucking were thought to be different from those of spontaneous mouthing, it was expected that the two types of rhythmical mouthing would have entirely different temporal patterns. Yet the serial order of pacifier sucking in sleep was exactly the same as that of spontaneous mouthing, and the two patterns were statistically indistinguishable.

Twenty full-term infants, who were delivered to healthy mothers after uncomplicated deliveries and tested on the fourth day after birth, all mouthed the pacifier at a mean frequency of about two sucks per second during regular sleep (range 1.9-2.3 sucks per second). Variation in mean frequency from burst to burst were extremely small for any one infant and slight across individuals (for the twenty infants the standard deviations varied from 0.09 to 0.24 sucks per second).[1] The mean frequency per second in a burst was the most constant feature of the sucking rhythm but the mean number of sucks in a burst, and the mean duration of rest periods were also stable values which constituted a second rhythm of lower frequency superimposed on basic rate.

Despite the invariance of mean values per burst, the individual sucks of a burst were not all equal in length, and varied systematically around the mean for that burst. Peak times (*i.e.*, the distance between two adjacent sucks in a burst—see Figure 3) at the start of the burst were invariably shorter than those near the end, whether the recording was taken from a normal full-term neonate, a premature, or an older infant. This rise in peak time was shown by graphing intervals between successive sucks within the burst as continuous function and plotting each burst as a separate line (Figure 4). The same rise was demonstrated by dividing all bursts of a record, regardless of their lengths, into three equal segments and comparing the mean frequency of the first, second and third segments. In all twenty infants (and in other normal infants tested subsequently) the

[1]Mean frequency of sucks was calculated by dividing the number of sucks in a burst by the total duration of that burst; standard deviations were calculated from mean frequencies per burst, rather than from individual sucks, for reasons to be indicated below.

sucks at the end of a burst were consistently slower than those near the start (p = .001 by Friedman 2-Way Analysis of Variance). One might, of course, attribute this rise in peak time to muscle fatigue, and assume that during the rest period the infant recovered from fatigue. The sucking performance of premature infants, however, indicated that this interpretation was unsatisfactory. During the early portion of a record, very young prematures of 31-32 weeks gestation who sucked for only 10 or 15 bursts, and then either stopped sucking altogether or else sucked in unanalyzable patterns, showed the *same* rather than a *greater* rise in peak time from the start to the end of a burst as normal infants, even though their sucking was clearly susceptible to fatigue. Full-term infants who sucked for one-half hour or more without any signs of tiring, showed the same relative rise in peak times as prematures, whereas the rise in peak time after one-half hour of continuous recording was the same as at the beginning in the babies born at term.

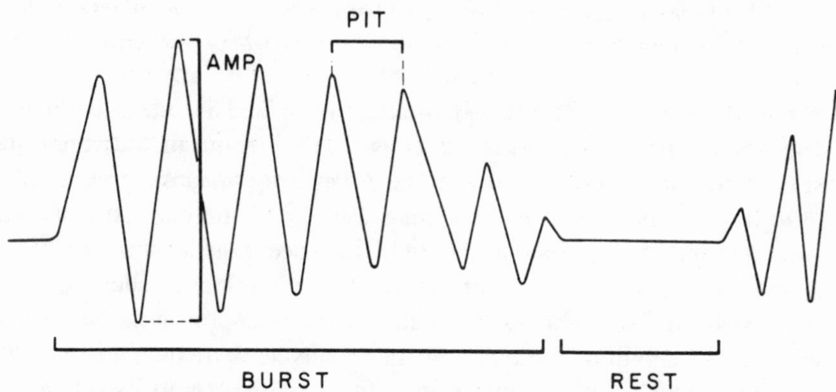

Figure 3. Diagrammatic representation of sucking pattern on pacifier–peak time (PIT), amplitude, burst length, and rest period.

Further support for the conclusion that fatigue was not responsible for the rise in peak time came from the performance of infants with chronic or progressive brain disease. One infant who had received four intrauterine transfusions and another three exchange transfusions after birth, because of an Rh incompatibility, was brought to the hospital at two months of age because he had failed to gain weight. This infant sucked on the pacifier in unusually long bursts of 30-40 sucks, yet the peak times remained relatively *constant* throughout the burst until the last three or four sucks when it rose significantly. Other infants with diffuse brain damage,

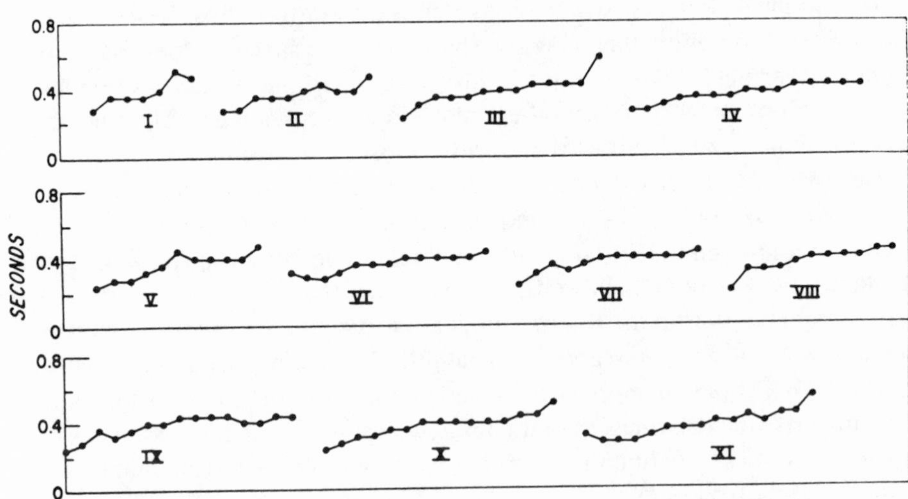

Figure 4. Progressive rise of peak times in a burst. Each of 11 consecutive bursts is represented by a line, every peak between 2 consecutive sucks in a burst by a point on that line; distance between lines does not indicate length of rest periods.

leukodystrophy, subacute encephalitis, also sucked in excessively long bursts and the peak times remained constant throughout the burst until the last three to four sucks, when again there was a significant increase. Were one to assume that a rise in peak time was due to fatigue, patients with central nervous system disease should be as susceptible as normal children and should show its effects after at least 10-15 continuous sucks. Yet the rise in peak time was always associated with the approaching *end,* rather than with the length of the burst. A more satisfactory explanation for the rise seemed to be the assumption that there is one mechanism which is responsible for both the increase of peak times and the termination of a burst; that this mechanism is central in origin (since it can be altered by central nervous system disease); and that it first slows down, and eventually arrests rhythmical sucking in the manner of a positively dampened oscillator. Acquired disease of the central nervous system may destroy this inhibitory mechanism selectively, and leave the basic pacemaker for sucking intact. In other diseases of the central nervous system, such as Down's Syndrome, the pacemaker itself may be altered without destroying the mechanisms responsible for the rise in peak times of the grouping of sucks in bursts (21).

The sucking performance of infants with congenital defects of the face, jaw and mouth represented an "experiment in nature," with which to test the role of sensory feedback in controlling the basic sucking frequency and the segmentation of sucking in bursts and rest periods. If the feedback from motor end organs were a significant determinant of serial order in sucking, one would expect that sucking pattern of infants with cleft palates and hare lips, or of infants with Pierre Robin's Syndrome, should differ from that of normal children. All such children who were at all capable of sucking, however, sucked at the *same* rate, in the *same* pattern of bursts and rest periods, and with the *same* rise in peak time from the start to the end of a burst, as normal infants.

The infant's performance on the pacifier during deep sleep also suggested that the pulses which trigger bursts of sucking at regular intervals were central in origin. One can, for example, calculate the mean number of sucks per burst for a particular infant, and predict with reasonable accuracy when a new burst is likely to start, and how long it will last. When such an infant is allowed to suck on the pacifier for as long as he will in regular sleep with the pacifier tied in place, he usually stops sucking altogether 10-15 minutes after an episode of restful sleep starts, although he can be made to resume sucking at any point by an arousing stimulus. Once sleep has inhibited mouthing proper, the infant may continue to show rapid tremors of the tongue and jaw, which have a frequency of seven to eight per second, and are organized in bursts of 5-15 separate movements. Such tremors appear in many normal infants after they have sucked for at least ten minutes, and much more frequently in children with presumptive minor cerebral dysfunction or gross neurological damage, where the tremors may start as soon as the infant begins to suck. Tremors may precede or follow a burst of sucking or, in pathological cases, may be imposed on the sucking movement itself. Their only relevance to this discussion is that they involve motor coordination patterns which are entirely different than those for mouthing activity proper, and that they, too, may appear at regular intervals. In deep sleep, bursts of tremors appeared at intervals which corresponded exactly to the moment when a burst of sucking would have started in lighter sleep. It would seem, therefore, that the appearance of activity bursts at regular intervals was not specific to spontaneous and pacifier-provoked rhythmical mouthing, but that some central pacemaker which has a lower frequency than that for the basic sucking rate activates a variety of different peripheral motor patterns at the same rate. Which motor pattern is activated depends on the level of arousal, but the pacemaker for episodic bursts of activity is extrinsic to, or autonomous of, sucking itself.

When the pacifier was removed right after the start of a burst of sucking, the infant often continued to make empty mouthing movements as if the pacifier were still in his mouth. In such an experiment, the number of empty mouthing movements after the pacifier was removed, plus the number of sucks before the pacifier was removed, usually equalled the mean number of pacifier sucks in a burst for that infant. Once a burst had been triggered, it therefore ran its course regardless of changes in peripheral feedback, as if the length of a burst represented a finite potential for activity that was independent of sensory feedback from the pacifier.

Clinical evidence and *ad hoc* experiments suggest that the temporal organization of non-nutritive sucking is to a large extent regulated by central mechanisms which determine or co-determine (1) the basic rate of sucking; (2) the rise of peak time in the burst; (3) the onset and termination of bursts, and (4) the duration of rest periods.

Graduating by one step to a higher level of integration, one finds that the rhythms which are characteristic for the activity of one motor end *organ* can spread to control the rhythmical organization of other reflexes at the same time. Peiper (26) has shown, for example, that *nutritive sucking* ''drives'' swallowing and breathing whenever all three reflexes are simultaneously active, as they must be during feeding. When nutritive sucking begins, the rate of respiration changes until a 1-1 or a 1-2 ratio is established (26).

Both Prechtl (25) and Peiper (26) have observed a phase-relation between sucking and kneading movements of the front paws in nursing kittens, as well as between sucking and grasping in premature human infants. In two-month-old human infants with suspected minor cerebral dysfunction, I have found a one-to-one correspondence between nutritive sucking and blinking that is constant at the start of a feeding, but breaks down as the infant's hunger is satisfied. The rhythm of sucking thus controls not only the physiologically dependent functions of swallowing and breathing, but can spread to anatomically and physiologically unrelated reflexes which have their own natural rhythm when acting alone, but under special motivational conditions are locked in phase with nutritive sucking.

Stereotypes

Several neonatal motor patterns have been described so far whose stable and relatively fixed rhythms were compatible with the hypothesis that the rhythms observed in reflex behavior are intrinsic, and do not depend either on experience or specific sensory inputs. From the simple reflex rhythms of the neonate it is, however, a big jump to the stereotypic mannerisms of older children, since the latter involve more complex motor coordinations, and are more easily influenced by experience, perceptual input, and motivational disposition than congenital reflexes. Since stereotypies are nevertheless stable and relatively simple motor rhythms whose temporal sequences can be analyzed directly, their relation to personality development was relegated to a secondary position for the purposes of this essay, and the rhythmical features were stressed.

Dynamic psychology defines stereotypes as autoerotic activities, with the implications that their primary function is the discharge of instinctual drive tension, and that their aim of tension reduction is fused with the means for achieving it. In specific clinical contexts, sterotypies are also called autisms when they occur in autistic children, and blindisms when they appear in blind children. The neutral term *mannerism* seemed more appropriate than any clinical designation because the behavior patterns to be described were not pathological formations as such, but could occur among normal adequately cared for children, children with *acquired* central nervous system lesions, and retarded children raised in good homes, as well as among institutionalized mongoloid children.

Both the relatively high incidence of stereotypies among institutional children, and the successful inhibition of mannerisms by social-therapeutic interventions, point to a causal relation between mannerisms and social deprivation (27-30). This relation, however, cannot account for the frequent occurrence of mannerisms among blind and feeble-minded children who have been properly cared for, or for the emergence of mannerisms in children who showed no stereotypic activity until the onset of progressive neurological signs and symptoms, or for the instrumental (adaptive) function of mannerisms at particular stages in sensorimotor development.

The observations to follow were selected from a collaborative study, in which Dr. Sadako Imamura and I studied the development of stereotypic mannerisms in a homogeneous population of institutionalized mongoloid children. We traced the transformation of different stereotypic motor patterns over time; investigated the changing relation of form and function in the mannerisms; and compared the forms of mannerism in one diagnostic group with those in normal children and children with other organic illnesses. The primary population for the study was a group of infants with Down's Syndrome, all residing in the same institution. We did not attempt to define mannerisms precisely at the outset, but with certain qualifications scored as mannerisms all movements involving the head or the face, one or more limbs, or one of its parts, the entire body, or any combination among these that were repeated in approximately the same form at regular, short intervals.[2] The abnormality or uniqueness of a mannerism was not a defining criterion for its inclusion in the tabulation since almost every type observed among the mongoloid children also occurred either as a transient phenomenon in normal children, or as a persisting preoccupation in children with organic or functional pathology. With the exception of the intricate rhythmical behavior patterns invented by older autistic children which most of us could not imitate without a great deal of practice, the stereotypies were in no way unusual in form.

Although the specific rates of mannerisms was the primary issue for this essay, our preliminary impressions concerning the functional significance of mannerisms will be summarized briefly before turning to the quantitative data, in order to give some substance to the otherwise sterile numbers, and in order to indicate the range of different functions which these motor patterns can assume.

Early in the observations it became clear that new stereotypies did not appear in the child's motor repertory at random, but that the sequence of their emergence closely paralleled the overall sequence in motor development.

The development of mannerisms adhered closely to Werner's heuristic ordering principle (the "orthogenetic law") which made it possible to arrange the sequential changes of mannerisms in a rational order (31). Most of the mongoloid children began between the sixth and the twelfth month with an intermittent stiffening and relaxation of the entire body that was not rhythmical beyond a global activation and relaxation of variable length. As the extensor rigidity abated, the infants began to move the separate body parts independently in simple stable rhythms. Eventually the component parts were reintegrated as articulated patterns and in complex temporal sequences.

Mannerisms were also not simply modes of self-gratification, or goals in their own right. Some infants used a particular rhythmic pattern as long as they were content, but stopped as soon as they became unhappy or began to cry; others used the same motor repetition when they first encountered a familiar person; another group started the mannerism at the moment when

[2]The tabulation also included a group of repetitive motor patterns like intermittent hyperextension and relaxation of the entire body, even though they had no discernible rhythmical pattern; repetitive reflex actions like eye-blinking and respiration, which could be observed in any normal child or adult under the most varied conditions, were not included.

they were abandoned; and still others started rocking only after they had been alone and "bored" for some time. To the degree that the meaning of the mannerisms could be inferred from the context by direct observation, stereotypies were used as motor expressions of affect and modes of social encounter as often as they represented executive actions for tension discharge.

A child often used the same mannerisms in distinctly different ways at different stages in development, and the form-function relation of sterotypic mannerisms changed systematically over time. Mannerisms which at first were simple empty repetitions with no apparent relation to external objects, might become not only the instrument but also the target of the activity. An empty grasping movement, for example, was transformed into a movement of hitting the face; empty kicking was replaced by kicking one leg with the other. At a more advanced stage, the infants directed their motor activities away from their own bodies and toward objects in the environment. A child who had been rubbing his body began to rub the sheet of the bed in the same repetitive manner; the child who had kicked one leg with the other now kicked the bars of his crib in the same way and at the same rate. Some children eventually incorporated the bodies of other persons as an essential part of the total configuration. A child who had previously hit her mouth with her hand while opening and closing the mouth rhythmically, now banged Dr. Imamura's hand against her own mouth in the same form and at about the same frequency as she had previously used her own hand. An infant who had persistently rubbed his ear back and forth against the sheet as he lay on his side, now used Dr. Imamura's body as the adequate surface, and while being held rubbed himself repetitively against Dr. Imamura's chest.

The mannerisms thus went through systematic structural and functional changes. At first they might serve as channels for drive tension discharge, but eventually they were often used as motor means toward a concrete goal. To the extent that mannerisms became the means for exploring the physical environment, and for contacting the people in it, they reflected not only a child's social condition, motor and postural development, but also his intellectual performance (32).

A quantitative assessment of *rates* revealed that different mongoloid children performed a particular mannerism consistently at the same frequency. The similarity between these rates and rates of pacifier sucking in normal neonates suggested to me that the basic rhythm of spontaneous mouthing observed in infancy might be preserved even after the motor patterns themselves have undergone structural modifications.

When hand and mouth movements were coordinated, the new mannerisms (*e.g.,* tapping the chin with the dorsal surface of the hand) usually took twice as long as mouthing alone (range 1.0-1.4 movements per second). Similarly, children who previously had kicked their legs by extending and flexing them at the rate of one full kick per second, later kicked their legs against an object, and then mean rate was 0.5-0.7 movements per second.

One of the common mannerisms seen among mongoloid children, which I have called ''rocking proper,'' was also observed in normal children and children with other organic illnesses. To perform it the child supported himself on his hands and knees facing the mattress, and rocked back and forth on his haunches in a continuous back and forth motion. All mongoloid children who engaged in ''rocking proper'' did so at a rate of 1.0 complete movements per second, with no variation from day to day, or from child to child. When children assumed this posture but kept their bodies at rest and nodded their heads up and down, the rate varied from 1.8-2.2 movements per second.

Children with other illnesses rocked at about the same rate as those with Down's Syndrome. Three autistic children, who rocked in this fashion, did so at the same constant rate of 1.0 movements per second. At other times two of them also nodded their heads at the rate of two movements per second while at rest in this position. Several normal infants between 9-12 months, and one child of 18 months with suggestive signs of minor cerebral dysfunction, rocked in the same pattern and at the same rate except at the start or end of a period of rocking.

For three normal infants who were starting to crawl, ''rocking proper'' was clearly a point of transition from sitting to physical displacement. For these infants rocking was an end in itself during the early weeks after onset. Eventually, however, it became the child's means for propelling his body forward. Once he was in motion he crawled in the usual fashion; but when an obstacle arrested his progress he briefly resumed rocking back and forth before moving in a new direction.

There would be little point in reporting the rate for each type of mannerism, or in extending the list of their possible functions. So far I have found no children in whom the rate of a familiar mannerism deviated significantly from the rates reported above. The findings converge on the tentative conclusion that every mannerism has its own rate, regardless of individual experience or diagnostic category. From isolated clinical instances it would, of course, be specious to argue for a discrete endogeneous oscillator specific to each stereotypy of a particular frequency which is immune to external influences. Children who rock habitually can be started off by music, and the musical rhythm may modify, even if it does not control their rates. Mechanical factors related to body structure, muscle tension, elasticity, fatigue and level of excitation, as well as external synchronizers and other environmental distractions thus influence the manifest rhythm of stereotypic mannerisms to a significant degree, and it would be misleading to assume that motor rhythms are the direct expression of endogenous central pacemakers. They may nevertheless represent "natural" frequencies instigated by central oscillator of a fixed frequency and modified by environmental and physiological factors. Barring opportunities for experimental stimulation during neurosurgical procedures, one must rely on the comparison of minor variations in frequency among many instances of the same stereotypy, to derive the natural frequency of particular forms.

Earlier I mentioned that the patterns and manifest rhythm of mannerisms did not differ significantly in normal and pathological children. What did distinguish the mannerisms was their persistence in the pathological children, and the gradual transformation into more complex rhythms in the normal children. Normal infants eventually stopped repeating a particular mannerism after they had acquired the new locomotor pattern or posture for which the mannerism seemed to be a prelude. Pathological children either continued the repetitive motor rhythm at the expense of developing the corresponding motor skill, or else they continued to rock in the archaic pattern despite the acquisition of the new motor skill. Except in the case of the elaborate mannerisms invented by some autistic children (which may well be qualitatively novel forms), stereotypic repetitions were nothing more than perseverations of the usual sensory motor schemata, long after repetition for the sake of practice or "cumulative assimilation" had lost its adaptive function (33).

The behavior of individuals in a state of neurological regression provided circumstantial evidence for the assumption that the rhythms associated with particular mannerisms were preserved as potential regulators of serial order after the motor patterns themselves had been integrated in more complex sequences. At the most primitive level this became apparent in the behavior of an adult patient with chronic encephalitis and a total loss of voluntary motor functions. When given a pacifier, she *chewed* it rhythmically at exactly the same rate and in the same pattern of alternating bursts and rest periods as the young infant sucks on the pacifier. For the sake of comparison, I asked normal adults to suck on the pacifier, but they were totally incapable of reproducing the typical infantile pattern. In the same vein, children between the ages of four and six years with severe obstructive hydrocephalus sucked in stable infantile patterns, while age mates with a mild form of the disease responded to the pacifier exactly like their normal peers, and either refused altogether to suck or produced erratic patterns.

At a more complex level, children with diagnoses varying from suspected third ventricle tumors, to demyelinizing diseases, to "nonspecific" chronic encephalitis, who had as one of their presenting symptoms the onset of stereotypic mannerisms, showed the same forms of motor repetition as normal, mongoloid and autistic children—rocking back and forth in sitting position, "rocking proper," head nodding, mouthing, leg kicking, and the like. Whenever mannerisms associated with the onset of the neurological disease resembled those observed in normal home reared or institutionalized mongoloid children, the rates of performance were the same. In most cases, the parents of children with acquired neurological lesions reported that their children had shown no mannerisms for several years before the onset of other neurological symptoms. Thus, the clinical evidence on patients with acquired neurological lesions also favors the interpretation that a specific motor mannerism is associated with a particular rhythm, regardless of age or diagnosis.

Motor development may then be viewed as the transformation of simple rhythmical repetition or "circular reaction" into integrated actions (33), whose rhythmical origins are no longer apparent exactly because the component motor parts have been integrated and the associated rhythms have been submerged in complex phase sequences. In keeping with Lashley's thesis, but unprejudiced by fact, I have assumed that the simple rhythms of neonatal behavior are not *replaced* by qualitatively different regulations of serial order, but that the endogenous rhythms are dissociated from their manifest reflex patterns, and enter into complex phase relations with other dissociated rhythms which can then control the sequence of internalized actions and thought patterns. Empirical support for these assertions is hard to come by from the study of humans alone. One would not expect the resultant complex rhythms in behavior to be obvious to direct observations, but with refined instrumentation designed to detect subtle phase interactions, and by developmental studies focusing on the transformation of simple rhythms, it should be possible to investigate the problem empirically.

Conclusions

The systematic observation of neonates has shown that some reflex activities of the young infant are organized in remarkably stable, high frequency rhythms. Circumstantial evidence was presented which admits, even if it does not prove, the proposition that the human central nervous system instigates motor rhythms analogous to the endogenous automatisms described by von Holst and Weiss for lower species, and that the influence of these rhythms is not limited to one motor end organ alone, but can influence anatomically unrelated motor activities as well. At a primitive level of integration, motor rhythms of different frequencies are known to interact so that one drives the other by a "magnet effect." Two rhythms may also interact to generate rhythms whose temporal properties differ entirely from those of either component rhythm, although no instances for such phase interactions in human behavior have yet been described. The interaction of *more* than two distinct rhythms should give rise to a complexity of sequences in behavior which could only be detected with the use of refined experimental techniques, but would nevertheless be rhythmical in its organization.

From the comparative study of normal and neurologically damaged individuals, it was concluded that a regression in neurological function is associated with the reemergence of simple motor rhythms and mannerisms. Stereotypic motor rhythms may thus be viewed as segments of the behavior repertory which have either not been integrated with other motor patterns, or else have "de-differentiated" in the course of neurological regression. Extrapolating from the disintegration of complex behavior patterns and the parallel reappearance of simple rhythms, it was proposed that the apparent suppression of rhythms in behavior is achieved by a phase interaction of two or more discrete rhythms as these motor patterns are coordinated. Finally it was speculated that after appropriate developmental transformation, about which nothing is known at present, the derivatives of simple high frequency rhythms may regulate the serial order of thought patterns and voluntary movements in the adult.

Preliminary results from the study of mannerisms in mongoloid children also suggested that rhythmical repetition may function not only as a consumatory behavior (in the sense of tension discharge) but also as the motor means by which the retarded child explores his surroundings. Especially among blind, and probably among autistic children, stereotypic mannerisms may dominate the child's motor repertory so completely that they interfere with lawful cognitive and social development.

These speculations about the developmental significance of high frequency rhythms may have some peripheral implication for the treatment of stereotypic mannerisms in disturbed and defective children. Techniques of negative reinforcements for the suppression of mannerisms have the advantage that they yield concrete results and rapid success; and wherever the intensity of mannerisms make their persistence incompatible with physical health or life, such suppressive techniques must be considered an essential clinical tool. In less dramatic instances, however, it might be more fruitful to recognize the biological substrate of motor mannerisms, and to devise methods for converting stereotypic mannerisms from global ends into motor means. This seems to be what Dr. Bruno Bettelheim has accomplished in his treatment of autistic children at the Orthogenic School in Chicago; it is the method by which Dr. Lukas Kamp successfully treated an autistic twin; and it is the method by which Dr. Bibace and his students at the Worcester State Hospital have sought to establish social contact with their juvenile and young adult schizophrenic patients. In each instance it seems to the outsider that the therapist has entered into the apparently aimless self-sufficient stereotypy with the patient, and has then converted the mannerism into a behavior that can be entrained on external synchronizers (for example, music), or related to concrete events and persons in the environment. While I must assume responsibility for this interpretation of the therapeutic endeavors, it offers a developmentally consistent formulation about the significance of stereotypic mannerisms wherever they may occur, and it may provide guidelines for an organismic approach to their treatment when their preponderance interferes with normal developmental differentiation.

REFERENCES

1. Sollberger, A. *Biological Rhythm Research*. New York: Elsevier, 1965.
2. Uexküll, Jacob von. *Umwelt und Innenwelt der Tiere*. Berlin: Springer, 1909.
3. Piaget, Jean. "Les Trois Structures Fondamentales de la vie Psychique: Rhythme, Regulation et Groupement," *Revue Suisse de Psychologie* 1:9-21, 1942.
4. Fraisse, Paul. *Les Structures Rhythmiques*. Louvain: Nauwelaerts, 1956.
5. Lashley, K. S. "The Problem of Serial Order in Behaviour," in F. A. Beach and others, eds., *The Neuropsychology of Lashley*. New York: McGraw-Hill, 1960, pp. 506-528.
6. Pittendrigh, C. S. and V. G. Bruce. "An Oscillator Model for Biological Clocks," in Dorothea Rudnick, ed., *Rhythmic and Synthetic Processes in Growth*. Princeton: Princeton University, 1957.
7. Cloudsley-Thompson, J. L. *Rhythmic Activity in Animal Physiology and Behavior*. New York: Academic Press, 1961.
8. Bunning, Erwin. *The Physiological Clock*. New York: Academic Press, 1964.

9. Richter, C. P. *Biological Clocks in Medicine and Psychiatry*. Springfield, Ill.: Charles C. Thomas, 1965.
10. Anliker, James. ''Simultaneous Changes in Visual Separation Threshold and Voltage of Cortical Alpha Rhythm,'' *Science* 153:316-318 (1966).
11. Holst, E. von. ''Versuche zur Theorie der Relativen Koordination,'' *Pfluger's Archiv.* 237:93-121 (1936).
12. ———. ''Bausteine zu einer Vergleichenden Physiologie der Lokomotorischen Reflexe bei Fischen: II. Mitteilungen,'' *Z. Vergl. Physiol.* 24:532-565 (1937).
13. Weiss, P. A. ''Autonomous versus Reflexogenous Activity of the Central Nervous System,'' *Proc. Amer. Phil. Soc.* 84:53-64 (1941).
14. ———. ''Further Experiments with Deplanted and Deranged Nerve Centers in Amphibians,'' *Proc. Soc. Exp. Biol. Med.* 46:14-15 (1941).
15. ———. ''Specificity in the Neurosciences,'' *Neurosciences Research Program Bulletin,* Vol. 3, No. 5 (1965).
16. Potter, R. K., et al. *Visible Speech*. New York: Van Nostrand, 1947.
17. Truby, H. M. and J. Lind. ''Cry Sounds of the Newborn Infant,'' *Acta Paediatrica Scandinavica,* Suppl. 163, 1965, pp. 7-59.
18. Wolff, P. H. ''The Natural History of Crying and Other Vocalizations in Early Infancy,'' in B. M. Foss, ed., *Determinants of Infant Behavior*. London: Methuen, in press.
19. ———. ''The Causes, Controls and Organization of Behavior in the Neonate,'' *Psychological Issues,* Vol. 5, No. 1, Monograph No. 17 (1966).
20. ———. ''La Theorie Sensori-Montorie de L'intelligence et la Psychologie du Development General,'' in *Psychologie et Epistemologie Genetiques: Themes Piagentiens*. Paris: Dunod, 1966, pp. 235-250.
21. ———. ''The Serial Organization of Sucking in the Young Infant.'' In preparation.
22. Lenneberg, E. H. *Biological Foundations of Language*. New York: Wiley, 1967.
23. Lieberman, Philip. *Intonation, Perception and Language*. Cambridge: MIT Press, 1967.
24. Prechtl, H. F. R., et al. ''Polygraphic Studies of the Full-Term Newborn Infant: I. Technical Aspects and Qualitative Analysis,'' *Developmental Med. and Child Neurol.* In press.
25. Prechtl, H. F. R. ''Angeborene Bewegungsweisen Junger Katzen,'' *Experientia,* Vol. 8 (1952).
26. Peiper, Albrecht. *Cerebral Function in Infancy and Childhood*. New York: Consultants Bureau, 1964.
27. Bakwin, Harry. ''Emotional Deprivation in Infants,'' *J. Pediat.* 35:512-521 (1949).
28. Bowlby, John. *Maternal Care and Mental Health*. Monograph #2. Geneva: World Health Organization, 1951.
29. Provence, Sally Ann, and R. C. Lipton. *Infants in Institutions*. New York: International Universities Press, 1962.
30. Spitz, R. A. *The First Year of Life*. New York: International Universities, 1965.
31. Werner, Heinz, ''The Concept of Development from a Comparative and Organismic Point of View,'' in D. B. Harris, ed., *The Concept of Development*. Minneapolis: University of Minnesota Press, 1957, pp. 125-147.
32. Spitz, R. A., and K. M. Wolf, ''Auto-erotism: Some Empirical Findings and Hypotheses on Three of Its Manifestations in the First Year of Life,'' *Psychoanal. Study of the Child* 3/4:85-120 (1949).
33. Piaget, Jean. *The Origins of Intelligence of Children*. New York: International Universities Press, 1952.

Dr. Peter B. Neubauer

Dr. Neubauer has been the Director of the Child Development Center in New York City since 1951. Dr. Neubauer is John Turner Lecturer at Columbia University and Clinical Professor at the Downstate Medical Center of the State University of New York, and was the President and Founding Member of the Association for Child Psychoanalysis.

Dr. Neubauer was born in Austria and came to the U.S. in 1941. He received his training, which includes a medical degree, at the University of Vienna, the University of Berne, Bellevue Hospital and New York University.

INDEX

A

B

C

D

E

F

G

H

I

J

K

L

M

N

O

P

Q

R

S

T

U

V

W

Z